出国留学书系

SAT、AP备考书系

Barron's 巴朗

AP经济学

（第5版）

Barron's AP MICROECONOMICS/ MACROECONOMICS 5th Edition

[美] 马斯格雷夫（Musgrave，F.） 卡克皮尔（Kacapyr，E.）
雷德尔斯海默（Redelsheimer，J.） 著

世界图书出版公司

北京 · 广州 · 上海 · 西安

图书在版编目（CIP）数据

Barron's AP经济学：第5版 /（美）马斯格雷夫（Musgrave，F.），（美）卡克皮尔（Kacapyr，E.），（美）雷德尔斯海默（Redelsheimer，J.）著；陈英，米睿译.
--北京：世界图书出版公司北京公司，2015.12（2018. 3 重印）
书名原文：Barron's Microeconomics/Macroeconomics，5th edition
ISBN 978-7-5192-0564-5

Ⅰ. ①B… Ⅱ. ①马… ②卡… ③雷… ④陈… ⑤米… Ⅲ. ①经济学–高等学校–入学考试–美国–自学参考资料 Ⅳ. ①G634.663

中国版本图书馆CIP数据核字（2015）第 299948 号

Barron's 巴朗 AP 经济学（第5版）

著　　者：[美] 马斯格雷夫（Frank Musgrave, Ph.D.）
[美] 卡克皮尔（Elia Kacapyr, Ph.D.）
[美] 雷德尔斯海默（James Redelsheimer, M.A.）
责任编辑：梁沁宁

出版发行：世界图书出版公司北京公司
地　　址：北京市东城区朝内大街137号
邮　　编：100010
电　　话：010-64038355（发行）　64015580（客服）　64033507（总编室）
网　　址：http://www.wpcbj.com.cn
邮　　箱：wpcbjst@vip.163.com
销　　售：新华书店
印　　刷：三河市国英印务有限公司
开　　本：880 mm × 1230 mm　1/16
印　　张：22.5
字　　数：552千
版　　次：2016年2月第1版　2018年 3 月第 3 次印刷
版权登记：01-2015-5576

ISBN 978-7-5192-0564-5　　定价：58.00元

目　录

宏观经济学

CONTENTS

INTRODUCTION

MACROECONOMICS

Introduction

导言

The AP Exams in Microeconomics and Macroeconomics

AP微观经济学和宏观经济学考试

1

→ WHERE TO FIND MICRO AND MACRO
→ MULTIPLE-CHOICE QUESTIONS
→ ANSWERING STRATEGIES
→ FREE-RESPONSE QUESTIONS

INTRODUCTION 导言

Economics is a fascinating and enlightening subject that provides students with valuable insights to help understand the world and analyze problems, while also helping one make better decisions. That being said, your most immediate concern is not likely solving complex world issues but preparing for the Advanced Placement (AP) Economics exam. Whether you are feeling extremely confident or in serious need of help preparing for the AP Economics exam, you have already made a wise economic decision by using this very book right now to prepare for the AP Economics exam. Like the tens of thousands of students around the world preparing for AP Economics exams this year (nearly 200,000 AP Economics exams were taken around the world in 2014), you may be feeling a bit overwhelmed by the extensive content in Economics, or thinking, "Where do I even begin to start studying?" Rest assured that in using this book you have turned to a fantastic resource to study for the AP exam. This book will help you learn the essential content in a clear and concise format. It highlights the important material to know based on a careful analysis of past AP Economics exams, as well as provide tips for success on either the AP Macroeconomics exam, AP Microeconomics exam, or both. It is clearly organized and written to help you focus on what you will actually be tested on and will prepare you for success for the AP Economics exam.

MICROECONOMICS, MACROECONOMICS, OR BOTH? 只是微观经济学、宏观经济学，还是两者都有？

To make sure you are efficient with your review, let's make sure you are in the correct section of the book. Some students take both the AP Microeconomics and AP Macroeconomics exams, but others may just take one of these. Please see Table 1.1 for the correct chapters to focus on for your specific test(s). *Note:* The basic economics section is the same for both AP Microeconomics and Macroeconomics, so all students should study Chapters 1–4.

Table 1.1

What Chapters Should You Study?

Micro	Macro
Chapters 1–13, with a full practice exam after Chapter 13.	Chapters 1–4, then skip to Chapters 14–21, with a full practice exam after Chapter 21.

THE EXAMS: WHAT TOPICS ARE TESTED?
考试：要考查哪些方面的题目？

The College Board is very specific about what information will appear on the exams. For instance, an entire 55–70 percent of the AP Microeconomics exam is made up of the nature and function of product markets! Spending time studying product markets is obviously a smart decision. Table 1.2 shows the approximate percentage of the multiple-choice questions that will come from each content area, as stated by the College Board. For example, you can be assured that, as 55–70 percent of the AP Microeconomics exam is the nature and function of product markets, anywhere from 33 to 42 of the 60 multiple-choice questions on the exam will come from this content area. For more specific details about the exam topics in, see Table 1.2. You find the entire AP Microeconomics and Macroeconomics course outline on The College Board's AP webpage (*http://apstudent.collegeboard.org/home*).

Table 1.2

Micro and Macro Exam Topics and Approximate Percentage (Multiple-Choice)

Micro	Macro
Basic economic concepts (8–14%)	Basic economic concepts (8–12%)
Nature and functions of product markets (55–70%)	Measurement of economic performance (12–16%)
Factor markets (10–18%)	National income and price determination (10–15%)
Market failure and the role of government (12–18%)	Financial sector (15–20%)
	Inflation, unemployment, and stabilization policies (20–30%)
	Economic growth and productivity (5–10%)
	Open economy: international trade and finance (10–15%)

On both AP Economics exams, well over half of your test grade comes from the multiple-choice section; the other third comes from the free-response questions (FRQs), with one long and two short questions (Table 1.3). More details and strategies for the multiple-choice and free-response questions are given later in this chapter.

Table 1.3

Exam Breakdown: Both Microeconomics and Macroeconomics

Section	Questions	Allotted Time
1. Multiple-choice questions (66.7% of final score)	60	70 minutes
2. Free-response questions (33.3% of final score)	1 long, 2 short FRQs	10 minute planning time, 50 minute answer time

You may also be wondering what percent of questions one needs to answer correctly for a 4 or 5 on the exam. The AP Economics exam does have a significant curve on it. In fact, only 5 out of more than 70,000 students who took the AP Microeconomics exam in 2014 got a perfect score! (If you do beat the odds and get a perfect score, you, your principal, and your teacher will receive a personalized letter of congratulations from the College Board on your achievement.) So now that we have established that well over 99 percent of students will get at least one question wrong, you can see Table 1.4 for the minimum correct percent of correct answers you need to earn for different AP scores (1–5). Keep in mind that the averages may change slightly from year to year due to different test questions being used and variations in student performance.

Table 1.4

Percent Correct Needed on Exam for Different AP Scores: Both Microeconomics and Macroeconomics

AP Score	Minimum Correct Points Earned on Ecam (%)
5	80
4	60
3	50
2	33
1	0

MULTIPLE-CHOICE QUESTIONS 选择题

The first part of the AP Economics exam is the multiple-choice section. In this section students are given 70 minutes to complete 60 questions. Each multiple-choice question works out to be 1.1 percent of your final AP exam grade, so every question is important. Even though students today have grown up in a era of standardized testing and have taken no shortage of multiple-choice tests, it's a good idea to refresh your skills or learn some new ideas in this section (some of which are relevant directly to the AP Economics exam). Here are some tips and suggestions:

1. **YOU'VE GOT 60 PROBLEMS, SO MAKE SURE RUNNING OUT OF TIME ISN'T ONE MORE.** Of the 60 questions, don't allow yourself to become stuck on or obsessed with one or two questions. Most students run out of time not because of the overall difficulty level but because of spending too much time on too few questions. If you don't know the answer, star it, and return to it later. The time limit works out to be around 70 seconds per question, yet no one question is worth more points than the other. Of the two sections of the test, the multiple-choice part is the one that you must be most mindful of the time.
2. **GRAPH IT OUT, REMOVE ALL DOUBT.** You will definitely be required to draw graphs in the free-response section, but drawing graphs can be very helpful in the multiple-choice section as well. A brief graph drawn in the margins can easily lead to the correct answers. For example, let's look at the following sample question:

   Which of the following changes in the demand of and the supply for widgets will definitely result in a decrease for both the equilibrium price and quantity of widgets?

Supply	Demand
(A) Increase	Increase
(B) Increase	No change
(C) No change	Decrease
(D) Decrease	Increase
(E) Decrease	Decrease

   Trying to visualize all of those options can seem overwhelming; however, a well prepared student could do a quick sketch of these supply and demand graphs. Visualizing five different scenarios can be confusing, and graphing it out can easily clarify the correct answer. Even economic experts are fond of drawing out graphs to be sure of an answer. By the time a student has drawn option C, he or she will have identified the correct answer and can move on to the next question.
3. **NO QUESTION LEFT BEHIND.** Answer every question. There is no penalty for incorrect answers, only points for right ones. So if you have no clue about the answer, guess anyway. Each question will have five choices, and you at least have a 20 percent chance at getting it right.
4. **ABSOLUTELY NOT THE RIGHT CHOICE.** Be careful when dealing with a question that uses absolutes. Anytime a possible answer uses absolute phrases such as *always, never, rarely,* and *none,* that choice is usually not the correct one.

5. **STAY POSITIVE, BUT RECOGNIZE THE NEGATIVES.** Make sure to read every word of the question carefully. A common way test writers employ negatives is found in this sample question:

The long-run growth rate of an economy will be increased by an increase in all of the following except

(A) capital stock.
(B) labor supply.
(C) real interest rate.
(D) rate of technological change.
(E) spending on education and training.

A student could possibly miss the word *except* at the end of the question, and just put answer A, which would be correct if there was no *except*. Another similar technique to confuse students is "which of the following is NOT..."

6. **DON'T BE INTIMIDATED BY A QUESTION'S LOOKS.** Some questions can look overwhelmingly difficult, but when approached correctly, they are usually less intimidating than their looks. Here is a sample of a question that can initially appear very difficult:

An opportunity cost is entailed in which of the following situations?

I. A student decides to attend college full-time.
II. A family uses its $20,000 savings to purchase an automobile.
III. A farmer decides to grow more wheat and less corn.

(A) I only
(B) II only
(C) III only
(D) I and III only
(E) I, II, and III

Consider questions of this nature to be merely glorified true / false questions. Walk through all of the options, and cross out the false ones. In this case, all three are true, making E the correct answer. Here is another sample of a question type that can appear intimidating:

ECONOMIC DATA (MILLIONS OF DOLLARS)

Government $1,000
Consumption $4,000
National Income $5,900
Investment $700
Consumption of Fixed Capital $30
Exports $300
Imports $500
Indirect business taxes $2,000

Based on the economic figures in the table above, what is the total gross domestic product, in millions of dollars?

(A) $5,500
(B) $5,700

(C) $5,900
(D) $6,150
(E) $6,950

Just because there are eight different options under economic data does not mean all of them need to be calculated. In this case, a student should recognize that the expenditure formula for calculating Gross Domestic Product is adding Consumption, Investment, Government Spending, and Net Exports. Hence, you can ignore four of the options under economic figures, and a simple calculation gives you the correct answer, A.

7. **EASY DOES IT, SOMETIMES.** Sometimes a few questions really are simple to answer. On past released AP Economics exams, the difficulty level of the multiple-choice questions tend to increase toward the second half of the section. So if questions at the beginning of a test appear especially easy, don't be surprised, it happens. Just be ready for some more difficult ones coming.

FREE-RESPONSE QUESTIONS 开放式题目

After the multiple-choice section and a short break, you move on to the free-response questions. This section makes up one-third of your AP score. This section is unique in that it begins with a 10-minute planning session; you can look at the questions but cannot record your official answers. Use this time wisely to plan and organize your answers. You then have 50 minutes to answer the questions. This section is comprised of one long question, worth about 16 percent of your final AP score, and two short questions, each worth about 8 percent. Try to use no more than 25 minutes for the long question, and 12.5 minutes for each of the two short questions. Past students report that they are more likely to run out of time on the multiple-choice section as opposed to the free-response questions, so be sure to double-check all of your answers in the free-response section. Here are some general tips for success on both the AP Microeconomics and the AP Macroeconomics free-response questions.

1. **YOU GET SECOND CHANCES.** They don't come only in life but also on the AP Economics exam. A very important thing to know about the free-response questions is that even if you answer the first part of a question incorrectly, it is still possible to earn "consistency" points on other parts of the question related to the initial incorrect answer. To give you an example from a question similar to one on a recent AP Microeconomics exam, let's look at the monopoly graph in Figure 1.1. Students were asked to begin by identifying the profit-maximizing quantity for the monopolist. From there, students were asked to identify the price, total revenue, and total cost of production; all of these answers are based on the profit-maximizing quantity chosen at the beginning. If a student chooses the wrong quantity, technically all of the following answers will be wrong as well. However, if a student incorrectly identifies the wrong quantity of 25 (The correct answer is a quantity of 15 and a price of 40.), he/she missed that point but is still eligible to get the other questions correct! The other answers are now based on the incorrect quantity of 25, which would result in different price, cost, and revenue answers that could be counted as correct. Despite this initial incorrect answer, several consistency points could be earned.

   Here is another example of how students can earn consistency points despite a wrong answer, this time from the AP Macroeconomics exam: The question reads "*Interest rates increase in the United States relative to Japan. Based on this change, What will*

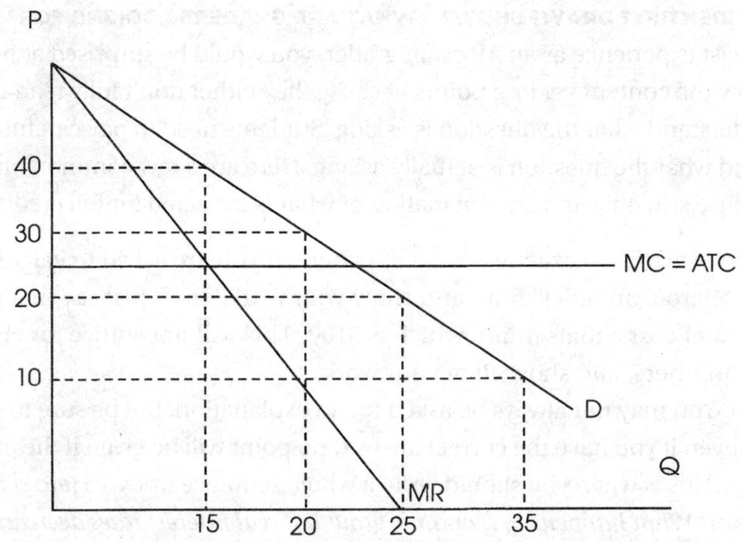

Fig. 1.1 Free-Response Example: Sample Monopoly Graph

happen to the value of the U.S. dollar vs. the Japanese Yen, and exports from the U.S. to Japan? Explain." The correct answer is the demand for the U.S. dollar would increase, making the U.S. dollar appreciate in value vs. the Yen. As the U.S. dollar appreciates vs. the Yen, exports to Japan decrease, because U.S. goods are now relatively more expensive for the Japanese. However, if a student incorrectly claims the U.S. dollar depreciates, one point is taken off, but not all is lost. The student can still earn a consistency point by stating that exports to Japan would increase, based on the initial wrong answer of a depreciated U.S. dollar.

2. **MIND YOUR Ps AND Qs.** Pay attention to price and quantities on the graphs you draw. Always completely label your graphs. You are guaranteed to have to draw graphs on the free-response section, and you will get several points on the AP exam for labeling your graphs correctly. At a minimum, this means putting the correct label on the *x*- and *y*-axes and all your curves. Also, be sure to show with an arrow when the curve shifts, and clearly identify any changes in price or quantity. For example, if the demand curve increases leading to an increase in price, you could label the first curve D 1, and the new curve D 2, just like the graphs you will see in this book. The same goes for price and quantity, or any other item you are asked to label. Also, the graders of AP exams will take off points for not drawing dotted lines to the *x*- and *y*-axes to show price and quantity; be sure to do this. To be sure of how to correctly label a graph, see any graph in this book.
3. **SAVE THE FIVE-PARAGRAPH ESSAY FOR ANOTHER AP EXAM.** Being verbose, which means using far more words than are required, is a common mistake students make. If a question asks you to identify a price or quantity, all that is required is to list the answer, (e.g., price of $5, quantity of 20). The amount of writing required for full credit on a question is actually quite minimal. See more information on what is required for a correct answer in item 5 below.
4. **A WELL-DRAWN GRAPH IS WORTH A THOUSAND WORDS.** OK, maybe not a thousand words, but it is worth a few points on the AP exam. AP graders are looking for specific labels and information when grading your exam, and a well-drawn, neat graph with correct shifts can clearly display your understanding of content. There are just a few graphs to memorize and know. Draw them neatly and correctly, and this will lead to success on the exam.

5. **EXPLAIN? IDENTIFY? DRAW? SHOW?—WHAT ARE GRADERS LOOKING FOR?** Speaking from my vast experience as an AP exam grader, you would be surprised at how many students know the content yet lose points because they either don't fully read the question or misunderstand what the question is asking. Students need to pay careful attention to understand what the question is actually asking. Here are a few common phrases that often confuse students and an explanation of what is expected for full credit when asked.

   - *Show your work.* Do exactly what it says here. If you are asked to calculate profit on the AP Microeconomics exam and show your work, don't just say that total revenue minus total cost equals profit, which is $100. This will not suffice for credit. Plug in all the numbers, and show all of your work.
   - *Explain.* You may not always be asked for an explanation, but be sure to give one if asked. Even if you have the correct answer, no point will be given if the explanation is missing. This is when you should write a whole sentence or two. Here is an example question: "*What happens to economic growth if real interest rates decrease? Explain.*" You will not receive full credit by merely stating that economic growth will increase because interest rates decreased. A correct answer for full credit would say: "*Economic growth will increase, because lower real interest rates will lead to increased investment and capital formation.*" Explain your whole line of reasoning, such as this answer does. **Note:** if the question does not ask you to explain, it's not required for credit.
   - *Identify or determine.* When you see these words, graders are expecting a straightforward answer that requires little writing. The question may ask to identify the price, quantity, or profit.
   - *Draw or show.* This is when graders are looking for a graph or a change on a graph. A question using these words may look like this: "*Draw a correctly labeled loanable-funds graph, and show how an increase in government borrowing affects the real interest rate on the graph.*" Here a student should label all axes and curves, and clearly show all shifts with arrows. See the previous labeling section for more information on graphing.
   - *Show your work.* Here it is insufficient just to write a generic formula, like $P \times Q = 20$. You actually need to use the numbers given in the problem, such as $5 \times 4 = 20$.

Here are a few other tips and reminders going into the AP Economics exam's free-response section:

- Be sure to practice free-response questions in this book. The questions in this book have been carefully developed to be similar to what you can expect to see on the actual exam.
- Be neat and organized. AP Economics graders are looking for specific words, numbers, or labels on a graph, and clear, legible answers will help your cause. Also, clearly label the question number you are answering. If you are answering question 2(ii), label it as such before your answer.
- Memorize the various graph labels and curves. You will get several points just by labeling your graphs correctly. There are only a few graphs to know for both the Microeconomics and Macroeconomics exams. Know them well.
- Don't repeat the question in your answer.
- Write your answers in the correct designated answer section. AP graders an instructed not to grade answers written in the wrong section. You would be surprised how many times students lose points for writing their answers or drawing graphs in the wrong section of the answer booklet. The location of the test booklet designated for answers is clearly labeled, but always double-check.

Here are some tips that are specific to either the Microeconomics or Macroeconomics free-response questions:

MICROECONOMICS FREE-RESPONSE 微观经济学开放式题目

- Know the four market structures. The long free-response question frequently asks students about one of these three market structures: perfect competition, monopoly, and monopolistic competition. The fourth, oligopoly, has been frequently asked about in one of the short questions, applying game theory.
- The other two short questions can come from a wide range of topics from the course outline. Common past topics for these questions in recent years have included comparative advantage and terms of the trade, nominal vs. real interest rates, the foreign exchange market expansion, and monetary expansion using money multiplier. Please note that any topic from the course outline could potentially be asked in this section.

MACROECONOMICS FREE-RESPONSE 宏观经济学开放式题目

- Know the Big 5 graphs. When you have to draw a graph, most likely it will be one of the Big 5. They are aggregate supply and demand, the Phillips curve, the money market, the loanable-funds market, and the foreign exchange market.
- Of the Big 5, the one that almost always appears is the aggregate supply and demand graph.
- Question number 1 (the long one) almost always starts by asking students to draw an economy at full employment, in a recession, or with inflation using the aggregate supply and demand model. It then moves on by asking for an appropriate monetary of fiscal policy for the situation. It will usually ask students to draw a second graph as well, likely the Phillips curve, the loanable-funds market, or the money market.
- The other two short questions can come from a wide range of topics from the course outline. Common past topics for these questions in recent years have included comparative advantage and terms of the trade, nominal vs. real interest rates, The foreign exchange market, banking money expansion using the money multiplier, gross domestic product, price indexes, the balance of payments. Please note that any topic from the course outline could potentially be asked in this section.

Table 1.5

Supplies

Items to Bring to the Exam

- No. 2 pencils (for multiple-choice answers)
- Black or dark-blue ballpoint pens (for free-response answers)
- Watch

Items that Are Strictly Forbidden

- Calculators
- Scratch paper
- Rulers, correction fluid, compasses, dictionaries, and the like
- Cellular phones, MP3 players, or iPads
- Food and drinks

The Discipline of Economics 经济学学科

2

→ WHAT IS ECONOMICS?
→ MICRO vs. MACROECONOMICS
→ POSITIVE vs. NORMATIVE ECONOMICS
→ OPPORTUNITY COST
→ PRODUCTION POSSIBILITIES FRONTIER
→ COMPARATIVE ADVANTAGE

ECONOMICS DEFINED 经济学的定义

Economics is a social science that studies how resources are used and is often concerned with how resources can be used to their fullest potential. Is it wise to use our resources to explore outer space or should we build low-income housing instead? Should we explore for oil fields in the United States or should we use our resources for other endeavors while we import the oil we need?

Consider the case of a student who has only 24 hours to spend each day. Some of this precious resource (time) must be spent on the necessities of life such as eating and sleeping. But of the hours remaining, how many should be devoted to studying? Socializing? Relaxing? Too much socializing and relaxing will not allow the student to live his or her life to its fullest potential. Neither will going overboard on the study time. One problem every student faces is just how much time should be allocated to each of the various activities that make for a full life. This is an economic problem, since the student must decide how the resource (time) will be used to its maximum potential.

The discipline of economics is not directly concerned with money or politics or the stock market; however, economic problems abound in each of these areas. People want to spend their money in the best way. Politicians want to make decisions to achieve the maximum benefit, and investors want the highest return from their savings. Any time someone is trying to make the most out of what he has, we are in the realm of economics.

Notice that our resources are scarce compared to our unlimited wants. There must be some resources that are unlimited. Air? Water? Time? No, all resources have their limits. You might contend that your material wants are modest, but then don't you have friends and relatives you would like to help? Economics is about how we deploy our resources to deal with scarcity.

It is only natural for families, firms, and nations to strive for the best outcomes, given their endowments of resources. For that reason every person and institution must grapple with economic problems every day.

TIP

The general distinction between macroeconomics and microeconomics is that the former deals with the overall economy whereas the latter is concerned with particular individuals, firms, industries, or regions within the economy.

Macroeconomics vs. Microeconomics 宏观经济学与微观经济学

The discipline of economics is broken into two fields: macroeconomics and microeconomics. Macroeconomics involves economic problems encountered by the nation as a whole. For example, do we spend too many of our resources on national defense and not enough on education of our youth? If households are required to pay fewer taxes, will national savings be affected? Will prices rise or fall because of a tax cut? Will increasing the money supply increase production levels in the economy?

Microeconomics is concerned with the economic problems faced by individual units within the overall economy. Here we will be focusing in on particular families, individuals, and firms. Some examples of microeconomic issues are: Does a particular family save enough to provide for its future needs? How will a tax break affect XYZ Corporation's output? If the Smiths win the lottery, how will their spending patterns change?

Positive vs. Normative Economics 实证与规范经济学

The discipline of economics can be split in another way—positive and normative economics. Positive economics is based on the scientific method. That means hypotheses are formulated and tested. For instance, one theory holds that if a family's income increased, their spending will increase but not by as much as the increase in income. There are several ways that this theory could be tested. One way is to observe how a group of families behave when their income is increased. Another might be to survey lottery winners to see how they disposed of their winnings.

Normative economics involves value judgments. Someone may feel that resources are better spent exploring outer space than providing free breakfasts for elementary school children. If this is the person's opinion, not based on a scientific investigation of the matter, then we are in the realm of normative economics. Normative economics is economics based on the way someone believes things *ought* to be.

It may appear as if positive economics is a superior form of the discipline since it is grounded in the scientific method and normative economics is based on opinions. However, normative economics is a crucial part of the economics discipline. Any scientific study will require an experiment, and experiments can be designed to highlight a scientist's prejudices. Even if an economist can keep his biases out of a study, why did he choose this particular question to investigate? However much economists strive to be like biologists and physicists, there will always be a large normative aspect to economics. Some economists claim that the normative side of the economics discipline is the more interesting.

RESOURCES 资源

Economists, like most professionals, have special words and phrases that are used to describe concepts and ideas that occur frequently in their work. In order to understand economics, one must master the jargon. Familiar words and expressions can take on new meaning as economic jargon. The term "resource" is a case in point. To the layperson, a resource is something that can be used or drawn upon in a particular situation or endeavor. Economists do not dispute this definition, and use the word "resource" to mean much the same thing. However, the economist gives the term a special, more particular definition. *A resource is anything that can be used to produce a good or service.* This definition is broad enough to cover such dissimilar things as farmland, crude oil, machinery, and even intellectual ability.

In macroeconomics every resource is classified into one of three categories: land, labor, or capital.

- **Land** does not only refer to the ground we walk on, but all natural resources. Therefore, resources such as farmland, crude oil, timber stands, oceans, and mineral deposits are all classified under the term "land."
- **Labor**, the second classification, encompasses all human attributes that are productive. Humans have the ability to perform a multitude of tasks, so there are many forms of this type of resource. Labor can be the person pounding nails at a construction site or the neurosurgeon in the operating room. Any time anyone is performing a service, function, or task, it is the resource "labor" at work. The professor in the classroom is using his intellectual capability to provide a service, just as a professional basketball player uses her athletic ability to produce points. In both cases, humans are using their attributes to produce things society finds valuable.
- **Capital**, in the economic sense of the term, is productive equipment or machinery. Again, many disparate items can fit into this classification: factory buildings, forklifts, computers, and paper clips are a few examples.

Not all resources fit neatly into this classification scheme. Resources such as time, health, money, adventurousness, and the willingness to take risks would all be difficult to categorize. Some economists have added categories to the classification system so that hard-to-classify resources have a place of their own, but most economists stick with the jargon and maintain that the productive assets of an economy are land, labor, and capital.

OPPORTUNITY COST 机会成本

Opportunity cost is what must be sacrificed to obtain something. The concept of opportunity cost is quite general and ubiquitous in everyday life. When someone decides to spend two hours studying—obtaining wisdom or better grades—something must be sacrificed. For some individuals this might be two hours of watching TV; for others the opportunity cost of two hours of study time may be two hours of lost quality time with the family.

When someone decides to attend college, costs are always a consideration. Even if the money cost of tuition and books is not an issue for the student, the opportunity costs are. The opportunity costs of attending college will be different for each student, since each student sacrifices something different to attend. For most students the opportunity cost of college is the work experience or leisure activities that must be foregone in order to be in college.

In the macroeconomic sphere, opportunity cost takes on a more specific meaning. If a nation decides to produce one more unit of product A, how many units of product B will have to be sacrificed? Producing another unit of product A will use up resources. Exactly how many units of product B could have been produced with those resources?

Table 2.1

Hypothetical Production Possibilities

Point	Guns	Butter
A	0	30
B	3	25
C	6	20
D	9	15
E	12	10
F	15	5
G	18	0

Table 2.1 shows various combinations of guns and butter that an economy could produce using all of its resources fully and efficiently. Using resources efficiently means that they are not used foolishly or wasted in the production process. Efficiency implies using resources to their maximum potential.

It may seem peculiar that this society produces only guns and butter. Guns can be thought of as all types of national defense, while butter represents consumer goods. The number of products in our example could be increased, but that would complicate the analysis unnecessarily.

Notice that each time the country portrayed in Table 2.1 produces three more guns, it must give up five pounds of butter. If it were decided to produce one more gun, then 1.67 pounds of butter would have to be sacrificed. Therefore, the opportunity cost of guns is 1.67 pounds of butter for this nation.

Conversely, if one more pound of butter were produced, society would have to forego the production of 0.6 guns. The opportunity cost of butter is 0.6 guns.

To calculate the opportunity cost of guns, divide the change in butter production by the change in gun production as you move from one line of Table 2.1 to the next.

$$\textit{opportunity cost of guns} = \frac{\textit{change in butter production}}{\textit{change in gun production}} = \frac{5}{3} = 1.67 \textit{ pounds butter}$$

The opportunity cost of butter is the reciprocal of the opportunity cost of guns.

$$\textit{opportunity cost of butter} = \frac{\textit{change in gun production}}{\textit{change in butter production}} = \frac{3}{5} = 0.6 \textit{ guns}$$

The concept of opportunity cost illustrates the simple fact that some amount of one product must be given up when more of another product is desired.

PRODUCTION POSSIBILITIES FRONTIER 生产可能性边界

The production possibilities frontier is the graphical portrayal of the information contained in Table 2.1. It shows the combinations of two goods that can be produced if the economy uses all of its resources fully and efficiently. Figure 2.1 is the production possibilities frontier that corresponds to Table 2.1. Points A through G are plotted with gun production measured on the vertical axis and butter production along the horizontal axis.

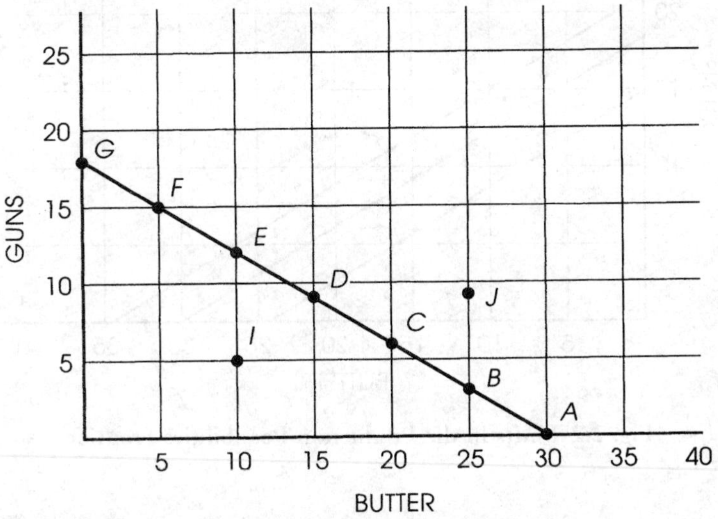

Fig. 2.1 Production Possibilities Frontier

The economy has the option of producing any combination of guns and butter along the frontier. At Point B most of the economy's resources are devoted to butter production. Only three guns are produced. At Point F gun production is predominant. Still, the economy is using its resources fully and efficiently at both points. A normative analysis is required to determine which point is preferred. On efficiency grounds all the points along the frontier are equal.

Points inside the frontier (Point I) are possible also. However, if the economy is operating at a point inside the frontier, resources are not being used fully or efficiently. Consider Point I, where 10 pounds of butter and five guns are being produced per year. By the definition of the production possibilities frontier we know that when the economy produces 10 pounds of butter, 12 guns could be produced if resources were used fully and efficiently (Point E). Point I represents a combination of guns and butter that does not require full or efficient resource utilization. The economy could do better by producing some combination of the two goods that lies on the frontier.

Points outside the production possibilities frontier (Point J) are unobtainable. Point J represents a combination of 25 pounds of butter and nine guns per year. By the definition of the production possibilities frontier we know that if 25 pounds of butter are produced, only three guns can be produced (Point B) if resources are used fully and efficiently. Therefore, points outside the frontier cannot be attained at this time.

Points outside the production possibilities frontier may be attained at some future date because the frontier may shift so that points like J lie along the new frontier. The frontier can also shift inward representing a change for the worse. Two factors cause the production possibilities frontier to shift:

1. changes in the amount of resources in the economy, and
2. changes in technology and productivity.

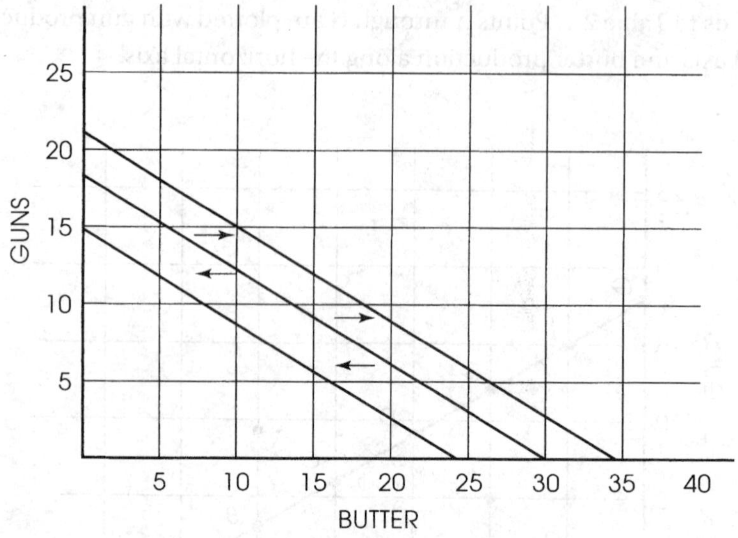

Fig. 2.2 Shifts in the Production Possibilities Frontier

TIP

A decline in unemployment does not shift the production possibilities frontier. If unemployment exists, then the economy is operating inside the frontier. A decline in unemployment would move the economy to a point closer to or onto the frontier.

It stands to reason that if the economy obtains more resources, larger combinations of guns and butter could be produced. This would shift the frontier to the right as in Figure 2.2. Similarly, a technological advance that made a given amount of resources more productive would also shift the frontier to the right.

The amount of resources in a country can increase for a variety of reasons. The amount of labor could increase through population growth. New territories could be acquired or existing land could be opened up for oil exploration or mining. The amount of capital could be increased by producing and putting in place more equipment and machinery.

The production possibilities frontier would shift to the left if the amount of resources were decreased or technology took a step backward. It is easy to imagine the amount of resources in an economy decreasing due to devastating weather, war, or a decline in population. But why take a technological step backward? However, economies sometimes do use less efficient production techniques because of government regulation or tradition.

Government regulations to ensure worker safety or protect the environment often force firms to use less efficient production techniques. Hopefully, the benefits of increased worker safety and a less polluted environment are worth the cost of lower output. By tradition, Amish farmers still use horses to plow their fields. When less efficient production techniques are adopted, the production possibilities frontier shifts to the left. Again, the costs of maintaining this tradition (less output) might be worth the benefits (a more wholesome life).

LAW OF INCREASING COSTS 递增成本规律

The production possibilities frontier is not typically a straight line as in Figures 2.1 and 2.2. You may have noticed that each time gun production increases by three in Table 2.1, butter production decreases by five. The opportunity cost of gun production is $5/3 = 1.67$ pounds of butter between all points. In other words, opportunity cost is constant throughout Table 2.1. This gives rise to the straight-line production possibilities frontier.

However, there is a good reason why opportunity cost will not be constant in the real world. The law of increasing costs states that as more of a product is produced, the opportunity cost increases. Table 2.2 presents data that comply with the law of increasing costs. The opportunity cost of guns is ⅔ = 0.67 pounds of butter between Points A and B, and rises to 3⁄3 = 1 pound of butter between Points B and C. A quick check will show that the farther down Table 2.2 we go, the higher the opportunity cost of guns. The more guns we are initially producing, the more expensive it will be to produce one more gun in terms of butter production lost.

Table 2.2

Hypothetical Production Possibilities with Increasing Costs

Point	Guns	Butter
A	0	25
B	3	23
C	6	20
D	9	15
E	12	10
F	15	5
G	18	0

This holds true for butter production also. In this case we move up Table 2.2 since more butter is produced as we go toward the top of the table. Between Points D and C the opportunity cost of butter is ⅗ = 0.6 guns, whereas the opportunity cost is ⅔ = 0.67 between Points B and A. These numbers are in line with the law of increasing costs, which states that the more of a product that is initially being produced, the higher the opportunity cost will be to produce still more.

When the numbers in Table 2.2 are graphed to form the production possibilities frontier the result is a line that is curved concave to the origin. This is shown in Figure 2.3. Concave-to-the-origin production possibilities frontiers are due to the law of increasing costs.

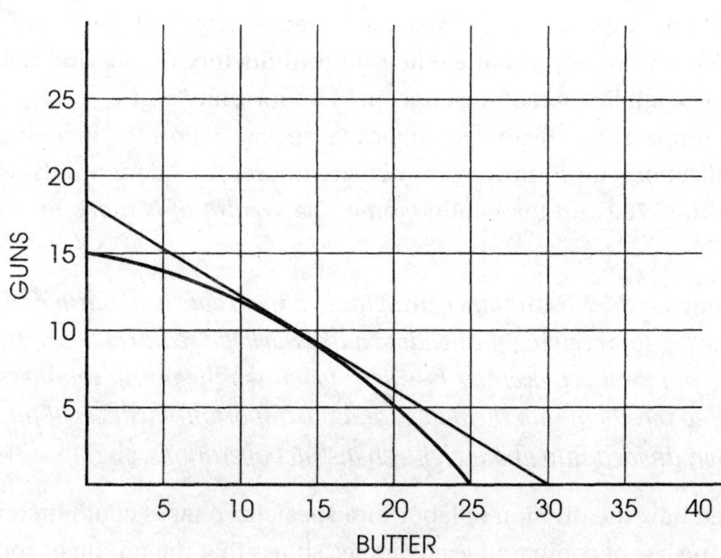

Fig. 2.3 Concave to the Production Possibilities Frontier

Causes 起因

But what is the cause of the law of increasing costs? Why does it cost more (in terms of butter) to produce another gun when a lot of guns are already being produced? To see the answer to these questions you must imagine the situation in an economy that is already producing a lot of guns. Most of the resources in the economy will be devoted to gun production, while only a few resources, such as farmers, cows, milking machines, and so forth, are engaged in butter production. Now, if that society wants to produce more guns, resources will have to be taken from butter production and used to produce guns. This means some farmers and cows will be employed in gun manufacture. (The cows could be used to turn mills that polish gun bores.) But farmers and cows are good at making butter and are not used in gun production, so when the resources are shifted from butter to gun production, not many more guns are produced, but a lot of butter must be sacrificed. In short, the opportunity cost of producing guns is high when gun production is already at a high level.

When gun production is low, the opportunity cost of increasing gun production is low. That is because most of society's resources are employed making butter. Imagine gunsmiths and gunmaking equipment being used to make butter since they are not needed to make the small number of guns being produced. Now, when gun production is increased, the resources that are adept at making guns can be shifted off the farm and into gun production—not much butter will be lost, but many more guns are produced. The opportunity cost of guns is low when a low level of guns is being produced.

The law of increasing costs is due to the fact that some resources are more adept at the production of one good than another. When resources are forced to work in an industry where they are not proficient, they are less productive. Thus, the opportunity cost of producing a good becomes greater as more resources are forced into industries where they are not as productive. This causes the production possibilities frontier to be concave to the origin.

COMPARATIVE ADVANTAGE 比较优势

A survey of economists undertaken in the early 1990s indicates that 93 percent of them believed that restrictions to free trade, such as tariffs and quotas, reduce economic welfare. The basis for this widespread support of free trade is the law of comparative advantage.

The law of comparative advantage was delineated convincingly by David Ricardo in the early 1800s. The law is an important element in introductory micro- and macroeconomics courses. It is also an application of the concept of opportunity cost.

The law of comparative advantage advocates specialization for increased output. The idea that specialization can improve productivity impressed Adam Smith when he visited a pin factory in the 1700s. In his famous tome *The Wealth of Nations* he wrote about his observations:

> *One man draws out the wire, another straights it, a third cuts it, a fourth points it, a fifth grinds it at the top for receiving the head; to make the head requires two or three distinct operations; to put it on is a peculiar business; to whiten the pins is another; it is even a trade by itself to put them into the paper; and the important business of pin making is, in this manner, divided into about eighteen distinct operations, . . .*

Smith showed how the division of labor into specialized tasks could increase productivity and output. The law of comparative advantage shows that the notion of specialization for increased productivity and output applies to nations as well.

When David Ricardo wrote about the benefits of free trade it was in opposition to the Corn Laws of England. The Corn Laws prohibited the importation of grains from outside England in order to protect domestic farmers. Ricardo, like 93 percent of today's economists, felt that the economic well-being of England suffered because of this restriction of trade.

To prove his point, Ricardo set up a scenario very similar to the one depicted in Table 2.3.

Table 2.3

A Hypothetical Example of Production Costs

	Labor Hours Needed to Produce a Unit of:	
Country	**Wheat**	**Cloth**
Portugal	10	20
England	20	60

The table shows how many hours of labor are required to produce one unit of wheat or cloth in England and Portugal. According to Table 2.3, Portugal can produce both products more efficiently than England. In Portugal, a unit of wheat can be produced with 10 hours of labor, while it requires 20 hours in England. One unit of cloth can be produced in Portugal with 20 hours of labor, while the corresponding number in England is 60.

Portugal is said to have the absolute advantage in the production of both wheat and cloth. Absolute advantage implies that the product can be produced more efficiently, that is, with fewer inputs. You might wonder why Portugal would want to trade with England at all, as England is an inefficient producer of both products. That was the genius of Ricardo's exposition—trade can be mutually advantageous to both countries even if one country has the absolute advantage in all products, because mutually advantageous trade is based on comparative advantage, not absolute advantage.

Comparative advantage means that a nation can produce the good with a lower opportunity cost. Consider the opportunity cost of wheat in Portugal. It takes 10 hours to produce a unit of wheat. If it was decided to produce another unit of wheat in Portugal, then half a unit of cloth would have to be given up since the labor would be pulled off cloth production and it takes 20 hours to produce a unit of cloth.

Opportunity cost, you will recall, is how much of one thing must be sacrificed in order to obtain a unit of something else. Here half a unit of cloth must be given up in order to obtain an extra unit of wheat. By similar reasoning, the opportunity cost of cloth in Portugal is two units of wheat. Table 2.4 outlines the calculations required to determine the opportunity costs of wheat and cloth in Portugal and England.

Portugal has the lower opportunity cost in cloth production (two units of wheat), and England has the lower opportunity cost in wheat production (1/3 unit of cloth). Portugal has the comparative advantage in cloth, and England in wheat. Ricardo showed that if each country produced only the good in which it held a comparative advantage and traded for the other product, then both countries could consume more of both goods.

Table 2.4

Calculations of Opportunity Costs from Table 2.3

Portugal
Opportunity cost of wheat = 10/20 = 1/2 cloth
Opportunity cost of cloth = 20/10 = 2 wheat
England
Opportunity cost of wheat = 20/60 = 1/3 cloth
Opportunity cost of cloth = 60/20 = 3 wheat

You might convince yourself of this by assuming that each nation has 120 hours of labor to divide between the production of both goods. For instance, England could use 120 hours to produce a unit of cloth and three units of wheat; Portugal could produce five units of cloth and two units of wheat. Total cloth production by both countries would be six units, and total wheat production would be five units.

Table 2.5

Production of Wheat and Cloth in 120 hours

In Isolation		Wheat	Cloth
	Portugal	2	5
	England	3	1
Total		5	6
Specialization		**Wheat**	**Cloth**
	Portugal	0	6
	England	6	0
Total		6	6
With Trade		**Wheat**	**Cloth**
	Portugal	2.5	5
	England	3.5	1

However, if Portugal devoted its entire 120 hours to cloth production, there would be six units produced and England could use 120 hours to make six units of wheat. This is specialization according to comparative advantage. Notice that total cloth production is six units as it was before specialization, but total wheat production is now six units, not five. The extra unit of wheat could be shared by the citizens of each country through specialization of production and trade.

In fact, we could determine what the terms of trade would have to be so that the extra unit of wheat would add to the welfare of at least one, if not both, countries. Suppose England offered to trade 2 units of wheat for 2 units of cloth. Portugal would not accept since she would be left with 4 units of cloth and the 2 units of wheat. In isolation she could have enjoyed 5 units of cloth and 2 units of wheat.

The terms of trade would have fallen somewhere between 2 units of wheat for 1 unit of cloth (which would leave Portugal no better off than in isolation) and 3 units of wheat for 1 unit of cloth (which would leave England no better off than in isolation). Let's say the two countries strike a deal to trade 2.5 units of wheat for 1 unit of cloth. Then both countries would consume 0.5 units more wheat than in isolation and the same amount of cloth. In other words, the countries would share the extra unit of wheat production that was gained by specialization according to comparative advantage and trade.

Notice that the terms of trade must fall between the opportunity costs of both countries. Portugal's opportunity cost of cloth from Table 2.4 is 2 wheat and England's is 3 wheat. So the terms of trade must lie between 2 and 3 wheat, for one unit of cloth. It amounts to the same thing to state the terms of trade as falling between 1/2 and 1/3 cloth for one unit of wheat.

The idea that trade is beneficial to all parties involved even when one party has an absolute advantage in everything has an analogy in microeconomics. Consider a lawyer who happens to be very fast and accurate at keying legal documents. It would still pay for the lawyer to hire a secretary to do the keying, even if the secretary is not as efficient. That is because the secretary has the comparative advantage (lower opportunity cost) in keying. If the lawyer does her own keying, the opportunity cost is the income that could have been earned writing law briefs.

SUMMARY 小结

- Economics is about using resources wisely. When we focus on one individual or one household or one firm and analyze its use of resources, we are practicing *microeconomics*. When we study whether a nation is allocating its resources in an efficient manner, we are practicing *macroeconomics*.
- Both macro- and microeconomics will require some normative analysis. That is, value judgments will have to be made at some point to answer most economic questions, but there is a tendency to be as positive as possible. Being positive means sticking to the scientific method of reaching conclusions and avoiding personal biases and opinions.
- Even if you have never studied economics before, you are well acquainted with it because everyone strives to make the most out of what they've got. Many people associate businesspeople or stocks and bonds with economics. That is correct because businesspeople are trying to make the most out of their company's resources, while stock and bond traders are trying to maximize their returns—but economics is so much more than that. Whenever a person, a firm, or a nation tries to make the most of its resources, it is practicing economics.
- Remember that the next time you have to decide between studying and watching TV. There's nothing wrong with watching TV. But you should realize that there is a cost to watching TV that goes beyond the cost of the electricity. The opportunity cost of watching TV is the study time you sacrifice. If you think it's worth it, then go for the TV, especially if you have a headache and wouldn't get much out of studying anyway. It's not just businesspeople and Wall Street players who make economic decisions.
- The idea that something must be sacrificed in order to pursue an alternative is captured in the concepts of opportunity cost and the productions possibilities frontier. The law of increasing costs suggests that the production possibilities frontier will be *bowed and concave to the origin as opposed to a straight line.*

TERMS 术语

Absolute Advantage the ability to produce something more efficiently

Capital productive equipment or machinery

Comparative Advantage the ability to produce something with a lower opportunity cost

Economics a social science that studies how resources are used and is often concerned with how resources can be used to their fullest potential

Efficiency using resources to their maximum potential

Labor all human activity that is productive

Land all natural resources

Law of Increasing Costs law that states that when more of a product is initially being produced, the higher the opportunity cost will be to produce still more

Macroeconomics economic problems encountered by the nation as a whole

Microeconomics economic problems faced by individual units within the overall economy

Normative Economics economics involving value judgments

Opportunity Cost the amount of one good that must be sacrificed to obtain an alternative good

$$\text{Opportunity Cost of Good X} = \frac{\text{Change in Good Y production}}{\text{Change in Good X production}}$$

Positive Economics economic analysis that draws conclusions based on logical deduction or induction; value judgments are avoided

Production Possibilities Frontier the combinations of two goods that can be produced if the economy uses all of its resources fully and efficiently

Resource anything that can be used to produce a good or service

Terms of Trade the amount of one good a country is willing and able to trade for another

MULTIPLE-CHOICE REVIEW QUESTIONS 选择题

1. Economics is a social science that

(A) is primarily concerned with money.
(B) is primarily concerned with how resources are used.
(C) relies solely on the scientific method for analysis.
(D) is primarily concerned with maximizing spiritual well-being.
(E) is purely normative.

2. *Macroeconomics focuses on*

(A) government and its laws that affect commerce.
(B) individuals and their resource use.
(C) corporations and their production levels.
(D) the resource use of the entire nation.
(E) money.

3. Given the table below what is the opportunity cost of wheat in France?

Country	Labor hours needed to produce a unit of: Wheat	Cloth
France	5	10
England	20	60

(A) 1/2 cloth.
(B) 1/2 wheat.
(C) 2 cloth.
(D) 2 wheat.
(E) 1/4 cloth.

4. Given the table below, which statement is true?

Country	Labor hours needed to produce a unit of: Wheat	Cloth
France	5	10
England	20	20

(A) England has the absolute advantage in both products.
(B) France should specialize in and export wheat while England should specialize in and export cloth.
(C) France has the comparative advantage in cloth.
(D) England has the comparative advantage in wheat.
(E) France has the absolute advantage in wheat while England has the absolute advantage in cloth.

5. Which of the following statements is positive?

(A) An economy that produces more butter than guns is better off than an economy that produces more guns than butter.
(B) Nations should concentrate their resources on producing wholesome consumer goods as opposed to the weapons of war.
(C) The production possibilities frontier is concave to the origin because of the law of increasing costs.
(D) Nations ought to devote at least some of their resources to national defense.
(E) Nations would do better by producing toward the middle of their production possibilities frontiers as opposed to the extreme points near the axes.

6. The primary focus of microeconomics is

(A) families and how they make money.
(B) firms and how they make profits.
(C) individual units within the overall economy.
(D) government.
(E) small countries.

7. Economists use the term "capital" to mean

(A) money.
(B) plant and equipment.
(C) where the central government is located.
(D) the center of the economy.
(E) a major idea.

8. Land refers to

(A) all productive resources.
(B) all natural resources.
(C) farmland only.
(D) real estate.
(E) chattels.

9. What you give up to pursue another alternative is known as

(A) capital.
(B) land.
(C) money cost.
(D) the price of the product.
(E) opportunity cost.

10. Given the following table, (combinations that can be produced using resources fully and efficiently)

Apples	Oranges
0	20
7	10
14	0

the opportunity cost of apples is

(A) $10/7$ oranges.
(B) $7/10$ oranges.
(C) $10/7$ apples.
(D) $7/10$ apples.
(E) 70 percent.

11. Given the following table,

(combinations that can be produced using resources fully and efficiently)

Soup	Nuts
0	15
1	10
2	5

the opportunity cost of soup is

(A) 5 nuts.
(B) 5 soup.
(C) 20 percent.
(D) 500 percent.
(E) not constant.

12. Production possibilities frontiers are concave to the origin because

(A) of inefficiencies in the economy.
(B) of opportunity cost.
(C) of the law of increasing costs.
(D) of constant opportunity costs.
(E) the extreme points are not as well established.

13. When opportunity cost is constant across all production levels, the productions possibilities frontier is

(A) concave to the origin.
(B) convex to the origin.
(C) undefined.
(D) shifted.
(E) a straight diagonal line sloping downward from left to right.

14. When an economy produces a combination of goods that lies on the production possibilities frontier,

(A) resources are being used fully and efficiently.
(B) prices are constant.
(C) opportunity cost is constant.
(D) resources will never be depleted.
(E) prices will rise.

15. The law of increasing costs

(A) does not apply to guns and butter.

(B) is the result of resources not being perfectly adaptable between the production of two goods.

(C) implies that prices will rise when the costs of making a good rise.

(D) causes the production possibilities frontier to be a straight line.

(E) implies that opportunity costs will rise as production levels fall.

MULTIPLE-CHOICE REVIEW ANSWERS 选择题答案

1. (B)	**4.** (B)	**7.** (B)	**10.** (A)	**13.** (E)
2. (D)	**5.** (C)	**8.** (B)	**11.** (A)	**14.** (A)
3. (A)	**6.** (C)	**9.** (E)	**12.** (C)	**15.** (B)

FREE-RESPONSE REVIEW QUESTIONS 开放式题目

I. The law of increasing costs states that the opportunity cost of producing a good will rise as more of the good is initially being produced. Explain why this is so.

II. Select two goods for which the law of increasing costs might not apply. Explain why the law would not apply in this case.

III. Select two goods for which it is clear the law of increasing costs would definitely apply. Explain why the law is definitely applicable in this case.

Free-Response Review Answers 开放式题目答案

I. The law of increasing costs indicates that the opportunity cost of producing a good will be higher when more of the good is being produced. This is because when the economy is devoting a significant amount of its resources toward the production of a particular product, all the resources that are proficient in the production of the good are already being used to produce it. If more of the good is to be produced, resources that are not as proficient will have to be drawn into the production process. You won't get much more production of this good but production of other goods will fall significantly. This means the opportunity cost of producing more of the good is high. The situation is reversed when production levels of the good are low to begin with.

II. The law of increasing costs would not apply to refrigerators and freezers because the resources required for the production of these two goods are essentially the same. Since the resources are perfectly adaptable between the two goods, we always have to give up the same amount of refrigerators to produce one more freezer, regardless of how many freezers we are producing to begin with.

III. The law of increasing costs would most likely apply to milk and computers. Most of the resources required to produce milk are not very useful in computer production. Therefore, when most of the economy's resources are already being used to produce computers, only cows, farmland, tractors, and farmers are left producing milk. In order to produce still more computers you will have to take these resources off the farm and use them to make computers. You will have to give up quite a bit of milk just to produce one more computer.

Economic Systems 经济体 3

- → COMMAND ECONOMY
- → CAPITALISM
- → ALLOCATIVE EFFICIENCY
- → MIXED ECONOMY
- → CIRCULAR FLOW DIAGRAM

FUNDAMENTAL ECONOMIC ISSUES 基本经济问题

In every nation there are a variety of issues that demand attention: What can be done about poverty and unemployment? Pollution? The national debt? Inflation? And so on. Yet before these questions can be addressed—indeed, before these problems even crop up—there are some fundamental economic questions that each and every country will have to contend with.

Even Robinson Crusoe had to deal with economic issues on his deserted island. What resources were on hand to provide food and shelter? Was clothing necessary? Crusoe had to decide how to best employ his meager resources to ensure his survival. In the same manner, each nation must decide what is the best way to use the resources at its disposal.

Would it be wise for Crusoe to spend all his time keeping a signal fire burning and searching the horizon for a rescue ship? Or should the same wood that might be used in the signal fire be used to build a shelter? Should the United States use its resources to explore Mars or to build low-income housing? One of the most fundamental questions any economy will have to address, whether it is one man trapped on an island or a highly industrialized nation, is what should be produced given its resources.

In Cuba it is virtually impossible to get cosmetic surgery, while the United States devotes a significant amount of its resources to this. Part of the reason why this is so has to do with the fact that the United States has so many resources compared to Cuba, but another reason why Cuba spends hardly any resources on plastic surgery is because of the way the decision is made about what will be produced in Cuba.

Opportunity Costs 机会成本

Before exploring further the differences in the way economic decisions are undertaken in Cuba versus in the United States, let us consider some other fundamental economic questions. Once it is decided to produce a certain set of goods and services, how much of each item should be produced? The concept of opportunity cost comes into play here. If it is decided to produce more than one item, then some amount of another item must be sacrificed.

Not only that, but many goods and services are related to one another. For instance, if it is decided to produce more wheat, this will require an increase in the production of tractors, seed, fertilizer, and other products needed to produce wheat. Considering opportunity costs and the fact that many products are related, the decision of how much to produce of each good and service becomes an extremely complex issue.

WHO GETS WHAT? 谁得到什么?

After having decided what and how much of each item is to be produced, there is still another basic question: Who is going to get how much of each good and service? In the United States, a medical doctor can obtain more and higher-quality goods and services than a schoolteacher. In Cuba doctors and teachers have roughly equal living standards. Certainly a person's income is important in determining how many goods and services can be obtained. But why do doctors receive so much more income than teachers in the United States and not in Cuba? The answer to that question involves how each economy responds to the basic economic issue of "who gets what?"

So there are two fundamental economic questions that any society will have to address:

1. How much, if any, of each good and service should be produced?
2. Who will get how much of each good and service?

In order to appreciate the complexity of these questions, imagine yourself shipwrecked on a desert island with 11 other people. It is possible to produce only a limited number of items with the resources on hand. The necessities of life will have to be produced: food, clothing, and shelter.

Should you attempt to build a boat large enough to take 12 people back to civilization? Or is a signal fire more logical? It would be possible to provide haircuts, and makeup could be manufactured, however crude. Exactly what should be produced?

If the production of cosmetics and haircuts is forsaken in order to produce more food, it will be necessary to produce more tools for working the land and harvesting the crops.

Who will get how much of each item produced? Should the doctor get more than the food production manager? Should the sick people get more or less than the others?

Now try and imagine coping with these questions when there are 350 million people and the array of goods and service encompasses everything from rubber bands to super computers. The organization of large economies is a mind-boggling task. How is it accomplished?

STRATEGIES FOR ADDRESSING ECONOMIC QUESTIONS 处理经济问题的策略

There are three basic ways to address the economic questions that are imposed upon a society: (1) government commands, (2) capitalism, and (3) a blend of government commands and capitalism.

The Command Economy 指令性经济

A command economy is one in which the central government dictates what will or will not be produced. The government also stipulates how much of each item is to be produced and finally, who is to get how many of the final products. Cuba and North Korea are examples of nations that rely heavily on the command system. The terms *communism* and *socialism* are sometimes used to describe economies that use central commands to address the fundamental economic questions.

Cosmetic surgery is not available in Cuba because the central government does not allow resources to be used on this service. Through the use of quotas and production plans, the Cuban government dictates how much of each good and service will be available. This is no simple task since thousands of items are produced.

Moreover, the production levels of the various goods and services must be coordinated so that if more sugar is to be produced, then more arable land, fertilizer, farm labor, and so on must be provided.

Finally, by setting the prices on almost all goods and services, and by setting the wage rates for almost all citizens, the Cuban government can dictate who gets what share of these products.

Setting prices and wages and stipulating how much of each item is to be produced for the whole economy are Herculean tasks. It is done with the help of computers by a large bureaucracy. Often, mistakes are made. The quota of sugar cannot be met because not enough tractors are available. Without sugar, the rum quota cannot be met.

On the other hand, the command system has some commendable features. Wages can be set so that there is no lower class. However, if everyone makes about the same income, incentives to work hard and develop new lines of business are discouraged. Still, the price of alcohol can be set high to curtail alcoholism, while the price of textbooks can be established artificially low to encourage education.

The Cuban economy is not a pure command economy. There is some experimentation with households and firms being allowed to sell their excess production in markets where prices are not fixed by the government. And there are many transactions between households that the government cannot control. Some products and a variety of services are provided on the "black market."

Capitalism 资本主义

Capitalism has been defined by different writers in remarkably different ways. Some point to the importance of private property in capitalist economies, while others note the emphasis on risk-taking and entrepreneurial skills. The best definition of capitalism, however, is in regard to how the basic economic questions are addressed. Capitalism is an economic system where supply and demand determine prices. These prices coordinate the economy by resolving what and how much will be produced. Supply and demand will also determine a person's income and therefore how much of the production the person can obtain for his or her own use.

In this type of system, the government does not run the economy but, instead, attempts to create an environment where prices can be determined in free markets. Amazingly, these prices coordinate the economy.

In a capitalist economy, prices determine how much of each item will be produced. If consumers want more baggy, pleated pants instead of blue jeans, then the price of baggy, pleated pants increases and the price of jeans falls. Producers, with an eye on profit possibilities, then manufacture more baggy, pleated pants and fewer jeans. In fact, textile manufacturers who do not respond to the price changes could go out of business.

Consumers, not the government, determine how much of each item will be produced. They do this by purchasing the products they like. When consumers demand and purchase products, they are voting for those products. The prices of consumers' favorite products rise and this sends a signal to suppliers to provide more of that product.

An individual's income determines how much of the production he can obtain and enjoy, but income is largely determined by the wages an individual receives. And the wage rate is just another price in the economy: the price of labor.

Notice that the government does not have to get involved in setting prices and wages in capitalist economies. Prices and wages are determined in free markets and these prices serve to coordinate the economy and answer the basic economic questions. Prices govern the behavior of consumers and producers who seek to make the most out of their respective resources. Just the right goods and services are produced in just the right amounts. This is known as "allocative efficiency" in economic jargon.

ALLOCATIVE EFFICIENCY 配置效率

A market is a mechanism that allows buyers and sellers to exchange a good or service. A free market is unfettered by interference from anyone not directly involved in the exchange. The hallmark of a capitalist economy is prices determined in free markets. Markets that are regulated by the government or any other agency are not truly free. By this definition, the market for beef in the United States is not free because it is regulated by several agencies including the U.S. Department of Agriculture. However, because Americans mostly want to buy inspected beef, we can argue about whether or not the market for inspected beef in America is truly free.

In the next chapter, we shall see in great detail how prices are determined in perfectly competitive markets—free markets with many buyers and sellers. The more perfectly competitive markets there are in an economy, the closer the economy is to perfect capitalism.

When the prices of products are determined in perfectly competitive markets, an amazing thing happens: The economy's fundamental problems are answered. Consider the question of how much of a particular good is to be produced. In the market for tulips, if the most any buyer is willing to pay is two cents per tulip, then none will be produced. But if buyers have a mania for tulips and are willing to pay a lot, then many will be produced, and the amount of resources devoted to tulip production will be vast.

The other fundamental question is Who will get how much of each good or service? If our tulip-crazed society is capitalist, then competitive markets will answer this question as well. A person's income will determine how many tulips he gets, and those incomes are determined in competitive markets. Labor is another product, and if the most any buyer is willing to pay is two cents an hour, then little or no labor will be supplied. But if buyers (or shall we call them employers?) are willing to pay quite a bit for an expert in tulip production, then a lot of experts will step forward offering their labor services in this industry. Indeed, a lot of resources will be devoted to tulip production in this society, and those with agricultural skills or fertile land or green houses will be handsomely rewarded.

Not only does capitalism answer the fundamental economic questions, it does so in a decentralized way. No authority has to be on the lookout that enough tulips are produced. When buyers offer high prices, sellers respond to the profit motive and bring a bounty to market. But sellers are discouraged from bringing too much because in that case they would not be able to sell all their stock. They would begin to lower their asking price. The new lower price would caution others from entering the market as sellers, and current sellers would have less incentive to work over a period of time to bring so many tulips next time.

Capitalist societies respond very well to changes in the population's preferences. Imagine that tulips become passé and now people want roses. Buyers offer low prices for tulips and high prices for roses. Sellers respond to the profit motive by bringing fewer tulips to market and more roses. In this way, resources are switched from tulip production to rose production.

When all of the prices in an economy are determined in competitive markets, resources will be deployed in the optimal way to ensure the right products are made in just the right amounts to satisfy the buyers. This result is truly amazing since it is the result of decisions made by buyers and sellers across the economy in a decentralized way. No central planning is required. The only necessity is that people pursue their own self-interest.

This fascinating result of competitive markets is known as allocative efficiency. The mathematical proof that capitalism results in allocative efficiency is attributed to Léon Walras, but Adam Smith understood the concept well and put it in a very memorable way in 1759:

> *Every individual . . . neither intends to promote the public interest, nor knows how much he is promoting it . . . he intends only his own security; and by directing that industry in such a manner as its produce may be of the greatest value, he intends only his own gain, and he is in this, as in many other cases, led by an invisible hand to promote an end which was no part of his intention.*
>
> *The Theory of Moral Sentiments, Part IV, Chapter I, pp.184–185, para. 10.*

The fact that allocative efficiency follows from free markets leads some people to conclude that the government should not interfere in economic matters. Government intervention can only interfere with the working of the invisible hand. Once again, Adam Smith pointed out that there will always be a need for government. Who will ensure that markets are indeed competitive? Who will settle disputes between buyers and sellers? Who will protect people, their products, and their money while they are conducting market exchanges? In the next section, we explore why no economy can be purely capitalist.

The Mixed Economy 混合经济

All of the countries in the world today use a blend of government commands and capitalism to address the fundamental economic questions that arise. In the United States, capitalism is emphasized, but government commands are used when free markets break down. For instance, society benefits when people pursue education beyond high school. The government promotes higher education by providing scholarships, grants, and loans. Private colleges have competition from state schools. Our government doesn't trust the production of higher education to the market. It gets involved and increases the equilibrium quantity of college degrees granted.

TIP

There are several other instances where competitive markets break down. You will need to know these well only if you are taking the Microeconomics exam.

Similarly, there is no pure command economy on the planet; even Cuba and North Korea have some free markets. It is best to view the economies of the world on a spectrum with pure capitalism on the right and pure command economies on the left. The United States is closer to pure capitalism than France, and France is closer to pure capitalism than Cuba.

As we go forward we will focus on the fundamental macroeconomic concepts of capitalist economies such as the United States where the decentralized decision making of the price system predominates.

THE CIRCULAR FLOW DIAGRAM 流动循环图

In capitalist economies, most of the resources are owned by individuals and households. The government and business enterprises will own some resources in such a system, but not the lion's share. Moreover, since most of the large firms are owned by stockholders (individuals and households) and most government resources, such as Yosemite National Park, are considered to be jointly owned by everyone, it is fair to assume that all of the resources are owned by individuals and households.

The circular flow diagram portrayed in Figure 3.1 shows these resources (land, labor, and capital) flowing from households to firms. In return, households receive wages and profits. This exchange of resources for money is known as the market for resources.

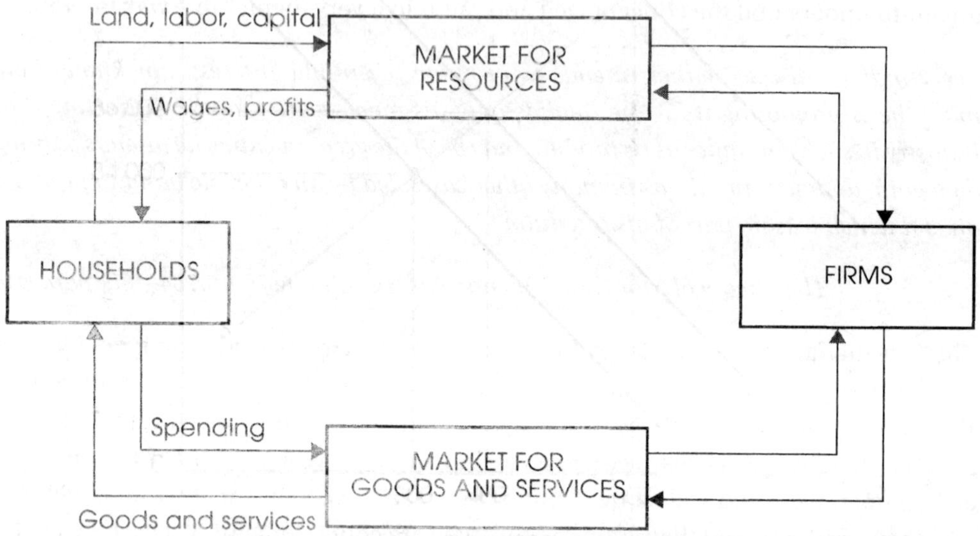

Fig. 3.1 The Circular Flow Diagram

Households spend their money income to purchase the goods and services supplied by firms. This exchange of income for products is known as the *market for goods and services*.

The circular flow diagram shows how resources are used to produce goods and services and how these goods and services are distributed. Essentially, individuals and households sell their resources to firms that use the resources to produce goods and services. Individuals and households use the proceeds from the sale of their resources to purchase the output of the firms.

The circular flow diagram can be expanded to include the government and banks. There would be more boxes and more lines representing flows of money and products, but no matter how complicated or simple, the circular flow diagram shows how institutions in capitalist economies are tied together.

SUMMARY 小结

Even if you drop out of society and go to live as a hermit on an isolated mountaintop, you will have to cope with the fundamental economic questions: What should be produced with the resources on hand and how much of each item should be produced? Hermits, however, do not have to deal with the other fundamental economic question: How much of the production should each member of society get?

- Government commands and capitalism are two general ways to address the fundamental economic questions. Each approach has its strengths and weaknesses. Basically, an economy organized by government commands can be more equitable while a market economy is more efficient.

- When supply and demand are allowed to determine prices in competitive markets, just the right amount of goods and services will be produced to satisfy society's wants. This is known as *allocative efficiency*. Resources are deployed in the production of the things society desires.
- No country in the world is purely capitalistic. Even in the United States the government does not allow free markets to determine all prices. Similarly, no nation is a pure command economy. Even Cuba has some free markets.

TERMS 术语

Allocative Efficiency when resources are deployed to produce just the right amount of each product to satisfy society's wants

Capitalism an economic system where supply and demand determine prices

Circular Flow Diagram diagram that shows how households and firms are related by the exchange of resources and products

Command Economy economy in which the central government dictates what will or will not be produced and who gets what

Law of Demand law that states that when the price of a product increases, the quantity demanded decreases, *ceteris paribus*

Law of Supply law that states that when the price of a product increases, the quantity supplied increases, *ceteris paribus*

Market a mechanism that allows buyers and sellers to exchange a good or service

Mixed Economy a blend of government commands and capitalism

MULTIPLE-CHOICE REVIEW QUESTIONS 选择题

1. Which of the following is a fundamental economic question?

(A) Who will get how much of each good and service?

(B) Who should pay taxes?

(C) Who will work?

(D) Who will make the economic decisions?

(E) Who will be allowed into the economy?

2. In a command economy

(A) the market dictates the answers to the fundamental economic questions.

(B) competition helps answer the fundamental economic questions.

(C) state and local governments respond to the fundamental economic questions.

(D) the central government dictates the answers to the fundamental economic questions.

(E) laws are set up to answer the fundamental economic questions.

3. Market economies

(A) rely on markets to coordinate economic activity.

(B) rely on the government to address the fundamental economic questions.

(C) rely on elected officials to make the most important economic decisions.

(D) rely on courts to ensure people and firms get what they deserve.

(E) are more equitable than command economies.

4. Prices in capitalist economies are

(A) unfair.

(B) determined in competitive markets.

(C) determined, in most cases, by the federal government.

(D) a reflection of our basic values.

(E) a means to achieve equality.

5. If the market for corn is competitive, then

(A) it is difficult for new suppliers to join in.

(B) buyers will get all they want at a good price.

(C) the market favors buyers.

(D) the market is fair.

(E) there must be many buyers and sellers.

6. Compared to a command economy, a capitalist economy emphasizes

(A) equity.

(B) planning.

(C) efficiency.

(D) centralization.

(E) human rights.

7. Allocative efficiency

(A) implies optimal resource deployment.

(B) means no inferior products will be produced.

(C) ensures the distribution of output is equitable.

(D) can only occur in pure command economies.

(E) defies the idea of the invisible hand.

8. Scarcity

(A) implies nonoptimal resource deployment.

(B) applies to some, but not all, resources.

(C) is an issue in every economy.

(D exists in command economies only.

(E) is eradicated by the invisible hand.

9. If buyers bid up the price of a good, then

(A) sellers will try to bring more of it to market.
(B) sellers will bring less to market anticipating less demand at the higher price.
(C) fewer resources will be devoted to its production.
(D) they must not want it.
(E) its price will eventually fall back to normal.

10. If a capitalist society wants more coffee, then the relative price of coffee will

(A) fall.
(B) rise.
(C) not necessarily change.
(D) remain unchanged.
(E) change indeterminantly.

11. If the relative price of coffee rises due to a change in tastes in a capitalist society, then

(A) less coffee will be consumed.
(B) more resources will be devoted to coffee production.
(C) less tea will be consumed.
(D) suppliers will bring less to market.
(E) the price will eventually return to where it was prior to the change in tastes.

12. The invisible hand

(A) works in command economies as well as capitalist economies.
(B) works in capitalist societies.
(C) is concerned with resource allocation when markets are regulated.
(D) refers to regulation in command economies.
(E) requires altruism.

13. In the market for resources in the circular flow diagram, households

(A) get goods and services from firms.
(B) send only labor to firms.
(C) send only land and labor to firms.
(D) send land, labor, and capital to firms.
(E) send spending to firms.

14. In the market for goods and services in the circular flow diagram, households

(A) get wages and profits from firms.
(B) get goods and services from firms.
(C) send only land and labor to firms.
(D) send land, labor, and capital to firms.
(E) send labor to firms.

15. In the market for resources in the circular flow diagram, households

(A) send only land and labor to firms.
(B) get goods and services from firms.
(C) get wages and profits from firms.
(D) send land, labor, and capital to firms.
(E) send their spending to firms.

MULTIPLE-CHOICE REVIEW ANSWERS
选择题答案

1. (A) **4.** (B) **7.** (A) **10.** (B) **13.** (D)

2. (D) **5.** (E) **8.** (C) **11.** (B) **14.** (B)

3. (A) **6.** (C) **9.** (A) **12.** (B) **15.** (C)

FREE-RESPONSE REVIEW QUESTIONS 开放式题目

I. What are the fundamental economic questions?

II. Contrast how the fundamental economic questions are addressed in command versus capitalist economies.

III. Cite the advantages and disadvantages of command economies.

Free-Response Review Answers 开放式题目答案

I. There are two fundamental economic questions that any society will have to address: (1) How much, if any, of each good and service should be produced? and (2) Who will get how much of each good and service?

II. In command economies the central government stipulates what and how much of most products will be produced. By setting prices and wages the central government can also dictate how much of the production is allotted to each household. In short, the central government controls production and income in command economies.

In capitalist economies free markets coordinate output and income. Supply and demand, which depend upon the decentralized decision making of all consumers and producers, determine what and how much will be produced. Supply and demand also determine incomes and, therefore, who gets how much of each good and service.

III. One disadvantage of command economies is that there can be a lack of incentive to work hard to get ahead. Since the government decides one's income level, it may not pay to put one's nose to the grindstone—the government may reward you all the same, anyway. One advantage of command economies is that prices can be set to achieve social goals. For example, the price of textbooks could be set low to promote education. Another advantage of command economies is that incomes can be set more equitably than capitalist economies.

Capitalist economies are typically more allocatively efficient than command economies; also, they do not require the large bureaucracy of command economies.

Demand and Supply: The Basics
需求与供给：基础知识

4

- → CHANGES IN DEMAND AND SUPPLY
- → COMPETITION
- → PRICE CEILINGS AND PRICE FLOORS
- → LAW OF DEMAND AND LAW OF SUPPLY
- → EQUILIBRIUM
- → CHANGES IN QUANTITY DEMANDED AND QUANTITY SUPPLIED

INTRODUCTION 导言

Economics is sometimes said to be "common sense made complicated." This description is somewhat true of the concepts of supply and demand. Supply and demand are fundamental to the study of economics, and understanding supply and demand is essential for performing well on both the AP Microeconomics and Macroeconomics exams. At the heart of economics is the role of prices in decision making and in the allocation of scarce resources through supply and demand. By mastering the basics of supply and demand, essential concepts in AP Microeconomics and Macroeconomics are understood much more easily. This chapter will cover the basics of supply and demand for you in detail, and with a little effort, it should be common sense made simple.

THINGS TO KNOW 要了解的事

Based on the most frequently asked questions on previous advanced placement exams, the following are the most important concepts. In this chapter, we will expand on these and other concepts and examples.

1. **CHANGES IN DEMAND VERSUS CHANGES IN QUANTITY DEMANDED, AND CHANGES IN SUPPLY VERSUS CHANGES IN QUANTITY SUPPLIED.** Changes in demand or supply show how nonprice determinants cause a shift in the demand or supply curve. Changes in quantity demanded result from only a price change in the good being analyzed, and there is no shift of a curve, just a movement along a fixed curve.
2. **MARKET EQUILIBRIUM.** This is the level of output and price at which the quantity demanded equals the quantity supplied. This provides a reference point for discussion of shortages and surpluses as well as a base of government policies.
3. **NONPRICE DETERMINANTS OF SUPPLY AND DEMAND.** Examples follow in this chapter on what factors influence increases or decreases in demand (supply).

4. **SIMULTANEOUS CHANGES IN DEMAND AND SUPPLY.** Examples and a table will follow to illustrate this situation.
5. **GOVERNMENT INDUCED CHANGES IN THE FORM OF PRICE CEILINGS AND PRICE FLOORS.** Examples and graphs will follow in this chapter.

DEMAND AND THE LAW OF DEMAND 需求与需求定律

A market's **demand** shows the quantity of a product a consumer is willing and able to purchase at each and every price. The demand for a product is shown graphically as a demand curve (see Figure 4.1). The demand curve performs one important job, and that is showing the quantity consumers want to buy at every price. You likely already know that at higher prices, people tend to buy less of a product, and at lower prices, people buy more (common sense!). If so, then you also already know the **law of demand,** which states that when the price of a product increases, the quantity demanded decreases, and vice versa (ceteris paribus— "all other things remaining unchanged"). This relationship is shown in the down-sloping demand curve shown in Figure 4.1. An easy way to remember the demand curve's slope is "DEmand DEclines."

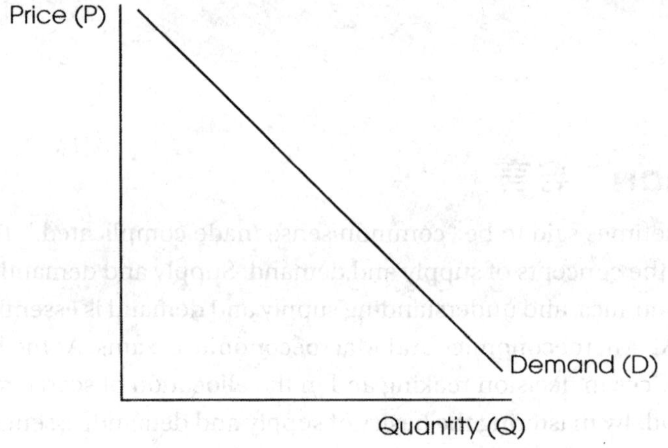

Fig. 4.1 A Demand Curve

Reasons for the Law of Demand 需求定律的原因

There are two important reasons why people buy less of a good when the price increases and more when a price decreases, giving the demand curve its downward slope.

1. **THE INCOME EFFECT.** When prices fall, consumers can afford to buy more of a particular good or service. When prices rise, consumers' income will not buy as many goods and services, and the quantity people will buy of a product decreases. This is known as the income effect.
2. **THE SUBSTITUTION EFFECT.** When the price of a good increases, its price has also gone up relative to the prices of other goods, all else equal. If we assume apples and oranges are substitutes, a increase in the price of apples will lead consumers to purchase more oranges and fewer apples. This is known as the substitution effect and further reinforces the notion of a downward sloping demand curve and the law of demand.

Change in Quantity Demanded vs. Change in Demand 需求量的变化与需求的变化

One of the most confusing topics for students to comprehend about supply and demand is when there is a change in the quantity demanded or a change in demand. These two phrases have different meanings although they sound similar. When the market for a product only has a price change, there is not a shift in the demand curve, but a movement along an existing curve. This is known as a change in the **quantity demanded.** As shown in Figure 4.2, as the price decreases from P_1 to P_2, the quantity demanded increases from Q_1 to Q_2. As price is the only variable that changes, this is just a change in the quantity people would buy at the new price (the quantity demanded), and no shift in the curve occurs. A change in price is just a movement along a fixed demand curve, a change in the quantity demanded.

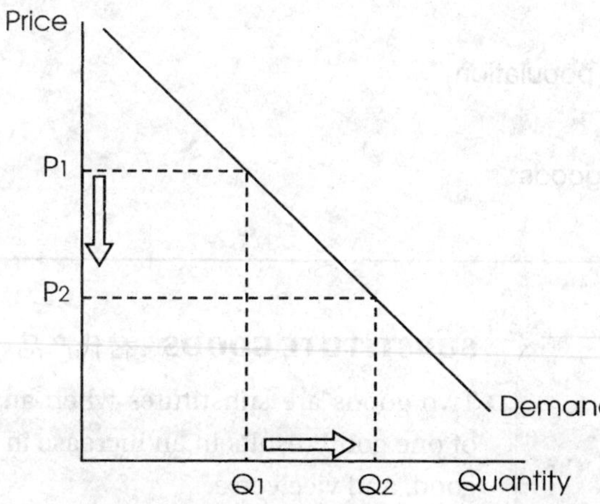

Fig. 4.2 A Change in Quantity Demanded

Shifts of the Demand Curve: The Determinants of Demand
需求曲线的变动：需求的决定因素

There are other scenarios where people will want to purchase more or less of a good at the same price. These are not just price changes that result in a change in the quantity demanded but variables that cause consumers to buy more or less of a product at the same price. These are called the **determinants of demand** (also called shifters of demand). As shown in Figure 4.3, an increase in one of these determinants of demand would shift the demand curve to the right (D_1 to D_2), and a decrease would shift the curve to the left (D_1 to D_3).

USEFUL HINT

Useful Hint regarding curve shifts: "Less to the left, more to the right."

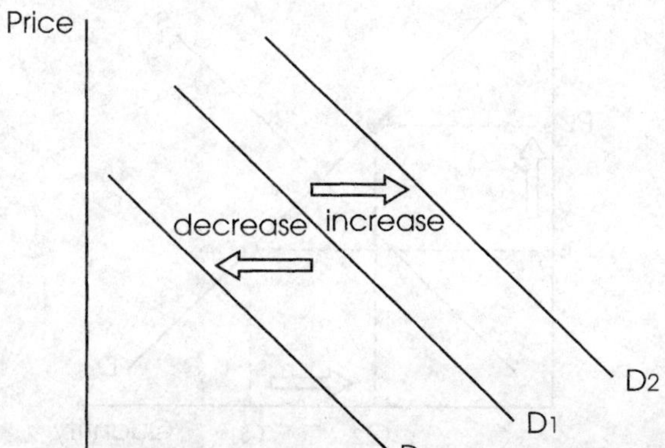

Fig. 4.3 Shifts in Demand

The determinants of demand can be learned by the acronym SPICE shown in Table 4.1, followed by an explanation of each with examples.

Table 4.1

Determinants of Demand——SPICE (Shifter of the Demand Curve)
S—Substitute goods
P—Preferences and population
I—Income
C—Complementary goods
E—Expectations

USEFUL HINT

Price and demand for substitute goods have a direct relationship: if the price of one goes up, the demand for the other product goes up.

SUBSTITUTE GOODS 替代产品

Two goods are substitutes when an increase in the price of one good results in an increase in demand for the other good, and vice versa.

EXAMPLE

Assume consumers view apples and oranges as perfect substitutes. If the price of apples increases while the price of oranges remains constant, the quantity demanded of apples decreases, and consumers will now demand more oranges at each price, shifting the curve for oranges to the right (see Figures 4.4 and 4.5). (*Note*: The demand curve for apples will not shift, this is just a decrease in the quantity demanded, a movement along a fixed apple demand curve. The demand curve for oranges will increase and shift to the right.)

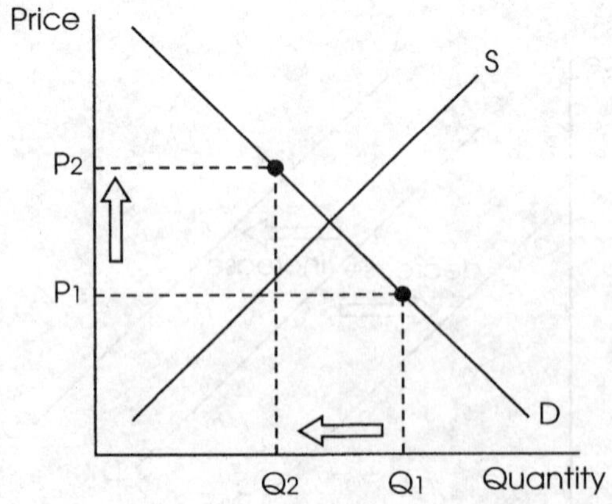

Fig. 4.4 Market for Apples

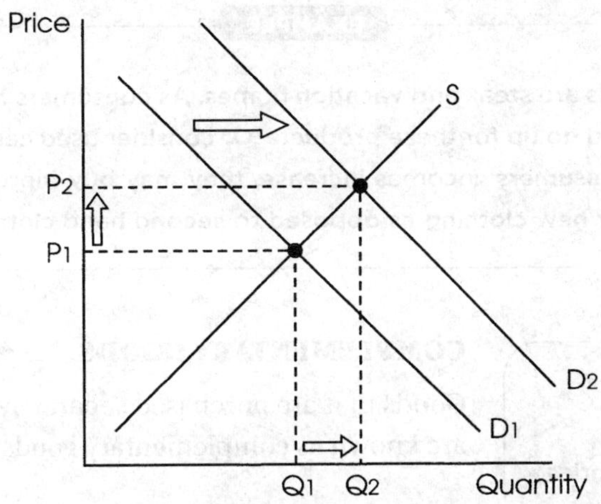

Fig. 4.5 Market for Oranges

PREFERENCES 偏好

Preferences refers to a consumer's tastes or preferences for a good or service. If people's preferences for a specific product increase, the demand curve will shift to the right.

EXAMPLE

A successful advertising campaign for a product by a celebrity movie star may increase the demand for a product, making consumers want to buy more at each price level (a shift from D_1 to D_2 on Figure 4.3). Other examples of preferences changing demand are the latest fads in fashion, coolness of a product, or a decline in popularity for out-of-date technology.

POPULATION 人口

Sometimes also referred to as the number of consumers in a market, population refers to the total number of buyers in a specific market. A bigger market will mean more demand.

EXAMPLE

If there is a huge baby boom in a country, there will be more demand for baby supplies. Conversely, an increase in the number of people older than 65 would lead to more demand for retirement and nursing homes.

INCOME 收入

When people have more income, they generally increase their demand for most products. Most goods are **normal goods**, where as income increases, the demand for a product increases. Some goods, however, are **inferior goods**, where an increase in income leads to a decrease in demand.

EXAMPLE

Some normal goods are steak and vacation homes. As consumers have more income, their demand would go up for these products. Or consider used cars or goods sold at thrift stores. As consumers' incomes increase, they may buy more new cars instead of used or shop for new clothing as opposed to second hand clothes.

USEFUL TIP

The price and demand for complementary goods have an inverse relationship. If the price of one increases, the demand for the other good decreases, and vice versa.

COMPLEMENTARY GOODS 互补商品

Goods that are purchased separately but are used together are known as complementary goods.

EXAMPLE

Consider the market for large cars and gasoline. If the price of gas rises significantly, consumers will find it more expensive to own a large, gas-guzzling car. The demand for large cars would decrease due to the increase in price for gas. Another example would be hot dogs and hot dog buns. If the price of hot dogs decreases, the quantity of hot dogs purchased would increase, and the demand for buns would increase, shifting the bun demand curve to the right.

EXPECTATIONS 预期

Consumers' expectations of future prices can have a large effect on current demand for a product. An expectation of higher prices in the future will cause an increase in current demand.

EXAMPLE

If consumers expect prices of new houses to increase dramatically in the future, the present demand for new houses will increase, shifting demand to the right. If people feel that home prices will decrease significantly next year, that would decrease current demand for housing, as consumers will wait until next year.

SUPPLY AND THE LAW OF SUPPLY 供给与供给定律

Buyers dislike high prices, but they are likely to make sellers happy. Since buyers and sellers feel differently about prices, the supply curve will have a different meaning and slope than the demand curve. A market's **supply** shows the quantity of a product a producer is willing and able to offer for sale at various prices. The supply for a product is shown graphically as a supply curve, as in Figure 4.6. The supply curve performs one important job, which is showing the quantity producers want to offer for sale at every price. The **law of supply** states that when the price of a product increases, the quantity supplied increases, ceteris paribus. An easy way to remember the positive slope of the supply curve is "Supply to the sky."

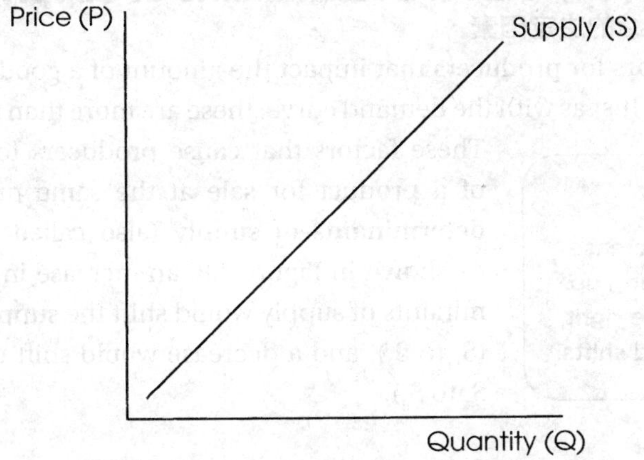

Fig. 4.6 A Supply Curve

Reasons for the Law of Supply 供给定律的原因

When prices increase, sellers have greater opportunities for increasing their profits. This is one reason to explain why as prices rise, so does the quantity supplied. Also, as producers increase production, the cost of producing each additional unit generally increases as sellers face rising marginal costs of production. Hence, it takes a higher price for the product to induce producers to offer more for sale. Conversely, if the price falls for a product, there is less incentive or motivation to offer a product for sale and the quantity brought to market will decrease. As prices fall, firms find it harder to cover costs of production and earn smaller profits, so less is offered for sale.

Change in Quantity Supplied vs. Change in Supply 供给量的变化与供给的变化

Similar to demand, supply also makes a distinction between a change in quantity supplied vs. a change in supply. When the market for a product only has a price change, there is not a shift in the supply curve, but a move along an existing curve. This is known as a change in the **quantity supplied.** As shown in Figure 4.7, as the price increases from P_1 to P_2, the quantity supplied also increases from Q_1 to Q_2. Because price is the only variable that changes, this is just a change in the quantity supplied, and no shift in the curve occurs. There is a change in the quantity producers will offer for sale, but the curve does not shift. A change in price is just a movement along a fixed supply curve.

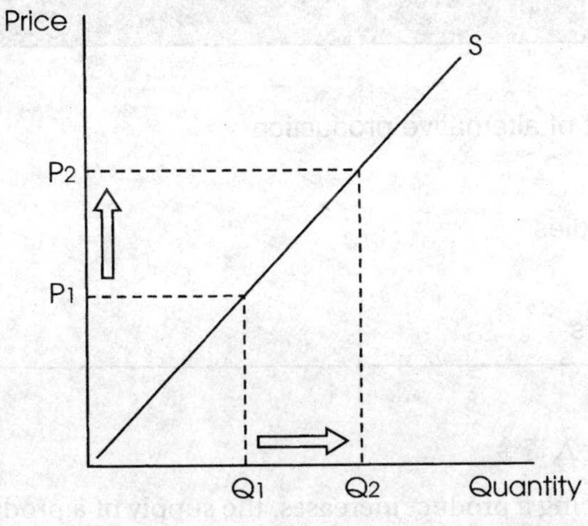

Fig. 4.7 A Change in Quantity Supplied

Shifts of the Supply Curve: Determinants of Supply

供给曲线的变动：供给的决定因素

There are many factors for producers that impact the amount of a good that will be offered for sale at each price. Just as with the demand curve, these are more than mere price changes. These factors that cause producers to offer more or less of a product for sale at the same prices are called the **determinants of supply** (also called shifters of supply). As shown in Figure 4.8, an increase in one of these determinants of supply would shift the supply curve to the right (S_1 to S_2), and a decrease would shift the curve to the left S_1 to S_3).

> **USEFUL HINT**
>
> **Students sometimes mistakenly shift an increase in supply to the left, as it looks like it is going up. However, an increase in supply shifts to the right, and a decrease to the left, just like demand shifts.**

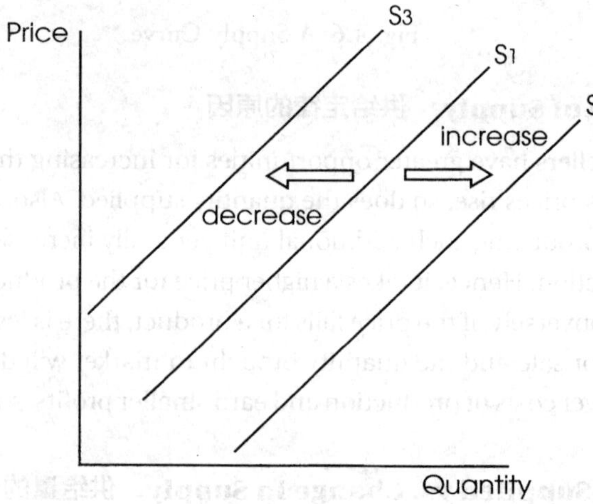

Fig. 4.8 Shifts in Supply

The determinants of demand can be learned by the acronym COTTEN shown in Table 4.2, followed by an explanation of each with examples.

Table 4.2

Determinants of Supply——COTTEN (Shifter of the Supply Curve)
C—Cost of Inputs
O—Opportunity cost of alternative production
T—Technology
T—Taxes and subsidies
E—Expectations
N—Number of sellers

COST OF INPUTS 投入资金

When the cost of producing a product increases, the supply of a product decreases, and vice versa. A change in the cost of producing a product affects the supply of a good or service.

EXAMPLE

If the cost of fertilizer used in the production of corn increases, the supply of corn would decrease (shown by a shift from S_1 to S_3 on Figure 4.8). If labor costs decrease for smartphones producers, resource costs fall, and the supply of phones would increase (shown by a shift from S_1 to S_2 on Figure 4.8).

OPPORTUNITY COST OF ALTERNATIVE PRODUCTION 可选产品的机会成本

Sometimes a firm can easily switch between production of several different products. Profit-maximizing firms will choose to produce what gives them the most profit or where their opportunity cost is lowest.

EXAMPLE

A farmer who has a fixed amount of land is producing corn but can use his land to grow either corn or wheat. If the price of wheat increases significantly relative to corn, the farmer will switch from producing corn to producing wheat. The opportunity cost of producing corn increased, thus the switch to wheat. This would decrease the supply curve for corn, and shift to the left.

TECHNOLOGY 技术

New technology can decrease production costs and increase productivity that results in the supply curve shifting to the right.

EXAMPLE

Many automobile factories today use robots and other machines in the production process, increasing productivity and shifting the supply curve to the right. Several hundred years ago, the invention of the cotton gin drastically increased the supply of cotton.

TAXES AND SUBSIDIES 税收与补贴

A **tax** on the production of a good will result in increased production costs, which will decrease supply. If a firm is fortunate enough to get a **subsidy**, a payment from the government to produce a product, profits increase at each price level that induce increased supply.

EXAMPLE

A farmer receives a subsidy for producing corn and now has an incentive or motivation to increase supply. Conversely, a cigarette producer may be taxed on each unit produced, thus increasing the cost of production and decreasing supply, shifting the supply curve to the left.

EXPECTATIONS 预期

Similar to buyers, sellers also include future price considerations into their actions in a market. If sellers think the price will increase in the future, they may hold back the amount offered for sale, decreasing current supply, with the ultimate goal of increasing profits in the future. The converse holds true if producers think the price of a good may fall. They would increase current production today, increasing supply, shifting the supply curve to the right.

EXAMPLE

A cotton farmer who thinks the prices will rise next year may not bring his current harvest to market, with the hope of selling for higher prices in the future. This would decrease the current supply curve for cotton.

NUMBER OF SELLERS 卖方的数量

As more sellers and competition enter a market, the supply increases. While the extra competition may be difficult for sellers, the extra supply usually is good for consumers, who receive more choice and lower prices as the supply curve shifts to the right.

EXAMPLE

The opening of new pizza restaurants in a college town increases the supply of pizzas, shifting supply to the right. Students benefit from more choice and lower prices from the extra competition.

MARKET EQUILIBRIUM: SUPPLY AND DEMAND TOGETHER 市场均衡：供给与需求

The establishment of prices in a competitive market comes about by trial and error—sellers initiating a price only to discover a surplus has occurred. A **surplus** exists when the quantity supplied is greater than the quantity demanded, which is above the equilibrium price. In a competitive market with a surplus, prices will eventually fall to the equilibrium price. A **shortage** is below the equilibrium price when the quantity demanded is greater than the quantity supplied, and buyers want more products than are offered for sale. In a competitive market, prices will increase to the equilibrium price.

Increases in the price reduce the shortage (buyers or consumers "bid" against one another) until it disappears at equilibrium. This equilibrium (illustrated below) has the following characteristics:

1. There is no tendency for change; the demand and supply stay the same or constant.
2. The amounts demanded equal the amounts supplied (at the intersection of supply and demand).
3. There is no surplus or shortage; the equilibrium price "clears" the market.

Equilibrium—The Illustration 市场均衡——图解

Equilibrium occurs at E (Price = \$5; quantities exchanged = 300), the intersection of S and D (supply and demand), where the quantities demanded = quantities supplied. The characteristics of equilibrium (above) apply.

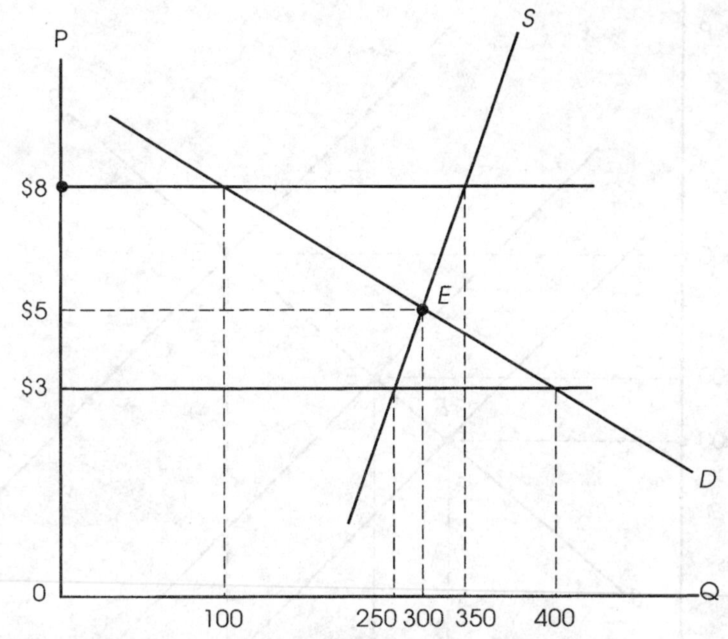

Fig. 4.9 Market Equilibrium

Disequilibrium 非均衡

If the price is \$8, then there is disequilibrium since the quantities demanded at \$8 would equal 100 and the quantities supplied would equal 350; therefore, there would be a surplus of 250. As the market (suppliers) react to the surplus, the price will drop until it equals \$5 (equilibrium price) at which the market is "cleared" of the surplus. The converse holds, when the price is *below* the equilibrium, such as \$3, when a shortage of 150 would develop. At \$3, the quantities demanded exceed the quantities supplied (400 > 250) and the consumers (buyers) would bid the price up until it reaches \$5 (equilibrium price) and the market is cleared of any shortage.

Changes in Equilibrium 均衡的变动

1. When given a problem on supply and demand, the first step is to figure out whether an event affects either the supply or demand curve (or both if it is a double shifter—watch out for those!). Knowing the acronyms for the determinants of supply (COTTEN) and demand (SPICE) are necessary. Once you discern what curve is affected, is it an increase or decrease? Then for the final step, just shift it, noting your new equilibrium price and quantity.
2. Demand and/or supply shifts will cause new equilibrium positions (new intersections of supply and demand). With supply constant, changes in the demand determinants would cause shifts in the demand curve. These shifts would cause new equilibrium price and equilibrium quantity positions. For example, if there is an increased preference for SUVs, then the demand for SUVs would increase in the form of a shift in the demand curve (as illustrated in Figure 4.10).

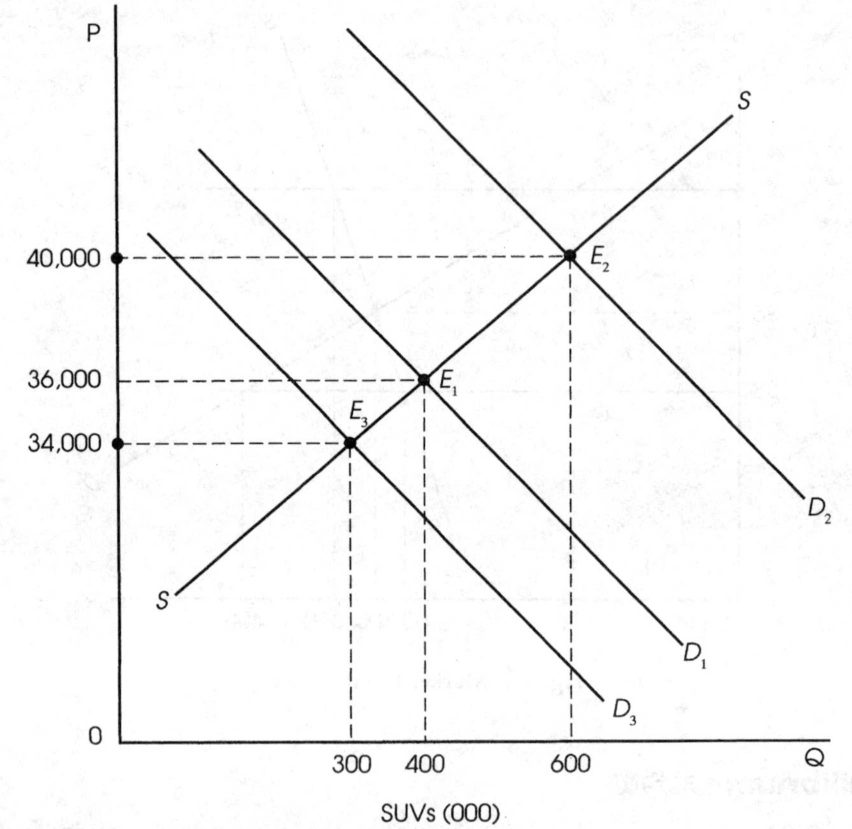

Fig. 4.10 Market for SUVs: Equilibrium Changes

The demand curve would shift (increase) from D_1 to D_2 (with supply constant at S). As illustrated above, the new equilibrium is at E_2 with the equilibrium price of $40,000 (up from $36,000) and the equilibrium quantity at 600,000 SUVs (up from 400,000 SUVs). This same kind of effect would occur if one of the other determinants of demand changed in the same direction; for example, if there was a sharp increase in the number of buyers with very high incomes.

USEFUL HINT

With supply constant, an increase in demand will cause an increase in equilibrium price and quantity. Conversely, a decrease in demand leads to a decrease in equilibrium price and quantity.

3. With supply again given at S, and with the expectation that the prices of SUVs *will* decrease very soon since the market is becoming saturated with new models from competitors, demand for SUVs will now decrease as potential buyers wait for a better deal. This is illustrated (above) with a shift of D_1 to D_3 and a new equilibrium at E_3 (equilibrium price at $34,000, down from $36,000, and equilibrium quantity at 300,000, down from 400,000 SUVs).

4. In brief, we will now analyze shifts (increases or decreases) in supply with demand as given or constant.

With demand constant, an increase in supply will lead to a decrease in equilibrium price and an increase in equilibrium quantity; conversely, a decrease in supply will lead to an increase in equilibrium price and a decrease in equilibrium quantity.

Thus, if a producer of a particular form of steel faces increasing costs of coking coal (an input in steel production), he will decrease his supply of steel. This is illustrated in Figure 4 .11.

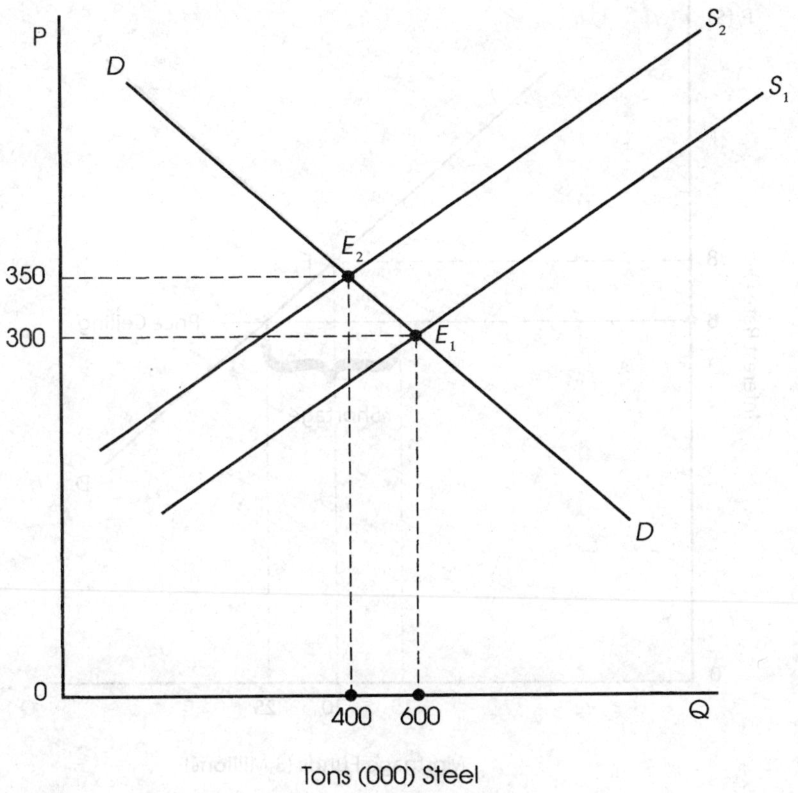

Fig. 4.11 Steel Market

As a result of a supply shift (decrease) from S_1 to S_2, the equilibrium price increases to $350 a ton (from $300) and the equilibrium quantity decreases to 400 tons (from 600).

5. What happens if there are changes in demand and, simultaneously, in supply? Table 4.3 is a schedule of which effects on price and quantities are determinable.

Table 4.3

Effects on Price and Quantity

Change in Demand	Change in Supply	Effect on Equilibrium Price	Effect on Equilibrium Quantity
Increase	Increase	Indeterminate	Increase
Decrease	Decrease	Indeterminate	Decrease
Increase	Decrease	Increase	Indeterminate
Decrease	Increase	Decrease	Indeterminate

Government-induced Changes—Price Ceilings and Price Floors

政府引导的变动——最高价格和最低价格

For varying reasons, a government may wish to establish a **price ceiling**, which prohibits prices to rise above a certain level as in rent (city-controlled prices or rents for apartments), or as in the establishment of a ceiling or interest rates for mortgage loans. In other situations,

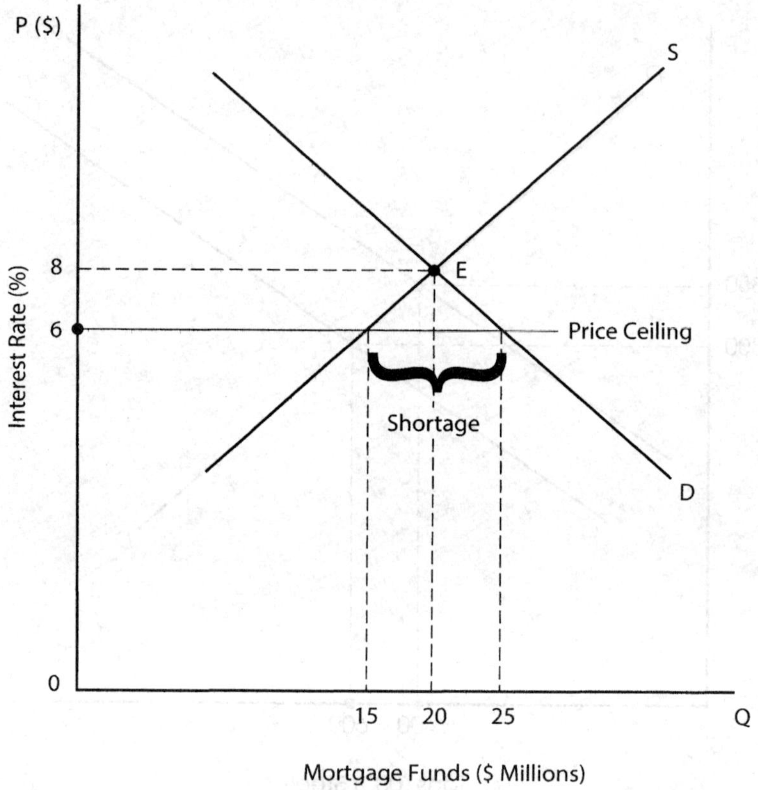

Fig. 4.12 Market for Mortgage Loans

a government may wish to establish a **price floor** making it illegal, for example, to hire workers at a wage lower than the minimum wage. Thus, as illustrated in Figure 4.12, if the state government sets 6 percent as the maximum rate that can be charged on mortgage loans, and if the market equilibrium price would be 8 percent, the amount of mortgage loan funds actually exchanged would decrease to $15 million from $20 million.

This is an example of an effective price ceiling that would produce a shortage of mortgage funds relative to the amounts desired by borrowers.

A price floor might be instituted by the federal government for agricultural prices in order to support farmers who take losses under market prices and to maintain an adequate supply of agricultural products to the population. The floor would be established above the equilibrium or market price while a price ceiling would be established under the equilibrium or market price. See Figure 4.13. With the equilibrium price of $8, a total of 100 bushels of wheat are exchanged (the amounts demanded are equal to amounts supplied). At the price floor, by government, of $10, suppliers are willing to provide 140 bushels. Thus a surplus develops.

Note: A price ceiling is meant to set a price above the equilibrium and a price ceiling below. If for some reason a government sets a price floor below or a price ceiling above the equilibrium price, it will have no effect, or be a nonbinding price floor/ceiling. For example, in the oil boom areas of North Dakota, the wage being paid to fast-food workers and other low-skilled labor is much higher than the minimum wage. Here the minimum wage (a price floor) has no effect as the equilibrium wage is far above the government-set minimum wage. A price ceiling or price floor that does work as intended is known as an effective price ceiling/floor.

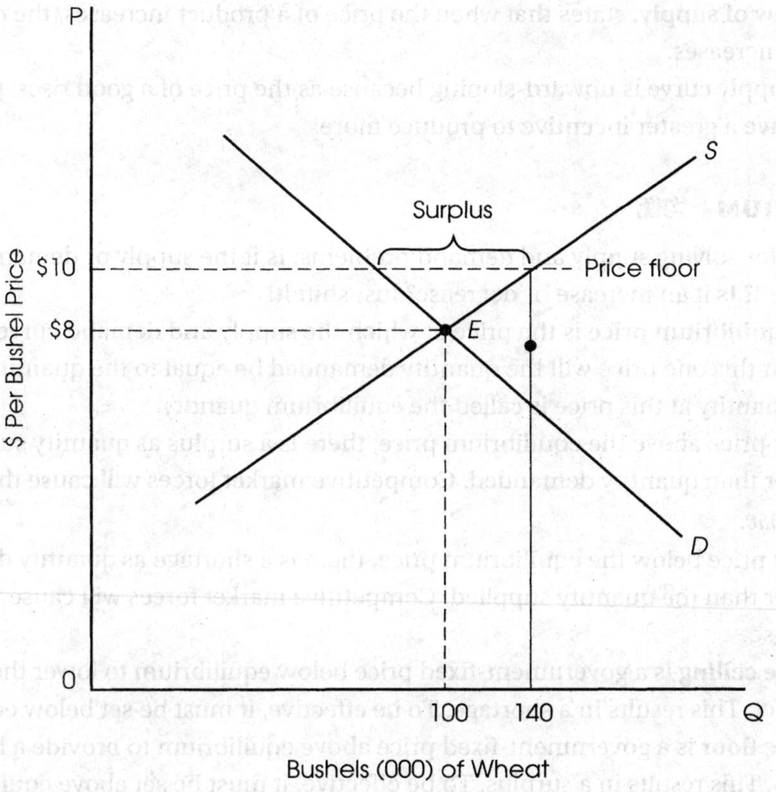

Fig. 4.13 Wheat Market

SUMMARY 小结

DEMAND 需求

1. A market's **demand** curve shows the quantity of a product a consumer is willing and able to purchase at various prices.
2. If the price of a good changes, move along an existing demand curve for that good. A price change does not shift the curve. This is called a **change in quantity demanded**.
3. A nonprice change in demand, one of the determinants of demand (remember the SPICE shifters), shifts the demand curve. Shift to the right for an increase or left for a decrease. This is called a **change in demand**.
4. The **law of demand** states that when the price of a product increases, the quantity demanded decreases, and vice versa.
5. The demand curve is downward-sloping due to the **income** and **substitution effects**.

SUPPLY 供给

1. A market's **supply** curve shows the quantity of a product a producer is willing and able to offer for sale at various prices.
2. If the price of a good changes, move along the existing supply curve of the good. A price change does not shift the curve. This is called a **change in quantity supplied**.
3. A nonprice change in supply, one of the determinants of supply (remember the COTTEN shifters), shifts the supply curve. Shift to the right for an increase or left for a decrease. This is called a **change in supply**.

4. The **law of supply**, states that when the price of a product increases, the quantity supplied increases.
5. The supply curve is upward-sloping because as the price of a good rises, producers will have a greater incentive to produce more.

EQUILIBRIUM 均衡

1. Steps for solving supply and demand problems: Is it the supply or demand curve affected? Is it an increase or decrease? Just shift it!
2. The **equilibrium price** is the price at which the supply and demand curves intersect.
3. Only at this one price will the quantity demanded be equal to the quantity supplied. The quantity at this price is called the equilibrium quantity.
4. At any price above the equilibrium price, there is a surplus as quantity supplied is greater than quantity demanded. Competitive market forces will cause the price to decrease.
5. At any price below the equilibrium price, there is a shortage as quantity demanded is greater than the quantity supplied. Competitive market forces will cause the price to increase.
6. A **price ceiling** is a government-fixed price below equilibrium to lower the price of a product. This results in a shortage. To be effective, it must be set below equilibrium.
7. A **price floor** is a government-fixed price above equilibrium to provide a high price for sellers. This results in a surplus. To be effective, it must be set above equilibrium.

TERMS 术语

Ceteris Paribus holding all other factors or conditions constant

Determinants of Demand the factors that cause consumers to buy more or less at the same price; these are substitutes, preferences, population, income, complements, and expectations

Determinants of Supply the factors that cause sellers to offer more or less for sale at the same price; these are cost of inputs, opportunity cost of alternative production, technology, taxes and subsidies, expectations, and number of sellers

Equilibrium Price price at which quantity supplied equals quantity demanded

Income Effect a reason for the law of demand, the purchasing power of income is inversely related to the price of a product; If the price of a particular good decreases, a consumer may buy more of this good as his income has more buying power

Inferior goods where an increase in income leads to a decrease in demand

Law of Demand law that states that when the price of a product increases, the quantity demanded decreases and are inversely related

Law of Supply law that states that when the price of a product increases, the quantity supplied increases and are directly related

Market place where buyers and sellers meet to exchange goods and services

Normal goods where as income increases, the demand for a product increases

Price Ceiling a maximum legal price established below the equilibrium price

Price Floor a minimum legal price established above the equilibrium price

Quantity Demanded has an inverse relationship with changes in the price of a particular good

Quantity Supplied has a direct relationship with changes in the price of a particular good

Shortage when the quantity demanded is greater than the quantity supplied; in a competitive market with a surplus, prices will fall to the equilibrium price

Substitution Effect a reason for the law of demand, as the price of a particular good decreases, a consumer may buy more of this good relative to higher-priced goods

Surplus when the quantity supplied is greater than the quantity demanded, which is above the equilibrium price; in a competitive market with a surplus, prices will fall to the equilibrium price

MULTIPLE-CHOICE REVIEW QUESTIONS 选择题

1. An effective price ceiling is characterized by

(A) a price set below the current (or equilibrium) market price of the good.
(B) a price set above the current (or equilibrium) market price of the good.
(C) a shift of the demand curve (function).
(D) a shift of the supply curve.

2. Which of the following would cause the price of a good to increase above the equilibrium price and stay there permanently?

(A) Consumers' incomes decreased
(B) An effective price ceiling
(C) Taxes for producers increased
(D) The price of a substitute product decreased
(E) An effective price floor

3. If the government subsidizes the production of halogen headlights,

(A) the demand curve will shift to the left.
(B) the demand curve will shift to the right.
(C) the supply curve will shift to the left.
(D) the supply curve will shift to the right.
(E) the quantity supplied will increase along a fixed supply curve.

4. If consumers are advised that multi-grained bread will substantially lessen the risk of cancer, which of the following will happen in the market for multi-grained bread?

(A) The demand curve will shift to the left, decreasing the price of multi-grained bread.
(B) The supply curve will shift to the left, increasing the price of multi-grained bread.
(C) The demand curve will shift to the right, increasing the price of multi-grained bread.
(D) The supply curve will shift to the right, decreasing the price of multi-grained bread.
(E) None of the above.

5. Assume the supply of bananas decreases due to rising costs of production, while demand increases due to consumer preferences. What will happen to the new equilibrium price and quantity?

	Price	Quantity
(A)	Increase	Increase
(B)	Increase	Indeterminate
(C)	Decrease	Decrease
(D)	Decrease	Increase
(E)	Indeterminate	Increase

MULTIPLE-CHOICE REVIEW ANSWERS
选择题答案

1. (A) **2.** (E) **3.** (D) **4.** (C) **5.** (B)

FREE-RESPONSE REVIEW QUESTIONS 开放式题目

I. For each of the following simultaneous changes in demand and in supply for a product, indicate the effect on equilibrium price *and* equilibrium quantity.

A. increase in demand and an increase in supply

B. decrease in demand and a decrease in supply

C. increase in demand and a decrease in supply

II. Assume the market for leather baseball gloves is in equilibrium.

A. Draw a correctly labeled graph of the market for leather baseball gloves, labeling the price P_E and the quantity Q_E at equilibrium.

B. Now assume the price of leather increases, and it is an input used to produce baseball gloves. Using a correctly labeled supply and demand graph, show how this event affects the new equilibrium price and quantity for baseball gloves, labeled P_2 and Q_2.

III. Assume the market for chicken wings is in equilibrium.

A. Draw a correctly labeled graph of the chicken wing market, labeling the price P_E and the quantity Q_E at equilibrium.

B. Assume the government now decides the price of chicken wings is too high and decides to set an effective price ceiling in the market. Draw the price ceiling on the same graph drawn in A, labeling the new price P_C, the new quantity supplied Q_S, and the new quantity demanded Q_D.

C. At the new price, is the chicken wing market in equilibrium, or does it have a shortage or a surplus? Explain.

Free-Response Review Answers 开放式题目答案

I. A. An increase in demand and an increase in supply would result in an increase in equilibrium quantity; the effect on equilibrium price is indeterminate.

B. A decrease in demand and a decrease in supply will result in a decrease in equilibrium quantity, and the effect on equilibrium price is indeterminate.

C. An increase in demand and a decrease in supply would result in an increase in equilibrium price; the effect on equilibrium is indeterminate.

II. Cost of inputs is a determinant of supply. So as the costs of producing gloves increases, supply decreases and shifts to the left. This results in a decrease in equilibrium quantity and an increase in price, as shown in Figure 4.14. Be sure to check that you have labeled price and quantity, the supply and demand curves, and the supply decreasing, as in Figure 4.9.

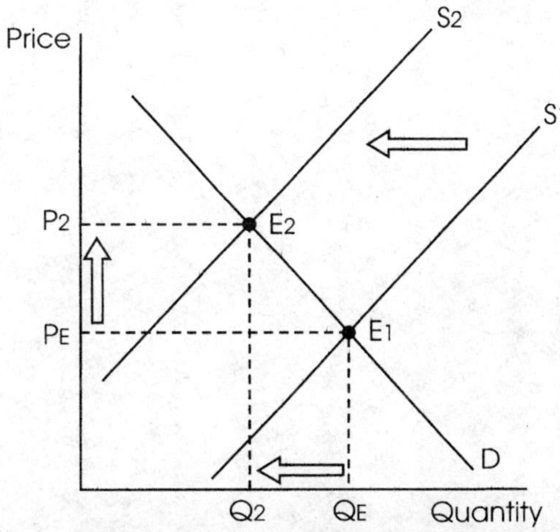

Fig.4.14 Free-Response II Answer

III. A, B. See Figure 4.15 for the correct graph.

C. An effective price ceiling is below the equilibrium price and leads to a shortage. At the price ceiling, the quantity demanded increases, as consumers want to buy more at a lower price. However, the quantity supplied decreases at the lower price as it is no longer profitable for some firms to produce at price P_C.

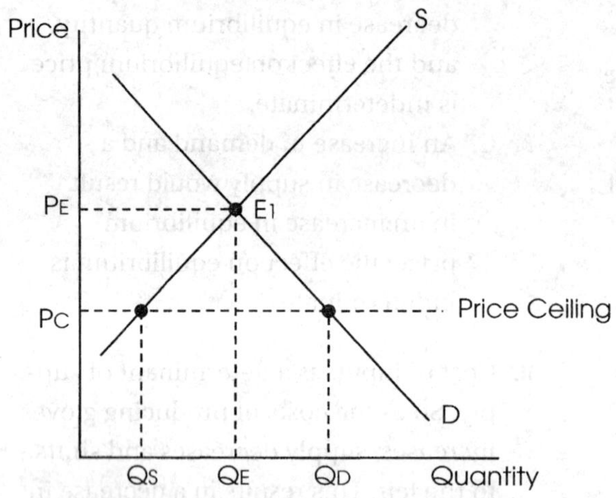

Fig. 4.15 Free-Response III Answer

Microeconomics

微观经济学

As you work toward achieving that 5 on your AP Microeconomics exam, here are five essentials that you **MUST** know above everything else:

Barron's Essential 5

巴朗总结的五个要点

1

Characteristics of the 4 market structures: You will be asked specific questions on these characteristics as well as questions about pricing, output, and the effects of government regulation. These questions may constitute as much as 25 percent of the multiple-choice questions and more than 50 percent of the free-response questions.

- Know how to both correctly graph and interpret the following markets: perfect competition, monopoly, and monopolistic competition. Also, be sure to fully understand an oligopoly's game theory payoff matrix.
- Be sure to know how these markets differ on the degree of efficiency, price elasticity, barriers to entry, economic profits, availability of substitutes, the numbers of sellers, and the independence or interdependence (the latter as in Game Theory) in pricing strategy among sellers.
- Be sure to know how government regulation of monopolies affects prices, profits, and output.

2

Basic relationships of costs and production and their application to output and price decisions. Marginal analysis is central in this context.

- You should know the law of diminishing marginal returns, the relationships between average and marginal costs and product curves, and the distinctions between the long and short run.
- Pay attention to economies of scale particularly in the adjustment from the short run to the long run in plant capacity.
- Be able to demonstrate the relationship of production to costs (e.g., the relationship of MP and AP to AVC and MC).

3

The applications of demand and supply to elasticity and consumer choice in economic decision making.

- You should know the concept of diminishing marginal utility and the utility-maximizing rule. You will be expected to find the utility-maximizing combination of two goods given the constraints.
- You should be able to explain and graph consumer and producer surplus. Know the income and substitution effects of a downward sloping demand curve.
- Know the concepts and the formulas for price, cross price, and income elasticity of demand. Also, know the formulas for the numerical coefficient of elasticity and the price elasticity of supply.

4

The connections between product markets and labor markets, as they frame the bases for many exam questions. Know the relationships between costs, production and supply, and the relationships among prices, costs, and revenue as in Essentials points #1 and #2 above.

- Know the laws and measurement of labor as a derived demand.
- Know cost minimization and profit maximization for hiring labor.
- Expect a question on MRP and MFC and know how to draw a labor market graph.

5

Basic functions of government in a market-oriented economy. The bases for government roles can be based on positive or normative considerations and involve the following concepts that appear in AP exams. Know these concepts and how to apply them.

- Market failure to produce desired outcomes.
- The presence of externalities, positive or negative.
- The nature and significance of public and private goods.

Applications of Demand and Supply—Elasticity and Taxation 5
需求与供给的应用——弹性与税收

→ PRICE ELASTICITY OF DEMAND AND OF SUPPLY
→ INCOME ELASTICITY OF DEMAND
→ CROSS PRICE ELASTICITY OF DEMAND
→ BURDEN OF TAXES ON CONSUMERS AND SUPPLIERS
→ TRADE, TARIFFS, AND QUOTES

INTRODUCTION 导言

The law of demand states that consumers will buy more of a product when the price falls and less when the price increases. In the real world, however, people may still buy a product when the price of a product increases. How much more or less will people buy with price changes? Why do people still heat their homes in the winter when energy costs rise but buy less Pepsi when it goes up in price? These questions can be addressed by studying **elasticity**, which shows how sensitive consumers and producers are to changes in price.

THINGS TO KNOW 要了解的事

Based on the most frequently asked questions on previous AP exams, the following are the most important concepts.

Consider the following as a guide:

1. Total Revenues (TR) Test: P × Q = TR
   - Thus, if price (P) increases by 20 percent and quantity demanded (Q) decreases by 20 percent, total revenue (TR) will stay the same. This is called a *unit elasticity*.
   - If P increases by 20 percent and Q decreases by 25 percent, then TR will decrease. This is called *elastic demand.*
   - If P increases by 20 percent and Q decreases by 10 percent, then TR will increase. This is called an *inelastic demand.*

Table 5.1

Total Revenues Test (P × Q = Total Revenue) and Elasticity

Type of Elasticity	Relationship Between Price (P) and Total Revenue (TR)
Elastic	P and TR are inversely related
Inelastic	P and TR have a direct relationship
Unit elastic	TR does not change when P changes

2. Price Elasticity of Demand $= \dfrac{\%\ \Delta \text{ Quantity Demanded}}{\%\ \Delta \text{ Price}}$

(The percentage change in the quantity demanded of a particular good divided by the price of the same good.) Using the three examples above (number 1), in the first case, the value of the coefficient or ratio = 1 since the percentage change (Δ) in quantities demanded equals the percentage change in price. This is called *unit elastic*. In the second case, the value of the ratio = 25/20 or 1.25. Since the change in Q is more than proportional to the change in P, the response is relatively *elastic* or greater than 1. In the third case, the value of the ratio = 10/20 or .5. Since the change in Q is less than proportional to the change in P, the response is relatively inelastic or a ratio value of less than 1. If demand for a good is perfectly inelastic, a price change has no impact on quantity demanded, and the elasticity coefficient is 0. If demand is perfectly elastic, a price change has an infinite change in quantity demanded, and the coefficient is ∞ (infinity). The elasticity coefficient numbers are always positive, so ignore a negative sign if present when calculating the value. **Note:** Recent AP exams have made the distinction between perfectly and relatively elastic/inelastic demand. You can find respective elasticity values in Table 5.2.

Table 5.2

Elasticity Coefficient Value

Type of Elasticity	Elasticity Value
Perfectly inelastic	= 0
Relatively inelastic	< 1
Unit elastic	= 1
Relatively elastic	> 1
Perfectly elastic	∞ (infinity)

3. Price elasticity of supply uses essentially the same formula except that as *P* increases, Q supplied also increases, rendering the total revenue check useless in the supply case. For Elasticity of Supply:

$$\frac{\%\ \Delta \text{ Quantity}}{\%\ \Delta \text{ Price}}$$

NOTE

To calculate a percentage, change in price (P), or quantity demanded (Qd), take the amount of the change in P or Qd divided by the original P or Qd – as shown in these formulas. For example, an increase in the Qd from 10 to 20 would be calculated as 20 - 10/10 = 1 or a 100% increase in Qd.

Qd(New) - Qd(Old)/Qd(Old)

P(New) - P(Old)/P(Old)

In brief, the relationship of price changes, elasticity, quantities demanded, and total revenue can be summarized as follows:

Price	**TR**	**Price Elasticity of Demand**
increases	decreases	>1, relatively elastic
increases	increases	<1, relatively inelastic
increases	stays the same	=1, unit elastic
decreases	increases	>1, relatively elastic
decreases	decreases	<1, relatively inelastic
decreases	stays the same	=1, unit elastic

Note: The negative sign is ignored so that the nature of the response—elastic, inelastic—will not be confused with a negative slope or inverse relationship.

PROBLEM TO SOLVE (FREE-RESPONSE QUESTION)

An out-of-state tourist uses a laundromat in Langley, Washington. A large, handwritten sign advises the users of this service that the owner was experiencing some economic difficulties including rising costs of water and propane gas. The monthly charge to the owner for water use was $2,225 and the cost for propane gas was $542 a month. Thus, the owner felt justified in increasing the price for the use of a washer from $1.50 to $1.75. The owner advised the users that her service represented a monopoly since it was the only laundromat on the southern end of the island. She claimed that she was not taking undue advantage of the customers but she wanted to be able to continue serving them while "making a living." Please answer the following:

1. **What percentage of decrease in quantities demanded of the owner's services would allow her to maintain the same level of total revenue (given the increase in the price of use of a washer)?**
2. **What percentage of decrease in quantities demanded would realize an increase in total revenue?**
3. **What percentage of decrease in quantities demanded would result in a decrease in total revenue?**
4. **For numbers 1, 2, and 3 above, indicate whether the price elasticity of demand is elastic, inelastic, or unit elastic.**
5. **What are the connections between her increase in costs of providing the service and the price elasticity of supply? What are the connections between her increase in cost and the supply of her service?**

Answers:

1. **The increase in price is 16.67 percent (.25 on a basis of $1.50). Thus, the owner could experience the same (16.67 percent) decrease in quantities demanded to maintain the same level of total revenue P × Q = TR and**

$$\text{Price elasticity of demand} = \frac{\%\ \Delta\ \text{Quantity Demanded}}{\%\ \Delta\ \text{Price}}$$

2. **Less than 16.67 percent**
3. **More than 16.67 percent**
4. **For number 1, unit elastic; for number 2 inelastic; for number 3 elastic.**
5. **She must cover her costs; in other words, the higher the price/cost ratio, the more willing she is to supply more. Also, the closer she is to a monopolist, the more she can determine the price.**

LIMITS AND DEGREES OF ELASTICITY 弹性的限度与程度

If perfectly elastic, the coefficient of elasticity is infinity. This means that the buyer is so sensitive to price changes that if one seller raises his price, the buyer will switch to another seller. This situation implicitly assumes that there are many sellers so that no one seller or group of sellers can exercise any significant control over the terms of exchange: prices, quantities, market share, etc. Nowhere is this better exemplified than in the norm for competition in product markets, that is perfect competition (more on this later in Chapter 9). The seller is a "price taker," that is, the market of *all* buyers and *sellers* for a *particular* product determines the price that the seller must charge or lose business to other competitors who produce the identical product that becomes a perfect substitute. It is illustrated below in Figure 5.1. (An easy way to remember the slope of a perfectly inelastic demand curve, is to call it "Mr. Flat.")

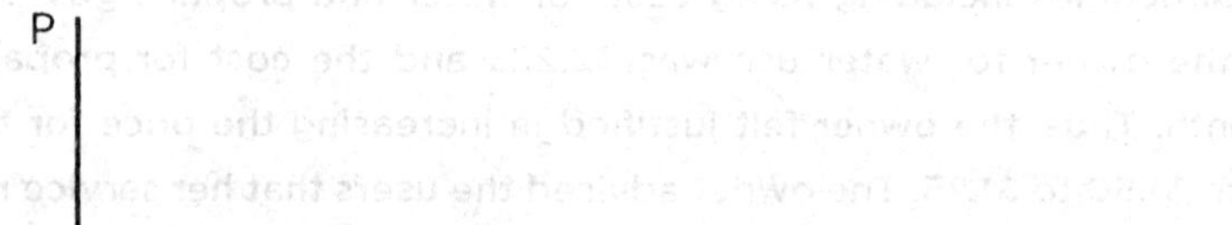

Fig. 5.1 Perfectly Competitive Firm (Perfectly Elastic Demand)

As demand curves approach this horizontal slope, they become relatively more elastic until they reach the horizontal shape. As demand curves approach the perfectly vertical slope (*perfectly inelastic*), they become relatively more inelastic. Hence, the perfectly elastic and imperfectly elastic curves set the mathematical or graphical limits on elasticity. The perfectly inelastic demand curve would be illustrated as follows in Figure 5.2. (To remember the slope of a perfectly inelastic demand curve, call it "Mr. Stick.")

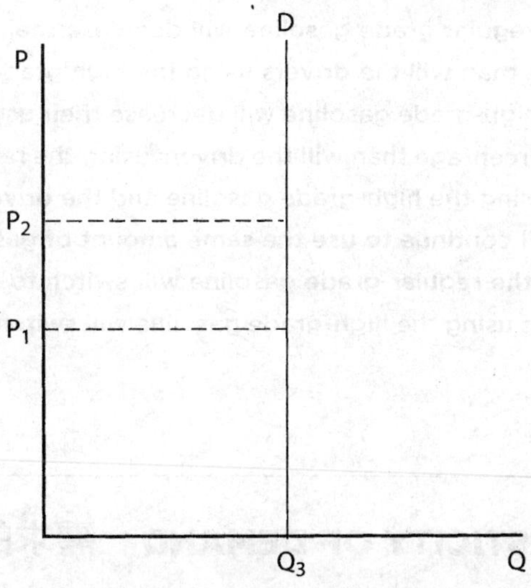

Fig. 5.2 Perfectly Inelastic Demand

Price elasticity of demand can vary along a demand curve. The slope does not change along a linear curve but elasticity does change along a linear curve. This is illustrated by the following:

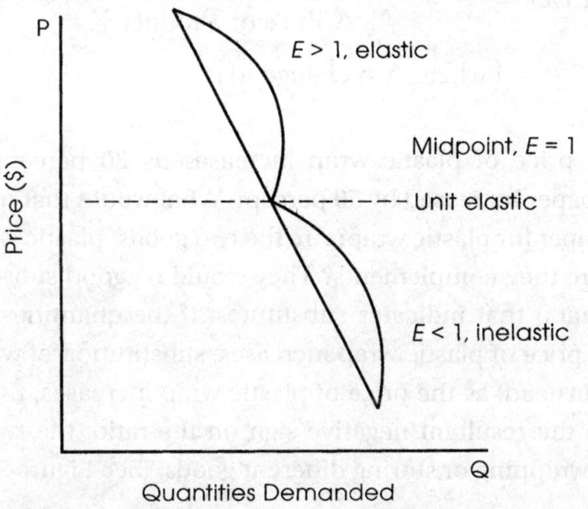

Fig. 5.3

SAMPLE QUESTION

As the price for regular grade (octane), unleaded gasoline increases from $3.00 to $3.25 per gallon, and higher grade (octane) unleaded gasoline increases from $3.25 to $3.75 per gallon, which is most likely to occur?

(A) Drivers using the regular grade gasoline will decrease their use of gasoline by a higher percentage than will the drivers using the high grade octane.
(B) Drivers using the high-grade gasoline will decrease their use of high-grade gasoline by a higher percentage than will the drivers using the regular-grade gasoline.
(C) Both the drivers using the high-grade gasoline and the drivers using the regular-grade gasoline will continue to use the same amount of gasoline.
(D) The drivers using the regular-grade gasoline will switch to the high-grade gasoline and the drivers using the high-grade gasoline will switch to the regular-grade gasoline.

(Answer: B.)

CROSS-PRICE ELASTICITY OF DEMAND 需求的交叉价格弹性

Another important type of elasticity is cross-price elasticity of demand. The essential question to which this concept is addressed is, "What effect on quantities demanded of one product will a price change in another product have?" The answer to this question will, in turn, give us clues to market share, the degree of competition that may extend from one market to another, and to what effect a dominant product in one market may have on products in another market. First, the relationship in ratio form:

Cross Price Elasticity of Demand = CPED

$$\text{CPED} = \frac{\%\ \Delta\ \text{Quantity Demanded of Product Y}}{\%\ \Delta\ \text{Price of Product X}}$$

$$(\text{where } \Delta = \text{change in})$$

Suppose that the price of plastic wrap increases by 20 percent, and the quantities demanded of waxed paper increased by 50 percent. What would that tell us about the ability to substitute waxed paper for plastic wrap? Are the two goods, plastic wrap and waxed paper, good substitutes or are they complements? They would be good substitutes because of the positive sign on the ratio that indicates substitutes: If the quantities demanded of waxed paper increase as the price of plastic wrap increases, substitution of waxed paper for plastic wrap is occurring. If instead, as the price of plastic wrap increases, the quantities of waxed paper decreases with the resultant negative sign on the ratio, the two goods are complements: both used for wrapping or storing different goods. (See Figure 5.4.)

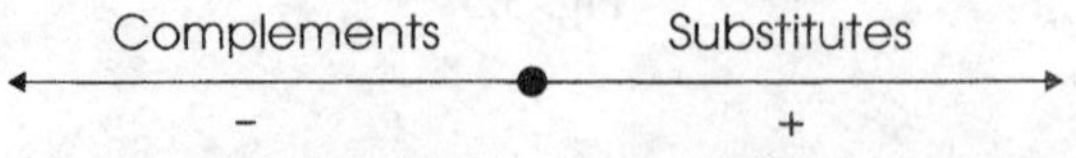

Figure 5.4 Cross-Price Elasticity of Demand

Determinants of Price Elasticity of Demand 需求价格弹性的决定因素

1. **THE PERIOD OF ADJUSTMENT, OR THE LONG RUN VS. THE SHORT RUN.** The short run is the time over which supply cannot fully adjust to changes in demand so that there is a relative scarcity of goods compared to the change in demand for the goods. Therefore, in the short run, prices act as rationers of the relatively scarce goods; in other words, the prices are "bid up" by the excess demand; there are more buyers willing to purchase these goods than there are goods available, the result being that the goods go to the highest bidders. In the 1970s fuel-efficient automobiles, produced mostly by the Japanese, were in high demand, particularly during the oil shortage crisis. Since the supply of these automobiles was limited relative to the demand, retail automobile dealers were able to charge prices well above the suggested list ("sticker") price rather than to charge prices at some typical discount. Over the long run, when more choices are available (supply having adjusted to the increase in demand), consumers have more choices and are more sensitive (higher price elasticity of demand) to price changes. Also, price elasticity of demand will vary between the short run and the long run. In the short run, buyers have more limited choices because of the relative scarcity of products and resources. Over the long run (when supply fully adjusts to changes in demand), the choice of products and resources becomes greater and hence, buyers are more resistant to price increases for any given product or resource.

   Therefore, the long run demand curve for any given product will be relatively more elastic than the demand function in the short run.

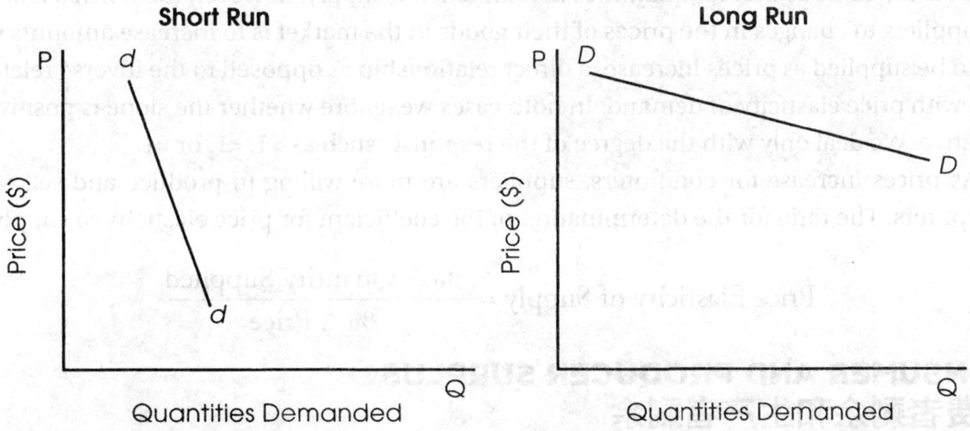

Fig. 5.5

TIP

Remember, that as a demand curve approaches the perfectly horizontal shape (perfectly elastic), it becomes relatively more elastic.

2. **ARE THERE ADEQUATE SUBSTITUTES AVAILABLE, OR IS THE GOOD A NECESSITY?** If a good is a necessity without substitutes, a consumer is likely to purchase the same quantity as the price changes. Diabetics who need a shot of insulin to survive do not have adequate substitutes; their demand for insulin is inelastic, as there are no substitutes available. If the price of Toyota cars increases, buyers likely can find a close substitute and buy a different brand. Hence, demand would be relatively elastic for Toyota cars.

INCOME ELASTICITY OF DEMAND 需求的收入弹性

In addition to consumers being constrained by prices in their purchasing decisions, they are also constrained by their budgets or incomes. Thus, we consider consumers' sensitivity in terms of their responses to changes in both prices and incomes. Income elasticity of demand is defined as:

$$\frac{\%\ \Delta \text{ Consumption of a Good}}{\%\ \Delta \text{ Consumer Income}}$$

This ratio for normal goods will have a positive sign, that is, as consumer income (I) increases, we expect that consumption of a normal good will also increase. If the increase in consumption is more than proportional to increase in income,* then the value of the ratio is greater than one (>1) and the response is more than proportional to the change in income, making the response elastic (>1). If the change in consumption is less than proportional to the change in income (ratio is <1), then the response is inelastic but still with a positive sign. If the change in consumption is exactly proportional to change in consumer income, then the value of the ratio is one and the response is unit elasticity (=1). (See Figure 5.6.)

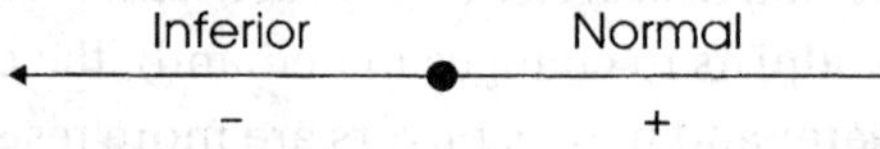

Fig. 5.6 Income Elasticity of Demand

PRICE ELASTICITY OF SUPPLY 供给的价格弹性

The basic relationship of the degree of the response of quantities supplied to changes in prices is the same as that for quantities demanded. For supply, however, the normal reaction of suppliers to changes in the prices of their goods in the market is to increase amounts willing to be supplied as prices increase, a direct relationship as opposed to the inverse relationship with price elasticity of demand. In both cases we ignore whether the slope is positive or negative. We deal only with the degree of the response, such as >1, <1, or =1.

As prices increase for computers, suppliers are more willing to produce and sell more computers. The ratio for the determination of the coefficient for price elasticity of supply is:

$$\text{Price Elasticity of Supply} = \frac{\%\ \Delta \text{ Quantity Supplied}}{\%\ \Delta \text{ Price}}$$

CONSUMER AND PRODUCER SURPLUS 消费者剩余和生产者剩余

An important way economics measures the effectiveness of markets is to highlight and calculate consumer surplus and producer surplus. When both consumer and producer surplus are maximized, economists consider this an efficient outcome. The **consumer surplus** is the difference between the highest price a consumer would pay for a product and the actual price paid. For example, if you bought a concert ticket for $20, but you would have paid as much as $50, the consumer surplus is $50 – $20 = **$30**. The demand curve displays the maximum price each consumer will pay, so this can be easily calculated and displayed graphically using the supply and demand graph. For example, in Figure 5.7, the market for a bag of peanuts, the area of consumer surplus is the triangular area below the demand and above the equilibrium price of $5, or area ABC. You can also calculate the dollar value of total consumer surplus in the peanut market. To calculate the exact value of the consumer surplus, take the difference between $9 and $5 on the price axis times the quantity sold, and multiply by ½. Or, ½ × ($9 – 5) × 30 = **$60**. The total value of consumer surplus is $60.

The **producer surplus** is the difference between the lowest price a producer would sell a product and the actual price received. If you have an old cell phone that you sell on the Internet for $100, but would have sold for as low as $50, your producer surplus is $100 – $50 = **$50**. In Figure 5.7, the equilibrium price for a bag of peanuts is $5, but many sellers would have sold for less than that and received producer surpluses. The area of producer surplus is above the supply curve and below the equilibrium price of $5, or area CBD. To calculate the exact value of the producer surplus, take the difference between $5 and $1 on the price axis times the quantity sold, and multiply by ½. Or, ½ × 4 × 30 = **$60**. Adding the Consumer and Producer surplus together gives you the total surplus of $120.

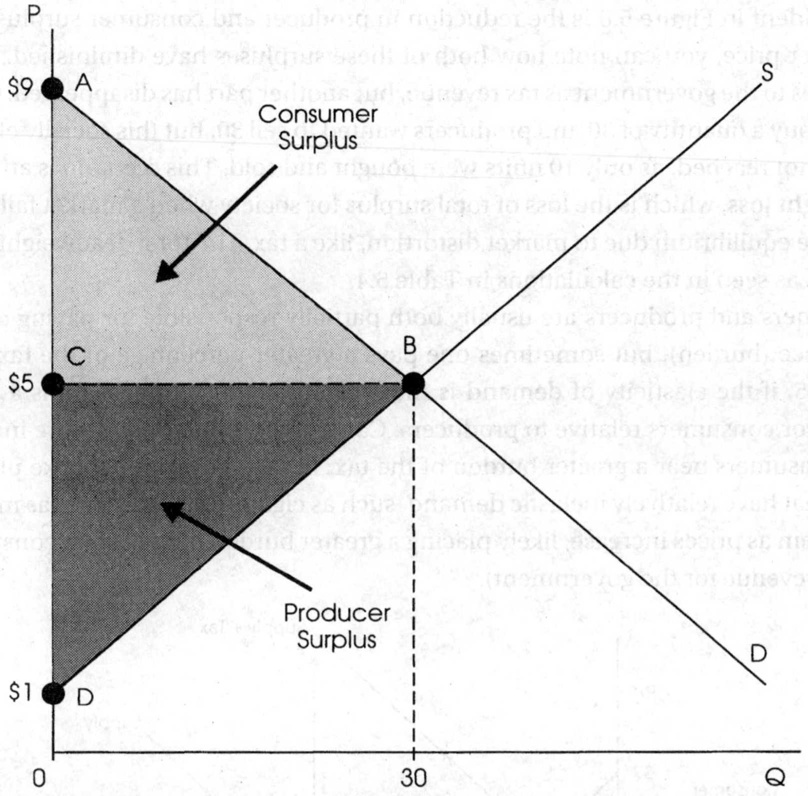

Fig. 5.7 Consumer and Producer Surplus in the Peanut Market

Table 5.3

Consumer and Producer Surplus (from Figure 5.7)	
Equilibrium price and quantity	**$5, 30**
Consumer surplus	**Area: A B C**
	½ × ($9 – $5) × 30 = **$60**
Producer surplus	**Area: C B D**
	½ × ($5 – $1) × 30 = **$60**
Total surplus	**$60 + $60 = $120**

IMPACT OF TAXES ON CONSUMER AND PRODUCER SURPLUS 向供给商和消费者征税带来的后果

All governments need tax revenue to provide public services, but taxation does result in a reduction of total surplus. Taxes can have varying impacts on consumers and producers depending on their respective price elasticity of demand or supply. In Figure 5.8, the equilibrium price of a pound of beef is $4. Suppose, however, that the government places an excise tax of $4 on the production of beef, measured graphically by the vertical distance between the supply curves. An **excise tax** is a per-unit tax on production. After the tax, the consumers pay a price of $6 for beef, but sellers only get $2 from the sale; the other $4 goes to the government as tax revenue. Many people think consumers will pay all the $4 tax; however, it actually is divided up between buyers and sellers. In this example, total tax revenue is $40 [($6 – $2) × 10 = $40], whereas consumers pay and buyers both split the tax evenly, $20 each ($2 × 10 = $20).

Also evident in Figure 5.8 is the reduction in producer and consumer surplus. As buyers pay a higher price, you can note how both of these surpluses have diminished. Part of this surplus goes to the government as tax revenue, but another part has disappeared. Consumers wanted to buy a quantity of 30 and producers wanted to sell 30, but this socially efficient outcome was not reached, as only 10 units were bought and sold. This scenario is an example of a **deadweight loss**, which is the loss of total surplus for society when a market fails to reach a competitive equilibrium due to market distortion, like a tax. The total deadweight loss in this case is $40, as seen in the calculations in Table 5.4.

Consumers and producers are usually both partially responsible for paying a tax, or the tax incidence (burden), but sometimes one pays a greater percentage of the tax. As shown in Table 5.5, if the elasticity of demand is more elastic than supply, there is a smaller tax incidence for consumers relative to producers. Conversely, if demand is more inelastic than supply, consumers bear a greater burden of the tax. In fact, governments like placing taxes on items that have relatively inelastic demand, such as cigarettes or gasoline, as many people still buy them as prices increase, likely placing a greater burden of the tax on consumers (and providing revenue for the government).

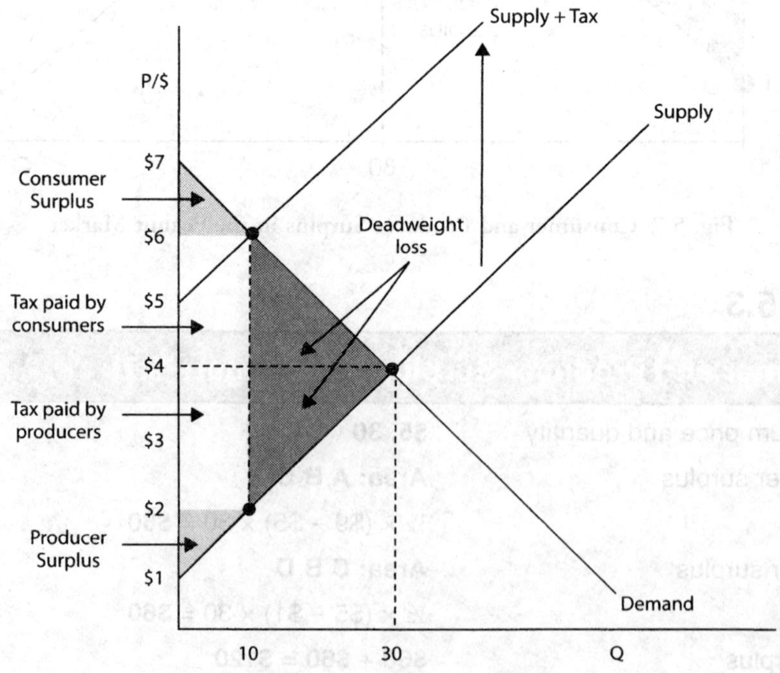

Fig. 5.8 Incidence of the Tax on the Beef Market

Table 5.4

Before and After Tax Analysis of Figure 5.8

Before Tax		After Tax	
Price and quantity	**$4, 30**	Total size of tax	**$4**
Consumer surplus	1⁄2 × ($7 – $4) × 30 = **45**	Price for consumers	**$6**
Producer surplus	1⁄2 × ($4 – $1) × 30 = **45**	Price received by sellers	**$2**
Total surplus	$45 + $45 = **$90**	Consumer surplus	1⁄2 × ($7 – $6) × 10 = **5**
		Producer surplus	1⁄2 × ($2 – $1) × 10 = **5**
		Total tax revenue	($6 – $2) × 10 = **40**
		Tax paid by consumers	($6 – $4) × 10 = **20**
		Tax paid by producers	($6 – $4) × 10 = **20**
		Deadweight loss	1⁄2 × ($4 – $2) + (30 – 10) + 1⁄2 × ($6 – $4) × (30 – 10) = **$40**

Table 5.5 summarizes who is responsible for paying a tax, or the tax incidence. This table is for elasticity of demand; for elasticity of supply, you would just switch the amounts of tax paid by buyers and sellers.

Table 5.5

Tax Incidence

Elasticities	Tax incidence: Who pays the tax, consumers or producers?
Elasticity of demand > elasticity of supply	Producers pay more of the tax than consumers.
Elasticity of demand < elasticity of supply	Consumers pay more of the tax than producers.
Perfectly inelastic demand (Ed = 0)	**Consumers pay all the tax.**
Perfectly elastic demand (Ed = ∞)	**Consumers pay none of the tax.**
Perfectly inelastic supply (Es = 0)	**Producers pay all of the tax.**
Perfectly elastic supply (Es = ∞)	**Producers pay none of the tax.**

TRADE, TARIFFS, AND QUOTAS 贸易、关税和配额

If you have taken Macroeconomics in addition to Microeconomics, you likely have learned about international trade in detail. However, for the purposes of Microeconomics, the section of the book you are in right now, you need to understand the effects of international trade on surpluses and how tariffs and quotas influence a market. To better understand the benefits of international trade, let's look at the market for bananas in Figure 5.9. Here you can see the price and quantity before ($4, 40) and after trade ($2, 60). Note at the world price the total surplus (area ABCDE) is greater than before trade (area ABC). At the world price, consumers receive huge gains from the lower prices, but a peculiarity of the trade graph is that producer surplus shrinks from area BC to C. Despite the fact the producer surplus decreases in size, there is still a large net positive gain in total surplus, from the large increase in consumer surplus. The amount of domestic consumption increases from 50 to 80 after trade, and the total amount of imports is 60 – 20 = **40**. See Table 5.6 for more details from the graph.

Let's assume that domestic suppliers successfully lobby the government for a tariff on imported bananas due to their decline in producer surplus due to international trade. A **tariff** is a tax on imports or exports, and a **quota** has a similar effect on trade that sets a limit on the quantity of goods imported or exported. As shown on Figure 5.10, the imposition of a $1 tariff on imported bananas increases the price of bananas to $3 and reduces the quantity of domestic consumption from 60 to 50. Domestic producers are happy as their production

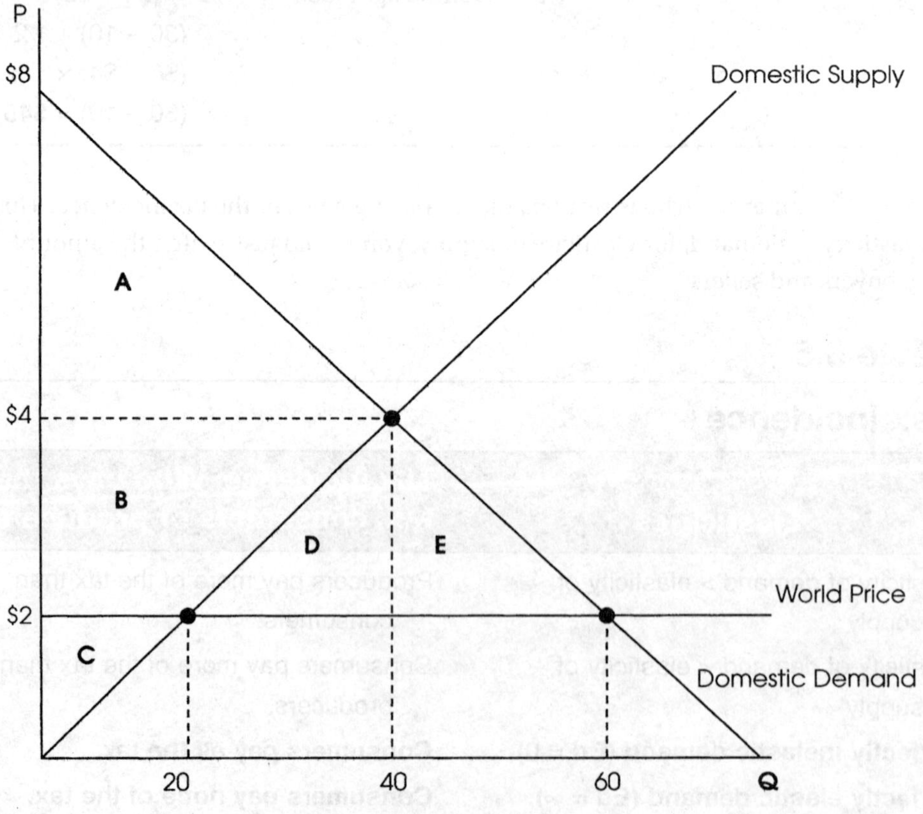

Fig. 5.9 International Trade

Table 5.6

Before and After Trade Analysis of Figure 5.9

Before World Trade		After Trade @ World Price	
Equilibrium price and quantity	$4, 40	Equilibrium price and quantity	$2, 60
Consumer surplus	A	Consumer surplus	A B C D E
Producer surplus	B C	Producer surplus	C
Total surplus	A B C	Total surplus	A B C D E
Quantity of imports	—	Quantity of imports	60 – 20 = 40
Net gains from trade	—	Net gains from trade	D E

increases from 20 to 30 and their producer surplus increases from C to BC. However, the tariff has an undesirable effect on total surplus and brings back a deadweight loss (areas D and G). A similar effect would take place if a quota set as opposed to a tariff, except a quota will not provide tax revenue for the government like a tariff (areas F_1 and F_2 are the tax revenue). See Table 5.7 for further analysis of the impact of the tariff.

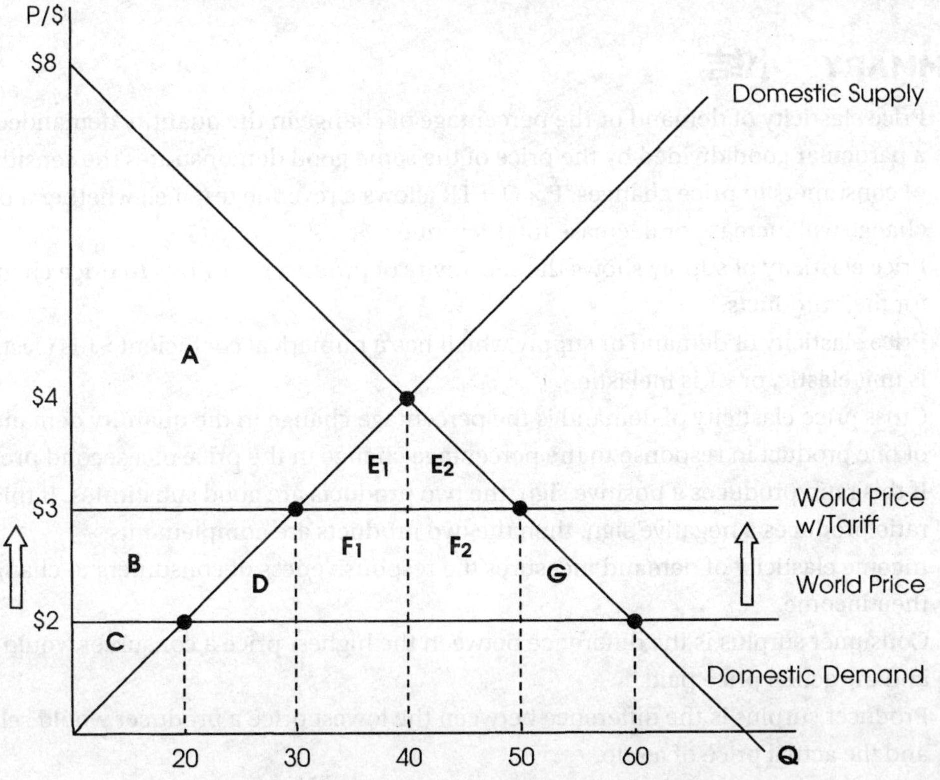

Fig. 5.10 World Trade Before and After Tariff

Table 5.7

An Analysis of Trade Before and After a Tariff

World Price Before Tariff		World Price After Tariff	
Equilibrium price and quantity	**\$2, 60**	Equilibrium price and quantity	**\$3, 50**
Consumer surplus	**A B D $E_{1,2}$ $F_{1,2}$ G**	Consumer surplus	**A $E_{1,2}$**
Producer surplus	**C**	Producer surplus	**B C**
Total surplus	**A B C D $E_{1,2}$ $F_{1,2}$ G**	Total surplus	**A B C $E_{1,2}$ $F_{1,2}$**
Net gains from trade	**D $E_{1,2}$ $F_{1,2}$ G**	Net gains from trade	**$E_{1,2}$ $F_{1,2}$**
Quantity supplied (domestic)	**20**	Quantity supplied (domestic)	**30**
Quantity of imports	60 – 20 = **40**	Quantity of imports	50 – 30 = **20**
		Deadweight loss (net loss from tariff)	**D G**
		Tax revenue	**$F_{1,2}$**

SUMMARY 小结

- Price elasticity of demand or the percentage of change in the quantity demanded of a particular good divided by the price of the same good demonstrates the sensitivity of consumers to price changes. P × Q = TR allows a revenue test, i.e., whether a price change will increase or decrease total revenue.
- Price elasticity of supply shows the sensitivity of producers or firms to price changes for their products.
- Price elasticity of demand or supply which has a numerical coefficient >1 is elastic, =1 is unit elastic, or <1 is inelastic.
- Cross price elasticity of demand is the percentage change in the quantity demanded of one product in response to the percentage change in the price of a second product. If this ratio produces a positive sign, the two products are good substitutes. If this ratio produces a negative sign, then the two products are complements.
- Income elasticity of demand measures the responsiveness of consumers to changes in their income.
- Consumer surplus is the difference between the highest price a consumer would pay and the actual price paid.
- Producer surplus is the difference between the lowest price a producer would sell for and the actual price of a sale.
- A tax on a good creates a deadweight loss, and the burden or incidence of the tax falls more on the person with the more inelastic demand or supply.
- A tariff does provide the government with tax revenue but also causes a deadweight loss.

TERMS 术语

Consumer Surplus the difference between the highest price a consumer would pay for a product and the actual price paid

Cross-Price Elasticity the percentage change in demand for good X if there is a price change for good Y. If the number is negative, they are complements, and if it is positive, they are substitutes.

Deadweight Loss the loss of total surplus for society when a market fails to reach a competitive equilibrium due to market distortion, like a tax

Elasticity a measure of how producers and consumers respond to changes in price

Excise Tax a per-unit tax on production

Income Elasticity of Demand how a change in income affects the quantity demanded for a product. If income goes up and the quantity demanded goes down, it is an inferior good. If the quantity demanded increases with income, it is a normal good.

Producer Surplus the difference between the lowest price a producer would sell a product and the actual price received

Total Revenue the amount of money taken in by a firm from its sales, which is the price of a product multiplied by the quantity sold

Total Revenues Test a way to determine elasticity by multiplying the price of a good times the quantity sold. If price and total revenues are directly related, a good is inelastic; if inversely related, a good is elastic; and if they equal each other, the good is unit elastic.

FORMULAS 公式

Price Elasticity of Demand:

$$E_d = \frac{\%\ \Delta\ \text{Quantity Demanded}}{\%\ \Delta\ \text{Price}}$$

Cross-Price Elasticity of Demand:

$$\text{CPED} = \frac{\%\ \Delta\ \text{Quantity Demanded of Product X}}{\%\ \Delta\ \text{Price of Product Y}}$$

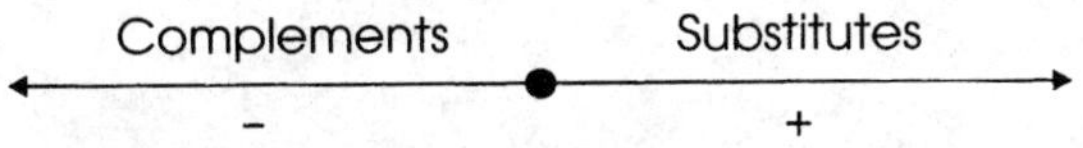

Income Elasticity of Demand:

$$E_i = \frac{\%\ \Delta\ \text{Quantity Demanded}}{\%\ \Delta\ \text{Consumer Income}}$$

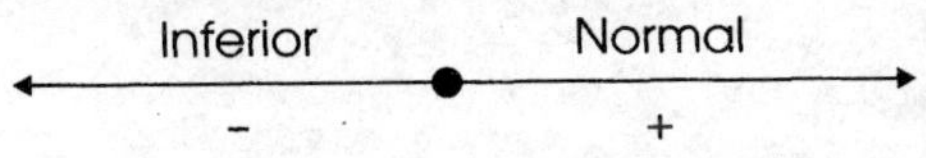

Price Elasticity of Supply:

$$E_s = \frac{\%\ \Delta\ \text{Quantity Demanded}}{\%\ \Delta\ \text{Price}}$$

% Change in Price:
P(NEW) – P(OLD)/P(OLD)
% Change in Quantity Demanded:
Qd(NEW) – Qd(OLD)/Qd(OLD)

MULTIPLE-CHOICE REVIEW QUESTIONS 选择题

1. When the price elasticity of demand coefficient ratio is 2, demand is

(A) unit elastic.
(B) relatively elastic.
(C) perfectly elastic.
(D) relatively inelastic.
(E) perfectly inelastic.

2. Price times quantity measures

(A) the international trade gap.
(B) the budget deficit.
(C) total revenue.
(D) price elasticity of demand.
(E) price elasticity of supply.

3. A positive sign on cross price elasticity of demand indicates that the two products are

(A) luxuries.
(B) necessities.
(C) substitutes.
(D) complements.
(E) independent.

4. If the quantity demanded of good X increases 25% while the price decreases 25%, this means the price elasticity of demand is

(A) unit elastic.
(B) relatively elastic.
(C) perfectly elastic.
(D) relatively inelastic.
(E) perfectly inelastic.

5. If an excise tax is imposed on a supplier, the tax incidence will fall more heavily on consumers if

(A) demand and supply are both unit elastic.
(B) the price elasticity of demand is more inelastic than supply.
(C) the price elasticity of supply is more inelastic than demand.
(D) the price elasticity of demand is more elastic than supply.
(E) the price elasticity of supply is perfectly elastic.

MULTIPLE-CHOICE REVIEW ANSWERS
选择题答案

1. (B) **2.** (C) **3.** (C) **4.** (A) **5.** (B)

FREE-RESPONSE REVIEW QUESTION 开放式题目

1. Analyze the following graph of the price of sugar in the United States before and after a tariff is imposed.

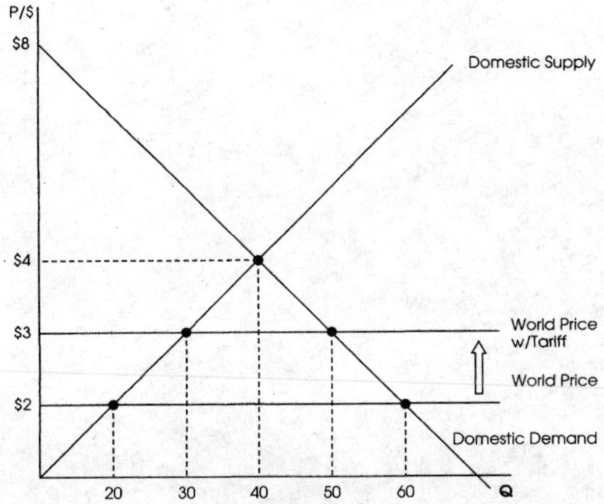

Sugar Market with Trade Before and After

(a) What is the price of sugar if there is no trade?

(b) Calculate the total consumer surplus both without trade *and* at the world price without a tariff. Show your work.

(c) Calculate the total tariff revenue at the world price with a tariff. Show your work.

(d) What is the quantity of domestic supply at the world price both with and without a tariff?

Free-Response Review Answers 开放式题目答案

(a) $4

(b) ½ × ($8 – $4) × 40 = $80 consumer surplus at the price before trade
½ × ($8 – $2) × 60 = $180 consumer surplus with trade at the world price

(c) ($3 – $2) × (50 – 30) = $20

(d) 20 at the world price without a tariff
30 at the world price with the tariff

Theory of Consumer Choice or Behavior 消费选择或消费行为理论

6

→ BASIC TENETS OF CONSUMER CHOICE THEORY
→ DIMINISHING MARGINAL UTILITY
→ UTILITY MAXIMIZING RULE

INTRODUCTION 导言

Economics is the study of choices involving decisions set in the context of scarcity limited by constraints. We buy a basket of goods knowing that we cannot buy as large a selection as we might want, given the constraints of prices and income. How do we make these choices? How does a consumer allocate a limited income among the many choices of goods and services?

THINGS TO KNOW 要了解的事

Based on the most frequently asked questions on previous advanced placement exams, the following are the most important concepts.

1. The basic tenets of the theory of **consumer choice**. This involves many subconcepts, including the **law of diminishing marginal utility**. The student needs to identify this law as being associated with **consumer choice**, as opposed to the law of diminishing marginal productivity, which is associated with producers.
2. The utility maximization rule, $MU_x / P_x = MU_y / P_y$. You can be sure you will be asked about the utility maximizing rule on the AP exam.

BASIC TENETS OF THE THEORY OF CONSUMER CHOICE 消费选择理论的基本原则

1. **THE CONSUMER CAN RANK GOODS** in order of preference: "I prefer a new cell phone to a pair of running shoes."
2. **THE CONSUMER UNDERSTANDS DIMINISHING MARGINAL UTILITY.** As a consumer buys a hot dog, her utility (satisfaction) increases (from zero); as she consumes a second hot dog, her total utility (satisfaction) from the second hot dog is likely to be less than the satisfaction she derived from the first. That is, satisfaction derived from a continuing consumption of hot dogs is going to increase at a decreasing rate, or each additional hot dog is going to add less to total satisfaction than that of the previous hot dog. The *marginal utility* (the addition

to total satisfaction) is decreasing, while the total satisfaction continues to increase up to the level of disutility when too many hot dogs lead to a point at which one more hot dog actually *decreases* total utility or satisfaction, that is, the marginal utility of the "one more hot dog" is negative. Diminishing marginal utility becomes a factor in a consumer's choice when comparing goods and their prices with a limited income. Diminishing marginal utility is also a factor in the determination of a pricing strategy for firms.

3. **THE CONSUMER FACES CONSTRAINTS OF PRICES AND INCOMES.** The factors of rationality, preferences, and diminishing marginal utility are not sufficient in order for the consumer to make final decisions about what to buy and how much to buy. The consumer is constrained from buying every good or service that meets the first three tenets of consumer choice listed above. She can be effectively prevented from purchasing every item on the "list" by a limited income and the prices of the goods and services.
4. **THE UTILITY-MAXIMIZING RULE.** Using the above tenets of consumer choice, the consumer wants to make choices from a variety of goods and services that will maximize her total utility or satisfaction relative to the constraints of prices and income. To do that, the consumer will want to obtain as much extra satisfaction for one good per its price as will be obtained from any other good per its price, given the amount of income available for "N" number of goods. Thus,

$$\frac{MU_X}{P_X} = \frac{MU_Y}{P_Y}$$

with as much income as is available being spent, given a discrete number of goods. In other words, whatever combination of two goods (for instance, four of good X and three of good Y) that meets this condition with the available income will maximize the consumer's total utility. The consumer would be in equilibrium with this combination. There would be no tendency to change this combination of the two goods. There would be no other combination of units of Good X and Good Y that would produce a greater total utility given the same prices of Goods X and Y and the same income for the consumer. Different consumers are going to have different tastes and preferences and therefore, different utility-maximizing combinations of the same two goods with the same prices and the same income. This holds for a particular time period only.

SAMPLE QUESTION

Table 6.1

Marginal Utility and Utility-Maximizing Combination

Units of J	MU_J	Units of K	MU_K
1	56	1	32
2	48	2	28
3	32	3	24
4	24	4	20
5	20	5	12
6	16	6	10
7	12	7	8

Given:

Consumer income = $52
Price of J 8
Price of K 4

The consumer will maximize her utility by purchasing

(A) 3 units of J and 6 units of K
(B) 6 units of J and 3 units of K
(C) 4 units of J and 5 units of K
(D) 5 units of J and 5 units of K
(E) 2 units of J and 7 units of K

(Answer: C.)

Based on Table 6.1, 4 units of J and 5 units of K =

4J @ $8 = $32
+
5K @ $4 = $20
$52

Here is a helpful table you can make when solving similar problems when given a problem similar to this sample question. Make a table of the marginal utility / price for each product, and circle the highest marginal utilities per price and continue until you have spent all the income, which is 4 of J and 5 of K with an income of $52.

Table 6.2

Total Units	Marginal Utility J / Price J	Marginal Utility K / Price K
1	⑦	⑧
2	⑥	⑦
7	④	⑥
4	③	⑤
5	2.5	③
6	2	2.5
7	1.5	0

TIP

For Table 6.1, first construct two additional columns: MU_J/P_J and MU_K/P_K. Next, find all the combination of units of J and units of K that satisfy the condition of $MU_J/P_J = MU_K/P_K$. The answer will be the combination that costs $52 or comes close to $52 without exceeding it.

SUMMARY 小结

- The basic tenets of the theory of consumer choice include ranking goods in order of tastes and preferences, understanding diminishing marginal utility, facing constraints of prices and income and making choices of goods on the basis of the utility-maximizing rule.
- Be sure to know the utility maximizing rule:

$$\frac{MU_X}{P_X} = \frac{MU_Y}{P_Y}$$

TERMS 术语

Diminishing Marginal Utility at some point in the consumption pattern of a good, each additional unit consumed yields less additional satisfaction (utility)

Total Utility the total satisfaction a consumer receives from the consumption of a good or service

MULTIPLE-CHOICE REVIEW QUESTIONS 选择题

Use this Table for Questions 1 and 2.

Table 6.3

Quantity of Pizza	Marginal Utility from Pizza	Quantity of Music Downloads	Marginal Utility from Music Downloads
1	10	1	8
2	8	2	6
3	6	3	4
4	4	4	2
5	2	5	1

1. Samantha consumes both pizza and music downloads. Table 6.3 shows her marginal utility from these. What is her total utility from purchasing four music downloads?

(A) 4
(B) 14
(C) 18
(D) 20
(E) 21

2. Now assume Samantha's weekly income is $12, the price of a pizza is $2, and the price of a music download is $1. What is the utility-maximizing quantity of pizza and music downloads if she spends her entire $12 on pizza?

	Pizza	Music Downloads
(A)	2	2
(B)	2	3
(C)	4	4
(D)	5	4
(E)	5	5

3. The utility-maximizing rule is to choose the basket of goods that

(A) has the highest marginal utility of each good in the basket.
(B) has the lowest prices for the goods.
(C) has the highest value of marginal utility to price for each good.
(D) the marginal utility to price ratio equal for all goods in the basket.
(E) the marginal utility to price ratio equal for all goods in the basket subject to the income constraint.

4. According to the principle of diminishing marginal utility,

(A) marginal utility stays the same.
(B) total utility stays the same.
(C) marginal utility decreases with each additional unit of a good that is consumed.
(D) marginal utility and total utility both decrease.
(E) total utility declines.

MULTIPLE-CHOICE REVIEW ANSWERS
选择题答案

1. (D) **2.** (C) **3.** (E) **4.** (C)

FREE-RESPONSE REVIEW QUESTION
开放式题目

See question and answer on pages 82–83.

Costs, Production, Supply
成本、生产、供给

7

→ LAW OF DIMINISHING MARGINAL RETURNS
→ PRODUCTION FUNCTION
→ RELATIONSHIP OF PRODUCTION CURVES TO COST CURVES
→ LONG RUN VS. SHORT RUN
→ ECONOMIES OF SCALE
→ IMPLICIT AND EXPLICIT COSTS
→ OPPORTUNITY COSTS
→ ECONOMIC PROFIT VS. ACCOUNTING PROFIT
→ AVERAGE COSTS AND MARGINAL COSTS, FIXED COSTS AND VARIABLE COSTS
→ TOTAL COSTS AND MARGINAL COST

INTRODUCTION 导言

All of the basic concepts of costs and production and their interrelationships upon which price and output decisions are made are the subject matter of this chapter. We are not able to fully analyze decisions on prices and outputs without the appropriate revenue data and the related market four structures (perfect competition, monopoly, monopolistic competition, oligopoly). The following chapters on product markets will allow us to complete the analysis.

Students sometimes get overwhelmed learning in this unit, with several different formulas and costs to learn. However, with a little practice and review of the important concepts, you can master these concepts.

THINGS TO KNOW 要了解的事

Based on the most frequently asked questions on previous AP exams, the following are the most important concepts.

1. **LAW OF DIMINISHING MARGINAL RETURNS.** In the short run, as variable inputs are applied to fixed inputs, production first increases at an increasing rate; then, production increases at a decreasing rate (diminishing marginal returns or additions to total production become less and less at the margin). Later, there is actually a decrease in total production or output as successively equal increments of variable inputs are added. Examples, graphs, and explanations will follow in this chapter.
2. **RELATIONSHIPS AMONG AVERAGE AND MARGINAL COST AND PRODUCT CURVES.** Marginal cost (MC) intersects both the average variable cost (AVC) and the average total cost (ATC) curves at their minimum points. This means that if MC > AVC, AVC must be rising (see Figure 7.1); if MC < AVC, AVC must be declining. Similarly, the marginal product curve (MP) intersects the average product curve (AP) at the maximum point of the AP curve (see Figure 7.2(a)).

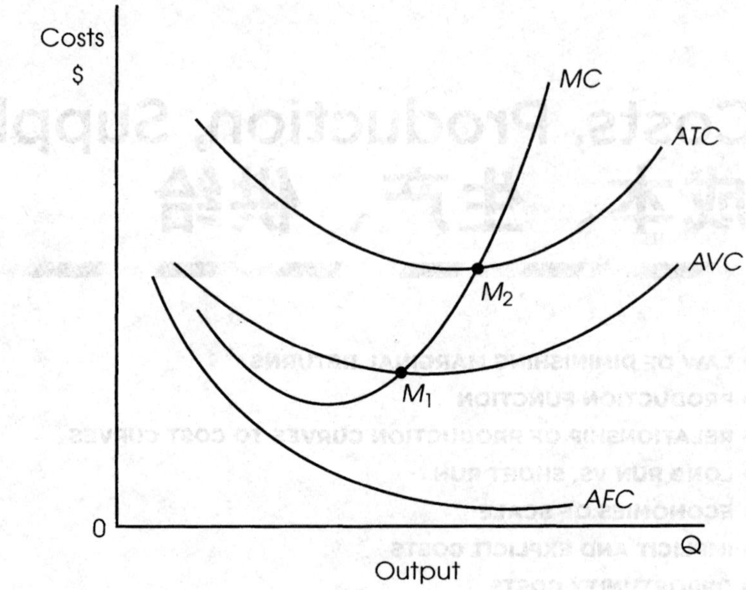

Fig. 7.1 Average Variable Cost, Average Fixed Cost, Average Total Cost, and Marginal Cost

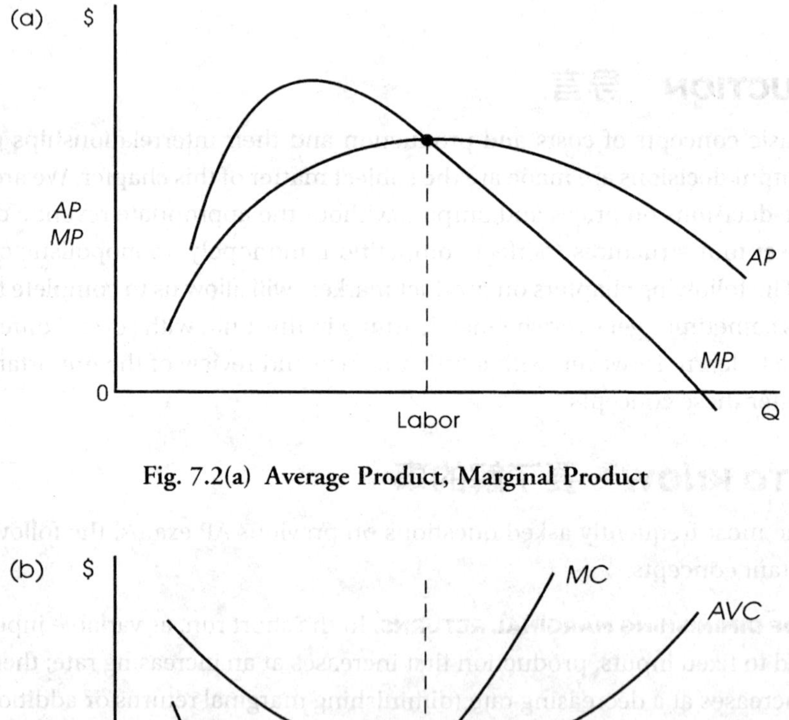

Fig. 7.2(a) Average Product, Marginal Product

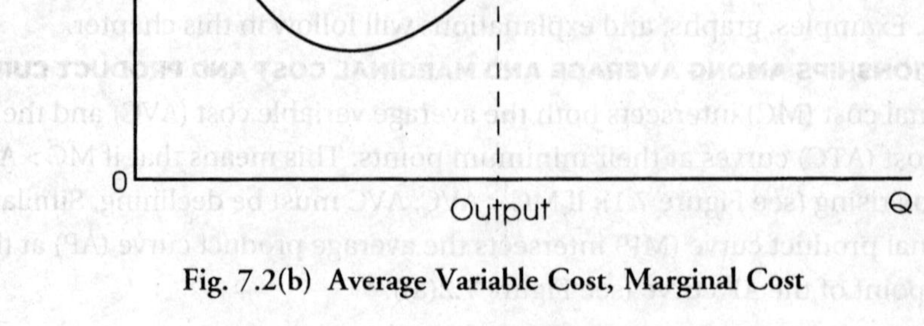

Fig. 7.2(b) Average Variable Cost, Marginal Cost

3. **ECONOMIES OF SCALE.** There are reductions in long-run average total cost (LRATC) as production increases. If a firm increases output and the long-run average total cost is decreasing, there are economies of scale. If output increases and the long-run average total cost curve is rising, there are diseconomies of scale, and if output increases and long-run average total cost curve remains constant, there are constant returns to scale.
4. **COSTS:** opportunity costs, economic costs versus accounting costs, economic profits versus accounting profits, and a normal profit. (This will be covered at the end of this chapter.)

PRODUCTION 生产

In the theory and practice of the firm, we start with the basic facts of the need of the firm to combine its resources into a product or a service. The resources are land, labor, and capital, and entrepreneurial ability. The latter suggests this task of combining resources with some "taking" or assuming of risks. The firm or entrepreneur needs to be innovative and able to adjust to changing technology, labor supply, and new sources of funding capital projects including venture capital. Before a firm can engage resources in any effective manner, it needs to know basic production concepts such as the relationship between resources (also known as inputs, factors of production, or agents of production) and output.

The Production Function and Diminishing Marginal Returns

产品功能与减少边际报酬

The distinction between the short run and the long run is significant in economics. It is *not* the difference declared by a student; the student posited that a long run was any run over one mile in distance. In economics, the distinction is that in the short run, supply cannot fully adjust to changes in demand, due to fixed resources. In the long run, supply does fully adjust to changes in demand as all resources are variable in the long run. The law of **diminishing marginal returns** is a *short run phenomenon.* Thus, as the firm adds more variable inputs to a fixed quantity of other inputs, each added input has less fixed inputs with which to work. If grapes are to be pressed for juice with the use of workers' feet, and there is a fixed supply of grape vats to stomp in, one can imagine that increasing the number of workers will, initially, greatly increase the amount of pressed grapes. However, at some point, there will be a scramble among workers to find a suitable space for the pressing of grapes. An increasing number of workers are competing for space and need to share space leading to smaller and smaller increases in output or **diminishing marginal returns.**

Relationship of Production to Costs 产品与成本的关系

In order to fully appreciate the nature of production and its relationship with costs, we need to define terms for production and then set forth the transition or connection between production and costs.

The relationship between average product (AP) and marginal product (MP) is illustrated in Figure 7.2(a). You will note that when AP is at its peak, AP intersects MP. Any further additions of variable inputs will be associated only with decreasing total product or output. Therefore, there can be no economic rationale for hiring any additional units of labor since these units will have some cost.

Table 7.1

Product Curves and Schedules

No. of Grape Pressers	Total Output (Grape Juice)	Average Product	Marginal Product
1	60	60	60
2	160	80	100
3	250	83.3	90
4	330	82.5	80
5	400	80	70
6	460	76.67	60
7	510	72.86	50
8	550	68.75	40
9	580	64.44	30
10	600	60.00	20
11	610	55.45	10
12	610	50.83	0
13	600	46.15	–10

On this table you will see that if the firm hires a twelfth grape presser, output remains at 610. If the firm hires at thirteenth presser, there is an associated decrease in output to 600 costs. Average product (AP) is defined as the total product or output divided by the number of units of variable input, e.g., labor, and

$$AP = \frac{\text{total output}}{\text{variable input}}$$

$$MP = \frac{\text{change in output}}{\text{change in input}}$$

where MP = marginal product. Marginal product is the more significant measure of these two. We need to know the impact of adding one more unit of input, such as labor, on output. As we identify costs and revenues later, we will be able to ascertain whether the additional cost of an additional unit of input relative to its marginal contribution to revenue is justified. We will reserve that analysis until the chapter on resource markets (Chapter 12). In this current chapter, and the chapters to follow on product markets, we will emphasize the various cost curves related to increases in product and their connection to prices and revenues.

TIP

Marginal analysis is crucial to economic decision-making. Decisions are made at the margin, not at the average. Firms want to know whether an additional unit of production adds more total costs or more to total revenue.

COSTS 成本

Relationship of MP and AP to AVC and MC:

In Figures 7.2(a) and 7.2(b), there is an illustration of this relationship. It is as if we are in a maximum/minimum symmetry. That is, the relationship of marginal product (MP) to average product (AP) is the exact opposite of the relationship of marginal cost (MC) to average variable costs (AVC). In both cases, as the marginal (MP, MC) is less than the average (AP, AVC), the average is declining. As the marginal (MP, MC) is greater than the average (AP, AVC), the average is increasing. However, the MP curve intersects the AP at the *maximum* point on AP, but the MC curve intersects the AVC curve at the minimum point on AVC. Thus, as MP declines, each additional unit of labor adds less and less to total product (think of MP as the addition to total product or the difference in total product as one more unit of labor is added). Regardless of the loss of an additional unit of labor, if each successive equal increment of labor adds less and less to total product, then MC will tend to rise as MP decreases.

A WORD OF CAUTION 警示词

Simply because MP is declining (diminishing marginal returns) and MC is rising does *not* necessarily mean that the firm should discontinue production. We need to have the comparison of marginal revenue (MR) with marginal cost. We will look at this in the unit on product markets (Chapter 8). If MR > MC, then the firm will want to continue since it is adding more to revenue than to cost at the margin of producing an additional unit of output.

This relationship of cost to production will be extended to economies of scale later in this chapter. The different measures are AFC, AVC, ATC, MC, TFC, TVC, TC:

1. **FIXED COSTS:** Total fixed costs are those that, in total, do not vary with changes in output. At zero output, total costs = total fixed costs. Examples would be depreciation costs, capital costs or building and equipment, property taxes, mortgage interest, administrative salaries, and sometimes employee salaries or wages (all or a portion of, such as, tenured faculty, high percent of nurses' salaries, etc.). Average fixed costs (AFC) are total fixed costs divided by output or TFC ÷ Q. As you might expect, since total fixed costs are constant over varying output, then average fixed costs are going to decline as output increases. So, if TFC are constant or

$$\frac{TFC}{Q}$$

then as output increases, AFC decline.

$$\frac{(TFC)}{Q\uparrow} \Rightarrow AFC\downarrow$$

where Q = output. This AFC along with the other marginal and average cost curves are depicted in Figure 7.1.

2. **VARIABLE COSTS.** Total variable costs are costs that, in total, vary as output changes. As we will see in the next section on economies of scale, these costs tend to decline initially, then reach a minimum, and then increase. Variable costs include the changes in number of employees, energy costs related to production changes, travel expenses,

materials related to production, etc. Average Variable Costs (AVC) equal Total Variable Costs (TVC) divided by Q where Q equals the output level. AVC is illustrated in Figure 7.1.

3. **TOTAL COSTS.** Total Costs = Total Fixed Costs + Total Variable Costs or TC = TFC + TVC. This relationship and the others identified in this section will become important as the readers will progressively complete a table of cost data; different columns will be blank in total or part on different tables. The correct or final table will appear in the chapter on perfect competition, Chapter 9; indeed, this final table will become the basis for a problem in best or optimal output in that chapter. Also, the total of the average costs is significant and necessary to know to complete the cost tables. Thus, ATC = AFC + AVC. As with TC = TFC + TVC, the above identity can be completed if one knows two of the three numbers or has progressively developed the necessary numbers. Thus, if one knows TC and TVC, one can determine TFC and so on. Before we expand the discussion to the long run, Figure 7.1 illustrates these cost curves (average and marginal) including their relationships. The reader will note that MC intersects both the average variable cost curve (AVC) and the average total cost curve (ATC) at their respective minimum points (M_1, M_2). *This is important to know*. Also, as in our previous discussion, the AFC curve declines rapidly approaching zero level as Quantity (Q) of output increases with total fixed costs constant. The location or level of average variable costs (AVC) and average total costs (ATC) are significant as you will need to know the shut-down position (minimum AVC) and the relationship of price to ATC at best output (P > ATC, profits; P < ATC, losses) under perfect competition (Chapter 9).

TAXES AND SHIFTING COST CURVES 税收和变动的成本曲线

One of the most important shifters of cost curves are taxes. Different types of taxes have differing effects on cost curves. For example, a per-unit tax places a tax on each additional unit produced. An excise tax, placed on the sales of a specific product, is an example of a per-unit tax. A per-unit tax increases only if output increases; thus, it is a variable cost, not a fixed cost. So it will not affect or impact a firm's fixed costs. If a per-unit tax is placed on the production of a firm in Figure 7.3, variable costs increase, shifting the MC, ATC, and AVC upward, but not the AFC. The amount produced at the profit-maximizing quantity (MR = MC, more on that in later chapters) will then decrease from Q_1 to Q_2 due to the tax. (**Note:** Try not to be confused by all of the shifts on Figure 7.3: it merely shows the increases in AVC, ATC, and MC and their shifts.)

Not all taxes will affect variable costs, however. If a lump-sum tax is imposed, that is a fixed amount of tax regardless of the amount a firm produces. This then affects the fixed, not variable, costs. With a lump-sum tax, marginal and variable costs are not affected. Note how the lump-sum will not affect the amount produced (Q_1) in Figure 7.4, as marginal cost does not change, and thus the profit-maximizing output (MR = MC) is not affected. The only curves that shift are the AFC and ATC, as ATC is the total of variable and fixed costs.

See Table 7.2 for a summary of the effect of lump-sum taxes and per-unit taxes on the different cost curves.

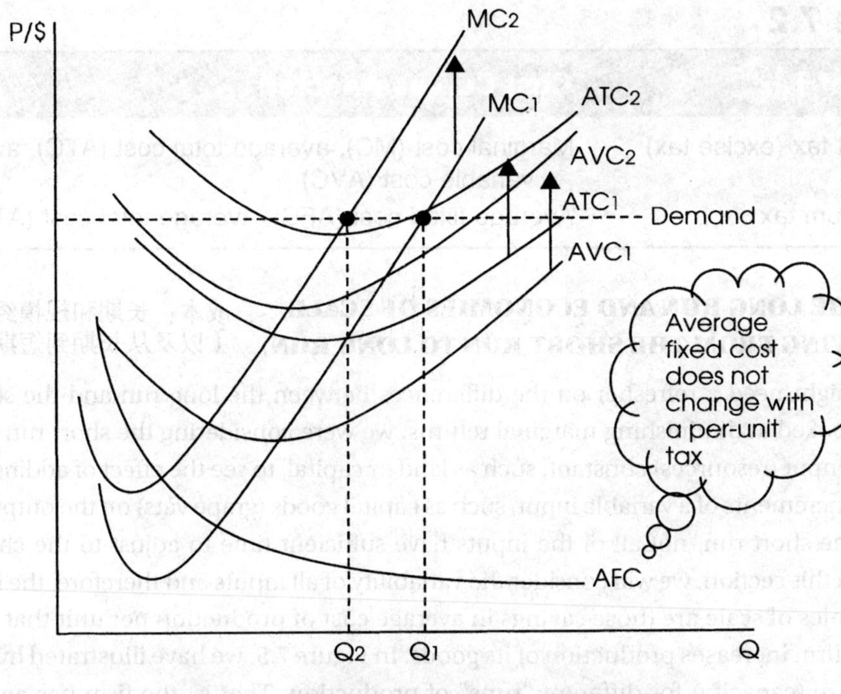

Fig 7.3. Shifting Cost Curves: A Per-Unit Tax

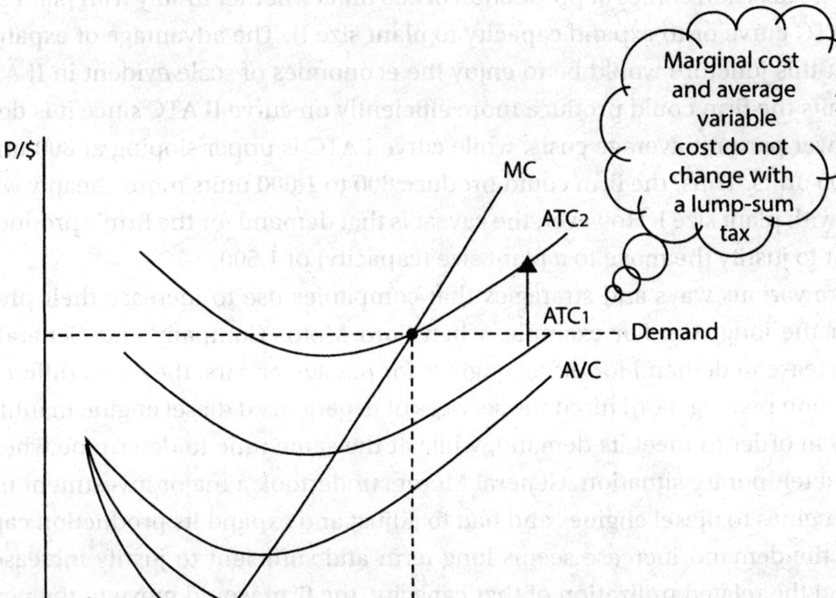

Fig 7.4. Shifting Cost Curves: A Lump-Sum Tax

Table 7.2

Type of Tax	Cost Curves Affected
Per-unit tax (excise tax)	Marginal cost (MC), average total cost (ATC), average variable cost (AVC)
Lump-sum tax	Average fixed cost (AFC), average total cost (ATC)

COSTS: THE LONG RUN AND ECONOMIES OF SCALE (AND MOVING FROM THE SHORT RUN TO LONG RUN) 成本：长期和规模经济（以及从长期到短期）

First, we might need a refresher on the differences between the long run and the short run. When we looked at diminishing marginal returns, we were considering the short run since we held some input (resources) constant, such as land or capital, to see the effect of adding successive equal increments of a variable input, such as capital goods (grape vats) on the output (grape juice). In the short run, not all of the inputs have sufficient time to adjust to the changes in demand. In this section, we will consider the variability of all inputs and therefore, the long run.

Economies of scale are those savings in average cost of production per unit that are realized as the firm increases production of its goods. In Figure 7.5, we have illustrated hypothetical plant size (capacity) for different "runs" of production. That is, the firm has an average total cost (ATC) curve I for production up to 1,000 units, ATC curve II for up to 1,500 units, and so on. The decision comes at production of 800 units whether to stay with plant size I and its related ATC curve or to expand capacity to plant size II. The advantage of expanding the plant size at this juncture would be to enjoy the economies of scale evident in II ATC. That is, at 800 units the firm could produce more efficiently on curve II ATC since it is downward sloping—lower per unit average costs, while curve I ATC is upper sloping at 800 units to its limit of 1,000 units. Thus, the firm could produce 800 to 1,000 units more cheaply with plant size II than with plant size I. However, the caveat is that demand for the firm's production will be sufficient to justify the move to a plant size (capacity) of 1,500.

There are various ways and strategies that companies use to increase their production capacity for the long run. For example, when Ford Motor Company and General Motors faced an increase in demand for diesel engines for passenger cars, they took different paths in their decision making. Ford hired the services of experienced diesel engine manufacturers in Germany in order to meet its demand, while at the same time to determine whether this was simply a temporary situation. General Motors undertook a major investment in changing piston engines to diesel engines and had to adjust and expand its production capacity.

Thus, if the demand increase seems long term and sufficient to justify increased plant capacity, and the related utilization of that capacity, the firm would move to the next-larger plant size when the ATC curve of one size intersected the ATC curve of the next-larger size (e.g., when ATC I intersects ATC II at 800 units of production rather than waiting until production reaches 1,000). The extent to which this becomes an on-going process, the long run average total cost curve becomes the envelope curve that touches base with these decision points—800, 1,300, 2,000, and 2,400 units.

VALUE OF A LARGE-SIZE FIRM 大型公司的价值

The value of having a large-size firm is that it can hire specialists in finance, marketing, distribution, public relations, corporate communications, information technology, and even economics! The sole proprietorship or "Mom and Pop" operation has to be "Jack and Jill of everything"—all those specialized areas listed above—and "master of none." Thus, the larger firm can become more efficient than the small firm simply on the basis of being able to hire more expertise. The other general internal efficiency is the gain that comes from the increase in volume that allows fixed costs to be spread over a larger output of goods and services lending to a decrease in average per unit costs.

In the chapter on imperfect competition, Chapter 11, we cite the case of too many gasoline stations at a busy intersection. The volume of sales, gallons of gasoline, is too low in total to provide any basis for economies of scale for any of the four gasoline stations. It is a classic example of underutilization or excess capacity as the major source of inefficiency in the long run under monopolistic competition. This situation could be illustrated with the graph in Figure 7.6(c). You will see on the economies of scale (the Long-run average total cost/LRATC) declining very quickly and then a long range of diseconomies of scale (the longer, upward sloping portion of the LRATC curve) rising. Each station simply cannot pump enough gallons of gasoline over which to spread its fixed costs. Figure 7.6(c) illustrates a relatively small firm. Conversely, a very large firm such as an automobile manufacturing company can enjoy an LRATC curve as illustrated in Figure 7.6(b) since it can cover its fixed costs over a very large number (millions) of its output or automobiles. This LRATC curve has a long downward declining shape with economies of scale. Also, the company can use the most modern technology that would be, in many cases, too expensive for smaller firms or the smaller firms would have to purchase smaller technology. This smaller technology would be more expensive per unit produced. For example, a machine with 1,000 horsepower would not cost twice as much as one with 500 horsepower.

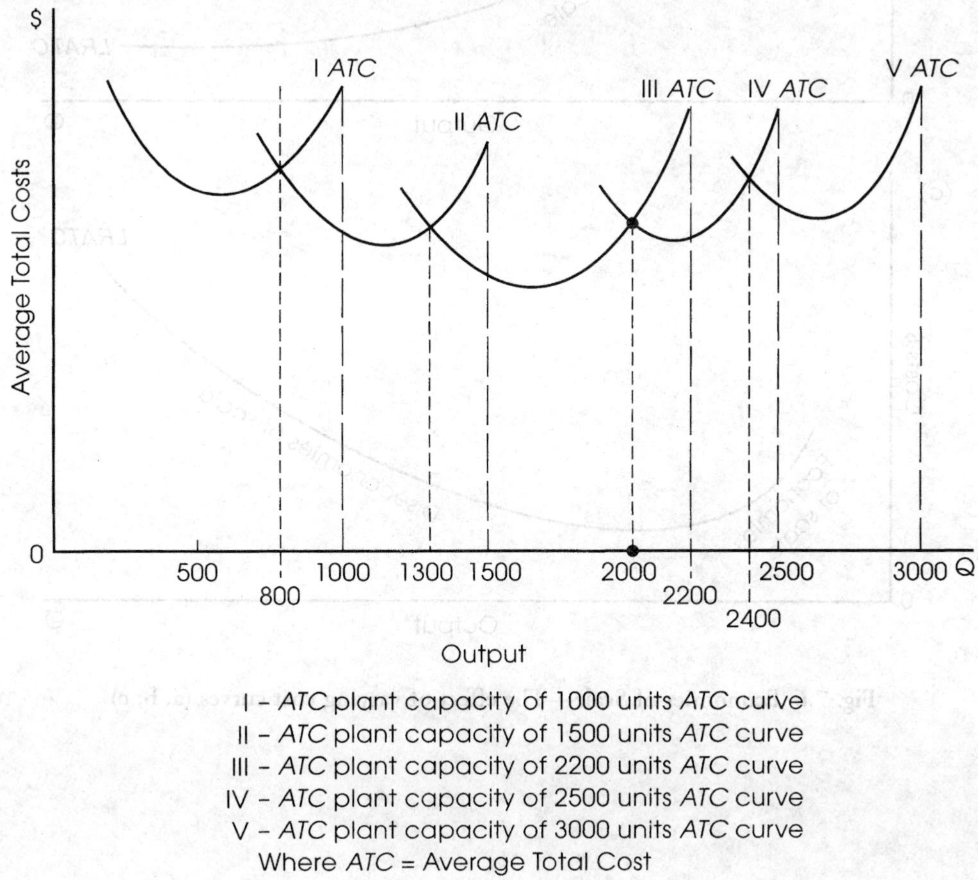

Fig. 7.5 Adjustment in Plant Size (Capacity) From Short-Run to Long-Run Cost Curves

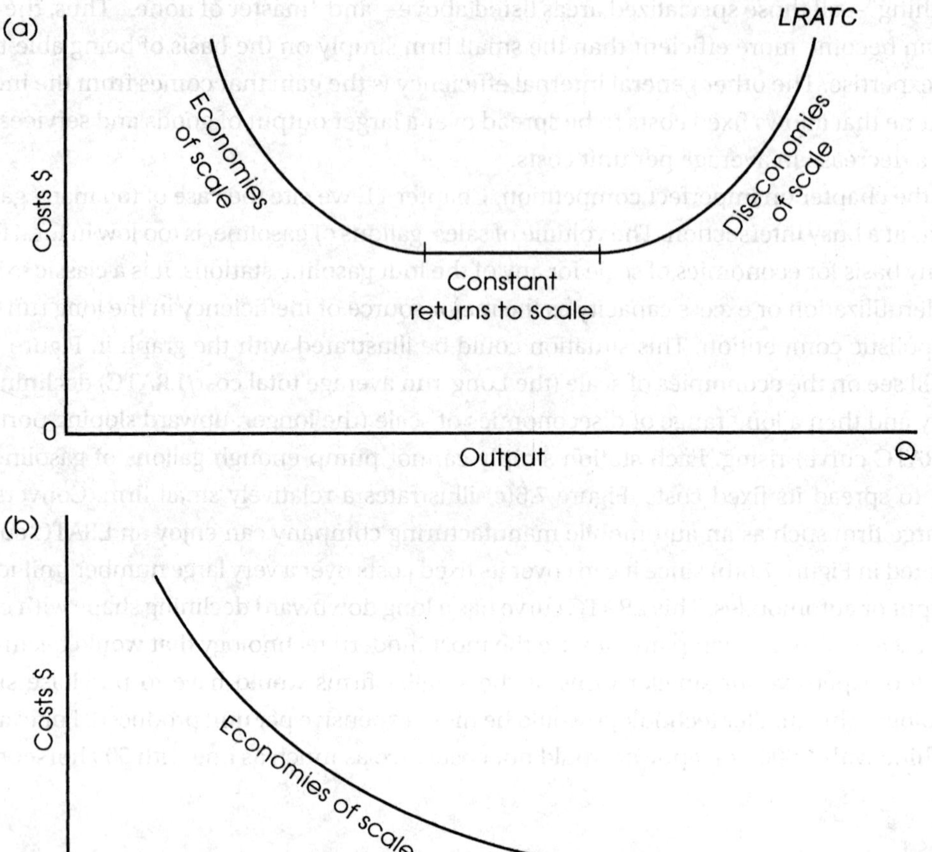

Fig. 7.6 Economies of Scale—The effect of varying cost curves (a, b, c)

ECONOMIC VS. ACCOUNTING PROFIT 经济与会计利润

There is a vast difference between the way economists and accountants view profit that is important to comprehend. The major difference between these two is the way they measure costs; while every business has explicit costs like labor, rent, and equipment, economists also consider implicit costs, those not directly visible (opportunity costs) when calculating profit. Accountants are, not surprisingly, concerned with **accounting profit**, which equals revenue – explicit costs. To an economist, economic profit equals revenue minus explicit *and* implicit costs.

Normal Profit 正常利润

Now that we know that economic profit is different from accounting profit, what happens if there is zero economic profit? Even though this situation sounds bad, it actually means a firm is doing well. What zero economic profit means is resources employed in a firm could not be put to better use anywhere else. If an entrepreneur has a normal profit, he could not be making more profit in another venture. This condition of zero economic profit is known as a **normal profit**, which means resources will not be better off in any other activity. Still confused? Here's another example. Let's say famous basketball player LeBron James retires from basketball to start a restaurant, Bron's Burritos. LeBron earns $3 million in revenue, has $2 million in explicit costs, for an accounting profit of $1 million in his first year ($3 million in revenues – $2 million in expenses). However, LeBron also could have earned $20 million playing basketball during the year. To an accountant, it looks like LeBron made a nice profit of $1 million. But to an economist, LeBron lost out big time, to the tune of $19 million, as seen in Table 7.3.

Table 7.3

Bron's Burrito Restaurant: Accounting vs. Economic Profit

Sales from restaurant (revenue)	$3 million
Explicit costs	–$2 million
Accounting profit (revenues – explicit costs)	$1 million
Implicit costs (basketball salary)	–$20 million
Economic profit or loss (revenues – explicit and implicit costs)	–$19 million

For one more scenario, assume in the next year LeBron earned a $20 million accounting profit at Bron's Burritos. In this case, his economic profit would be zero. You may be thinking why zero? While LeBron's accounting profit is positive ($20 million), his economic profit considers his implicit costs as well, the $20 million he could have earned playing ball if not running his restaurant (though it might be more fun). Considering this implicit cost ($20 million) gives LeBron zero economic profit, the point that is also called normal profit. Table 7.4 has a review of the two ways to measure profit, and since this is economics, the one on the left is most important (just don't tell an accountant I said that).

Table 7.4

The Difference Between Economic and Accounting Profit

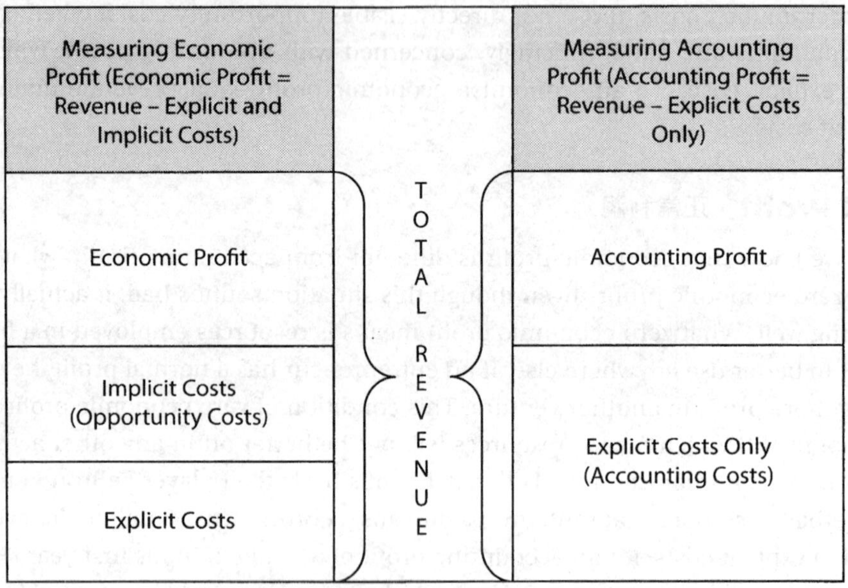

SUMMARY 小结

- Law of Diminishing Marginal Returns. This is the range of output over which production increases at a decreasing rate, i.e., the additional units of production become smaller and smaller.
- Relationships Among Average Cost (AC, AVC, ATC), Marginal Cost (MC), Average Product (AP) and Marginal Product (MP) Curves. The MP curve *always* intersects the AP curve at the maximum point of the AP curve. The MC curve *always* intersects the Average Cost Curve (AVC, ATC) at their minimum points.
- Economies of Scale. These reductions in average cost per unit of output as production increases may be in the form of constant, increasing, or decreasing returns to scale.
- Economic Profits vs. Accounting Profits. Accounting profits result from subtracting explicit costs from income or revenue. Economic profits produce a return that is less than a return of an alternative activity using the same resources (implicit costs).
- Economic Profits. Revenue minus explicit *and* implicit costs.
- Accounting Profits. Revenue minus explicit costs.

TERMS 术语

Accounting Profit the difference between total revenues and explicit costs only

Average Fixed Cost a firm's total fixed cost divided by total output

Average Product total product divided by the variable input used in production

Diseconomies of Scale at this stage of output, as a firm's output increases, its long-run average total cost (LRATC) curve increases. The upward sloping part of the LRATC.

Economic Profit total revenues subtracted by both explicit and implicit costs; this is the type of profit referred to in Economics

Excise Tax a per-unit tax placed on the sales of a specific product

Fixed Costs these costs do not change when quantity changes in the short run, but can change in the long run

Law of Diminishing Marginal Returns the range of output over which smaller and smaller additional units of output are produced as successive equal increments of a variable input are added to fixed quantities of other inputs in the short run

Long Run period of time over which supply can fully adjust to changes in demand

Lump-Sum Tax a fixed tax on producers regardless of the amount produced; affects average fixed cost and average total cost

Marginal Cost what it costs to produce an additional unit of output; equal to $\Delta TC / \Delta Q$

Marginal Product how much additional output is produced when an input is added by a firm

Normal Profit zero economic profit, where an entrepreneur will not be better off in any other venture

Per-Unit Tax a tax on each additional unit produced, and affects variable costs: marginal cost, average total cost, and average variable cost

Short Run period of time over which supply cannot fully adjust to changes in demand due to fixed resources

Total Costs the total of fixed and variable costs

Variable Costs these costs change as production increases

FORMULAS 公式

Total Cost (TC) = Total Variable Costs (TVC) + Total Fixed Costs (TFC)

Average Total Cost (ATC) = Average Variable Costs (AVC) + Average Fixed Costs (AFC) or Total Costs / Q

Marginal Cost (MC) = $\Delta TC / \Delta Q$

Average Fixed Cost (AFC) = TFC / Q

Average Variable Cost (AVC) = TVC / Q

MULTIPLE-CHOICE REVIEW QUESTIONS 选择题

1. Which of the following is true?
   (A) TC = TVC + TFC.
   (B) TFC = TC at all levels of output.
   (C) AVC + AFC = TC.
   (D) MC = TC − TFC.
   (E) ATC = AVC + MC.

2. If a business owner has a $100,000 accounting profit, and could have made exactly $50,000 in his next best business opportunity, he has earned
   (A) $100,000 in economic profits.
   (B) $150,000 in economic profits.
   (C) $50,000 in economic profits.
   (D) Neither an economic profit or loss.
   (E) None of the above.

3. With capital fixed at one unit with 1, 2, 3 units of labor added in equal successive units, production of the output increases from 300 (1 unit of labor), to 350 (2 units of labor) to 375 (3 units of labor). Which of the following is a correct interpretation?
   (A) This is long run increasing returns to scale.
   (B) This is long run decreasing returns to scale.
   (C) This is long run constant returns to scale.
   (D) This is short run diminishing marginal productivity.
   (E) This is short run increasing marginal productivity.

4. There are economies of scale when
   (A) the tripling of all inputs doubles the output produced.
   (B) long-run average total cost decreases as output increases.
   (C) short-run average total cost curve remains constant as output increases.
   (D) long-run average total cost curve increases as output increases.
   (E) short-run average total cost curve increases as output increases.

5. Marginal cost (MC) is equal to average variable cost (AVC) and average total cost (ATC) when:
   (A) marginal cost (MC) intersects AVC and ATC at their maximum points.
   (B) AVC and ATC intersect MC at its maximum point.
   (C) MC intersects AVC and ATC at their minimum points.
   (D) AVC and ATC intersect MC at its minimum point.
   (E) the economy is in the recovery phase of the business cycle.

Refer to the graph below for Question 6.

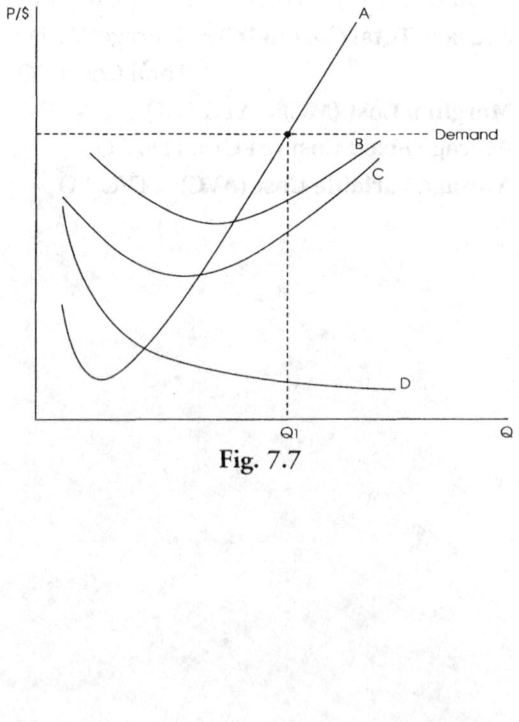

Fig. 7.7

6. Which cost curves do A, B, C, and D represent, in order from A to D?

(A) ATC, MC, AFC, AVC
(B) MC, AFC, AVC, ATC
(C) MC, ATC, AVC, ATC
(D) AFC, MC, ATC, AVC
(E) AFC, ATC, AVC, MC

7. Which of the following statements is true regarding the marginal cost (MC), average variable cost (AVC), and average total cost (ATC) curves?

(A) If MC is greater than ATC and AVC, then ATC and AVC must be decreasing.
(B) If MC is greater than ATC and AVC, then ATC and AVC must be increasing.
(C) If MC is decreasing, then ATC and AVC must be decreasing.
(D) If ATC and AVC are decreasing, MC must be decreasing as well.
(E) If ATC and AVC are increasing, MC must be increasing.

MULTIPLE-CHOICE REVIEW ANSWERS
选择题答案

1. (A) **2.** (C) **3.** (D) **4.** (B) **5.** (C)

6. (C) **7.** (B)

FREE-RESPONSE REVIEW QUESTION 开放式题目

1. A. Complete the table below.

Output	TC	AFC	AVC	ATC	MC
1		$400	$100		$100
2		200	75		
3		133	70		
4		100	73		
5		80	80		
6		67	90		
7		57	103		
8		50	119		
9		44	138		
10		40	160		

B. Determine what total costs (TC) would be for zero output.

Free-Response Review Answer 开放式题目答案

1. A.

Output	TC	AFC	AVC	ATC	MC
1	$500	$400	$100	$500	$100
2	550	200	75	275	50
3	610	133	70	203	60
4	690	100	73	173	80
5	800	80	80	160	110
6	940	67	90	157	140
7	1,120	57	103	160	180
8	1,350	50	119	169	230
9	1,640	44	138	182	290
10	2,000	40	160	200	360

B. At zero output, TC = $400.

Product Markets: Types, Characteristics, Pricing Strategies

产品市场：类型、特点、价格策略

8

- → PERFECT COMPETITION, MONOPOLISTIC COMPETITION, OLIGOPOLY, MONOPOLY
- → EFFICIENCY
- → BARRIERS TO ENTRY/EXIT
- → ELASTICITY AND PRODUCT MARKETS
- → AVAILABILITY OF SUBSTITUTES, SIMILARITY OF PRODUCTS, NUMBER OF SELLERS
- → PRICE-TAKERS AND PRICE-MAKERS

INTRODUCTION 导言

This chapter is an view of the four product markets in which firms operate. These four markets range from perfect competition to the imperfectly competitive real-world models of monopolistic competition and oligopoly to monopoly. For each of these product markets, there is a set of characteristics that will help you understand the different costs, efficiencies, and pricing strategies of the different markets.

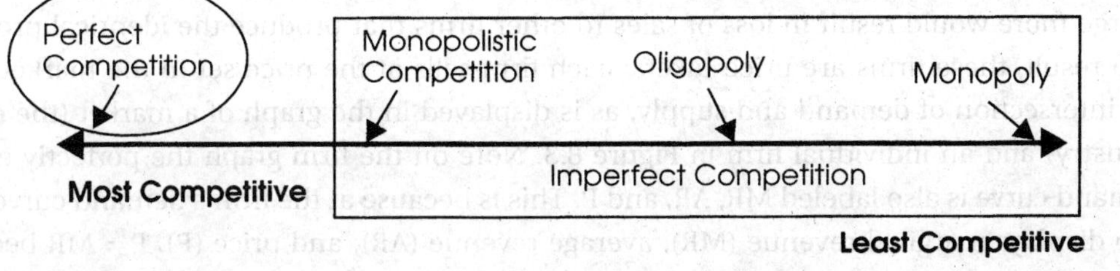

Fig 8.1

TIP

The largest number of questions on the AP Microeconomics exam come from these four markets.

THINGS TO KNOW 要了解的事

The four market structures make up the largest percentage of content on the AP Microeconomics exam. The four market structures have many differences as well as similarities. The market structures Venn diagram (Figure 8.2) gives a complete overview of these differences and similarities and is very helpful to review. Most of these details will be discussed in later chapters; be sure to mark this diagram and refer back to it as you move to later chapters.

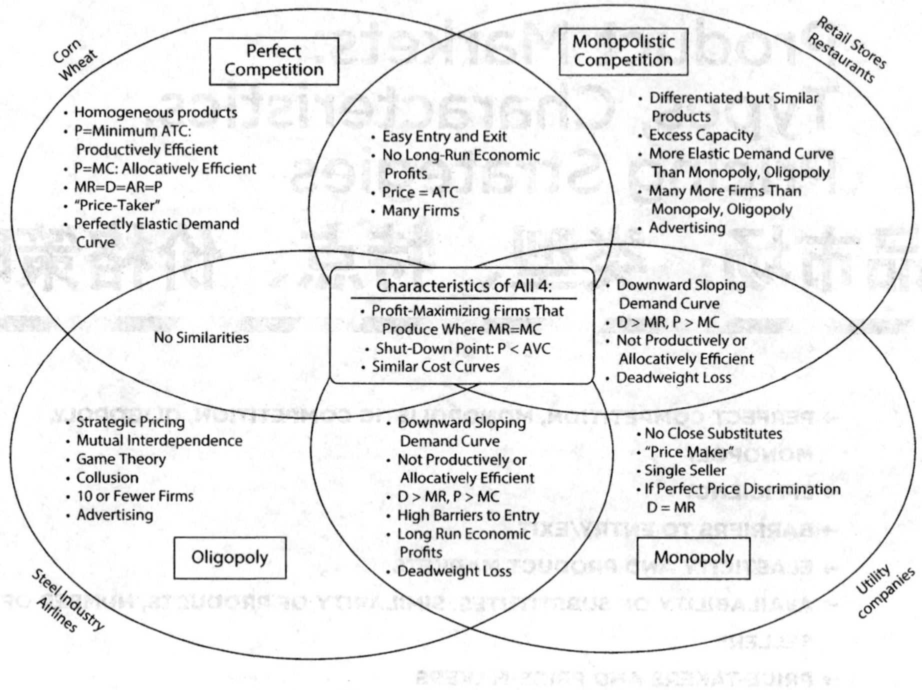

Fig. 8.2 Market Structures/Venn Diagram

PRODUCT MARKETS: DEFINITIONS 产品市场：定义

Perfect Competition 完全竞争

Perfect competition is characterized by a large number of sellers so that no one seller or group of sellers can have a significant effect on the market for a product. Perfectly competitive firms are "price-takers" where they have no influence on the price of the product they produce. Prices for each firm in this perfectly competitive environment are determined in the market where all firms (sellers) compete for the buyers of the same (homogeneous) product. That is, the price is set in this market and each firm must charge the "market price"; to charge more would result in loss of sales to other firms that produce the identical product. As a result, these firms are price-takers; each firm sells at the price set in the market or at the intersection of demand and supply, as is displayed in the graph of a market (the entire industry) and an individual firm in Figure 8.3. Note on the firm graph the perfectly elastic demand curve is also labeled MR, AR, and P. This is because at the firm's demand curve, this also displays marginal revenue (MR), average revenue (AR), and price (P). P = MR because

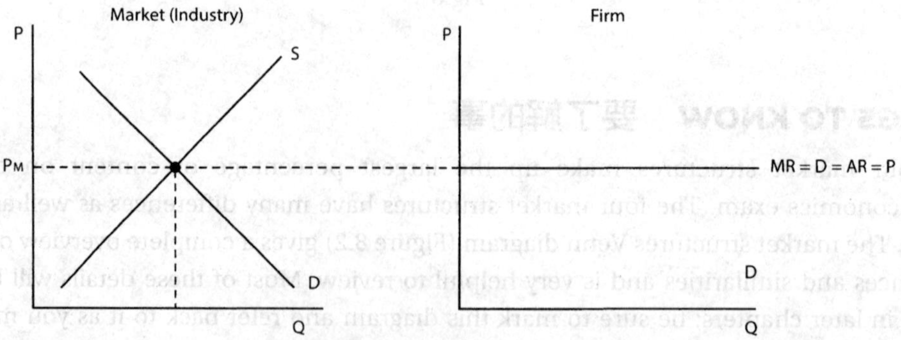

Fig. 8.3 Perfect Competition

regardless of how many units a firm sells, the price stays constant; each additional unit sells for the same price regardless of the quantity sold. (**Note**: Cost curves, ATC, MC, and so on that help determine profit or loss will be added to the market graphs in later chapters.)

To illustrate, under perfect competition, there are no barriers to entry for firms that want to enter the market—no technological secrets, no financial barriers, no legal or regulatory constraints, etc. Also, there are no barriers to exit, such as government subsidies, tax relief, import quotas, or high tariffs. Perfect competition is also characterized by homogeneous (identical) product; firms must use the currently available technology and fully utilize plant and equipment to maintain the competitive norm of costs and hence, be efficient. We will discover in the next chapter that a firm sets the ideal for efficient markets in long-run equilibrium under perfect competition.

Under perfect competition, there is no pricing strategy. The price elasticity of demand for each firm (see Chapter 5) is perfectly elastic, a horizontal curve indicating that the products are perfect substitutes. Each firm must produce and price at minimum cost or lose sales to the other firms. Each customer buys a product at its minimum average total cost. Thus, the more substitutes available, the more competitive the industry structure and the more elastic the response to price changes. The perfectly competitive model is one of price-takers with no pricing strategy or power independent of the market.

TIP

To remember the labels on a perfectly competitive firm, MR = D = AR = P, you can just remember Mister Darp, or label it MRDARP. This will get you credit for a correct label on the AP exam.

Monopoly 垄断

There are many forms that monopoly can take (see Chapter 10). It is important to note that we are on the opposite end of market structures than that of perfect competition. That is, monopolies are characterized as one seller of a product for which there are no close substitutes. As you can see in Figure 8.4, monopolies (and all imperfectly competitive firms) have down-sloping demand curves with marginal revenue less than demand. This will come into play in later chapters when discussing the profit-maximizing output (MR = MC). When a monopoly wants to sell more units, it must lower its price for all buyers; when price is lowered from, say $200 to $150, the additional (marginal) revenue received decreases faster than price, from which the demand curve is derived. Thus, we have the two separate demand and marginal revenue curves seen in Figure 8.4.

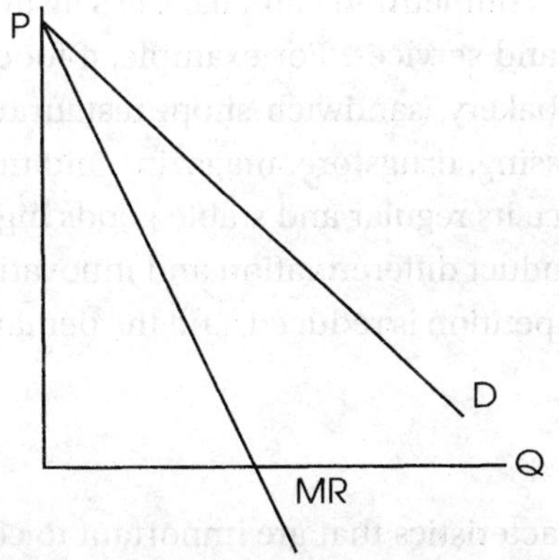

Fig. 8.4 Monopoly

Table 8.1 exemplifies the reasoning behind the differing marginal revenue and demand curves, that marginal revenue is less than price (the demand curve) and does not equal price. Note that marginal revenue eventually becomes negative. This is why the MR curve falls below the quantity axis in Figure 8.2 and is known as the inelastic range of demand. A monopolist will likely not sell a product in this range, as the additional revenue is negative.

Barriers to entry allow monopolists to increase prices and limit output; hence, no available close substitutes leads to lack of competition and the demand curve is less elastic than that of perfect competition. There are several types of monopolies and pricing strategies that we will review in later chapters.

Table 8.1

Price and Marginal Revenue

Price	Qd	Total Revenue	Marginal Revenue
$6	0	0	—
$5	1	5	5
$4	2	8	3
$3	3	9	1
$2	4	8	–1
$1	5	5	–3

Monopolistic Competition 垄断竞争

This market structure is the setting for many firms in the United States and other countries. Monopolistically competitive firms are monopolies, but only in the sense that they sell their own product that is slightly differentiated from competitors. Consider, for example, two different pizza restaurants selling slightly different tasting pizzas or McDonald's hamburgers being different from Wendy's. There are also many competitors due to easy entry into and exit from these industries. Hence the name "monopolistic competition." When graphing these firms, there are also down sloping demand and marginal revenue curves similar to a monopoly in Figure 8.4. Furthermore, they are characterized by many medium-sized firms that need to be innovative and differentiate their products in ways other than price. That is to say, a firm in monopolistic competition can take sales away from a rival with a variety of "price-distracting" products and services. For example, a food supermarket might develop a huge store complete with bakery, sandwich shop, restaurant, dry cleaner, specialty and take-home meals, film processing, drugstore, magazine and newspaper section, bulk foods, etc. This store could then price its regular and stable goods higher than its rival stores; thus, a strategy that is based on product differentiation and innovation that reduces competition. With few substitutes, the competition is reduced, and the demand curve becomes less elastic.

Oligopoly 寡头垄断

An oligopoly has several characteristics that are important to comprehend:

- **There are a few large producers** who have a large, but not total control over the market. Consider cable companies or a few large airlines.
- **Both identical or differentiated products may be produced.** This may be a standardized product like steel and natural gas, or differentiated products such as soft drinks or airplanes.

- **They are interdependent.** The pricing and output decisions of one firm have a huge impact on the profits of others in the industry. Due to this, oligopolies have a strong incentive to break the law by colluding and fixing prices.
- **There are high barriers to entry.** For example, the car industry is very difficult to enter, as only large firms can produce at a cost low enough to survive. It also requires a very large amount of money to make the capital investments required for this type of firm.

For the purposes of the AP exam, the good news is there is no graph to learn for an oligopoly; just the game theory payoff matrix discussed in Chapter 10.

PRICE-TAKERS VS. PRICE-MAKERS

Price-takers act at the direction of the market; they must charge the going price or face possible elimination. Price-makers are able to control or manipulate some markets; they can charge a price that is in excess of marginal costs that maximizes profits.

SUMMARY 小结

This chapter provides an overview of the different market structures that include perfect competition, monopoly, monopolistic competition, and oligopoly.

The basic reference guide to these market structures is in Figure 8.1. This Venn diagram compares the structures by numbers of sellers, availability of substitutes, degree of price elasticity of demand, similarity of products, pricing policy, barriers to entry/exit, efficiency, economic profits, price related to marginal cost, and price related to marginal revenue.

TERMS 术语

Monopolistic Competition market structure characterized by many medium-sized firms who need to be innovative and differentiate their products in price and nonprice ways

Monopoly one firm constitutes the market (industry) selling a product for which there are no close substitutes (a price-maker)

Oligopoly market structure characterized by relatively few sellers who act interdependently and/or collusively to be price-makers and to control markets

Perfect Competition market structure characterized by a larger number of sellers with a homogeneous product, infinitely elastic demand for firms, and no barriers to entry or exit (a price-taker)

MULTIPLE-CHOICE REVIEW QUESTIONS 选择题

1. For which of the following market structures are the most products available for consumers?

(A) Perfect competition.
(B) Monopolistic competition.
(C) Oligopoly.
(D) Monopoly.
(E) All of the above.

2. Which of the following market structures' demand curves has the greatest degree of elasticity?

(A) Perfect competition.
(B) Monopolistic competition.
(C) Oligopoly.
(D) Monopoly.
(E) All of the above.

3. Which of the following types of market structures is comprised of just a few firms?

(A) Perfect competition.
(B) Monopolistic competition.
(C) Oligopoly.
(D) Monopoly.
(E) All of the above.

4. Which of the following market structures is *not* a price-maker?

(A) Perfect competition.
(B) Monopolistic competition.
(C) Oligopoly.
(D) Monopoly.
(E) All of the above.

MULTIPLE-CHOICE REVIEW ANSWERS
选择题答案

1. (A) **2.** (A) **3.** (C) **4.** (A)

Perfect Competition 完全竞争

9

→ MARKET DEMAND CURVE AND FIRM'S DEMAND CURVE
→ LONG RUN EQUILIBRIUM
→ PRICE-TAKERS
→ PRICE AND MARGINAL COST
→ STRATEGIES FOR PROFIT MAXIMIZATION AND LOSS MINIMIZATION
→ OPTIMAL OUTPUT AND EFFICIENCY
→ EVALUATION OF PERFECT COMPETITION IN THE LONG RUN
→ ADJUSTMENT FROM SHORT RUN TO LONG RUN EQUILIBRIUM
→ CONSUMER AND PRODUCER SURPLUS
→ ALLOCATIVE AND PRODUCTIVE EFFICIENCY

INTRODUCTION 导言

Based on the most frequently asked questions on previous AP exams, the following are the most important concepts.

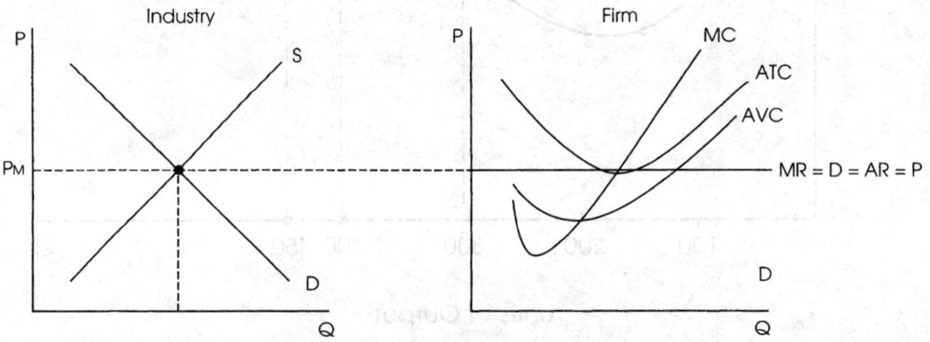

Fig. 9.1 Perfect Competition

THINGS TO KNOW 要了解的事

1. Demand curve of the *market* (or *industry*—all firms selling the same product) is downward sloping to the right but the demand curve of the firm is *horizontal* (perfectly elastic demand curve).
2. Since the demand curve of the individual firm is horizontal, P = MR for the firm.
3. Each firm takes its price from the industry, or market, and is a "price-taker."
4. The graph of a perfectly competitive market in long-run equilibrium shown in Figure 9.1 displays a situation that is unique to perfect competition and not found in other markets—efficiency. As a perfectly competitive firm produces where P = MC,

TIP

To calculate profits, go to the profit-maximizing quantity, *MR = MC*, and draw a straight dotted line to the optimal quantity. From that quantity, draw up to the firm's demand curve, which gives you the profit-maximizing price. Compare that price to the ATC curve at the same quantity. The formula for profit is the (Price − Average Total Cost) × Quantity, for either an economic profit or loss. And if price is below *AVC*, the firm should shut down.

it is **allocatively efficient. This means that the exact amount of a product is being produced to meet society's desires.** Another type of efficiency is also present. A perfectly competitive firm in long-run equilibrium also produces where P = minimum ATC. This is known as **productive efficiency, which means goods are being produced at the lowest possible cost using the fewest possible resources.**

5. Firms in all market structures maximize profits by producing where MR = MC. If we refer to the short run, price as reflected by the demand curve remains horizontal but can increase or decrease in the short run; therefore, there can be profits or losses in the short run. The firm wants to maximize profits or minimize losses by producing the optimal output: i.e., the level of output at which MR = MC. Thus, if you are given a graph, a table, or a set of output and price levels, you need to find the location of the optimizing output in the short run. For example, if Price is $14, find the optimal output in the diagram below:

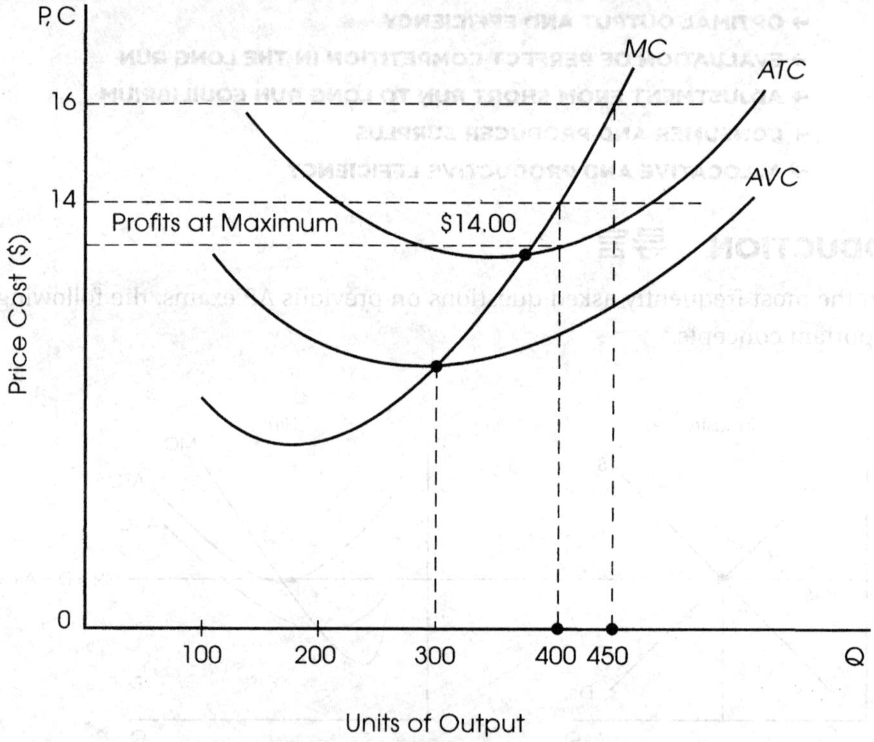

Fig. 9.2 Determination of Profits

The optimal output would be at the level at which MC = MR. Follow the horizontal demand curve over to where the price of $14 (MR) = MC (intersection of the MC function with Price or Demand). Drop a line perpendicular to the horizontal axis and the output of 400 would be the optimal output, the output level at which profits would be maximized or the level at which MR = MC. As a follow-up question, what would the firm do if the price increased to $16? (Again, refer to Figure 9.2). Would the firm produce at 300, 350, 400, 450, or 525 units of output? To determine the answer, follow the general criterion of best output @ MC = MR. Thus, with a price (MR) of $16, MR = MC at an output level of 450. Hence, the best (optimal) output level will be 450.

* Note that MC intersects both AVC and ATC at their minimum levels.

6. As mentioned in the chapter on costs (see Chapter 7) and as illustrated in point 5, ATC = MC when ATC is at its minimum point and AVC = MC when AVC is at its minimum point. That is, MC always intersects ATC and AVC at their minimum points. When MC > ATC, ATC must be rising since the additions to total cost (marginal costs) are greater than average costs. The converse holds with MC < ATC.
7. The following are conditions that are correct about firms operating under perfect competition:

   At *long-run* equilibrium,

   a. P = MR. No pricing strategy. Firms are price-takers.
   b. P = MC. This is the allocatively efficient quantity. Price at which product sells (at "market") equals the extra cost incurred.
   c. P = minimum average total cost: Productive efficiency.
   d. Firms realize zero economic profit or *normal* profits.
   e. Firms have no incentive to price their goods and services below the market price.
   f. The demand curve for each firm is horizontal.
   g. Products are homogeneous; therefore, no purpose for advertising.
8. Profits and competition. LR equilibrium under perfect competition leads to normal profits (zero economic profits).
9. The conditions (criteria) for continuing production, shut-down, profits, losses in the short run under perfect competition (expanded coverage later in this chapter). For each price (P = MR), in the short run:

   a. The **shut down point** for a firm is when P < AVC. If P ≤ AVC, firm should shut down and its total losses = total fixed cost (TFC). If P ≥ AVC, firm should continue production.

EXPANDED CONCEPTS 扩充概念

1. The individual firm as a price-taker (see Figure 9.1).

   The firm is a price-taker, that is, the price for the homogeneous (same) product is determined in the market, where all buyers and sellers meet, and "dictate" to each individual firm. Since there is a sufficiently large number of firms under perfect competition, no one firm or group of firms can determine its own price. The firms must sell at the market-determined price for two basic reasons: (1) If a firm increases its price above the market price, customers will buy the identical product from another seller at the market price; and, (2) If a firm lowers its price below the market price, it will incur losses and not increase its sales significantly, if at all, since each firm has a very small share of a very large number of sellers. (For more characteristics of perfect competition, see the introductory section of Chapter 8.)
2. Criteria and output strategies for profit-maximizing (and loss-minimizing) firms in the short run under perfect competition.

   - For the appropriate context, firms may incur some losses in the short run as long as they are covering average variable costs (those costs that increase as output increases) with the market price. Unless a firm can cover (equal to or greater than) average variable costs with its price, it is more economical to shut down production and simply incur fixed costs (those costs that, in total, do not vary with output changes).
   - The decision-making process to determine best (optimal) output, that is, the output level that maximizes total profits or minimizes total losses.

     a. The firm should produce if P ≥ Average Variable Cost (AVC). It should continue to produce as long as Marginal Revenue (MR) > Marginal Cost (MC). This means that the firm is adding more to its revenue than it is adding to its costs at the margin of producing one additional unit. Therefore, as long as MR > MC, the firm would, necessarily, be adding more to its profits or, in the situation of losses, be reducing losses. At the level of output at which MR = MC, profits would be maximized or losses minimized; hence, the optimal output would occur at MR = MC.

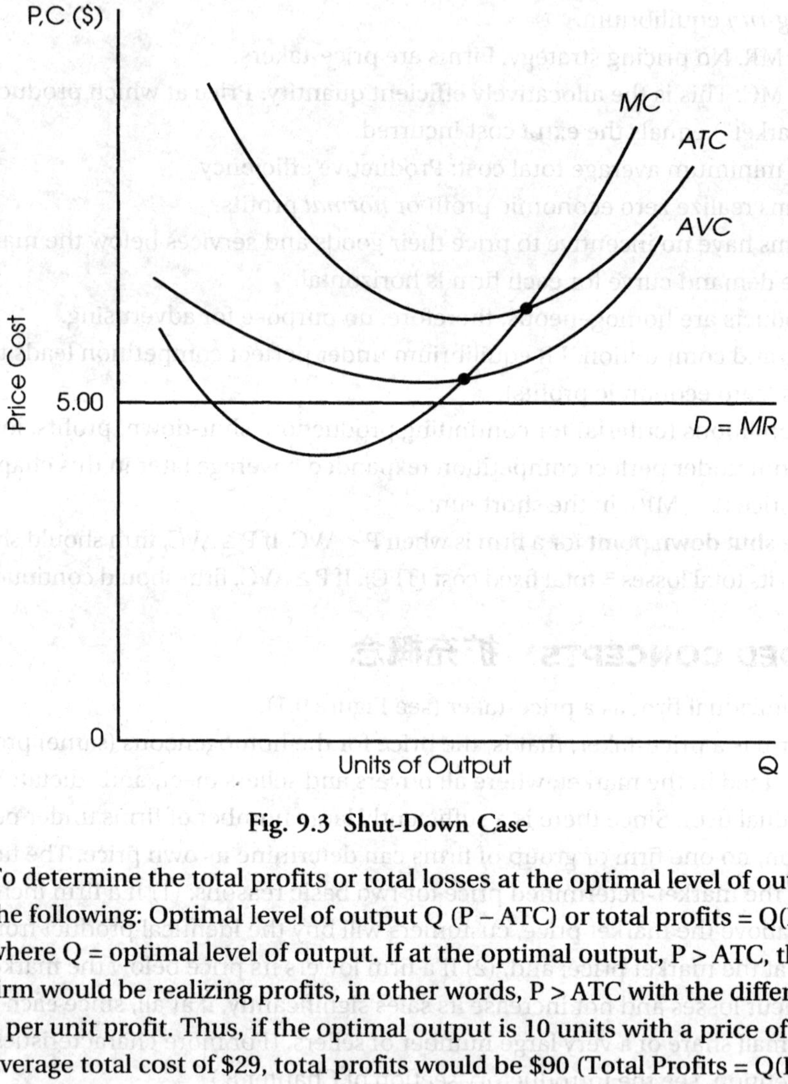

Fig. 9.3 Shut-Down Case

TIP

This is the exception to the general rule that the optimal (best) output occurs at the level at which MC = MR. Whenever price is less than average variable cost (AVC), zero output is optimal in the short run. In Figure 9.3, the price of $5 is less than AVC at all levels of output. The firm shuts down and takes its total fixed costs at zero output as its losses (minimizes total losses).

b. To determine the total profits or total losses at the optimal level of output, use the following: Optimal level of output Q (P – ATC) or total profits = Q(P – ATC) where Q = optimal level of output. If at the optimal output, P > ATC, then the firm would be realizing profits, in other words, P > ATC with the difference being a per unit profit. Thus, if the optimal output is 10 units with a price of $38 and average total cost of $29, total profits would be $90 (Total Profits = Q(P – ATC)) or (10 (38 – 29) = 10 × $9) = or $90. If, at the best output of 10 units with a price of $38 and average total cost at $40, losses would occur (ATC > P); total losses would be = Q(ATC – P) or 10(40 – 38) = $20.

In summary, to determine best output, use the following steps (for *each* price). Remember P = MR for the firm in perfect competition:

1. Compare the price with AVC; go down the AVC column to see if P = AVC or P > AVC. If so, the firm continues to produce as long as MR > MC up to the level of output at which MR = MC or the highest level of output at which MR > MC. This would be the optimal output. If AVC > P, then the firm would shut down and take at its losses, total fixed costs. The MR = MC criterion would not apply here—the best (optimal) output is zero units of output.

2. If the firm continues to produce (P > AVC), then the best output is where MR = MC.
3. To determine total profits or losses, first determine whether at best output P > ATC or ATC > P. In the former case, profits are realized. In the latter case, losses are incurred. If Q is the optimal output, then for total profits, Q(P – ATC); for total losses, Q(ATC – P).

There is a problem to solve, using hypothetical cost data, at the end of this chapter. You may wish to pause with your further reading of this chapter and take on the problem now. The table of costs is taken from Chapter 7, Costs, Production, Supply.

DECISION MAKING FOR THREE SITUATIONS

1. **Shut-down case (see Figure 9.3). (P < AVC, therefore, shut down; total losses = TFC). At the market price of $5, the average variable cost is higher than price at every level of output. Therefore, the firm should shut down (at least temporarily) since its cost of continuing production is greater than its revenue. It has no revenue to apply to fixed costs and cannot recover its variable costs at the price of $5 per unit. Its optimal or best output is zero and its minimal total costs are equal to its total fixed costs.**
2. **Profit maximization case (see Figure 9.4). P > AVC, which suggests that the firm should continue to produce as long as MR > MC up to the level of output at which MR = MC; this level of output will maximize profits.**

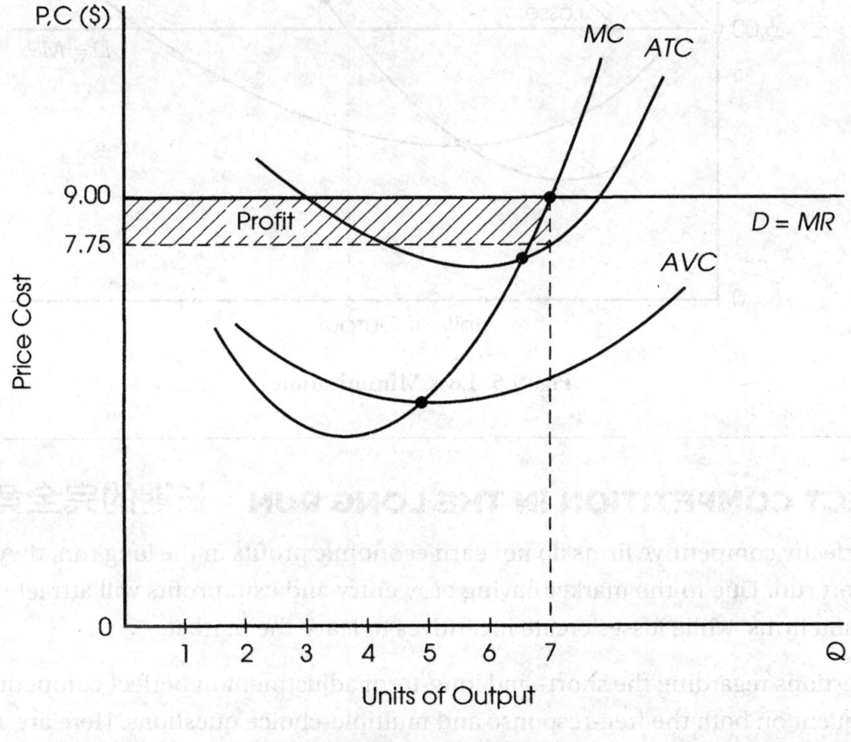

Fig. 9.4 Profit Maximization

At the market price of $9, the firm covers its ATC (P > AVC) and thus, continues to produce as long as MR > MC up to the level of output at which MR = MC (or if there is no level of output at which MR = MC, the highest level of output at which MR > MC would be the optimal output. In this case MR = MC at the $7 units of output. The optimal (best) output is 7 at which profits are maximized. Total profits at 7 units of

output would be Q*(P – ATC) = total profits. Profits are maximized when the Q* is the optimal level of output (MR = MC). So, Q*(P – ATC) becomes 7(9 – 7.75) = 8.75.

3. Loss minimization (see Figure 9.5). P > AVC, which suggests that the firm, in the short run, will continue to produce as long as MR > MC up to the level of output at which MR = MC even if there are losses, then we want the level of output at which we minimize the total losses (MR = MC).

   At a market price of $6 per unit this level would be at 5 units of output (MR = MC). Total losses would be Q*(ATC – P) where Q* is the optimal or best output, that is, total losses are minimized. Thus, Q*(ATC – P) becomes 5(7.60 – 6) = 8.00. This is the rectangular area in the graph above, noted as "losses" (loss permit at best output, x number of units).

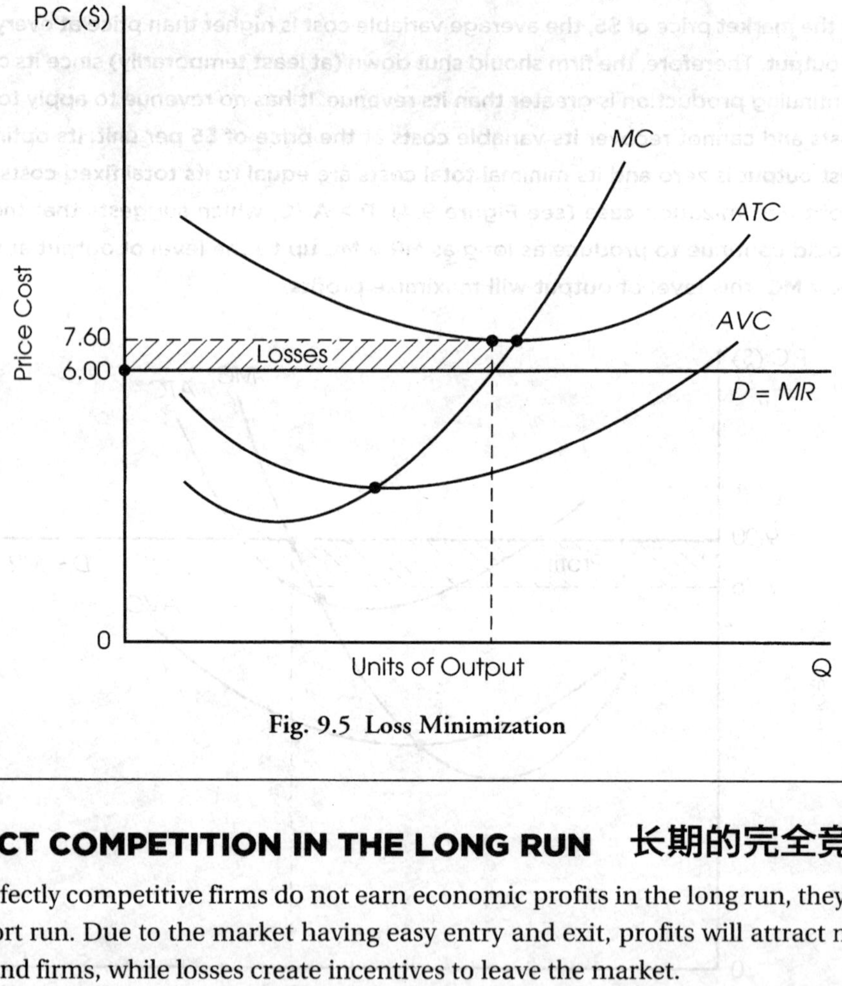

Fig. 9.5 Loss Minimization

PERFECT COMPETITION IN THE LONG RUN 长期的完全竞争

While perfectly competitive firms do not earn economic profits in the long run, they often do in the short run. Due to the market having easy entry and exit, profits will attract new competition and firms, while losses create incentives to leave the market.

- Questions regarding the short- and long-term adjustment in perfect competition are frequent on both the free-response and multiple-choice questions. Here are some scenarios with graphs for you to better understand this concept.

In this example, the market is made up of the world's corn farmers, and as corn is a global commodity the price of corn is traded on the world market. The firm graph comes from Farmer Bob's corn farm in the Midwest. Demand has currently gone up for corn in the world markets, causing the price of corn to rise (a move from E_1 to E_2 in the corn market on Figure 9.6). As Farmer Bob is a price-taker, he has no influence over the price of corn in the

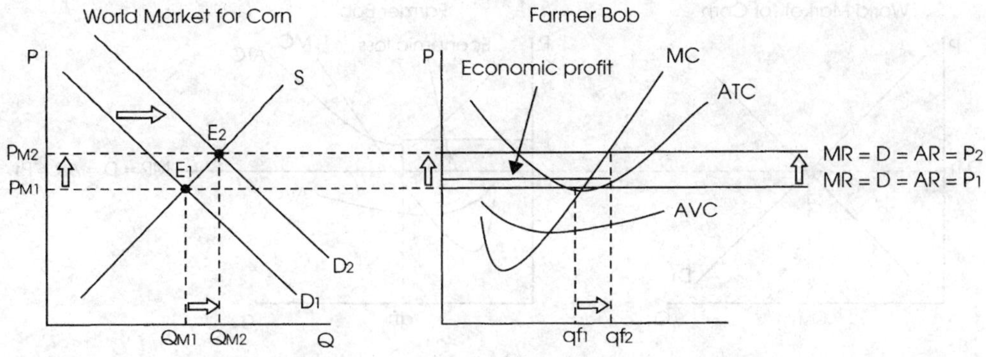

Fig. 9.6 Perfect Competition (SR Economic Profits)

world market. However, as he realizes the price of corn has increased, he increases production to the profit-maximizing quantity (MR = MC) and is earning economic profits for the first time in many years (see Figure 9.6).

Farmer Bob and other corn farmers are elated that they are earning economic profits. In an efficient market like corn, however, with easy entry and exit, when there are economic profits, competition is never far away. Entrepreneurs see profits to be made, and after an adjustment period, also known as the long run, many new firms enter the corn market. As shown in Figure 9.7, these new firms increase the supply in the world market, increasing from S_1 to S_2 and moving to a new equilibrium, E_2 to E_3, reducing the price in the Market from PM_2 to PM_3. Farmer Bob now sees his economic profits disappear. He has no choice to take the new price in the market, which makes his new perfectly elastic demand curve fall from $MRDARP_3$ to $MRDARP_2$. Farmer Bob and other firms will always produce at the profit-maximizing quantity of MR = MC, which is now qf_3, where he originally began producing in Figure 9.5. Even though economic profits for Farmer Bob have gone away, he still is breaking even, and earning a normal profit, so not all is lost.

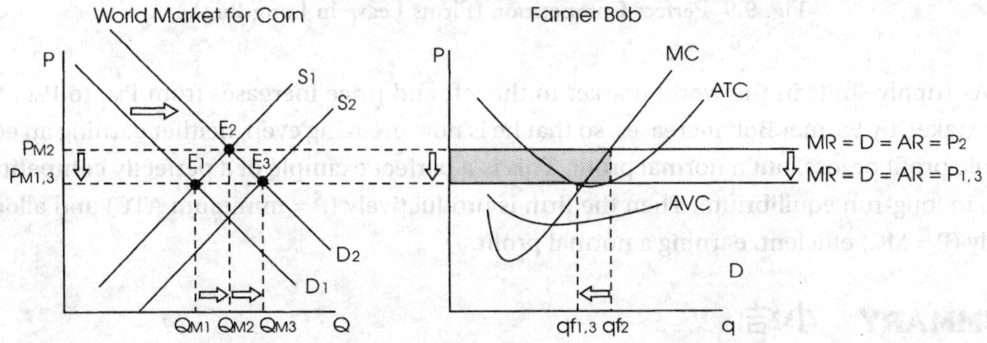

Fig. 9.7 Perfect Competition (Long-Run Adjustment)

Another situation perfectly competitive firms find themselves in is incurring an economic loss. Should the firm with an economic loss shut down? To review, if a firm is producing where price is above AVC, they should continue to produce in the short run. The firm incurs a smaller loss than if they were to shut down, as they can cover their variable costs, and some of their fixed costs. If production is where P < AVC, they should shut down. In this example, Farmer Bob is incurring economic losses, but P > AVC, so his firm will continue to produce, as is seen in Figure 9.8. The marginal cost curve is the supply curve for a firm, but there is no supply curve below AVC, as the firm will not produce.

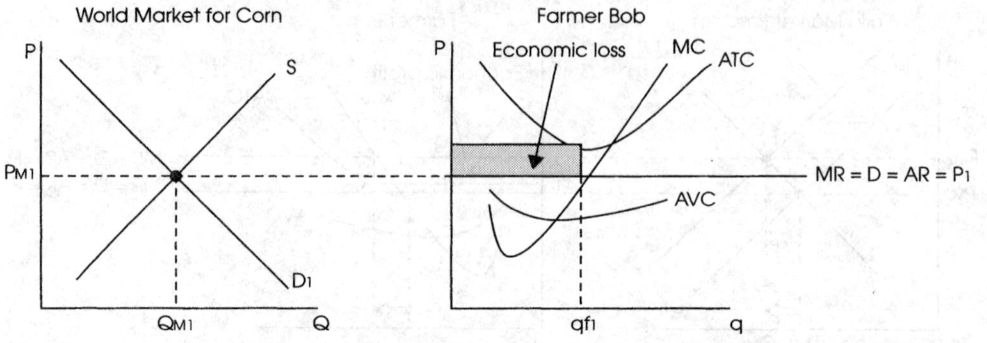

Fig. 9.8 Perfect Competition (SR Economic Profits)

In this scenario, price is < ATC, so the shaded rectangle shows the economic loss. Farmer Bob, however, realizes he is still above AVC and continues to produce corn, as he can still cover his fixed costs. Many other corn farmers see losses and decide to leave the industry. The industry again goes through a long-run adjustment; this time, as farmers leave the world market, the supply decreases and the world price increases, as shown on Figure 9.9.

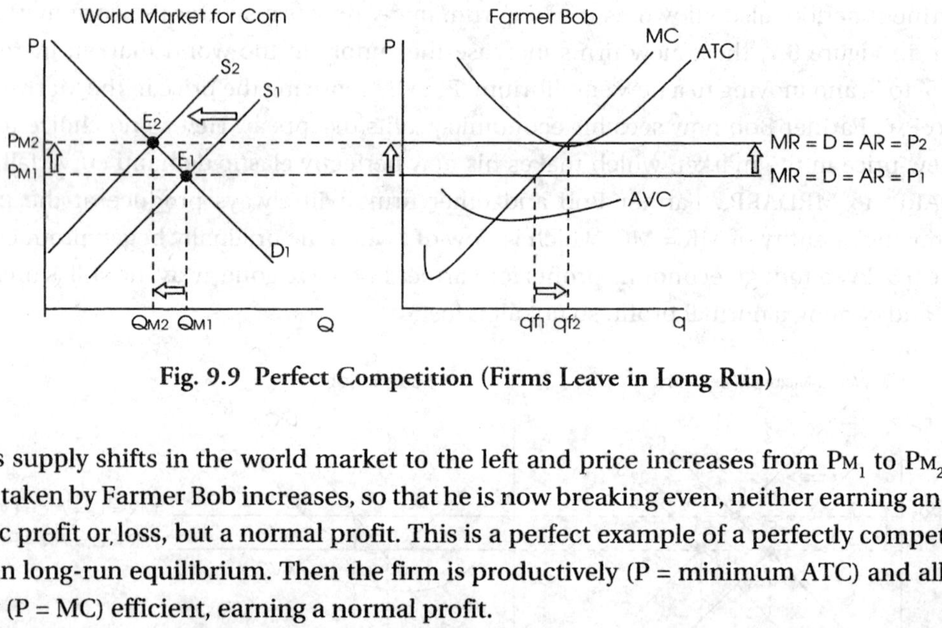

Fig. 9.9 Perfect Competition (Firms Leave in Long Run)

As supply shifts in the world market to the left and price increases from PM_1 to PM_2, the price taken by Farmer Bob increases, so that he is now breaking even, neither earning an economic profit or loss, but a normal profit. This is a perfect example of a perfectly competitive firm in long-run equilibrium. Then the firm is productively (P = minimum ATC) and allocatively (P = MC) efficient, earning a normal profit.

SUMMARY 小结

The perfectly competitive market is characterized by a large number of sellers, availability of perfect substitutes, perfectly elastic demand function, price-takers, no barriers to entry or exit, productive and allocative efficiency, zero economic profits, and pricing at marginal cost and at minimum average cost in the long run.

- The major criterion for determining the optimal (best) output for the firm operating under perfect competition, in the short run, is to produce that level of output at which MR = MC. The specific criteria and steps to determine the best output are:
  1. The firm will produce, in the short run, as long as price is greater than or equal to average variable cost (AVC). If price is less than AVC, the firm should shut down and take as losses its total fixed costs.

2. The firm (if number 1 is satisfied), will produce up to the level of output at which MR = MC. This will either maximize profits or minimize losses.

- The evaluation of perfect competition in the long run would reveal that firms are operating efficiently by utilizing the available technology with zero economic profits, price equal to minimum average cost, and price equal to marginal cost (socially efficient pricing). Firms are directed by the market in their pricing (price-takers).
- The adjustment of firms from the short run to the long run is accommodated by absence of barriers to entry or exit. The entry of new firms attracted by short run profits and exit of firms discouraged by losses ultimately results in the restoration of market equilibrium as described in the previous paragraph.

TERMS 术语

Economic Efficiency the allocation of resources to most productive and desired uses

Profit-Maximizing (Loss-Minimizing) Criterion the level of output at which marginal revenue (MR) equals marginal cost (MC)

Shut-Down Point in the short run, the firm should shut down when price is less than average variable cost (AVC)

FORMULAS 公式

P < AVC firms shut down in the short run

P = MR perfectly competitive firm's demand function

MR = MC profit maximizing criterion

P = MC socially optimal price (under perfect competition in the long run); efficiency

P = minimum average cost in the long run for a perfectly competitive firm

(P – ATC) Xq = profit or loss

MULTIPLE-CHOICE REVIEW QUESTIONS 选择题

1. The individual firm, operating under perfect competition, is characterized as:

(A) a price-maker.
(B) one of a few sellers.
(C) a price strategist.
(D) a price-taker.
(E) interdependent.

2. Firms maximize their profits by producing a level of output at which

(A) MC = AFC.
(B) MC = MR.
(C) P = ATC.
(D) MR = AVC.
(E) P = AVC.

3. In the short run, a firm should shut down if

(A) Price > ATC.
(B) Price < AVC.
(C) Price < ATC.
(D) Price = ATC.
(E) MR = MC.

4. The demand curve for the firm operating under perfect competition is

(A) upward sloping to the right.
(B) downward sloping to the right.
(C) perfectly vertical line.
(D) perfectly horizontal function.
(E) concave to origin.

5. Which of the following is not correct for the perfectly competitive firm, in the long run?

(A) price = minimum average cost.
(B) price = marginal revenue.
(C) price = minimum average variable cost.
(D) price = marginal cost.
(E) normal profits.

MULTIPLE-CHOICE REVIEW ANSWERS 选择题答案

1. (D) **2.** (B) **3.** (C) **4.** (D) **5.** (C)

FREE-RESPONSE REVIEW QUESTIONS
开放式题目

1. Using the table below (this table was developed progressively in the chapter on costs (the end of Chapter 7) and assuming that these cost data are for a firm in perfect competition for the short run, determine the profit maximizing output *and* the total amount of profits or losses at that output for *each* of the following prices:

Hint: P = MR for each price

Price	Output	Total Profit or Losses
a. $60.00		
b. $130.00		
c. $230.00		

Output	TC	AFC	AVC	ATC	MC
1	$ 500	$400	$100	$500	$100
2	550	200	75	275	50
3	610	133	70	203	60
4	690	100	73	173	80
5	800	80	80	160	110
6	940	67	90	157	140
7	1,120	57	103	160	180
8	1,350	50	119	169	230
9	1,640	44	138	182	290
10	$2,000	40	160	200	360

2. Assume the market for soybeans is perfectly competitive and in long-run equilibrium, and Sam's Soybeans is a small farm in the market.

(a) Draw correctly labeled side-by-side graphs of both the market for soybeans and the firm, labeling the market equilibrium P_M and Q_M, and Sam's Soybeans equilibrium P_F and Q_F.

(b) Is Sam's Soybeans earning economic profits, economic losses, or a normal profit?

(c) Now assume that in the soybean market there is a huge drought that ruins the soybean harvest of thousands of farmers, (but not Sam's). Show on the same graph as above what would happen to the new equilibrium price and quantity in both the market and firm, labeling the firm P_{M2} and Q_{M2} and Sam's Soybeans P_{F2} and Q_{F2}.

(d) Shade in the area of economic profit or loss for Sam's Soybeans at the new equilibrium.

Free-Response Review Answers
开放式题目答案

1. A. Zero output, P < AVC. Total losses = $400 = TC @ zero output

B. Five. Highest level with MR > MC. Total losses = $150 Q(ATC – P) or 5(160 – 130) = $150.

C. Eight. Total profits = Q(P – ATC) or 8(230 – 169) = \$488 (or \$490.00); TR – TC = \$1840 – 1350. Differences are due to rounding.

2. (a) See the graph and check for correct labels, prices, and quantities.

(b) Sam is earning a normal profit. A normal profit is the break-even point, where P = ATC and resources could not be put to better use anywhere else.

(c) Supply now shifts to the left in the market, causes the price to go up in the market, and as Sam's Soybeans is a price-taker the price for the firm increases as well.

(d) See the graph for the economic profit.

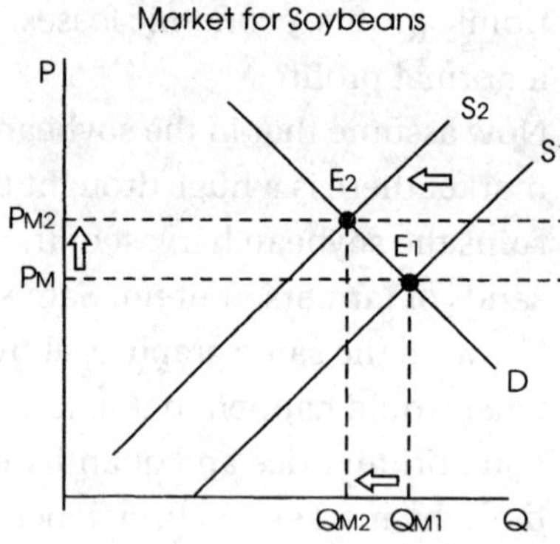

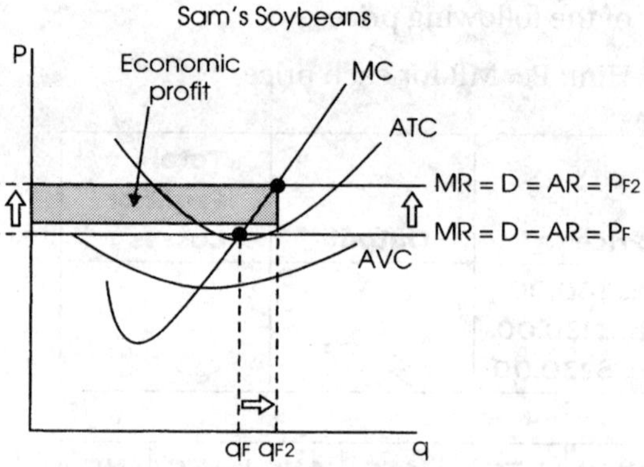

Monopoly 垄断

10

→ **MONOPOLY PRICING POLICY**
→ **PRICE-MAKERS**
→ **MISALLOCATION OF RESOURCES**
→ **INEFFICIENCY AND DEAD-WEIGHT LOSS**
→ **NATURAL MONOPOLY**
→ **PRICE DISCRIMINATION**
→ **REGULATION OF MONOPOLIES**

INTRODUCTION 导言

While it is important to know monopoly in terms of a definition—a market structure where one firm constitutes an industry and where no close substitutes exist for consumers, it is also important to know that a potential monopoly power can be found under oligopoly and monopolistic competition. Thus, firms can acquire power in imperfectly competitive markets if they can consistently price their goods in excess of marginal costs. Economists use the **Herfindahl Index**, the sum of the squares of the market shares of firms in a particular market or industry, to measure the concentrated power or power generated by shares of the market. In turn, these forms of monopoly reflect the characteristics of monopoly as illustrated in Table 8.1 in Chapter 8.

THINGS TO KNOW 要了解的事

Even though we will examine the major concepts in some detail as we progress through this chapter, the following are important things to know as evidenced on previous AP exams:

1. The monopolist faces a downward sloping demand curve that implies that price is greater than marginal revenue, which implies a pricing policy (in contrast to the perfect competition) that could actually lead to a lowering of price by the monopolist in order to induce more sales. A monopoly will always price on the elastic range of the demand curve.
2. The monopolist maximizes profits at the optimal level of output (MC = MR). By definition, the monopolist does control the supply of a product for which there are no close substitutes. However, the monopolist does not control the demand for the product but can exercise some influence on the quantity demanded by lowering or raising the price relative to price elasticity of demand.

3. Unregulated monopoly usually leads to
   a. higher than competitive prices
   b. lower than competitive output
   c. misallocation of resources, inefficiency, and dead-weight loss
4. Regulated monopoly can lead to
   a. a move toward outputs that are more efficient than in unregulated monopolies through subsidies that rise as output rises.
   b. a "fair" rate of return (as would prevail under competitive markets); P = ATC
   c. a socially optimal price and output, P = MC, which would require subsidies
5. It is important to know the characteristics of monopoly. You may make reference to these characteristics in Chapter 8 on the introduction to product markets.

THE NATURE OF MONOPOLY 垄断的性质

A **monopoly** by definition is a firm that is a single seller of a product for which there are no close substitutes. It is at the opposite end from perfect competition on the spectrum of market competitiveness.

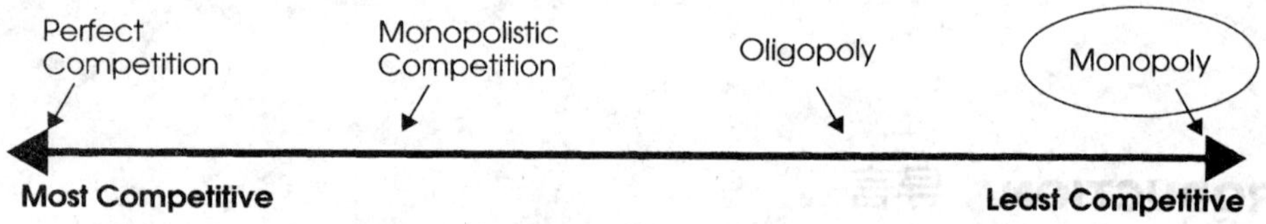

The key to the market power of a monopoly is the difficulty competitors have entering the industry. Here are a few reasons for these high barriers to entry:

- **Government power**. The government may give sole production rights to a single firm.
- **Resource control**. A firm may control the resources required for production of a product, such as a diamond company controlling all the diamond mines.
- **Economies of scale**. A firm that becomes very large may gain significant production advantages over its rivals by being able to produce with lower costs. (Reminder: Economies of scale means that long-run average total costs decrease as a firm grows in size.) Thus, competitors cannot compete as they may have higher production costs.
- **Copyrights or patents**. Here the government grants sole production rights of a product to a single firm, such as new medical drugs.

A MONOPOLIST'S DEMAND CURVE 垄断者的需求曲线

A profit-maximizing monopoly will always produce in the elastic range of the demand curve (the upper half of the demand curve). In this range, marginal revenue is positive; as a monopolist lowers prices to increase profits, total revenue increases. A monopolist will not produce in the inelastic range, as the marginal revenue is negative; a decrease in price here decreases total revenue. Note the position on Figure 10.1 where the marginal revenue curve travels below the quantity axis, at all prices below P_1, the inelastic range. (See Chapter 8 for more on the difference between the D and MR curves.) Also total revenue is at its highest point when marginal revenue is 0, shown at P_1 on Figure 10.1.

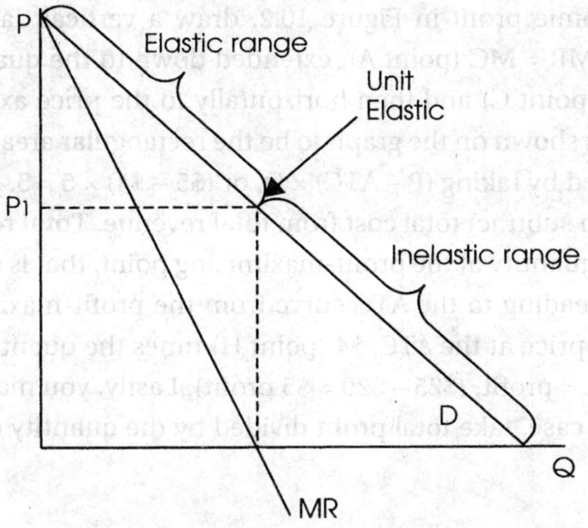

Fig. 10.1 Elastic and Inelastic Range

GRAPHING A MONOPOLY 用图表示垄断

A monopoly is unique in that it is both the firm and the industry, and "price-maker." In a monopoly, there is only one graph because the firm is the industry, which is sharply different from perfect competition's side-by-side graphs and perfectly elastic demand curve. Like all profit-maximizing firms, a monopolist determines price and output at where MR = MC. A monopoly graph is shown in Figure 10.2.

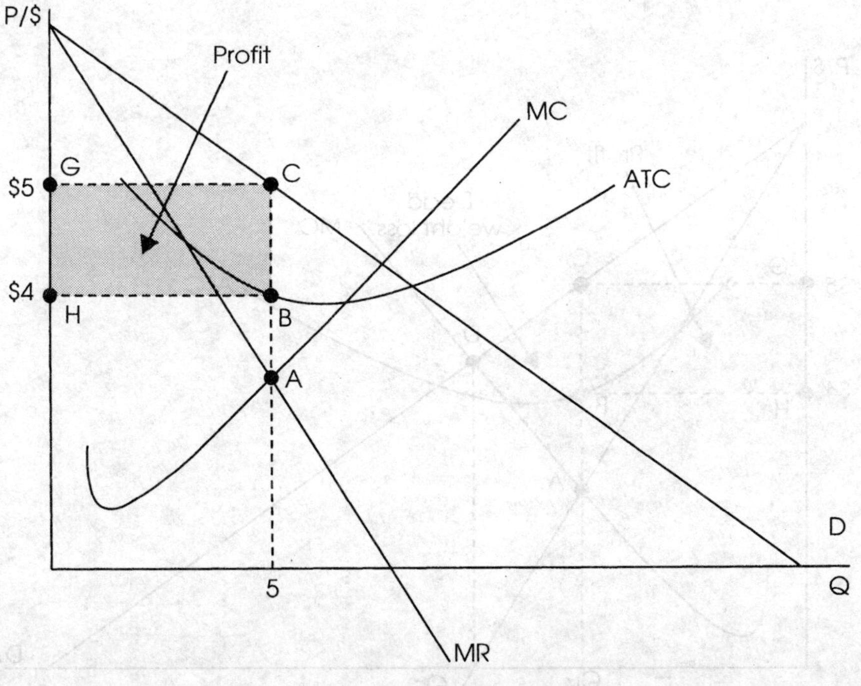

Fig. 10.2 Monopoly Profits

TIP

When answering monopoly graph questions, the first step is to locate the profit-maximizing quantity at MR = MC (Quantity of 5 in Figure 10.2). This is key to interpreting a monopoly graph.

To calculate economic profit in Figure 10.2, draw a vertical dashed line at the profit maximizing quantity, MR = MC (point A), extended down to the quantity of 5 and back up to the demand curve (point C) and then horizontally to the price axis (point G), where the price is $5. The profit is shown on the graph to be the rectangular area, HGCB. The numerical profit value is calculated by taking (P – ATC) × Q, or ($5 – $4) × 5 = 5. Another way to get this same exact answer is to subtract total cost from total revenue. **Total revenue** is calculated by taking the price times quantity at the profit-maximizing point, that is ($5 × 5 = $25). The **total cost** is calculated by heading to the ATC curve from the profit-maximizing quantity (point B) and then taking the price at the ATC, $4 (point H) times the quantity of 5. Total cost then is $4 × 5 = $20. TR – TC = profit, ($25 – $20 = $5 profit). Lastly, you may be asked to calculate **per-unit profit**. In this case, take total profit divided by the quantity ($5/5 equals a per-unit profit of $1).

Monopolies and Efficiency 垄断与效率

As you hopefully remember, **allocative efficiency** is producing the exact amount of units that society wants, where P = MC. **Productive efficiency** is also an optimal use of resources as goods are being produced at the lowest minimum cost, where P = ATC. Monopolies, however, price higher and produce at higher costs than is desirable, leading to a misallocation of resources. It is good to be *the* monopolist, but it is generally bad for consumers and society overall. This situation that is present in all imperfectly competitive markets (not perfect competition!) is known as the deadweight loss, which was introduced in Chapter 5 with taxation. To review, it is the loss to society resulting from market inefficiency resulting in the reduction of consumer and producer surplus. This is illustrated in Figure 10.3.

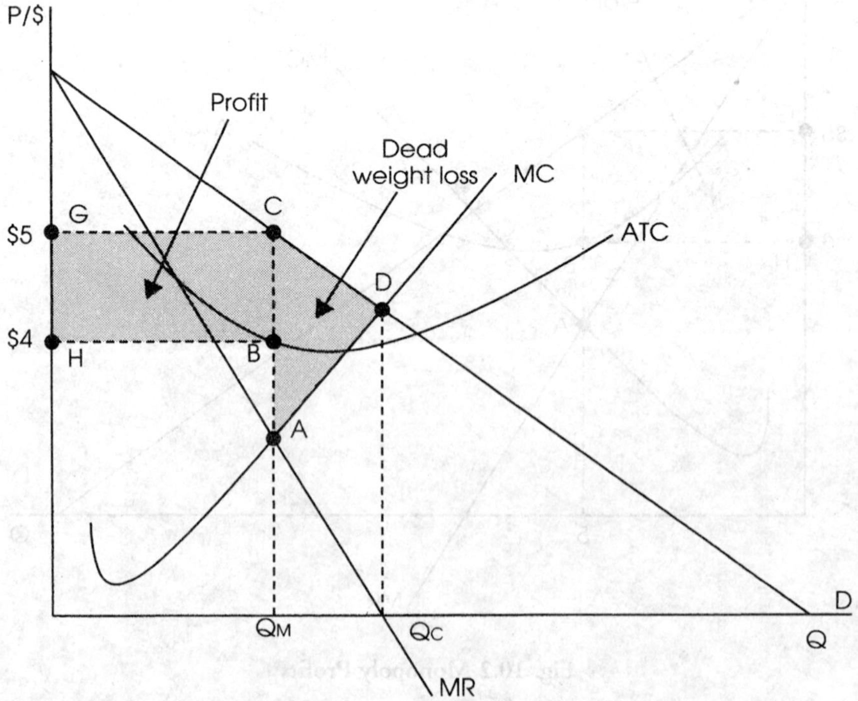

Fig. 10.3 Monopoly and Deadweight Loss

In Figure 10.3:

1. The deadweight loss is measured by the area of ACD. If this were a competitive market producing at Q_C, there would be no deadweight loss, and the area would be part of either consumer or producer surplus. The monopoly is not allocatively efficient as $P \neq MC$.
2. The monopoly also does not produce at minimum ATC. This means it is not productively efficient as $P \neq$ minimum ATC.
3. For help identifying and labeling deadweight loss, imaging drawing an arrow pointing at the output as if it were a competitive market. When labeling deadweight loss with a monopoly or monopolistically competitive firm, it will always be below the demand curve, above marginal cost, and to the right of the profit-maximizing quantity. Students have found this technique helpful in identifying the deadweight loss, as it is frequently asked on the AP Microeconomics exam.

INTERPRETING A MONOPOLY GRAPH 解释一张垄断图表

It is an important skill to be able to interpret several different versions of a monopoly graph. The graph shown in Figure 10.4 looks slightly different than the previous graphs in this chapter. Do you notice the difference? Well, if you haven't found it already, the marginal cost, average cost, and long-run average total cost curves have all the same perfectly elastic slope, for simplicity's sake, as opposed to their normal slope seen in Figures 10.2 and 10.3 and probably in your class. Don't let these different shaped curves distract you from the basics: firms still produce at MR = MC, profit is still calculated the same way, and so on.

TIP

A monopoly graph with flat cost curves similar to Figure 10.4 has appeared on several recent AP exams. Be sure to practice it.

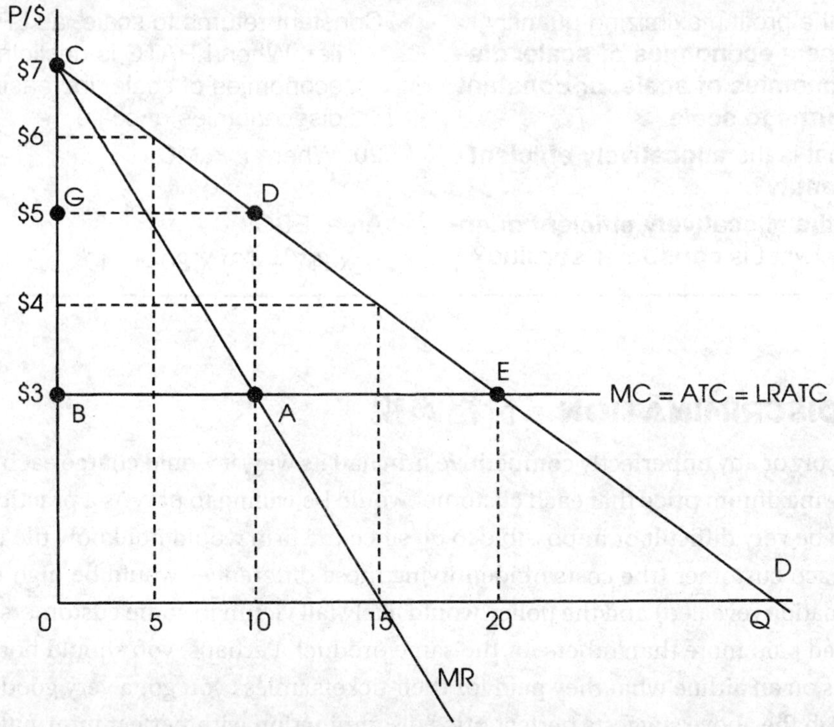

Fig. 10.4 Monopoly Graph with Flat MC, ATC, LRATC Curves

Please see Table 10.1 for questions and answers to several commonly asked questions using Figure 10.4.

Table 10.1

Monopoly Graph Questions and Answers From Figure 10.4

Question	Answer
1. What is the **profit-maximizing quantity**?	10, where MR = MC.
2. What is the **price** at the profit-maximizing quantity?	$5
3. Locate the area and calculate the **economic profit** at the profit-maximizing quantity.	Area: GDAB 10 x ($5 – $3) = $20
4. Locate the area and calculate the **deadweight loss** at the profit-maximizing quantity.	Area: DAE ½ (20 – 10) x ($5 – $3) = $10
5. Locate the area and calculate the **consumer surplus** at the profit-maximizing quantity.	Area: CDG ½ x ($7 – $5) x 10 = $10
6. Below what price is **marginal revenue** negative and in the **inelastic range of demand**?	$4 because below this MR is negative. A monopolist will always produce on the elastic portion of the demand curve, or ≥ $4 in this example.
7. At what quantity is there **unit elasticity**?	15, marginal revenue is neither negative or positive.
8. At the profit maximizing quantity, is there **economies of scale, diseconomies of scale, or constant returns to scale**?	Constant returns to scale, as LRATC is flat. When LRATC is declining, it's economies of scale, increasing it's diseconomies of scale
9. What is the **allocatively efficient quantity**?	20, Where P = MC
10. At **the allocatively efficient quantity,** what is **consumer surplus**?	Area: EBC ½ x ($7 – $3) x 20 = $40

PRICE DISCRIMINATION 价格歧视

If a monopoly or any imperfectly competitive firm had its way, it would charge each customer exactly the maximum price that each customer would be willing to pay. As a practical matter, this would be very difficult or impossible to do since the firm would not know the maximum price for each customer (the costs of identifying these differences would be high relative to any information revealed) and the policy would likely fall victim to some customers discovering they had paid more than others for the same product. Perhaps, you should not ask other passengers on an airline what they paid for their tickets unless you got a very good price.

Although the above suggests perfect price discrimination with perfect information about each consumer, we can still find many examples of price discrimination. For example, movie theaters may charge less for an afternoon (matinee) movie than for a movie in a more popular time such as evening or night. Senior citizens may be charged lower prices for lodging, museum attendance, and transportation. Some discounts simply promote better allocation of scarce commodities such as space on highways at commuter rush times or one's time. Price discrimination works best if the following conditions are operative:

1. Separate markets for consumers based on different price elasticities' relatively elastic demand. This really means that customers with demand have more choices of substitute products. Customers with relatively inelastic demand have less sensitivity to price of a particular product since they have fewer substitute choices.
2. There must not be opportunities for the resale of the product.
3. The price differences are not based on cost differences.
4. The firm is a price-maker—it has a pricing strategy that looks to charge a higher price and realize more profits.

PRICE DISCRIMINATION SHOWN GRAPHICALLY 用图表示价格歧视

For a monopolist who practices perfect price discrimination, the monopoly graph has a few distinctive features that are commonly asked on the AP exam:

1. **DEMAND = MARGINAL REVENUE.** An important distinction to make is that with perfect price discrimination, demand and marginal revenue are no longer separate curves. See Figure 10.5.
2. **NO CONSUMER SURPLUS.** Every consumer is paying the highest price he or she is willing to pay.
3. **PROFITS INCREASE.**

All of these are shown on Figure 10.5.

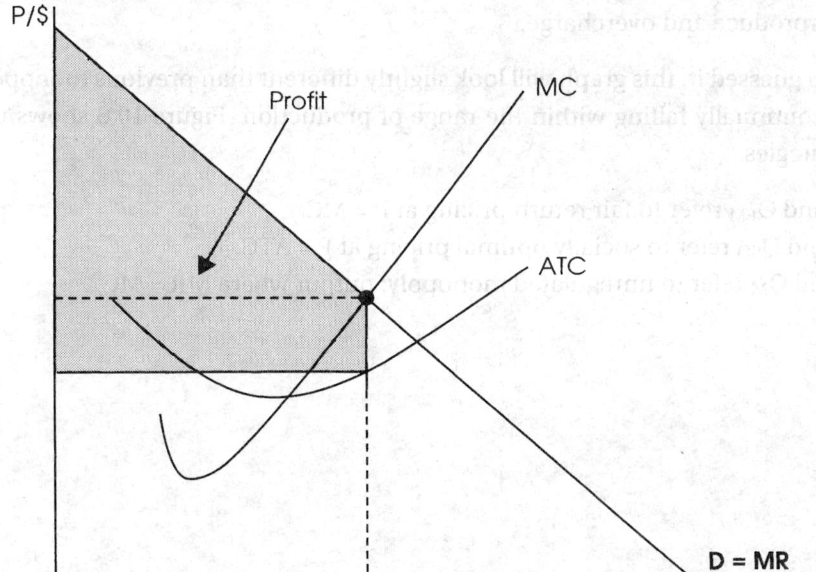

Fig. 10.5 Monopoly with Perfect Price Discrimination

Note that profit (shaded area) increases significantly at the profit-maximizing point (MR = MC) while the consumer surplus has disappeared and turned into profit for the monopoly.

NATURAL MONOPOLIES AND REGULATION OF MONOPOLIES 自然垄断与垄断的调控

Occasionally there is significant cost advantage when only one firm produces in a market. A firm in this situation is a **natural monopoly** and realizes economies of scale, where LRATC continues to decrease as output increases. Due to this and very high fixed costs that serve as barriers to entry, one firm can serve a market at lower costs than several firms. Electricity or water companies are examples of natural monopolies.

Due to the significant cost savings of having one producer in these industries, governments allow some monopolies such as utility companies to operate. However, that's not the end of the story. Due to the fear of high prices and poor quality and service (typical of markets with no competition), governments regulate natural monopolies with the goal of increasing efficiency and reducing deadweight loss.

Here are the two scenarios available for regulating a monopoly, with unregulated monopolies included for comparison.

1. **SOCIALLY-OPTIMAL PRICING.** Here government regulators will force the monopoly to have allocatively efficient pricing at P = MC. However, socially optimal is likely below the average total cost of production, which may force a firm to go out of business or require a large subsidy from taxpayers.
2. **FAIR-RETURN PRICING.** Regulators set the price = ATC wishing to let the monopoly break-even and earn a normal profit, covering its implicit and explicit costs. However, this price is higher than is socially optimal, but is less than the unregulated monopoly price.
3. **UNREGULATED MONOPOLY.** The bulk of this chapter has discussed unregulated monopolies, who produce at the profit-maximizing quantity of MR = MC, and underproduce and overcharge.

Yes, you guessed it, this graph will look slightly different than previous monopoly graphs, as ATC is continually falling within the range of production. Figure 10.6 shows these three pricing strategies.

- P_{FM} and Q_{FM} refer to fair return pricing at P = MC.
- P_{SO} and Q_{SO} refer to socially optimal pricing at P = ATC.
- P_M and Q_M refer to unregulated monopoly; output where MR = MC.

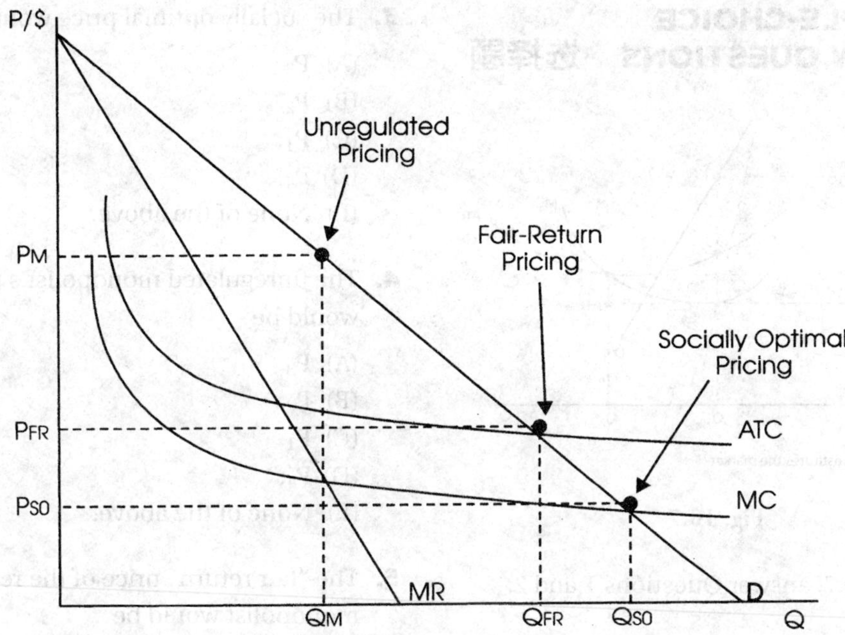

Fig. 10.6 Monopoly with Price Discrimination

TERMS 术语

Herfindahl Index the sum of the squares of market shares of firms in a particular market or industry; used to measure the level of concentrated power of firms in an industry

Monopoly one firm constitutes the market or industry where there are no close substitutes available for consumers; a monopolist is a price-maker

Natural Monopolies monopolies that have extensive economies of scale and can provide a product at a lower cost than can several firms

Price-Discrimination this practice charges different customers with different prices for the same product

FORMULAS 公式

MR = MC, profit maximizing level of output

REGULATED MONOPOLIES (PRICING AT):

a. Fair-Return Price:

Price = average total cost (at intersection of demand curve and average total cost curve)

b. Socially Optimal Price:

Price = marginal cost (at the intersection of demand curve and marginal cost curve)

MULTIPLE-CHOICE REVIEW QUESTIONS 选择题

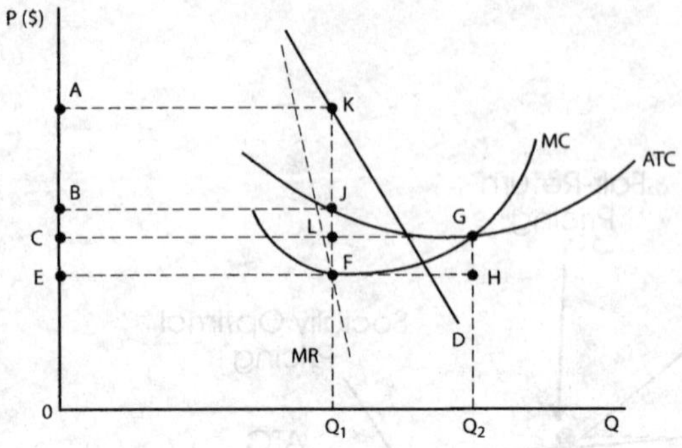

One firm constitutes the market

Fig. 10.7

For Fig. 10.7, answer Questions 1 and 2.

1. The total profits for this monopolist are identified by

(A) CEFL.
(B) ABJK.
(C) BCLF.
(D) CEHG.
(E) BEFJ.

2. The total costs for the monopolist are identified by

(A) CEFL.
(B) CEHG.
(C) ABJK.
(D) EOQ, F.
(E) BOQ, J.

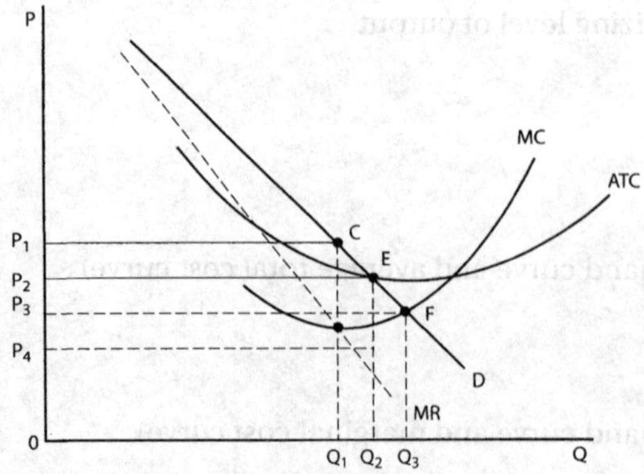

Fig. 10.8

For Fig. 10.8, answer Questions 3, 4, and 5.

3. The socially optimal price would be

(A) P_3.
(B) P_2.
(C) P_1.
(D) P_4.
(E) None of the above.

4. The unregulated monopolist's price would be

(A) P_3.
(B) P_2.
(C) P_1.
(D) P_4.
(E) None of the above.

5. The "fair return" price of the regulated monopolist would be

(A) P_3.
(B) P_2.
(C) P_1.
(D) P_4.
(E) None of the above.

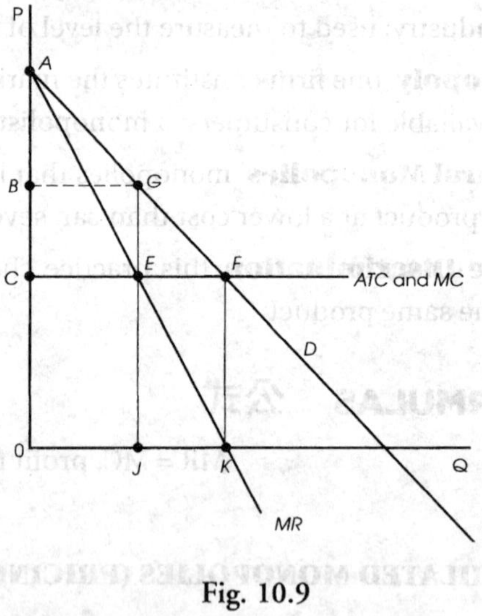

Fig. 10.9

For Fig. 10.9, answer Questions 6, 7, and 8.

6. In a perfectly competitive market, the original consumer surplus is

(A) ABG.
(B) ACF.
(C) BCEF.
(D) COKF.
(E) GEF.

7. After the monopolist takes over, the consumer surplus is
   (A) ABG.
   (B) ACF.
   (C) BCEG.
   (D) COKF.
   (E) GEF.

8. The deadweight loss is
   (A) ABG.
   (B) ACF.
   (C) BCEG.
   (D) COKF.
   (E) GEF.

MULTIPLE-CHOICE REVIEW ANSWERS
选择题答案

1. (B) **3.** (A) **5.** (B) **7.** (A)

2. (E) **4.** (C) **6.** (B) **8.** (E)

FREE-RESPONSE REVIEW QUESTION
开放式题目

Draw a correctly labeled graph of unregulated monopoly earning economic profits, and identify each of the following on your graph.

(i) The profit-maximizing quantity and price, labeled Q_M and P_M
(ii) The area of economic profit, shaded in
(iii) The deadweight loss also shaded in.
(iv) The allocatively efficient quantity, labeled Q_C.

Free-Response Review Answer
开放式题目答案

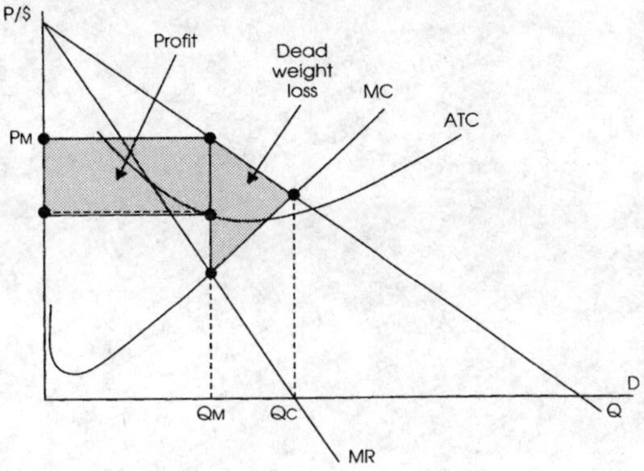

Fig. 10.10 FRQ Answer

Imperfect Competition: Monopolistic Competition, Oligopoly

不完全竞争：垄断竞争、寡头垄断

11

→ MONOPOLISTIC COMPETITION AND NON-PRICE COMPETITION
→ DIFFERENTIATED PRODUCTS
→ INEFFICIENCY
→ PRICE > MARGINAL COST
→ BARRIERS TO ENTRY AND EXIT
→ OLIGOPOLIES AND INTERDEPENDENCE
→ GAME THEORY AND STRATEGIES ON PRICES/OUTPUT
→ NASH EQUILIBRIUM

INTRODUCTION 导言

In the two previous chapters, we have reviewed the "bookends" of market structure: perfect competition and monopoly. Even though we have identified different forms of monopoly, monopoly is most importantly characterized for its monopoly pricing power (its sustainability of maintaining price over marginal cost) and its inefficiency compared to perfect competition. That is, the monopolist charges a higher price and restricts output to maximize profits as compared to the perfect competitor. Also, these restrictive actions of the monopolist as "price-maker" result in a deadweight loss to society.

Monopoly is the very antithesis of perfect competition. Firms and industries become more or less competitive as their behavior approaches or departs from the competitive model. Perfect competition sets the standard for efficiency. Thus, **oligopolies** and **monopolistic competitors** are inefficient since they are imperfect competitors. Monopolistic competition develops or fosters **excess capacity** in which there is underutilization of resources or inefficiency. Oligopolies, collusive and noncollusive, tend to set prices in such a way that P > MC, which is the standard identification and measure of monopoly pricing.

This chapter on monopolistic competition and oligopoly provides more real-world models and examples than perfect competition and monopoly. There are many more monopolistic competitors than there are oligopolies but oligopolies represent the most dominant industries in terms of market share, assets and control over prices, outputs, and allocation of resources.

THINGS TO KNOW 要了解的事

1. In the long run, monopolistic competition will be inefficient mainly due to excess capacity.
2. In the short run, it is possible for monopolistically competitive firms to earn economic profits; however, these profits attract new firms until economic profits have disappeared. However, zero economic profits do not imply the efficiency of perfect competition (long run). The monopolistic competitor has zero economic profits when average total cost (ATC) equals price at the profit maximizing level of output but not at minimum average total cost, implying the inefficiency due to excess capacity.
3. Inefficiency (allocative inefficiency) of monopolistic competition is also identified by price > marginal cost (P > MC). Unlike perfect competition, there is a tendency to price goods and services at a higher level than the costs to produce additional units.
4. Monopolistic competition is also inefficient compared to perfect competition since the monopolistically competitive firm restricts output level in order to maximize profits. Like all profit-maximizing firms, optimal output is at the level at which MR = MC, which results in a higher price and less output as compared to perfect competition in the long run.
5. Monopolistic competition is characterized by nonprice competition (advertising, unique products, warranties, coupons, appeal to brand or store name, etc.), differentiated products, innovation, large number of buyers and sellers, few barriers to entry and exit.
6. The profit-maximizing output and price for a firm under monopolistic competition is that level at which MR = MC. Also, unique to monopolistic competition is the long run tendency for zero economic profits but with the ATC curve tangent to the demand curve at the level of output at which MR = MC.
7. Under oligopoly, there is *interdependence* of firms as contrasted to the price-takers of perfectly competitive markets and the price-makers of monopoly power. Oligopolies must be keenly aware of their competition, as the output and price decisions of one firm can have a significant impact on the entire market, affecting output and profits.
8. Oligopolies have extensive market power, with high barriers to entry. If it were simple to enter the industry, you would have more than just a few firms.
9. Oligopolists can be noncollusive or collusive. In both models, an action of one rival is interdependent on the action of other rivals.

MONOPOLISTIC COMPETITION 垄断竞争

There are many sellers and buyers under monopolistic competition; thus, it is difficult for any firms to earn economic profits or emerge as price-makers. In order for a firm to gain an advantage in a market, it is often necessary to innovate or otherwise find a niche in the market. In other words, if a monopolistic competitor is able to distinguish its products or services from rivals, the firm will be successful. Most of any success for monopolistic competitors derives from non-price competition, such as brand name, store name, shoppers' cards, rewards for frequent customers, special amenities in lodging, etc. Wegman's Food Markets, a large and highly successful chain of stores in upstate New York, is known for its ability to attract customers on the basis of its varied and attractive displays of food and merchandise. The customers are not interested only in prices but almost everything else. Since the barriers to entry are relatively weak, rivals must continuously innovate to survive. There are many other fine supermarkets in upstate New York, including Tops, P&C, Price Chopper, A&P, and others. There is a highly competitive atmosphere with customers quite sensitive to prices since there are many good substitutes available and a relative ease of entry into the industry. Thus, each of these fine competitors has to find ways to distract the customers from prices and attract them to specialty features such as in-store brands of high quality, in-store bakeries, bulk food, etc.

These firms have downward sloping demand curves and they are characterized, as in monopolies, by price > marginal revenue and price > marginal cost.

From the Short to the Long Run 从短期到长期

In the short run, there are dynamic shifts in demand in an intense competitive environment. Thus, we can expect that some firms will realize profits as demand for their products increases, sometimes at the expense of rival firms, some of which will incur losses even to the extent of leaving the industry. Thus, in the short run, we can illustrate both situations with the following graphs:

In Figure 11.1 the firm is earning economic profits in the short run. As a result of these economic profits, new firms see opportunities for profit and enter the industry. In the long run, these new entrants to the industry reduce the market share of existing firms, and demand and marginal revenue for the existing firms decreases, resulting in a new long-run output level seen in Figure 11.3 at the break-even point.

In Figure 11.2, the firm is incurring losses in the short run. As firms are losing money, some start to leave the industry, as there is easy entry and exit. As firms leave the industry, market share increases for the remaining firms. Demand and MR then shift to the right for the existing firms, ending up in the long-run equilibrium shown in Figure 11.3.

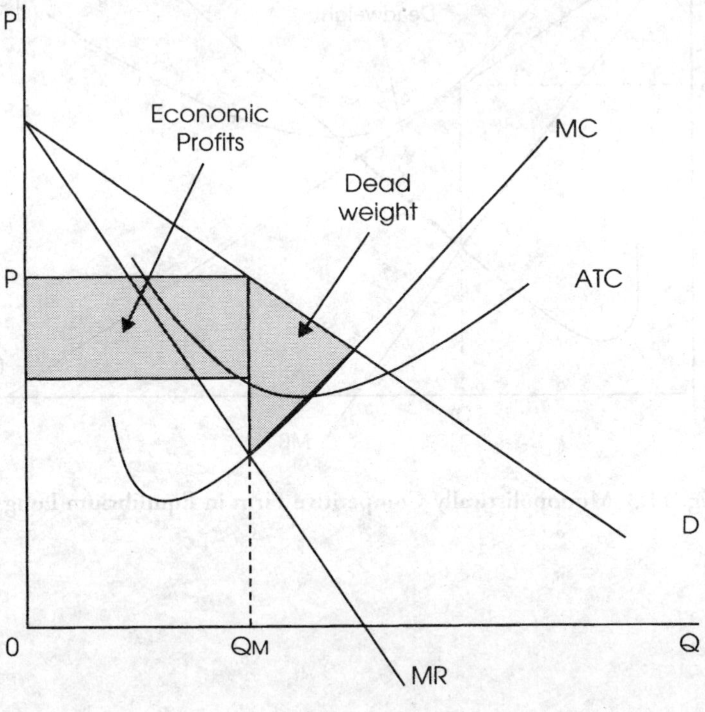

Fig. 11.1 Monopolistically Competitive Firm—Short-Run Profits

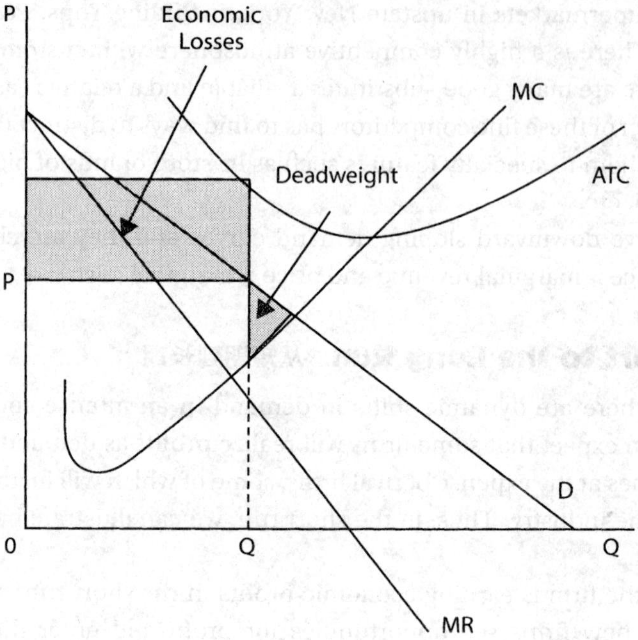

Fig. 11.2 Monopolistically Competitive Firm—Short Run Losses

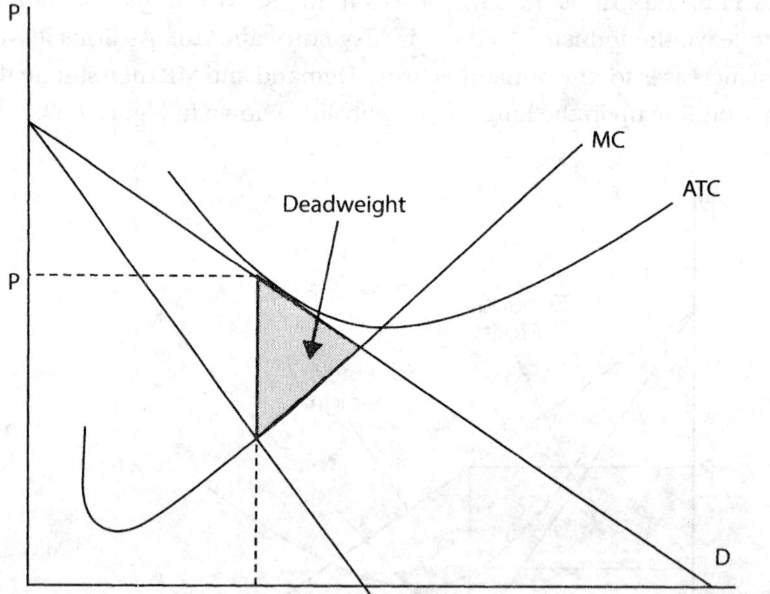

Fig. 11.3 Monopolistically Competitive Firm in Equilibrium Long Run

LONG-RUN EQUILIBRIUM AND EXCESS CAPACITY—MONOPOLISTIC COMPETITION
长期的平衡和过剩产能——垄断竞争

As seen in Figure 11.3, a monopolistically competitive firm in long-run equilibrium is neither allocatively efficient (P ≠ MC) nor productively efficient (P ≠ minimum ATC). A deadweight loss does exist as well, but it is generally not as large as a monopoly. Also, a monopolistically competitive firm earns a normal profit but no economic profits in the long run.

Another key feature of monopolistically competitive firms is the presence of excess capacity, shown graphically on Figure 11.4. A monopolistically competitive firm produces at Q_M, where a productively efficient firm (P = minimum ATC) would produce at Q_{ATC}. As an example of excess capacity, one might visualize four gas stations on the four corners of a busy intersection. The total demand, on average, for gasoline is considerably less than the available supply; therefore, each station is not able to utilize all of its pump capacity. Each station does not sell enough gas to spread its high fixed costs over the amount of gas sold, so the stations quickly exhaust any economies of scale and do not reach minimum ATC. This is a classic case of underutilization or excess capacity. Suppose that two gas stations would have the right capacity to handle the demand. They could then spend the fixed costs over a greater number of gallons of gas and achieve some efficiency. With easy entry and exit, there tend to be too many competitors given a certain demand. This is illustrated in Figure 11.4

TIP

When drawing a monopolistic competition graph in long-run equilibrium, make sure the demand curve is tangent with the *ATC* before its minimum point (See Figure 11.3 or Figure 11.4.)

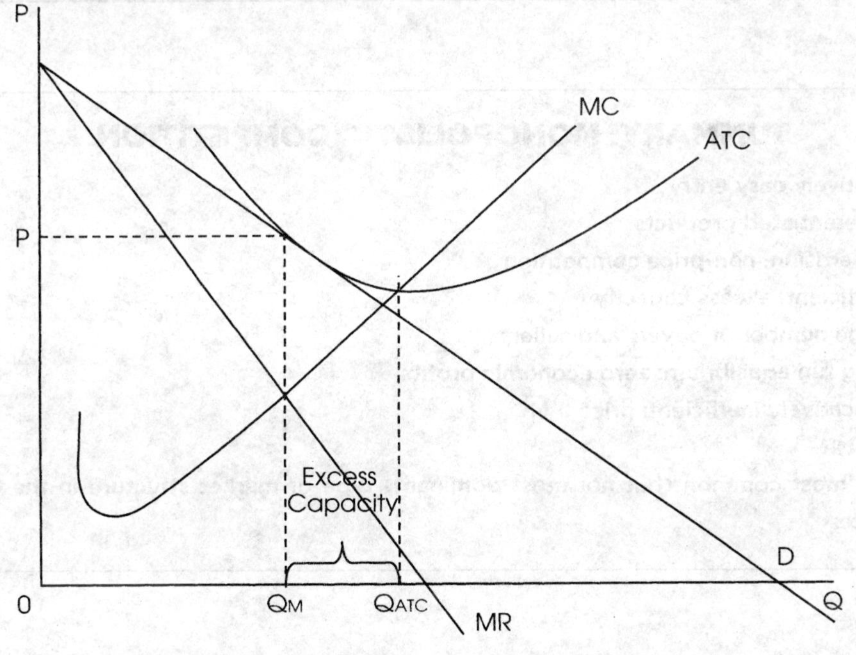

Fig. 11.4 Monopolistic Competition: Excess Capacity

Table 11.1

Long-Run Equilibrium

	Perfect Competition	Monopolistic Conpetition
Long-run profits (Economic)	Zero; Price = Minimum ATC	Zero; Price = ATC (*not* at minimum)
Efficiency/ inefficiency	Efficient = Market prices weed out the inefficient firms	Inefficient (excess capacity, underutilization of capacity)
Product differentiation	None. Products are homogeneous (identical in each product market)	Differentiation is necessary for survival.
Price/non-price competition	*Only price* competition. Firms are price-takers.	Nonprice competition is common.
P and MC	P = MC (socially optimal) efficient allocation of resources. Price = MC	P > MC. Allocatively inefficient.
P and MR	P = MR. No pricing strategy. All firms take prices from the market.	P > MR. Pricing strategy. Some extent of price making.

SUMMARY: MONOPOLISTIC COMPETITION

1. Relatively easy entry
2. Differentiated products
3. Advertising, non-price competition
4. Inefficient, excess capacity
5. Large number of buyers and sellers
6. Long run equilibrium: zero economic profits
7. Allocatively inefficient: price > MC
8. P > MR
9. The most common (but not most dominant) type of market structure in the United States

INTRODUCTION TO OLIGOPOLY 寡头垄断介绍

An **oligopoly** is a market structure characterized by a very small number of firms that have market dominance. Some examples of oligopolies in the real world can be found in the soft drink, airline, and cell-phone industries. The key to understanding an oligopoly is the "interdependence" of rival oligopolists. Oligopolists must closely consider the actions of other firms, as the output and price decisions of one firm can have a significant impact on an entire market. For example, Company X may want to raise its prices in an attempt to increase profits. However, if its oligopoly rival Company Y is expected to lower its prices to undercut the sales of Company X, then X may not raise its prices in the first place. This interdependence may actually lead to lower prices or, at least, no increase in prices.

The firms in this example and in oligopolistic markets have a strong incentive to collude. **Collusion** is an agreement (usually illegal) to agree on what price and the quantity will be produced in a market. Here are some other characteristics of oligopolies:

1. **PRICE LEADERSHIP.** If there is a price leader or dominant firm among the other oligopolists, the leader can "set" the price to maximize profits and other firms simply price at the same level since they are unable to gain market share by maintaining their previous prices. The other firms in the market face smaller profits given their lower volume of production.
2. **COLLUSIVE OLIGOPOLIES.** Oligopolies sometimes decide to form a **cartel**, which is a group of firms that act together and have a formal agreement not to compete. These oligopolists may decide that if "you can't beat 'em, you might as well join 'em." That is, rivals may divide markets among themselves according to regional areas or product specializations. Cartels, such as OPEC (Organization of Petroleum Exporting Countries) may have production limits or price agreements among its members in an effort to set or control prices (and act like a monopoly). However, oligopolistic firms that have colluded have a strong incentive to cheat, which is modeled in the next section in the game theory payoff matrix.

MODELING OLIGOPOLY: GAME THEORY 寡头垄断：博弈论

Game theory is the study of how people and firms act strategically in the context of a game. As rival oligopolistic firms attempt to maximize profits, the success of a strategy is dependent on the actions taken by the other firms. A firm may have a **dominant strategy**, which is the best choice for player regardless of what the other player chooses. See Figure 11.5 for an example of a payoff matrix between two firms in the same market.

		Firm B: High	Firm B: Low
Firm A	High	$25, $25	$0, $35
	Low	$40, $5	$10, $10

Fig. 11.5 Game Theory Payoff Matrix

TIP

Students find it helpful to circle or underline each player's respective numbers on the payoff matrix as to not mix up each firm's numbers, as shown for you in Figure 11.5.

Firm A's numbers are underlined, and Firm B's are circled. The first number will always be for the player on the left, and the last number, for the player on the top of the payoff matrix.

Figure 11.5 shows the potential profits for two competing firms when they price both high and low (assume each firm wants to maximize profit). Can you locate each firm's dominant strategy, if there is one? For Firm A, pricing low is the dominant strategy because if Firm B chooses a high price, firm A will receive a profit of $40 if they price low and a profit of $25 if they go high. If Firm B chooses a low price, Firm A will get $10 if it goes low but $0 if Firm A chooses a high price. As $40 > $25 and $10 > $0, Firm A is better off choosing a low price regardless of what Firm B does. Firm B's dominant strategy is also to go low, as this strategy is best regardless of what Firm A does ($35 > $25 if Firm A goes high and $10 > $5 if Firm A goes low).

Now assume that both A and B decide to collude and both price high and earn $25. Each side now has an incentive to cheat on their agreement. For example, if A prices high and B reneges on the agreement and switches to a low price, B's profits will increase to $35 from $25, while A will lose out, earning $0. This is why many collusive agreements in the real world are hard to maintain since the incentive to cheat is strong in oligopolistic markets.

NASH EQUILIBRIUM AND THE PRISONER'S DILEMMA
纳什均衡和囚徒困境

- In Figure 11.5, it turns out that both Firm A and Firm B have a dominant strategy of pricing low. As both firms have a dominant strategy of pricing low, they end up in the bottom right corner, with a profit of $10 each. The game has reached equilibrium with both players choosing their respective dominant strategies. When players choose the action that is best for them given the actions of the other players, it is said to reach a **Nash equilibrium**. Another way to think of Nash equilibrium is that it occurs when the game ends with both sides voluntarily choosing the same cell.
- The respective dominant strategies led both firms to set prices low and earn a profit of $10; however, if both sides had chosen high, they would each have had a greater profit of $25 each. As each firm acts in its own interest by choosing its best strategy considering the other player's actions, a less than ideal outcome results. This is known as the **prisoner's dilemma**. In a traditional prisoner's dilemma game, police arrest two suspects that they interrogate in separate rooms. A confession is the dominant strategy for both, yet when they both confess they receive longer prison sentences than if they had remained silent and not confessed.

A frequently asked question on the AP exam is to determine the dominant strategy, if any, for a player. A dominant strategy is not always present. A situation like this is depicted in Figure 11.6.

		Firm Y: High	Firm Y: Low
Firm X	High	$50, $45	$40, $35
	Low	$40, $10	$15, $20

Fig. 11.6 Game Theory Payoff Matrix

Can you locate the firm (X or Y) in Figure 11.6 that does not have a dominant strategy? (Once again, the numbers are underlined or circled for the respective players). If Firm X prices high, Y is better off pricing high as $45 is better than $35. However, if Firm X prices low, Y is better off pricing low, as $20 is greater than $10. It is clear Firm Y does not have a dominant strategy. Firm X does have a dominant strategy, as pricing high ($50 > $40 and $40 > $15) will leave it better off regardless of what Firm Y does.

If both players know the information in the matrix, a Nash equilibrium can still be reached despite Firm Y not having a dominant strategy. Firm Y knows X will choose its dominant strategy of pricing high. Aware of this, Firm Y will choose to go high, and the respective profits for Firms X and Y will be $50 and $45. So despite both sides not having a dominant strategy, a student can still discern what choice will be made by the players, given both sides know the information in the payoff matrix.

One more question that may appear on the AP exam is to show the effect of a subsidy (a government payment to producers) on the payoff matrix. If asked this, don't make this question harder than it really is. In Figure 11.7, the matrix shows the profits of each firm if they locate East or West. A question may ask what happens when the government awards a $5 subsidy to each firm who locates to the west of the city. Note the subsidy added only to each firm's West profits on the payoff matrix (shown as +5, you should add them together on the AP exam).

TIP

You will be sure to see Game Theory payoff matrix questions on the AP exam, certainly on the multiple-choice and maybe in the free-response section. The good news is you will not be required to graph an oligopoly, unlike the other market structures, but be sure you have the payoff matrix down pat.

		Firm Y: East	Firm Y: West
Firm X	East	$50, $45	$40, $35 + $5
	West	$40 + $5, $10	$15 + 5, $20 + $5

Fig. 11.7 Game Theory Payoff Matrix with Added Subsidy (West)

SUMMARY: OLIGOPOLY

1. Formidable barriers to entry
2. Differentiated or similar product
3. Interdependence
4. Few firms, controlling major shares of market
5. Allocatively inefficient: price > marginal cost, excess profits
6. Price > marginal revenue
7. Price-makers
8. Collusive activities and cooperative arrangements
9. An oligopolist's actions are influenced by the likely actions of rivals.

TERMS 术语

Cartel a group of firms that act together and have a formal agreement not to compete

Collusion an agreement (usually illegal) to agree on the price and the quantity produced in a market

Dominant strategy the best choice for one player regardless of what the other player chooses

Game theory the study of how people and firms act strategically in the context of a game

Monopolistic Competition this form of market structure is characterized by many medium-sized firms that need to innovate and differentiate their products in both price and non-price competition

Nash Equilibrium game theory outcome that occurs when both players choose the action that is best for them given the actions of the other players and reach the same payoff matrix cell

Oligopoly this form of market structure is characterized by relatively few sellers who act interdependently and/or collusively to be price-makers. There are strong barriers to entry and exit

FORMULAS 公式

MR = MC profit maximizing criterion for monopolistic competition and oligopoly

P > MC relationship between price (P) and marginal cost (MC) for both monopolistic competition and oligopoly

P = average total cost tendency for monopolistic competition in the long run

MULTIPLE-CHOICE REVIEW QUESTIONS 选择题

1. Which of the following is a characteristic of monopolistic competition?

(A) P > MC.
(B) Efficiency.
(C) Mostly price competition.
(D) P = MR.
(E) Homogenous or similar products.

2. Which of the following is *not* a characteristic of oligopoly?

(A) P = MC.
(B) Price-maker.
(C) Strong barriers to entry.
(D) Few firms.
(E) P > MR.

3. Which of the following is a characteristic of monopolistic competition?

(A) Economically efficient in the long run.
(B) Pricing at minimum ATC in long run.
(C) Excess capacity.
(D) Very few competitors.
(E) Most dominant market structure in United States.

Use Figure 11.8 to answer Questions 4 and 5:

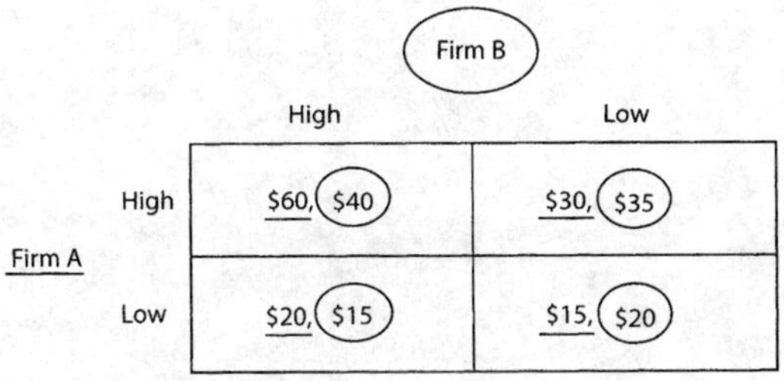

Fig. 11.8 Game Theory Payoff Matrix

4. Given the data in the game theory matrix (Figure 11.8), what are both firm's dominant pricing strategies?

	Firm A	Firm B
(A)	Low	No dominant strategy
(B)	High	Low
(C)	No dominant strategy	High
(D)	No dominant strategy	Low
(E)	High	No dominant strategy

5. Given the data in the game theory matrix (Figure 11.8), if both firms know all of the information in the matrix and cooperate in their pricing, what will each firm choose?

	Firm A	Firm B
(A)	High	High
(B)	High	Low
(C)	Low	High
(D)	Low	Low

MULTIPLE-CHOICE REVIEW ANSWERS 选择题答案

1. (A) **2.** (A) **3.** (C) **4.** (E) **5.** (A)

FREE-RESPONSE REVIEW QUESTION
开放式题目

1. Assume Carly's Cafe is a coffee shop that is operating in a monopolistically competitive industry. Carly's Cafe is earning economic profits.

   A. Draw a correctly labeled graph of Carly's Cafe, and include the following on the graph:

   (i) The profit-maximizing price and quantity, labeled P_M and Q_M.

   (ii) The area of Economic Profits, shaded in.

   (iii) The productively efficient output level, Q_P.

   (iv) The quantity of excess capacity.

   B. What will happen to the number of firms in this monopolistically competitive industry in the long run? Explain.

Free-Response Review Answer
开放式题目答案

A. See Figure 11.9. Note that productive efficiency is where MC and ATC meet. The area of overcapacity is between current output Q_M and Q_P.

B. As Carly's Cafe is earning economic profits, new firms will enter the industry, decreasing demand for the existing firm's products. The demand will decrease and shift left for Carly's Cafe and similar existing firms, returning to the long-run equilibrium with no economic profits or losses.

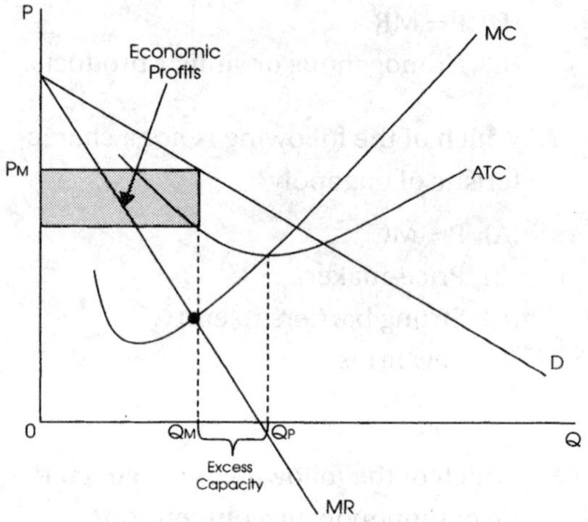

Fig. 11.9 Monopolistically Competitive Firm—Short-Run Profits

Resource Markets with Applications to Labor 劳动力资源市场

12

- → PRODUCT MARKETS AND RESOURCE MARKETS: THE CONNECTIONS
- → MARGINAL REVENUE PRODUCT
- → DERIVED DEMAND
- → MONOPSONY VS. COMPETITIVE LABOR MARKETS

INTRODUCTION TO FACTOR MARKETS 生产要素市场简介

If you are this far in the book, you probably have a good understanding of supply and demand and product markets. The good news is this unit applies fundamentals of supply and demand you have already learned. However, this section is concerned not with the product but with factor markets instead (land, labor, capital, and entrepreneurship). The key difference to note here is that the *firms are the demanders in the factor markets, not individuals, and suppliers are not firms but individuals with their labor*. The demand curve is now made of firms searching for inputs, not consumers in the market for goods and services. This unit explains issues such as why a career as a doctor is likely much more lucrative financially than one as a college professor. It is not the result of some type of conspiracy against professors, but the workings of supply and demand that determines wages.

THINGS TO KNOW 要了解的事

Here are the essential terms and concepts to know that will be discussed in greater detail later in the chapter.

1. **DERIVED DEMAND** relates the product and factor markets together. There is demand for the factors of production (land, labor, capital, entrepreneurs) as this demand is derived from the goods that are produced by these inputs. For example, there is demand for shoemakers because there is demand for shoes; the demand for shoemakers is derived from the demand from shoes from consumers (the product market).
2. **THE MARGINAL REVENUE PRODUCT (MRP)** is the addition to a firm's revenue when an additional input is employed. The MRP is represented graphically by a down sloping demand curve that tells a firm what hiring an additional unit of labor will contribute to their revenue.
3. **THE MARGINAL FACTOR COST (MFC)** (also sometimes called Marginal Resource Cost or MRC) is the additional cost employing an additional input like a machine or worker.

A firm maximizes its profits by continuing to hire inputs as long as MRP > MFC up until the point where MRP = MFC.

4. **THE LEAST-COST RULE** of multiple inputs states that to minimize costs (as any profit-maximizing firm will do) a firm will adjust the ratio of inputs until: (L is labor and K is capital)

$$\frac{MP_L}{P_L} = \frac{MP_K}{P_K}$$

5. A **MONOPSONY** occurs when there is a single buyer of labor. This is the "monopoly of the factor markets." Similar to how a monopoly overcharges and underproduces, a monopsony underhires and pays less than would occur in a competitive market.
6. **FACTORS** that can shift the demand and supply for resources. For example, an decrease in the cost of robots to produce cars will decrease the demand for assembly line car workers.

MARGINAL REVENUE PRODUCT (MRP) AND MARGINAL FACTOR COST (MFC) 边际生产收益和边际要素成本

Many employees feel they are extremely valuable and irreplaceable to their employer. Although this may be true, the more likely scenario is that the business owner is probably more concerned with whether the additional revenue generated from the employee is greater than the cost of hiring the worker.

The first step to determining the value of labor is to measure its Marginal Revenue Product (MRP). **The Marginal Revenue Product (MRP)** is the addition to a firm's revenue when an additional input is employed. This can also be calculated as follows:

$$MRP = \frac{\Delta \text{ in Total Revenue}}{\Delta \text{ in Resource Quantity}} \quad \textbf{Or MR * MP}$$

The next essential step to determining the value of labor in the factor market is to calculate the Marginal Factor Cost (MFC). **The Marginal Factor Cost (MFC)** is the additional cost to the firm from hiring an additional input like a machine or worker. If there is a competitive labor market, the MFC also equals the wage.

$$MFC = \frac{\Delta \text{ in Total Resource Cost}}{\Delta \text{ in Resource Quantity}} = \text{Wage}$$

A firm maximizes its profits by continuing to hire inputs as long as the MRP > MFC up until the optimal point where **MRP = MFC**. If MRP < MFC, the firm will no longer use that input, as it costs the firm more than it brings in revenue.

For a more detailed analysis of the profit-maximizing resource employment in a perfectly competitive labor market, look at Table 12.1. At 4 workers, the MRP of $30 is greater than the cost of the labor, $20. At this point, the firm would continue to hire workers until MRP = MFC at 5 units of labor. This is just an application of basic economic concepts, thinking at the margin, and weighing the marginal costs versus the benefits. If the costs are greater than benefits, a worker would not be hired, as is shown with the 6th unit of labor. The MFC ($20) is greater than the MRP ($10), so the optimal number of workers hired is 5 (MRP = MFC).

Table 12.1

How Many Workers Should Be Hired? *(product price = $10, wage = $20)*

Units of Labor	Total Product	Marginal Product (ΔQ / ΔL)	Marginal Revenue (P = MR)	Marginal Revenue Product (MP* MR)	Marginal Factor Cost (MFC = Wage)
0	0				
1	5	5	10	50	$20
2	16	11	10	110	$20
3	22	6	10	60	$20
4	25	3	10	30	$20
5	27	2	10	20	$20
6	28	1	10	10	$20
7	26	–2	10	–20	$20

THE THREE SHIFTERS OF RESOURCE DEMAND
导致资源需求变化的三个因素

In addition to **derived demand**, the demand in the product market that in turn creates a demand for the inputs used in production, there are other factors that influence the demand for labor. Here are the three shifters of resource demand.

1. **CHANGES IN THE PRODUCT DEMAND.** An increase in the price of a product then increases MRP and the resources used in production. An increase in the price of airplanes would also increase the MRP of airplane builders and would shift the demand curve (MRP) to the right, as shown in Figure 12.1. This would result in more labor being hired, as the optimal quantity increases from Q_1 to Q_2.

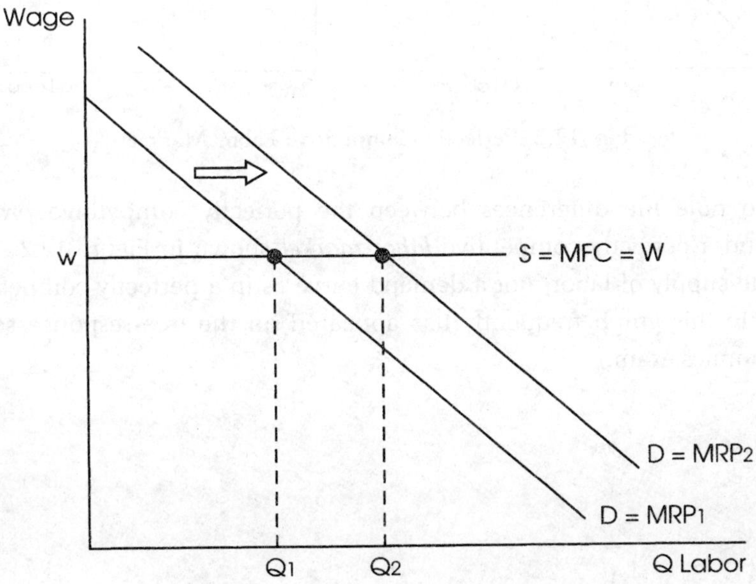

Fig. 12.1 The Demand for Labor

2. **CHANGES IN PRODUCTIVITY.** An increase in technological progress increases marginal product, and thus MRP as well (as MRP = MR * MP), shifting the MRP curve to the right from MRP_1 to MRP_2 (see Figure 12.1). Increases in productivity can make a firm more profitable and give them a greater incentive to employ more resources and utilize the increased productivity of resources.
3. **CHANGES IN THE PRICES OF OTHER RESOURCES.**
   - *Substitute resources.* If the price of farm machinery decreases relative to farm laborers, more machinery would be utilized, and this would decrease the MRP of farm labor, shifting the MRP from MRP_2 to MRP_1 in Figure 12.1.
   - *Complementary resources.* If the price of lumber used to build new houses decreases, more homes will be built, increasing demand and thus MRP for construction workers, shifting MRP curve to the right from MRP_1 to MRP_2.

PERFECTLY COMPETITIVE LABOR MARKET
完全竞争的劳动力市场

A **perfectly competitive labor market** is comprised of many firms hiring workers with similar skills and abilities. Just as perfectly competitive firms are price-takers in product markets, here the firms are **wage-takers**; each individual firm is only hiring a small, percentage of the industry total, has no influence on the market wage, and must pay its hired workers the market-determined wage rate. This wage is shown as w in the labor market, and as S = MFC = W for the firm in Figure 12.2.

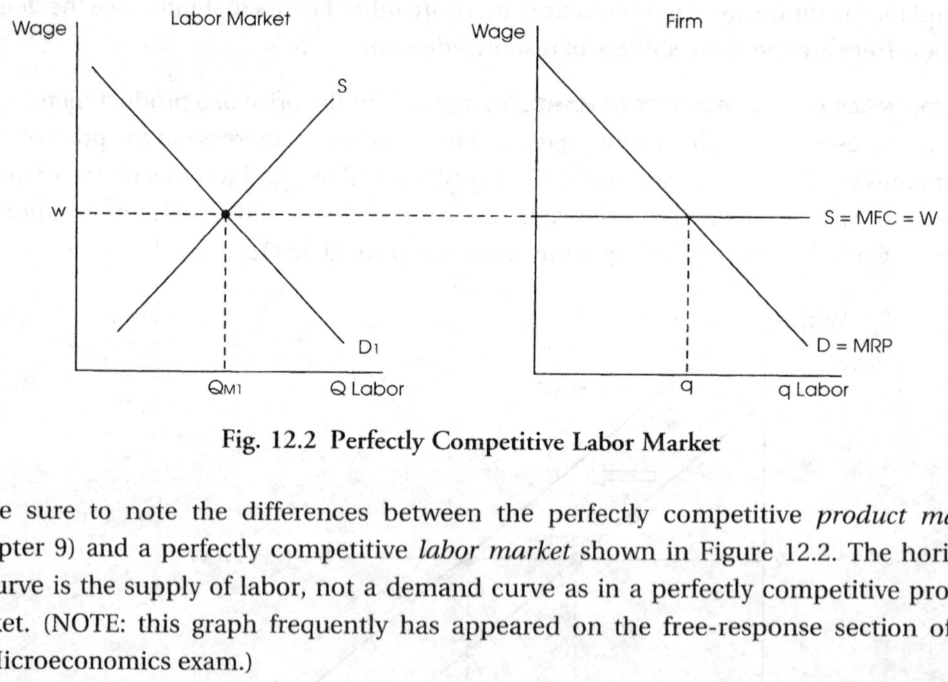

Fig. 12.2 Perfectly Competitive Labor Market

Be sure to note the differences between the perfectly competitive *product market* (Chapter 9) and a perfectly competitive *labor market* shown in Figure 12.2. The horizontal curve is the supply of labor, not a demand curve as in a perfectly competitive product market. (NOTE: this graph frequently has appeared on the free-response section of the AP Microeconomics exam.)

Minimum Wage 最低工资

An effective minimum wage can have a significant effect on a labor market and individual firms. If the government sets an effective minimum wage (which is a type of price floor, discussed in Chapter 4), the wage will increase, but the quantity hired in this labor market and the firm will decrease, as shown in Figure 12.3.

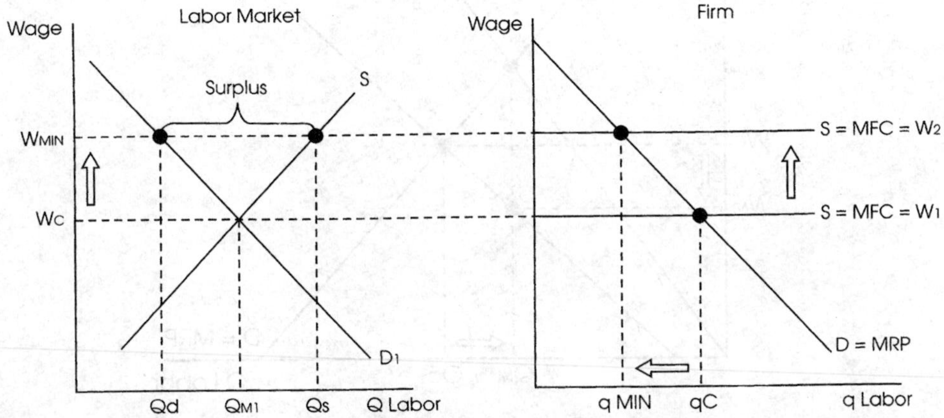

Fig. 12.3 Perfectly Competitive Labor Market with Minimum Wage

After the effective minimum wage is instituted in the labor market on the left, the quantity of labor supplied increases (Q_s), but the quantity demanded decreases to Q_d, which will be the new amount of labor hired in the market. As the individual firm on the right is a wage-taker, the wage increases shifting from W_1 to W_2, meaning that less labor is demanded as the quantity decreases from q_C to q_{MIN}.

MONOPSONY 买方垄断

Similar to the way a monopoly uses its market power to adversely affect product markets, a **monopsony** has a similar effect on factor markets. A monopsony is when there is a single buyer of labor, for example, a small town coal mine. Recall how a monopoly has two downward sloping curves, with marginal revenue less than demand, as it must lower its prices for everyone to increase sales, which decreases marginal revenue. A monopsony does not have two downward sloping curves but it does have two upward sloping curves, S and MFC (See Figure 12.4). The MFC curves increase at a faster rate than the supply curve as a monopsony cannot wage discriminate. As it hires additional workers, it must pay higher wages to them as well as to every other worker previously hired. This results in the MFC curve being higher than supply.

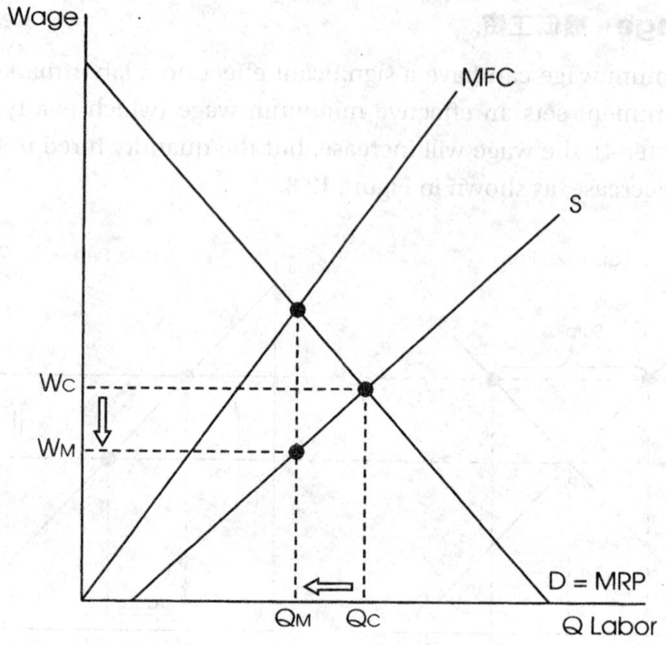

Fig. 12.4 Monopsony

In Figure 12.4, the quantity of labor hired in a monopsonistic labor market would be at Q_M, where MFC = MRP, but note the wage paid, W_M. They pay a wage based on the supply curve at Q_M, so a monopsony hires few workers and pays less than would occur in a competitive market (Q_C and W_C).

LEAST COST RULE 最低成本法则

You well know by now that firms maximize profits by pricing as high as possible and keeping costs low. Similar to when we learned about utility maximization by consumers in Chapter 6, producers attempt to find the cost-minimizing combination from two different inputs (labor and capital) used in production. (If you remember how to solve utility maximization problems from Chapter 6, it will come in handy.) Firms do this by applying the **least cost rule** of multiple inputs, which states that to minimize costs a firm will adjust the ratio of inputs until the marginal product of labor divided by the price is equal to the marginal product of capital divided by the price (L is labor and K is capital):

$$\frac{MP_L}{P_L} = \frac{MP_K}{P_K}$$

As firms use more and more of one resource, for example, labor, the productivity of the input (labor) eventually declines due to diminishing marginal returns. If $MP_L/P_L > MP_K/P_K$, the firm will hire more labor and decrease its use of capital. Eventually, however, the marginal product of labor will decline, and the ratios of marginal product per dollar will be equal as the formula states. The same holds true with the diminishing returns of capital usage. To solve a least cost rule problem, look at Table 12.2. If the firm has only $35, and a robot costs $10 and a factory worker costs $5, what is the optimal use of resources? Just as with consumers' utility maximization, make a chart of the MP/P for each; start by choosing the highest number and continue until all money has been spent (in this case $35).

Table 12.2

Least Cost Rule

Number of Robots / Factory Workers	MP_K (Robots)	MP_K/P_K (Price K= $ 10)	MP_L (Factory Workers)	MP_L/P_L (Price L= $ 5)
1	30	3	20	4
2	20	(2)	15	3
3	10	1	10	(2)
4	5	.50	5	1

In Table 12.2, hiring 2 robots and 3 factory workers is the optimal cost-minimizing point given the production constraint of $35. This is the point $\frac{MP_L}{P_L} = \frac{MP_K}{P_K}$ or 2 = 2 in this example.

SUMMARY 小结

- Marginal Revenue Product (MRP) of a resource represents the demand for labor and *marginal factor cost* (MFC) of a resource represents the cost of labor.
- The firm maximizes its profits by hiring the number of units of employees at which MRP = MFC.
- The three shifters of the labor demand curve are changes in the demand for the product, changes in productivity, and changes in the prices of other resources.
- The least cost rule is $\frac{MP_L}{P_L} = \frac{MP_K}{P_K}$.
- A monopsony is when there is a single buyer of labor, and graphically the MFC curve is higher than the supply curve. A monopsony hires labor at the quantity where MFC = MRP but pays a wage rate from the lower supply curve at the quantity hired.
- The demand for a resource is derived from the demand for a product to which the resource has contributed.
- The firm in the perfectly competitive labor (resource) market is a price-taker in terms of the wage rate paid by the firm for its workers. The supply (of workers) curve is perfectly horizontal at the competitive market wage rate.

TERMS 术语

Derived Demand the demand for a resource such as labor is derived from the product that the resource helps to produce

The Least-Cost Rule of multiple inputs that states that to minimize costs (like any profit-maximizing firm), a firm will adjust the ratio of inputs until (L is labor and K is capital)

$$\frac{MP_L}{P_L} = \frac{MP_K}{P_K}$$

Marginal Factor Cost (MFC) the additional cost for each additional unit of labor hired

Marginal Revenue Product (MRP) the addition to the firm's revenue as the result of an additional output for an additional unit of labor

Monopsony a market in which there is a single buyer of labor

FORMULAS 公式

Least Cost Rule

$$\frac{MP_L}{P_L} = \frac{MP_K}{P_K}$$

$$\text{Marginal Revenue Product} = \frac{\Delta \text{ in Total Revenue}}{\Delta \text{ in Resource Quantity}} \quad \textbf{or MR * MP}$$

$$\text{Marginal Factor Product} = \frac{\Delta \text{ in Total Resource Cost}}{\Delta \text{ in Resource Quantity}} = \text{Wage}$$

Optimal hiring point: MRP = MFC

MULTIPLE-CHOICE REVIEW QUESTIONS 选择题

Labor Units	Total Output	MP	Output* Price	TR	Labor** Price	MRP
1	5	5	10	50	60	
2	20	15	10	200	60	
3	30	10	10	300	60	
4	35	5	10	350	60	
5	35	0	10	350	60	

*Output price constant at $10 indicates a perfectly competitive product market.

**Labor price constant at $60 indicates a perfectly competitive labor market.

1. With the data in the table above, how many units of labor would the employer hire?

(A) 1
(B) 2
(C) 3
(D) 4
(E) 5

2. The basis for the answer in number 1 is

(A) Wage rate or P of labor > MRP of labor and with one additional unit of labor, wage rate < MRP.
(B) Wage rate or P of labor < MRP of labor and with one additional unit of labor W_L > MRP.
(C) total revenue is at a maximum.
(D) total output is at a maximum.
(E) marginal physical product is at a maximum.

3. A monopsonist is identified by one of the following:

(A) A wage payment lower than the marginal revenue product of labor.
(B) Employment level greater than that of a competitive labor market.
(C) A wage payment higher than that of a competitive labor market.
(D) A single seller of labor services.
(E) A marginal factor cost curve lower than the supply curve.

4. If for two resources, Labor (L) and Capital (K), the ratios of their marginal physical products are

$$\frac{MP_K}{P_K} > \frac{MP_L}{P_L}$$

the firm should:

(A) hire more capital (K) until the ratios are equal.
(B) hire more labor (L) until the ratios are equal.
(C) lower the price of capital (P_K).
(D) lower the price of labor (P_L).
(E) seek union membership for labor (L).

5. The backward bending supply curve is characterized by which of the following?

(A) As wage rates rise, the quantity of labor supplied continues to rise at every wage rate increase.
(B) The labor-leisure trade-off continues to favor the supply of more jobs, or the substitution effect.
(C) The labor-leisure trade-off favors the income effect or more leisure at higher wage rates.
(D) inexperienced, low-income, younger workers at the backward bending portion.
(E) discriminated workers.

MULTIPLE-CHOICE REVIEW ANSWERS 选择题答案

MRP in table going down the column starting with labor unit 2: 150, 100, 50, 0.

1. **(C)** 3, MRP (100) > labor price (60); at 4 labor units, MRP (50) < labor price (60).
2. **(B)** (see explanation in 1)
3. **(A)**
4. **(A)**
5. **(C)**

FREE-RESPONSE REVIEW QUESTION 开放式题目

1. A. Draw a monopsony graph.

B. Use this graph to contrast wage rates and units of labor employed under a perfectly competitive labor market and under a monopsony market.

C. Under what kind of market structure would the marginal factor cost of labor equal the wage rate (average cost of labor)?

Free-Response Review Answer 开放式题目答案

1. A.

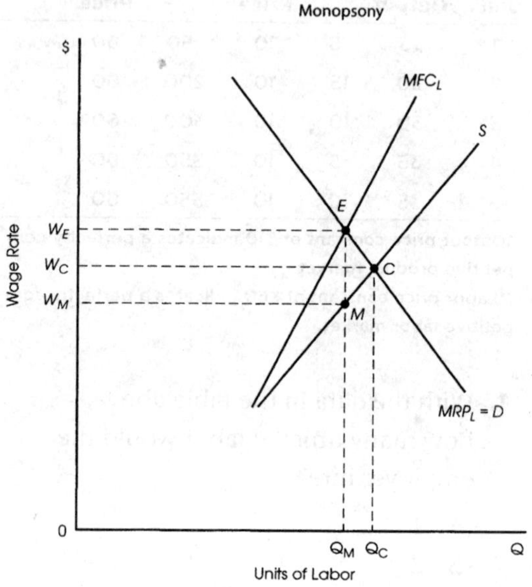

B. Q_M units of labor and Q_M wage rate for monopsony; Q_c units of labor and W_c wage rate for a perfectly competitive labor market.

C. perfectly competitive labor market

Government and Public Sector: Market Failure, Externalities, Public Goods, Efficiency

政府和公共部门：市场失灵、外部效应、公共产品、效率

13

- → POSITIVE AND NEGATIVE EXTERNALITIES
- → PUBLIC GOODS AND PRIVATE GOODS
- → MARKET FAILURE
- → INCOME DISTRIBUTION
- → TYPES OF TAXES

INTRODUCTION 导言

In previous chapters, we have discussed the benefits of markets in that they can lead to the efficient allocation of resources. However, there are situations where free markets fail to satisfy society's wants by producing too much or too little of a something. These situations are known as **market failures.** A market failure is when a market fails to provide an efficient allocation of resources, and there can be a role for government to intervene and attempt to promote a more desirable social outcome.

MARKET FAILURE AND EXTERNALITIES 市场失灵和外部效应

One argument for government involvement in a market is to increase efficiency by correcting market failures, leading to production where **marginal social benefit (MSB) = marginal social cost (MSC)**. With a market failure, private markets fail to produce at the efficient outcome where at MSB = MSC; this distortion results in **externalities**, the costs or benefits that affect people not involved in the production or consumption of a good. It is essential for the AP exam that you understand how to graph both positive and negative externalities, so let's go over examples of each type complete with graphs.

POSITIVE EXTERNALITIES 积极的外部效应

Even though a college student likely benefits from his or her education, the market does not realize all of the benefits of college education on society. A better educated population also results in lower crime rates, a more productive economy, and increased tax revenues; these spillover benefits to society make education a positive externality. A market with positive externalities like education means that if left alone, it will have a marginal social benefit (MSB) greater than the marginal private benefit (MPB) at the market quantity of production. For an example of a positive externality graph, look at Figure 13.1, the market for flu vaccines:

- The difference between the MSB and MPB curves is the **Marginal External Benefit (MEB)** received by society (MPB + MEB = MSB). At the quantity produced by the market (Q_{MKT}) in Figure 13.1, the MSB is greater than MPB, signifying underproduction.
- The difference between these two curves is the MEB received by society from the flu vaccine.
- The difference between Q_{MKT} and Q_S shows the amount the flu vaccine is being underproduced.
- The optimal quantity and price for the flu vaccine is found at Q_S, P_S, at the intersection of the ideal equilibrium, MSB = MSC.
- As the market is underallocating flu vaccines, the government can increase the quantity produced by giving a **per-unit subsidy** to producers equal to the marginal external benefit. A per-unit subsidy is a government payment for production of each unit of a product and gives a greater incentive for firms to increase production than a fixed subsidy not based on production quantity.

TIP

Students on past AP exams have especially had trouble locating the deadweight loss at the market equilibrium on externality graphs. A helpful tip is to imagine an arrow pointing the optimal output where "the socials meet," MSB = MSC, originating between the two demand curves.

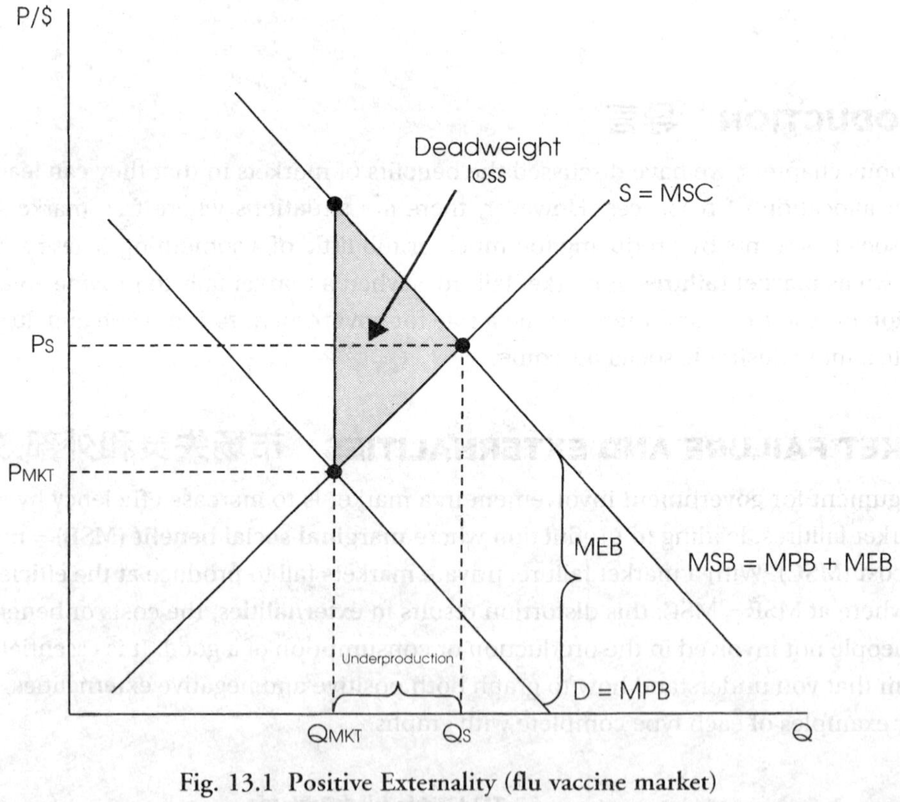

Fig. 13.1 Positive Externality (flu vaccine market)

NEGATIVE EXTERNALITIES 消极的外部效应

With a **negative externality**, the market is producing more of a good than is socially desirable. These externalities spill over to individuals who are neither consumers nor producers of a product yet incur costs. For example, consider a firm that is polluting and harming the environment. Without government intervention, the market is producing at a cost that is greater cost to society than the polluting firm. Some examples of negative externalities include secondhand smoke, airplane noise, or noisy neighbors. The most common example is pollution; let's analyze the polluting firm in Figure 13.2.

- The difference between the MPC and MSC curves is the **Marginal External Cost (MEC)** imposed on society by the negative externality (MPC + MEC = MSC). At the quantity produced by the market (Q_{MKT}) in Figure 13.2, the MSC is greater than MPC, signifying overproduction. (Most people are willing to deal with some pollution, as everyday activities such as driving or charging your smartphone uses energy that likely causes pollution.)
- The difference between these two curves is the MEC imposed by society from the polluting firm.
- The difference between Q_{MKT} and Q_S shows the quantity of pollution that is being overproduced.
- The optimal quantity and price for the polluting firm is found at Q_S, P_S, at the intersection of the ideal equilibrium, **MSB = MSC.**
- As the market is overproducing pollution, one government solution to this market failure is to place a **per-unit tax** equal to the marginal external cost on producers with the goal to decrease the amount produced by increasing the costs of production. A per-unit tax leads to increased costs of production of each additional unit produced and gives a greater incentive for firms to decrease production than a lump-sum tax that is fixed and not based on production quantity. This tax will decrease the firm's supply, which moves the graph toward the optimal equilibrium of **MSB = MSC.**

TIP

For help labeling the deadweight loss at the market equilibrium, imagine an arrow pointing the optimal output where MSB = MSC, originating between the two supply curves.

Fig. 13.2 Negative Externality: Output of Polluting Firm

One helpful way to remember the difference between the positive and negative externality graphs is to remember which graphs have two demand or supply curves. See Tables 13.1 and 13.2 for an acronym to help remember the curves and label for both the positive and negative externality graph.

Table 13.1

Positive Externalities: PED
P—positive
E—externality
D—demand (two demand curves, labeled MPB and MSB)

Table 13.2

Negative Externalities: NES
N—negative
E—externality
S—supply (two supply curves, labeled MPC and MSC)

Per-unit taxes or subsidies are not the only idea economists have to solve externalities, however. Economist Ronald Coase proclaimed that an efficient outcome can be reached without the aid of government. And you guessed it, his idea is named the **Coase Theorem.** According to the Coase Theorem, private parties can solve the issues created by externalities on their own. For example, a polluting firm may pay the affected parties to compensate for the harm of pollution. Or homes next to a new airport may receive soundproof windows from an airline company, all resolving the externalities without government intervention.

PUBLIC VS. PRIVATE GOODS 公共产品和私人产品

A **private good** both has exclusion and is a rival in consumption. For example, a person may be excluded from the benefits of private goods by not being willing or able to pay the price; if I bought the last seat to a sold-out major league baseball playoff game, someone else is denied the fun of watching the game in person. Also, if there are 40,000 seats available, one more ticket for me means one less for someone else. **Public goods** are nonexclusive and nonrival, as one person's consumption of a public good does not exclude others from benefiting from it, unlike a sold-out baseball game. Examples of public goods are national defense, police protection, and street lights. If a person pays no federal income tax, which funds the military, that person would not be denied any of the benefits of national defense. Everyone benefits from the public good of national defense, however, whether they have paid or not.

As public goods are nonexclusive, they do pose a dilemma known as the **free-rider problem**. This means that people know they can benefit from public goods without paying for them. If all consumers are free-riders, demand drops to zero for the product. For example, if a private company in your city wishes to put on a big fireworks show, they would have a hard time finding people willing to pay to watch. People who live nearby know they can see and benefit from the fireworks without paying and be "free-riders." Due to the free-rider problem, private firms will not supply public goods (or fireworks shows) and, if society wants a public good to be produced, it will have to direct government to do it. When this occurs, governments collect taxes for public goods and provide things, such as national defense, and even your city's taxpayer-funded fireworks show.

THE DISTRIBUTION OF INCOME 收入的分配

If you follow the news, you likely have heard debates over income inequality, or about the top 1% of income earners versus the bottom 99%. Economists debate many different factors that may cause income inequality; several frequently mentioned reasons include the increase in demand for highly skilled labor, global competition, past discrimination, education levels, and differences in ability and motivation.

At this stage of the book, you are probably not shocked to learn economics has a graph for income inequality, called the **Lorenz curve**, which shows how much of a country's total income is earned by the number of households. As shown in Figure 13.3, The 45-degree line represents perfect income equality, also shown at point B. At point B, 50% of families are receiving 50% of the total percent of income. The Lorenz curve part of the graph (shaped like a banana) shows the actual distribution of income. For example, at point A, 50% of the population has only 25% of the income, displaying income inequality. You can also infer from point A that the remaining 50% of the population earns 75% of total income. The bigger the gap between the Lorenz curve and the perfect equality line, the bigger the amount of income inequality (or the more the Lorenz curve has a banana shape, the more inequality).

TIP

The good news is students have never been asked in the past to draw the Lorenz curve from memory on the free-response section. The more likely scenario is that you will have to interpret it and know its meaning for the multiple-choice section.

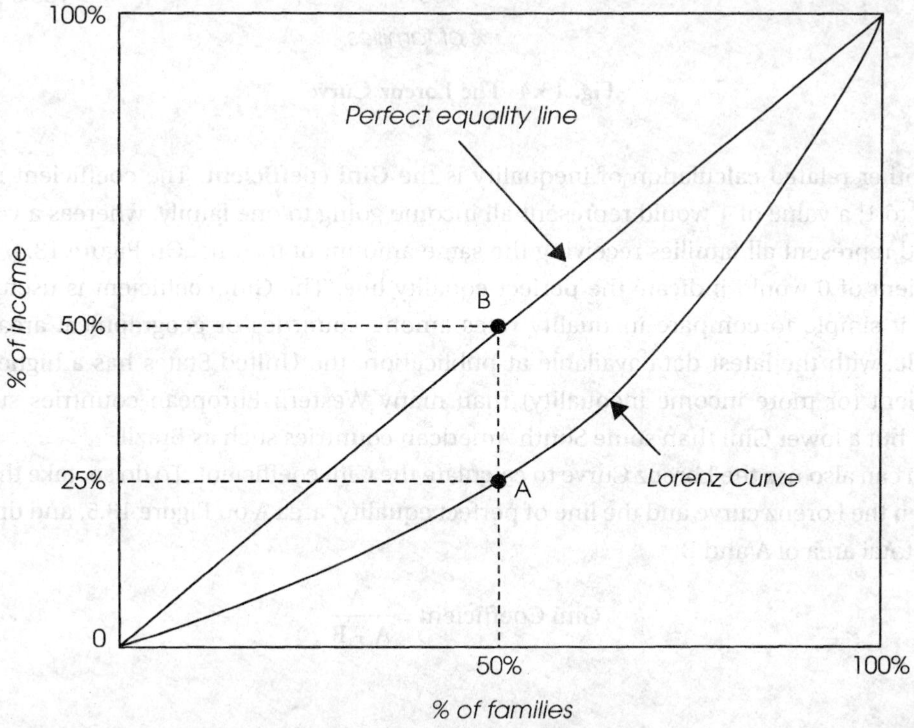

Fig. 13.3 The Lorenz Curve

In comparing Figure 13.4 to Figure 13.3, you can see the greater amount of separation between the Lorenz curve and the perfect equality line (or a bigger banana curve). If fact, at point A on Figure 13.4, 50% of the population earns only 10% of the income, where the remaining 50% earn 90% of total income.

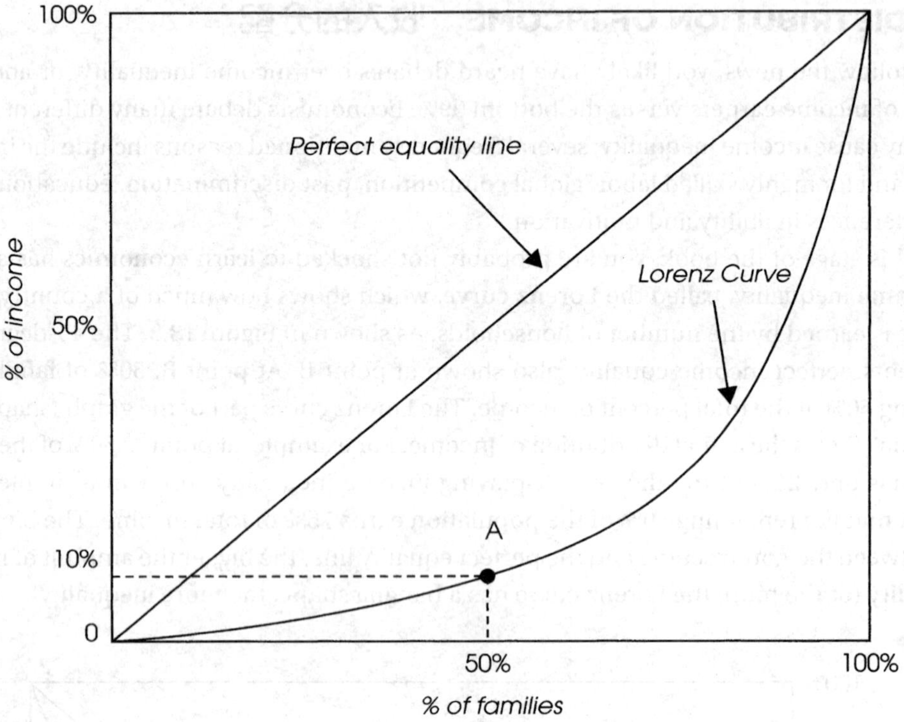

Fig. 13.4 The Lorenz Curve

TIP

A Gini coefficient closer to 0 would mean there is less income inequality, whereas a number closer to 1 would mean more inequality.

Another related calculation of inequality is the **Gini coefficient**. The coefficient ranges from 0 to 1; a value of 1 would represent all income going to one family, whereas a value of 0 would represent all families receiving the same amount of income. On Figure 13.4, a Gini coefficient of 0 would indicate the perfect equality line. The Gini coefficient is useful as it makes it simple to compare inequality rates among countries or geographical areas. For example, with the latest data available at publication, the United States has a higher Gini coefficient (or more income inequality) than many Western European countries such as France but a lower Gini than some South American countries such as Brazil.

You can also use the Lorenz Curve to calculate the Gini coefficient. To do so, take the area between the Lorenz curve and the line of perfect equality, area A on Figure 13.5, and divide it by the total area of A and B.

$$\text{Gini Coefficient} = \frac{A}{A + B}$$

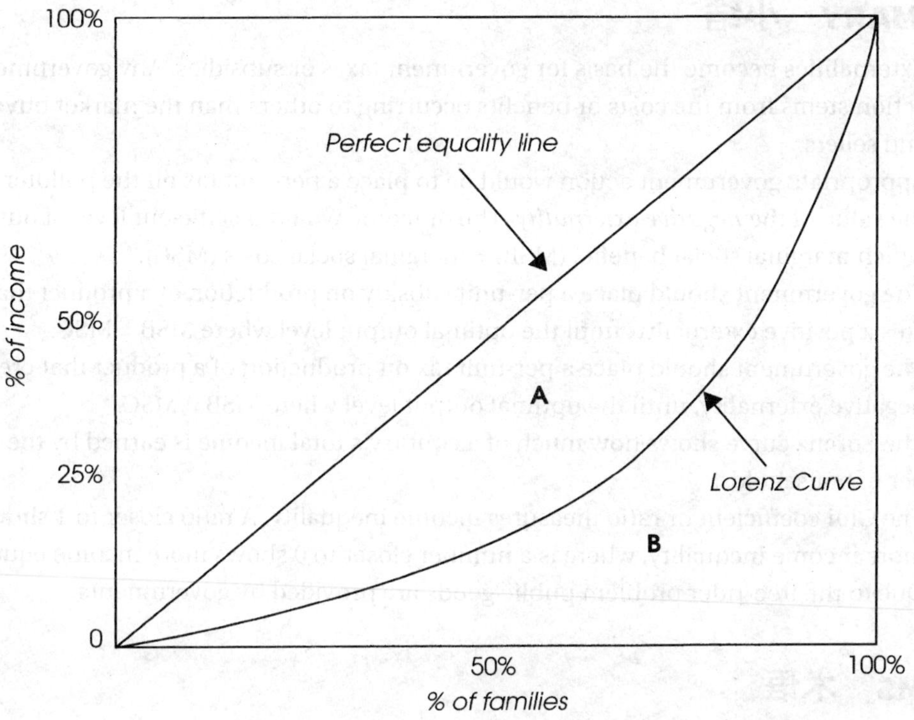

Fig. 13.5 The Lorenz Curve

TYPES OF TAXES 税收的种类

Taxation can be used by governments in an attempt to reduce income inequality. Some types of taxes may help reduce inequality; however, others can actually make the problem worse. Here are three types of taxes with examples:

- A **progressive tax** results in higher tax rates as income increases. The U.S. federal income tax is an example of a progressive tax. Published tax brackets range from 10% to 40% of income in 2014. The first few thousand dollars one earns is taxed at lower rates (even for very rich people like Bill Gates) and then every dollar earned at higher income levels is taxed at higher rates. By the time Bill Gates has earned more than $400,000 or so for the year (likely few seconds into the year), he is in the highest tax bracket. A progressive tax can lessen the amount of income inequality in a society.
- A **proportional tax** imposes the same tax rates on everyone regardless of income. Whether a person makes $100 or $100,000 a year, each person pays the same percentage of total income in taxes.
- A **regressive tax** is where the average tax burden decreases as a percent of income rises. The sales tax on consumption is a good example of a regressive tax. Higher-income earners are more likely to save some of their income, where low-income earners likely spend all or a greater percentage of their income earned. So as a percent of total income, a sales tax tends to have a greater burden on low-income earners, making it a regressive tax.

SUMMARY 小结

- Externalities become the basis for government taxes or subsidies. Any government action stems from the costs or benefits occurring to others than the market buyers and sellers.
- Appropriate government action would be to place a per-unit tax on the polluter for the value of the *negative externality*. The outcome would be efficient level of output at which marginal social benefits (MSB) = marginal social costs (MSC).
- The government should place a per-unit subsidy on production of a product that creates a positive externality, until the optimal output level where MSB = MSC.
- The government should place a per-unit tax on production of a product that creates a negative externality, until the optimal output level where MSB = MSC.
- The Lorenz curve shows how much of a country's total income is earned by the number of households.
- The Gini coefficient or ratio measures income inequality. A ratio closer to 1 shows more income inequality, whereas a number closer to 0 shows more income equality.
- Due to the free-rider problem public goods are provided by governments.

TERMS 术语

Coase Theorem theory that states private parties can solve the issues created by externalities on their own without government intervention

Free-Rider Problem because people know they can benefit from public goods without paying, government ends up providing public goods

Gini Coefficient a measure of income inequality that ranges from 0 to 1; a value of 1 would represent all income going to one family, whereas a value of 0 would represent all families receiving the same amount of income

Lorenz Curve curve that shows how much of a country's total income is earned by the number of households

Lump-Sum Tax a fixed tax on producers regardless of the amount produced

Marginal Social Benefit (MSB) the benefits that accrue to society when consuming a product; MPB + MEB = MSB

Marginal Social Cost (MSC) the costs that incurred to society when an additional unit is produced; MPC + MEC = MSC

Negative Externality when a third party outside of a market incurs some of the cost of producing a product. It causes the market to produce too much of the good from society's point of view as MSC > MPC

Per-Unit Subsidy a payment to producers from the government for each additional unit produced; a solution for positive externalities

Per-Unit Tax a tax on producers for each additional unit produced, adding to the marginal cost of production; a solution for negative externalities

Positive Externality the production or consumption of a good or service that creates benefits for third parties not involved in the transaction. It causes the market to produce too little of the product from society's point of view as MPB < MSB

Private Goods goods that are exclusive and rival in consumption

Progressive Tax tax that results in higher tax rates as income increases

Proportional Tax tax that imposes the tax rates on everyone regardless of income

Public Goods goods that are nonexclusive and nonrival, as one person's consumption of a public good does not exclude others from benefiting from it, like national defense.

Regressive Tax tax where the tax burden falls as income rises

FORMULAS 公式

MSB = MSC The Allocatively Efficient Quantity, considering externalities:

If MSB > MPB, it's a positive externality.

If MSC > MPC, it's a negative externality.

MPB + MEB = MSB

MPC + MEC = MSC

MULTIPLE-CHOICE REVIEW QUESTIONS 选择题

1. Which of the following is true about the public good?
   - (A) One person's consumption means others get less.
   - (B) Consumers can be excluded from its benefits by not paying for it.
   - (C) One more unit of a public good for some consumers means one less unit for other consumers.
   - (D) One person's consumption does not exclude others from consuming it.
   - (E) Everyone pays the same amount for the good.

2. If there is a negative externality associated with a firm's production of a private good, which of the following is an action by government that would most likely move the market to an efficient outcome?
   - (A) Shut down the firm.
   - (B) Give the firm a per-unit subsidy.
   - (C) Place a per-unit tax on the firm.
   - (D) Relocate the firm.
   - (E) None of the above.

3. If there is a positive externality associated with the production of a private good, which of the following is an action of government that would most likely move the market to an efficient outcome?
   - (A) Shut down the firm.
   - (B) Give the firm a per-unit subsidy.
   - (C) Place a per-unit tax on the firm.
   - (D) Relocate the firm.
   - (E) None of the above.

4. For a polluting steel company, a government action to most likely achieve an optimal or efficient outcome would produce what effect on the market equilibrium price and output?
   - (A) Output would increase; no change in price.
   - (B) Output would increase; price would decrease.
   - (C) Output would increase; price would increase.
   - (D) Output would decrease; price would decrease.
   - (E) Output would decrease, price would increase.

5. All of the following are true regarding externalities except?
   - (A) Marginal Social Cost = Marginal Private Cost + Marginal External Cost.
   - (B) Marginal Social Benefit = Marginal Private Benefit + Marginal External Benefit.
   - (C) A per-unit subsidy is a solution to a positive externality.
   - (D) If MSB > MPB, it is referring to a positive externality.
   - (E) The allocatively efficient production quantity is where MSB = MPC.

MULTIPLE-CHOICE REVIEW ANSWERS 选择题答案

1. (D) **2.** (C) **3.** (B) **4.** (E) **5.** (E)

FREE-RESPONSE REVIEW QUESTION
开放式题目

1. Assume Firm A has been polluting rivers and lakes near its factory while producing steel, causing a negative externality. Draw a correctly labeled market for Firm A showing each of the following for a, b, and c:

a. The private market equilibrium price and quantity, labeled P_M and Q_M.

b. The socially optimal quantity and price of production, labeled P_S and Q_S.

c. The deadweight loss at the market equilibrium.

d. Explain what government action could result in a socially optimal outcome.

Free-Response Review Answer
开放式题目答案

a, b, c.

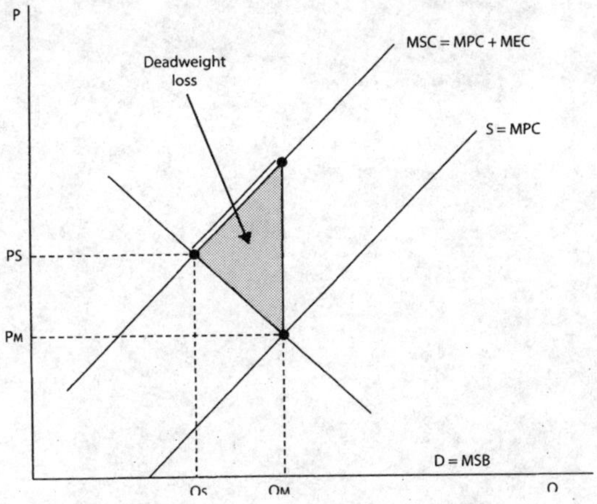

Fig. 13.6 Free-Response Review Answer

d. The government could place a per-unit tax on the production of steel, equal to the marginal external cost (the difference between the MPC and MSC curves).

Model AP Exam in Microeconomics

AP微观经济学考试样题

答题纸 ANSWER SHEET

微观经济学 Microeconomics

MULTIPLE-CHOICE QUESTIONS 选择题

1. Ⓐ Ⓑ Ⓒ Ⓓ Ⓔ
2. Ⓐ Ⓑ Ⓒ Ⓓ Ⓔ
3. Ⓐ Ⓑ Ⓒ Ⓓ Ⓔ
4. Ⓐ Ⓑ Ⓒ Ⓓ Ⓔ
5. Ⓐ Ⓑ Ⓒ Ⓓ Ⓔ
6. Ⓐ Ⓑ Ⓒ Ⓓ Ⓔ
7. Ⓐ Ⓑ Ⓒ Ⓓ Ⓔ
8. Ⓐ Ⓑ Ⓒ Ⓓ Ⓔ
9. Ⓐ Ⓑ Ⓒ Ⓓ Ⓔ
10. Ⓐ Ⓑ Ⓒ Ⓓ Ⓔ
11. Ⓐ Ⓑ Ⓒ Ⓓ Ⓔ
12. Ⓐ Ⓑ Ⓒ Ⓓ Ⓔ
13. Ⓐ Ⓑ Ⓒ Ⓓ Ⓔ
14. Ⓐ Ⓑ Ⓒ Ⓓ Ⓔ
15. Ⓐ Ⓑ Ⓒ Ⓓ Ⓔ
16. Ⓐ Ⓑ Ⓒ Ⓓ Ⓔ
17. Ⓐ Ⓑ Ⓒ Ⓓ Ⓔ
18. Ⓐ Ⓑ Ⓒ Ⓓ Ⓔ
19. Ⓐ Ⓑ Ⓒ Ⓓ Ⓔ
20. Ⓐ Ⓑ Ⓒ Ⓓ Ⓔ
21. Ⓐ Ⓑ Ⓒ Ⓓ Ⓔ
22. Ⓐ Ⓑ Ⓒ Ⓓ Ⓔ
23. Ⓐ Ⓑ Ⓒ Ⓓ Ⓔ
24. Ⓐ Ⓑ Ⓒ Ⓓ Ⓔ
25. Ⓐ Ⓑ Ⓒ Ⓓ Ⓔ
26. Ⓐ Ⓑ Ⓒ Ⓓ Ⓔ
27. Ⓐ Ⓑ Ⓒ Ⓓ Ⓔ
28. Ⓐ Ⓑ Ⓒ Ⓓ Ⓔ
29. Ⓐ Ⓑ Ⓒ Ⓓ Ⓔ
30. Ⓐ Ⓑ Ⓒ Ⓓ Ⓔ
31. Ⓐ Ⓑ Ⓒ Ⓓ Ⓔ
32. Ⓐ Ⓑ Ⓒ Ⓓ Ⓔ
33. Ⓐ Ⓑ Ⓒ Ⓓ Ⓔ
34. Ⓐ Ⓑ Ⓒ Ⓓ Ⓔ
35. Ⓐ Ⓑ Ⓒ Ⓓ Ⓔ
36. Ⓐ Ⓑ Ⓒ Ⓓ Ⓔ
37. Ⓐ Ⓑ Ⓒ Ⓓ Ⓔ
38. Ⓐ Ⓑ Ⓒ Ⓓ Ⓔ
39. Ⓐ Ⓑ Ⓒ Ⓓ Ⓔ
40. Ⓐ Ⓑ Ⓒ Ⓓ Ⓔ
41. Ⓐ Ⓑ Ⓒ Ⓓ Ⓔ
42. Ⓐ Ⓑ Ⓒ Ⓓ Ⓔ
43. Ⓐ Ⓑ Ⓒ Ⓓ Ⓔ
44. Ⓐ Ⓑ Ⓒ Ⓓ Ⓔ
45. Ⓐ Ⓑ Ⓒ Ⓓ Ⓔ
46. Ⓐ Ⓑ Ⓒ Ⓓ Ⓔ
47. Ⓐ Ⓑ Ⓒ Ⓓ Ⓔ
48. Ⓐ Ⓑ Ⓒ Ⓓ Ⓔ
49. Ⓐ Ⓑ Ⓒ Ⓓ Ⓔ
50. Ⓐ Ⓑ Ⓒ Ⓓ Ⓔ
51. Ⓐ Ⓑ Ⓒ Ⓓ Ⓔ
52. Ⓐ Ⓑ Ⓒ Ⓓ Ⓔ
53. Ⓐ Ⓑ Ⓒ Ⓓ Ⓔ
54. Ⓐ Ⓑ Ⓒ Ⓓ Ⓔ
55. Ⓐ Ⓑ Ⓒ Ⓓ Ⓔ
56. Ⓐ Ⓑ Ⓒ Ⓓ Ⓔ
57. Ⓐ Ⓑ Ⓒ Ⓓ Ⓔ
58. Ⓐ Ⓑ Ⓒ Ⓓ Ⓔ
59. Ⓐ Ⓑ Ⓒ Ⓓ Ⓔ
60. Ⓐ Ⓑ Ⓒ Ⓓ Ⓔ

Model AP Exam in Microeconomics
AP微观经济学考试样题

Two hours are allotted for this exam: 1 hour and 10 minutes for Section I, which consists of multiple-choice questions; and 50 minutes for Section II, which consists of three mandatory essay questions.

SECTION I—MULTIPLE-CHOICE QUESTIONS
第一部分——选择题

Time—1 hour and 10 minutes
Number of Questions—60
Percent of Total Grade—$66^2/_3$

Directions 说明

Each of the questions beginning on page 172 are followed by five suggested answers or completions. Select the one that is best in each case and then fill in the corresponding oval on the answer sheet.

1. Which of the following is NOT a characteristic of perfectly competitive industry?

(A) Free entry into the industry.
(B) Product differentiation.
(C) Perfectly elastic demand curve for firms.
(D) Homogeneous products.
(E) Many sellers and many buyers.

2. Which of the following is a characteristic of monopolistic competition in the long run?

(A) Strong barriers to entry.
(B) Homogeneous products.
(C) Zero economic profits.
(D) Minimum average total cost equals price.
(E) Allocative efficiency.

3. Which of the following is characteristic of oligopoly?

I. Formidable barriers to entry.
II. Mutual interdependence.
III. Relatively few sellers.

(A) I only.
(B) II only.
(C) III only.
(D) I and III only.
(E) I, II, and III.

4. Which of the following is a characteristic of monopoly?

(A) A price that is always in the elastic range of demand curve.
(B) Price equal to marginal revenue.
(C) Perfectly elastic demand curve.
(D) Weak barriers to entry.
(E) Zero economic profits.

5. Compared to perfect competition in the long run, monopoly has

(A) more choices of products for consumers.
(B) allocative efficiency.
(C) lower prices.
(D) a price less than marginal cost.
(E) a price greater than marginal cost.

6. With the presence of a negative externality, which of the following would correct the externality?

(A) A per-unit subsidy.
(B) A per-unit tax.
(C) A lower price.
(D) A higher level of output.
(E) A government-created task force.

7. With the presence of a positive externality, which of the following would correct the externality?

(A) A per-unit subsidy.
(B) A per-unit tax.
(C) A higher price.
(D) A lower level of output.
(E) A government-created task force.

8. Which of the following is true regarding externalities?

(A) Marginal Social Cost = Marginal Private Cost + Marginal Social Benefit.
(B) Marginal Social Benefit = Marginal Private Benefit – Marginal Social Cost.
(C) Marginal Social Cost = Marginal Private Cost + Marginal External Benefit.
(D) Marginal Social Cost = Marginal Private Cost + Marginal External Cost.
(E) Quantity of Externality = Marginal Private Costs.

9. Which of the following is true?

(A) Average total cost = total fixed costs divided by the number of units produced.
(B) Average total cost = average variable costs divided by the total number of units produced.
(C) Average total cost = average variable cost plus marginal cost.
(D) Average total cost = average variable cost plus average fixed cost.
(E) All of the above.

10. Which of the following is true about the relationship of the average total cost (ATC) curve and the marginal cost (MC) curve?

(A) ATC and MC are always equal.
(B) ATC and MC are never equal.
(C) The ATC curve intersects the MC curve at the minimum point of the MC curve.
(D) The MC curve intersects the ATC curve at the minimum point of the ATC curve.
(E) The MC curve intersects the ATC curve at the maximum point of the ATC curve.

Question 11 is based on the figure below:

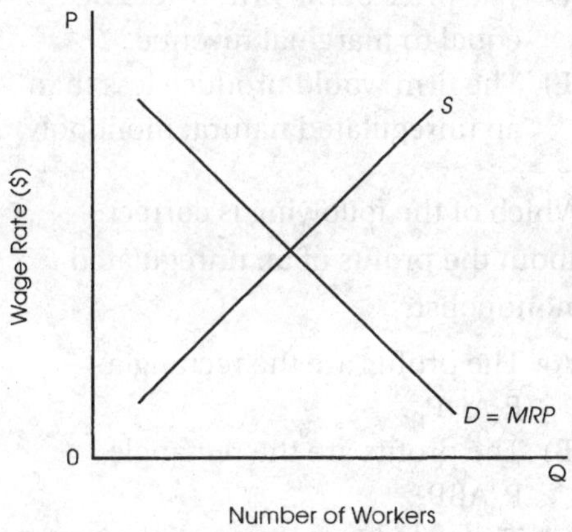

11. Which of the following will happen when a new computerized system for a firm increases the marginal productivity of its workers?

(A) The marginal revenue product curve will shift to the left, which will cause the wage rate to decrease.
(B) The supply curve will shift to the right, causing the wage rate to decrease.
(C) The marginal revenue product curve will shift to the right, causing the wage rate to increase.
(D) The supply curve will shift to the left, causing the wage rate to increase.
(E) The marginal revenue product curve will shift to the right and the supply curve will shift to the left, leaving the wage rate unchanged.

12. Which of the following is true about an effective price floor?

(A) It is used to correct government policy.
(B) It is used when the equilibrium price is too high.
(C) It will be located above the equilibrium price.
(D) It will be located below the equilibrium price.
(E) It is when the stock market has closed at a new low.

13. Which of the following is true about a price effective ceiling?

(A) It is used to correct government policy.
(B) It is used when equilibrium prices are too low.
(C) It will be located above the equilibrium price.
(D) It will be located below the equilibrium price.
(E) It is when the stock market has closed at a new high.

14. Which of the following situations best exemplifies the concept of consumer surplus?

(A) It refers to a consumer who no longer has any outstanding debts.
(B) The federal government has taken in more revenue than it has paid out in expenditures.
(C) A consumer does not buy a pizza as it costs more than the highest price she is willing to pay.
(D) A consumer pays less for a pizza than the highest price she is willing to pay.
(E) A consumer buys a pizza for the exact highest price she is willing to pay.

Number of Workers	Pair Sets Produced per Two Weeks
1	40
2	70
3	95
4	115
5	130
6	130

15. Given the data in the table above, and knowing that workers are paid $1,250 every two weeks and that the pair sets are sold to retailers at $50, how many workers would be hired?

(A) Two
(B) Three
(C) Four
(D) Five
(E) Six

Questions 16–19 are based on the figure below:

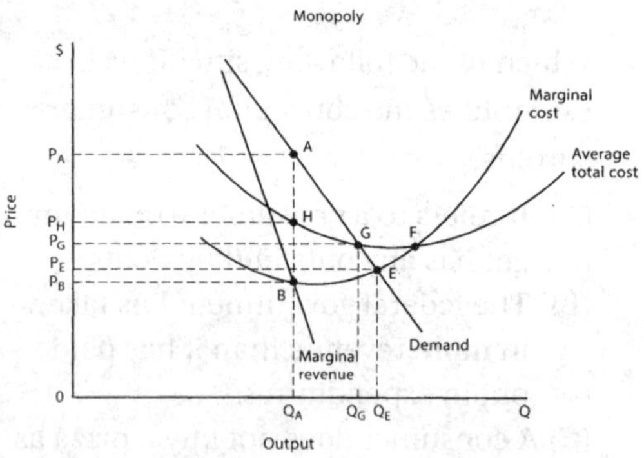

16. An unregulated monopoly would

(A) sell at price P_A and produce output at Q_A.
(B) sell at price P_G and produce output at Q_G.
(C) sell at price P_E and produce output at Q_E.
(D) sell at price P_B and produce output at Q_A.
(E) sell at price P_H and produce output at Q_A.

17. If this monopoly were regulated at the fair return price, what would be the correct quantity and output?

(A) Q_A, P_H
(B) Q_G, P_E
(C) Q_E, P_E
(D) Q_G, P_G
(E) Q_A, P_A

18. If regulation of a natural monopoly occurs where marginal cost intersects the demand curve, which of the following is correct?

(A) The firm would need to be taxed.
(B) The firm would realize profits.
(C) The firm would need to be subsidized.
(D) The price of the firm would be equal to marginal revenue.
(E) The firm would produce less than an unregulated natural monopoly.

19. Which of the following is correct about the profits of an unregulated monopolist?

(A) The profits are the rectangle P_AAHP_H.
(B) The profits are the rectangle P_HABP_B.
(C) The profits are less than those of a regulated monopoly.
(D) The profits are less than at a socially optimal output.
(E) None of the above.

Questions 20–23 are based on the figure below:

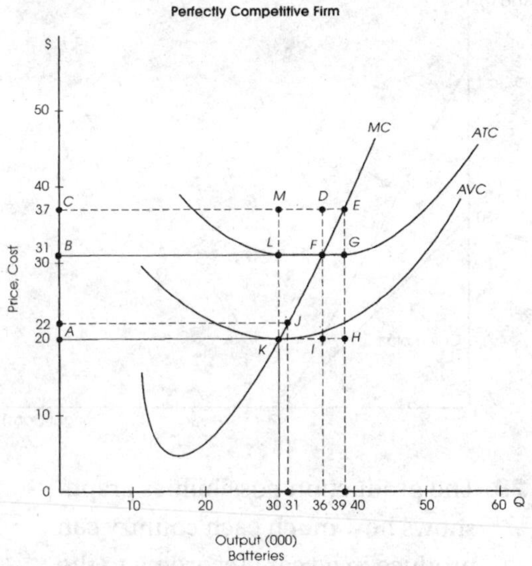

20. At a market price of $37, maximum profits are
(A) CBLM.
(B) CBFD.
(C) CBGE.
(D) BAKL.
(E) CAHE.

21. At a market price of $19, how many batteries will the firm produce?
(A) 20,000
(B) 29,000
(C) 36,000
(D) 28,000
(E) Zero

22. At a market price of $22, how many batteries will the firm produce?
(A) 20,000
(B) 26,000
(C) 31,000
(D) Zero
(E) 10,000

23. At the market price of $22, the output will result in
(A) economic losses.
(B) economic profits.
(C) normal profits.
(D) business profits.
(E) shut-down.

24. If the government announces that the drinking of red grape juice reduces the risk of heart attacks, which of the following will be correct in terms of changes in supply, demand, and the price of red grape juice?

	Supply	Demand	Price of grape juice
(A)	Increases	Decreases	Increases
(B)	No change	No change	Decreases
(C)	No change	Increases	Increases
(D)	Decreases	Increases	Decreases
(E)	Decreases	Decreases	Decreases

Questions 25–28 are based on the figure below:

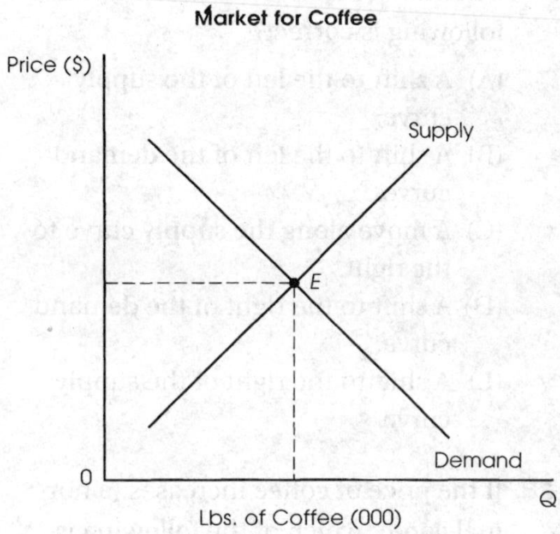

25. If the demand for coffee increases and at the same time increases in productivity lowered production costs, what would happen to the new price and quantity?

	Price	Quantity
(A)	Increase	Increase
(B)	Indeterminate	Increase
(C)	Increase	Decrease
(D)	Decrease	Indeterminate
(E)	Decrease	Decrease

26. If the government provides a subsidy to the producers of coffee, which of the following will occur?

(A) A shift to the left of the supply curve.
(B) A shift to the left of the demand curve.
(C) A move along the supply curve to the right.
(D) A shift to the right of the demand curve.
(E) A shift to the right of the supply curve.

27. If the producers of coffee have to pay an increase in wages and fringe benefits to their workers, which of the following is correct?

(A) A shift to the left of the supply curve.
(B) A shift to the left of the demand curve.
(C) A move along the supply curve to the right.
(D) A shift to the right of the demand curve.
(E) A shift to the right of the supply curve.

28. If the price of coffee increases (a normal good), which of the following is most likely to happen?

(A) An increase in the quantity of coffee consumers want to purchase.
(B) No change in the quantity of coffee consumers want to purchase.
(C) A decrease in the quantity of coffee consumers want to purchase.
(D) An increase (shift) in the demand for coffee.
(E) A decrease (shift) in the demand for coffee.

Use the following graph for Question 29:

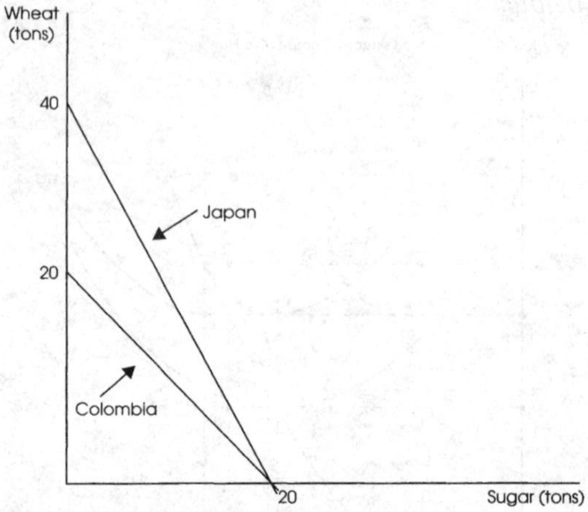

29. The production possibilities graph shows how much each country can produce in a year. According to the graph, which of the following is true?

(A) Colombia has an absolute advantage in the production of wheat.
(B) Japan has an absolute advantage in the production of sugar.
(C) Colombia has a comparative advantage in the production of wheat.
(D) Japan cannot benefit from trade with Colombia.
(E) Japan has a comparative advantage in the production of wheat.

Questions 30–31 are based on the figure below:

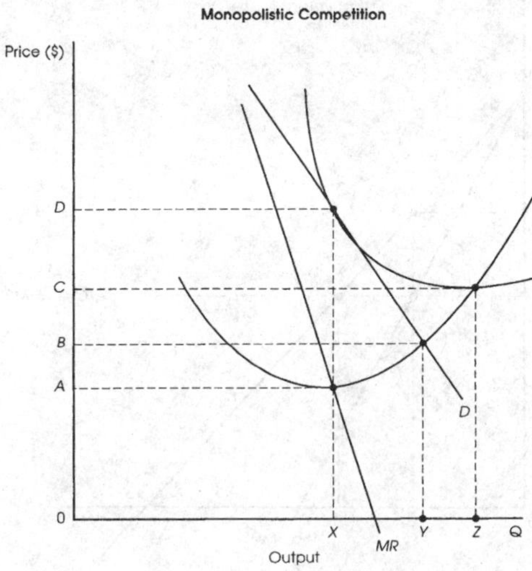

30. For this firm operating under monopolistic competition, which of the following is the profit-maximizing output and price?

(A) OX output and OA price.
(B) OX output and OD price.
(C) OX output and OB price.
(D) OZ output and OC price.
(E) OZ output and OA price.

31. At the profit-maximizing output, which of the following is correct?

(A) Economic profits are zero and the firm is operating efficiently.
(B) Economic profits are above normal and output is greater than under perfect competition.
(C) Economic losses are present.
(D) Price is less than marginal cost.
(E) Economic profits are zero and the firm is operating inefficiently.

32. Which of the following best exemplifies economies of scale?

(A) As a firm's output decreases, long-run average total cost decreases.
(B) As a firm's output increases, long-run average total cost increases.
(C) As a firm's output increases, long-run average total cost decreases.
(D) As a firm's output increases, long-run average total cost remains constant.
(E) As a firm becomes larger, it becomes less productive.

33. Which of the following is correct?

(A) In the long run, all inputs are variable.
(B) In the short run, all inputs are variable.
(C) In the long run, supply is not able to adjust fully to changes in demand.
(D) In the short run, supply is able to adjust fully to changes in demand.
(E) A short run is any distance less than one mile.

34. If a firm decreases its prices by 15 percent and its total revenue increases by 30 percent, which of the following is correct?

(A) The price elasticity of demand is unit elastic.
(B) The price elasticity of demand is perfectly elastic.
(C) The price elasticity of demand is relatively elastic.
(D) The numerical coefficient of elasticity is equal to one.
(E) The numerical coefficient of elasticity is less than one.

MODEL MICROECONOMICS EXAM

35. If one person has the only original signed copy of *The Wealth of Nations* by Adam Smith, which of the following would illustrate this situation?

(A) A downward sloping demand curve.
(B) An upward sloping supply curve.
(C) An invisible hand.
(D) A perfectly inelastic supply curve.
(E) A perfectly elastic demand curve.

36. When marginal cost equals price in a perfectly competitive product market at long run equilibrium, which of the following is NOT correct?

(A) There is allocative efficiency as price = marginal cost.
(B) There is productive efficiency as price = minimum average total cost.
(C) The perfectly competitive firm is earning economic profits.
(D) The market is producing the amount of goods desired by society.
(E) The firm is earning a normal profit.

37. Which of the following is a correct statement?

(A) Average total cost equals marginal cost plus average fixed costs.
(B) Average total cost equals marginal costs plus average variable costs.
(C) Average total cost equals average fixed costs plus average variable costs.
(D) Total fixed costs vary with output.
(E) Total fixed costs equal total variable costs at zero output.

38. Which of the following describes a monopolistically competitive market?

(A) A small number of firms with high barriers to entry and exit.
(B) A large number of firms with high barriers to entry and exit.
(C) A small number of firms and allocative efficiency.
(D) They produce products with no close substitutes.
(E) Low barriers to entry and exit and excess capacity.

Questions 39–41 are based on the figure below:

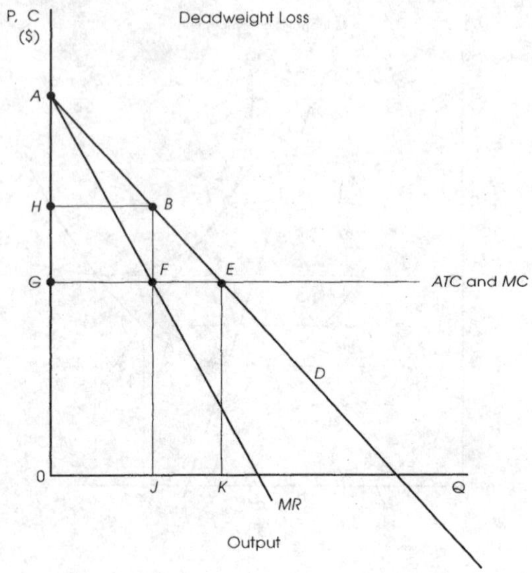

39. The original consumer surplus if this were a competitive market is

(A) AHB.
(B) BFE.
(C) AGE.
(D) HGFB.
(E) GOKE.

40. The deadweight loss as the result of monopoly is

(A) AHB.
(B) BFE.
(C) AGE.
(D) HGFB.
(E) GOKE.

41. The consumer surplus of the monopoly is

(A) AHB.
(B) BFE.
(C) AGE.
(D) HGFB.
(E) GOKE.

Use the following graph for Questions 42, 43, and 44.

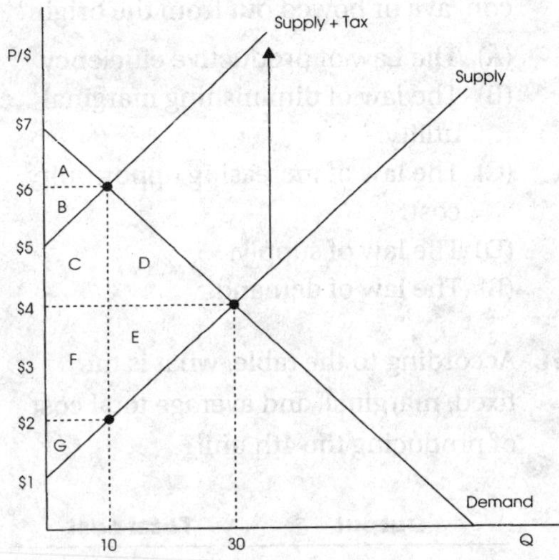

42. The market shown on the graph has had a per-unit tax placed on its production. What is the after-tax consumer and producer surplus?

	Consumer Surplus	Producer Surplus
(A)	ABCD	FEG
(B)	AB	FG
(C)	A	G
(D)	BCD	FE
(E)	ABCFG	DE

43. The market shown on the graph has had a per-unit tax placed on its production. What is the tax incidence, or burden of the tax paid by consumers and producers?

	Consumer Tax Incidence	Producer Tax Incidence
(A)	BC	F
(B)	ABCD	FEG
(C)	A	G
(D)	BCD	FE
(E)	ABCFG	DE

44. The market shown on the graph has had a per-unit tax placed on its production. What is the after-tax price paid by consumers and the after-tax price received by producers?

	Price for Consumers	Price Recieved by Sellers
(A)	$4	$4
(B)	$6	$2
(C)	$7	$1
(D)	$4	$2
(E)	$5	$1

45. If, for each additional unit of a variable input added, the increases in output become smaller, which of the following correctly identifies the concept?

(A) Diminishing marginal returns.
(B) Diminishing marginal utility.
(C) Increasing marginal utility.
(D) Increasing marginal productivity.
(E) Constant costs.

46. Which of the following is correct about the demand for labor?

(A) The demand for labor is independent of the demand for other inputs or resources.
(B) The demand for labor is independent of the demand for the products produced by labor.
(C) The demand for labor is independent of the availability of other inputs or resources.
(D) The demand for labor is derived from the demand for the products produced by labor.
(E) The demand for labor is derived from the demand for labor unions.

47. If an increase in the price of good Y causes the quantity demanded of good X to increase, this means the two goods are

(A) complementary goods.
(B) substitute goods.
(C) inferior goods.
(D) normal goods.
(E) independent goods.

Use the following graph for Question 48:

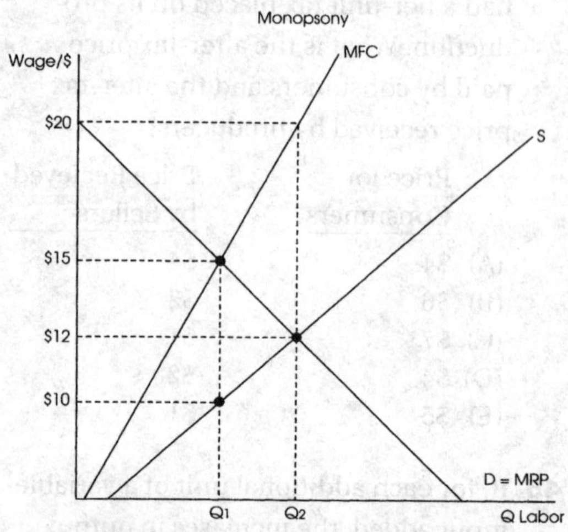

48. The graph shows a monopsony labor market. What is the profit-maximizing wage and quantity of workers hired by the monopsonist?

	Wage	Quantity
(A)	$12	Q2
(B)	$20	Q2
(C)	$15	Q1
(D)	$12	Q1
(E)	$10	Q1

49. Under what conditions would a firm continue to hire labor in a perfectly competitive labor market?

(A) When the marginal revenue product is greater than the marginal factor cost.
(B) When labor costs less than capital.
(C) When marginal revenue product is positive.
(D) When the marginal factor cost is greater than the marginal revenue product.
(E) When average product is increasing.

50. Why does the Production Possibilities Curve frequently have a shape that is concave or bowed out from the origin?

(A) The Law of productive efficiency.
(B) The law of diminishing marginal utility.
(C) The law of increasing opportunity cost.
(D) The law of supply.
(E) The law of demand.

51. According to the table, what is the fixed, marginal, and average total cost of producing the 4th unit?

Output	Total cost
0	$20
1	$30
2	$35
3	$50
4	$80
5	$115

	Fixed Cost	Marginal Cost	Average Total Cost
(A)	$20	$30	$20
(B)	$20	$50	$20
(C)	$20	$80	$60
(D)	$30	$30	$115
(E)	$110	$80	$47.5

Use the following game theory matrix for Questions 52 and 53:

		Firm Y High	Firm Y Low
Firm X	High	$60,$45	$50,$35
	Low	$40,$10	$15,$20

52. This game theory payoff matrix shows the possible profit for two firms deciding to price high or price low. Firm X will earn the profit to the left in each cell, and Firm Y's profit is to the right in each cell. Which of the following statements is correct?

(A) Firm X's dominant strategy is to price low.
(B) Firm X's dominant strategy is to price high.
(C) Firm Y's dominant strategy is to price low.
(D) Firm Y's dominant strategy is to price high.
(E) Neither firm has a dominant strategy.

53. This game theory payoff matrix shows the possible profit for two firms deciding to price high or price low. Firm X will earn the profit to the left in each cell, and Firm Y's profit is to the right in each cell. Assume each firm knows all the information in the payoff matrix. All of the following statements are correct *except*?

(A) if the two firms collude, Firm X will price high and Firm Y will price high.
(B) if Firm X prices low, then Firm Y will price low.
(C) if Firm Y prices high, Firm X will follow and price high.
(D) the game will reach a Nash equilibrium with both pricing high.
(E) if Firm Y prices high, Firm X will price low.

54. Assume Celine's Crab Shack earned an accounting profit of $20,000 this year. However, the owner and head chef, Celine, is also a talented artist who could have earned $30,000 painting, and $2,000 in interest from the money she invested in her restaurant. Based on this information, which of the following statements is correct about Celine?

(A) She has incurred an economic loss as a chef.
(B) She has gained economic profits as a chef.
(C) She has a negative accounting profits as a chef.
(D) She is earning a normal profit as a chef.
(E) Her explicit costs are $12,000 as a chef.

55. For a profit-maximizing, nonprice-discriminating monopolist, marginal revenue is

(A) equal to price.
(B) negative when the firm is maximizing profit.
(C) more than the price.
(D) a perfect elastic curve.
(E) less than the price.

56. Assume that people like mustard on their hot dogs. Due to increases in the cost of production, the supply of hot dogs decreases. How will this affect the market for mustard?

(A) The demand for mustard will increase as hot dogs and mustard are complements.
(B) The quantity demanded of mustard will increase as hot dogs and mustard are complements.
(C) The demand for mustard will go down as hot dogs and mustard are complements.
(D) The supply of mustard will increase to offset the hot dog market.
(E) The demand and supply of mustard will remain unchanged.

Use this graph for Question 57:

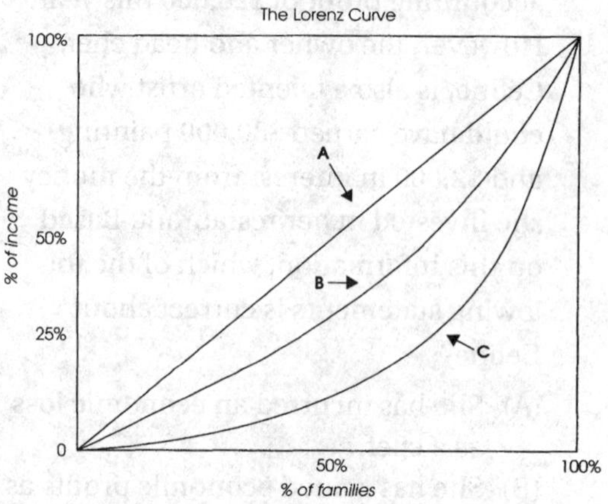

57. On the Lorenz curve, all of the following are true except

(A) Line A shows more income inequality than line B.
(B) Line A shows perfect income equality.
(C) Line B shows less income inequality than line C.
(D) Line C shows a greater income inequality than line A.
(E) On line A, 50% of the population earns 50% of the total income.

58. If a government passes an effective minimum wage law, in which of the following situations will the change in employment be the smallest?

(A) If labor demand is relatively elastic.
(B) If labor demand is unit elastic.
(C) If labor demand is relatively inelastic.
(D) If labor demand is perfectly elastic.
(E) If labor supply is relatively elastic.

59. Assume the government imposes 20% excise tax on all food sold in a country. Which of the following is true?

(A) This is a proportional tax.
(B) This is a regressive tax.
(C) This is a progressive tax.
(D) The quantity demanded for food will not change, as it is perfectly inelastic.
(E) There will be no additional tax revenue from this tax.

Use the following table to answer Question 60:

Number of Times	Marginal Utility from Movies	Marginal Utility from Trampoline Park
1	30	15
2	20	10
3	10	5
4	5	2
5	0	1

60. Assume Joe has only $45 to spend on entertainment. What combination of movies, that cost $10 per movie, and visits to the trampoline park, that cost $5 per visit, would maximize his utility?

(A) Going to the movies and trampoline park 2 times each.
(B) Going to the movies and trampoline park 3 times each.
(C) Going to the movies 2 times and the trampoline park 3 times.
(D) Going to the movies 3 times and the trampoline park 5 times.
(E) Going to the movies 4 times and the trampoline park 5 times.

SECTION II—FREE-RESPONSE QUESTIONS
第二部分——开放式题目

Planning Time—10 minutes

Writing Time—50 minutes

Percent of Total Grade—$33^1/_3$

Directions 说明

You have 50 minutes to answer all three of the following questions. It is suggested that you spend approximately half your time on the first question and divide the remaining time equally between the next two questions. In answering the questions, you should emphasize the line of reasoning that generated your results; it is not enough to list the results of your analysis. Include correctly labeled diagrams, if useful or required, in explaining your answers. A correctly labeled diagram must have all axes and curves clearly labeled and must show directional changes.

Students should consider doing a "sketch" (main points, quick graph, etc.) of the answer before actually answering the free-response questions. Good luck! When you use graphs on the free-response questions, label the axes and make direct references to any symbols, e.g., MR, P, output, on the graphs when you respond to questions.

NOTE

Advanced Placement exams require *three* Free-Response questions. Some of the questions may be based on material covered in the common chapters, such as production possibilities frontier or curve when applied to international trade. For these questions, please refer to those chapters.

1. Farmer Fred produces corn in a perfectly competitive market. Farmer Fred is earning economic profits.

(a) Draw correctly labeled, side-by-side graphs of both the market for corn and for Farmer Fred, showing each of the following:

(i) The equilibrium price and quantity in the corn market labeled P_{M1} and Q_{M1}.

(ii) The equilibrium price and quantity for Farmer Fred labeled P_{F1} and Q_{F1}.

(iii) Farmer Fred's economic profit shaded in.

(b) As Farmer Fred is earning economic profits, what will happen in the market for corn as the economy adjusts to long-run equilibrium? In two newly drawn, side-by-side graphs of the corn market and Farmer Fred, show the following with correct labels:

(i) The initial equilibrium price and quantity in the corn market labeled P_{M1} and Q_{M1}.

(ii) The initial equilibrium price and quantity showing short-run economic profits for Farmer Fred labeled P_{F1} and Q_{F1}.

(iii) Label the new long-run equilibrium price and quantity in the corn market P_{M2} and Q_{M2}.

(iv) Label the new long-run equilibrium price and quantity in for Farmer Fred labeled P_{F2} and Q_{F2}.

(c) At the new long-run equilibrium, is Farmer Fred earning an economic profit, an economic loss, or a normal profit?

(d) Now assume that in the corn market, the price of corn has decreased 20%, while the quantity demanded at that price has increased 40%. Is the price elasticity of demand unit elastic, relatively elastic, perfectly elastic, relatively inelastic, or perfectly inelastic? Explain.

2. The graph below is for a profit-maximizing monopolist.

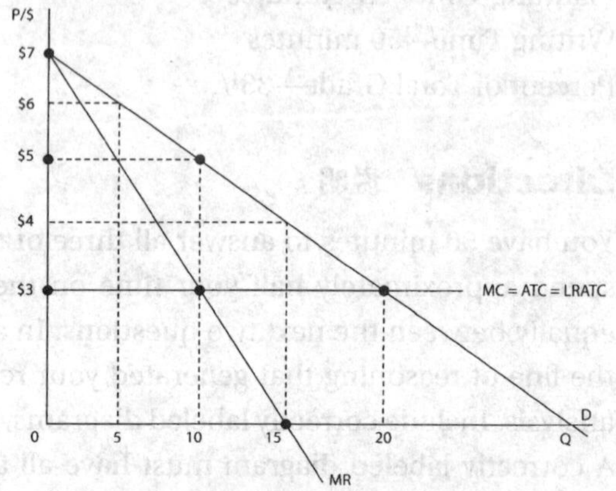

(a) Given the numbers in the monopoly graph, identify each of the following:

(i) The profit-maximizing quantity and price.

(ii) The difference in quantity between the profit-maximizing output and the allocatively efficient output level.

(iii) The area of deadweight loss, shaded in on the graph.

(b) At the profit-maximizing level of output, calculate the following. Please show your work and list your answer in dollars.

(i) The consumer surplus

(ii) The economic profit

(c) After what quantity of output would the monopolist not want to produce? Explain.

3. After an outbreak of the flu, a public relations campaign by the government is encouraging more people to get flu shots, arguing that it produces a positive externality.

(a) Draw a correctly labeled graph of this positive externality, showing each of the following.

(i) The equilibrium market price and quantity, labeled P_M and Q_M.

(ii) The socially optimal equilibrium price and quantity, labeled P_S and Q_S.

(iii) The area of deadweight loss, shaded in.

(b) At the market quantity, is the marginal social benefit greater than, less than, or equal to the marginal private benefit?

(c) What type of action would you recommend to bring production to the socially optimal quantity? Explain.

答案 ANSWER KEY
微观经济学 Microeconomics
MULTIPLE-CHOICE QUESTIONS 选择题

1. B	**16.** A	**31.** E	**46.** D
2. C	**17.** D	**32.** C	**47.** B
3. E	**18.** C	**33.** A	**48.** E
4. A	**19.** A	**34.** C	**49.** A
5. E	**20.** C	**35.** D	**50.** C
6. B	**21.** E	**36.** C	**51.** A
7. A	**22.** C	**37.** C	**52.** B
8. D	**23.** A	**38.** E	**53.** D
9. D	**24.** C	**39.** C	**54.** A
10. D	**25.** B	**40.** B	**55.** E
11. C	**26.** E	**41.** A	**56.** C
12. C	**27.** A	**42.** C	**57.** A
13. D	**28.** C	**43.** A	**58.** C
14. D	**29.** E	**44.** B	**59.** B
15. B	**30.** B	**45.** A	**60.** B

ANSWERS EXPLAINED
答案解析

MICROECONOMICS
微观经济学

Multiple-choice questions
选择题

1. **(B)** (Chapters 8,9) The other answers are all correct characteristics of a perfectly competitive industry. Products are homogeneous (the same, identical) under perfect competition.

2. **(C)** (Chapters 8,11) All of the other characteristics listed as choices are *not* appropriate for monopolistic competition. Choices **B**, **D**, and **E** are characteristics of perfect competition in the long run; choice **A** is characteristic of oligopoly and monopoly.

3. **(E)** (Chapters 8, 11) All of these are characteristics of an oligopoly. Review the Venn diagram in Chapter 8 for more characteristics of an oligopoly.

4. **(A)** (Chapters 8, 10) A profit-maximizing monopolist will always price in the elastic range of their demand curve. In the inelastic range of the demand curve, additional output will lower the price *and* decrease total revenue. (Unlike the elastic range or the demand curve, where total revenue increases as output increases.) Review the Venn diagram in Chapter 8 for more characteristics of a monopoly. To change the other choices to fit monopoly, you would have to rewrite choices **B**, **C**, **D**, and **E** as follows:

   B: P > MR
   C: downward sloping demand curve
   D: complete barriers to entry
   E: presence of economic profits

5. **(E)** (Chapters 8, 9, 10) With a monopoly, the price paid by consumers is greater than the cost of production, or P > MC. Thus, a monopolist is not allocatively efficient, which leads to monopolies having a deadweight loss. The optimal output from society's viewpoint is where P = MC, where perfectly competitive firms produce at long-run equilibrium. See the Venn diagram in Chapter 8 for more characteristics of a monopoly compared to perfect competition.

6. **(B)** (Chapter 13) The rule to follow is a tax for a negative externality and a subsidy for a positive externality. Both would internalize or correct the externality.

7. **(A)** (Chapter 13) See number 6.

8. **(D)** (Chapter 13) The marginal social cost is made up of the marginal private cost, but it also includes the costs imposed on other parties not involved in a transaction, known as marginal external costs. So the marginal private cost is added to the marginal external cost to equal the marginal social cost.

9. **(D)** (Chapter 7) This is simply definitional. See the chapter on costs for other definitions (Chapter 8).

10. **(D)** (Chapter 7) If marginal cost (MC) is less than average total cost (ATC), ATC will be decreasing as well. If MC is greater than ATC, ATC will be increasing. Therefore, MC intersects ATC at its minimum point. The exact same thing holds true for MC and average variable cost.

11. (C) (Chapter 12) If you look at the graph for this question, you will see the demand for workers curve (D) is equal to the marginal revenue product (MRP) of the workers. $MRP_L = MP_L \times P$/or MR_X). Thus, if the price for the product (P_X) stays constant and if the computerized system increases MP_L (marginal productivity), then MRP_L will increase illustrated as a shift of $D(MRP_L)$ to the right (shift to right, increase in demand for workers).

12. (C) (Chapter 4) The price floor is established since the market equilibrium price would be too low, e.g., when a \$5 market wage (price) for labor is deemed insufficient. So, the government says no one can be paid less than \$6 an hour (minimum wage).

13. (D) (Chapter 4) If interest rates for mortgage loans are 12% (market equilibrium) and the government says that this is too high, the government (state government under old usury laws) might establish a price ceiling of 10% (below the equilibrium rate).

14. (D) (Chapter 5) The consumer surplus is the difference between the highest price that a buyer would pay and the actual price paid. If you would have paid \$10 to see a movie but actually paid \$5, the consumer surplus would be \$5.

15. (B) (Chapter 12) First, construct a third column headed marginal product (MP), which would be the difference in pair sets for each additional worker hired (e.g., 30 MP as the difference between 40 pair sets for one worker, and 70 pair sets for two workers). Second, construct a fourth column headed MRP_L (marginal revenue product), which is the function of $MP_L \times P_X$. Then you will find the *number* of workers (first column) hired that will maximize the profits of the firm doing the hiring. This number will be the level of hiring at which $MRP_L \times P_L$ (or wage rate, which = \$1,250). Thus,

(1) Number of Workers	(2) Pair Sets Produced for Two Weeks	(3) MP_L	(4) MRP_L $MP_L \times P_L$
1	40	40	—
2	70	30	\$1,500
3	95	25	1,250
4	115	20	1,000
5	130	15	750
6	130	0	—

Since the pair sets are sold at \$50, column 4 is $MP_L \times P_L$(\$50). The profit-maximizing level is three workers whose MRP_L is \$1,250, which is equal to the wage paid every two weeks of \$1,250 per worker. If there is no level at which the wage rate = MRP_L, then the firm would hire the largest level of workers where MRP_L is greater than the wage rate paid.

16. (A) (Chapter 10) The reference is to the graph supplied for Questions 16–19. The profit-maximizing (best) output and the selling price are determined by the intersection of marginal cost and marginal revenue (MR = MC). The price, P_A, is read from the demand curve or by extending a vertical line from the intersection of MR and MC to the demand curve (point A); the related point on the price axis is P_A. Similarly, the best output is Q_A, which is found by dropping a vertical line from the intersection of MC and MR to the output (horizontal) axis.

17. (D) (Chapter 10) The fair return price is where price = average total cost, allowing the monopoly to break even and earn a normal profit, but zero economic profit.

18. (C) (Chapter 10) If a natural monopoly is regulated to produce where MC = D, this is the socially optimal output level, as the quantity being produced is the exact amount desired by society. However, at this point P < ATC, and thus the monopoly is incurring an economic loss and needs to be subsidized. The firm would be subsidized at the point at which P = MC (socially efficient, see 17 above) or the point of intersection of MC with the demand curve.

19. (A) (Chapter 10) We start with point A and the related point P_A (see answer 16). Then to complete the rectangle, we extend a vertical line from point B (MC = MR) to its intersection with average total cost (ATC) to find the per unit cost at point H. We then extend a line horizontally from H to its intersection with the price (vertical) axis at point P_H; thus, the rectangle P_AAHP_H. It is also helpful to know that profits or losses are (P – ATC) × Q.

20. (C) (Chapter 9) The correct answer is CBGE in reference to the graph supplied for Questions 20–23. Profits for the perfectly competitive firm are at the level of MR = MC. Remember, with perfect competition P = MR for the firm. The demand function is horizontal (P = MR). Also, MC intersects ATC at the minimum point of ATC. Thus, profits are maximized (with a market price of $37) at output level of 39 batteries. Point E is where MR = MC and a line dropped perpendicular to the output axis indicates a level of output of 39.

21. (E) (Chapter 9) With a price of $19, price is less than AVC at all levels of output. The minimum price of AVC (average variable cost) is $20 (point K). If the price is less than the average variable cost, the firm should shut down in the short run. Thus, the firm's best output is zero.

22. (C) (Chapter 9) At $22 (P = MR), MC = MR (intersection of MR ($22) with MC) at output level of 31,000 batteries. See point J.

23. (A) (Chapter 9) At a price of $22, P is less than ATC. This would result in a loss, yet is above the shut-down point.

24. (C) (Chapter 4) The government announcement would result in an increase in demand for red grape juice. With supply constant, the price for red grape juice would increase. The change would **not** be a change along a demand curve or a shift of the supply curve. There are only two choices that include an increase in demand with only one of them (C) showing an increase in price.

25. (B) (Chapter 4) We know for sure that the demand and supply curves will increase and shift to the right. This will definitely increase the new quantity, but price is indeterminate. On this question, it is not clear how far each curve will shift to the right, which determines the new price. So price is indeterminate.

26. (E) (Chapter 4) In the chapter on the basics of supply and demand, there is a list of factors that will cause shifts in supply and demand curves. When the government provides a subsidy to the producer, there is a decrease (in effect) in the cost of production that encourages more production (shift to the right of the supply curve).

27. **(A)** (Chapter 4) An increase in costs of production such as wage increases will lead to a decrease in supply.

28. **(C)** (Chapter 4) An increase in the price of coffee, a normal good, will cause the quantity demanded to decrease, moving along a fixed demand curve. Note that this is not a change in demand, as there is no shift in the curve, just a change in the quantity demanded.

29. **(E)** (Chapter 2) Absolute advantage is easy to find and is just the maximum amount that can be produced of a good. So it is a tie for sugar, but Japan has the absolute advantage in producing wheat. Even if one country has an absolute advantage in producing both products, a country can still benefit from trade. A country should specialize in the product in which it has a lower opportunity cost, which is a comparative advantage. To calculate comparative advantage, is it helpful to put the numbers in a chart (see following example) to calculate the opportunity cost. To calculate the opportunity cost, take the opposite number, and put it over the side for which you are calculating opportunity cost. For example, Japan's opportunity cost of producing wheat is 20/40, or ½. For Colombia, it's 20/20, or 1. So Japan has the comparative advantage in wheat, as their relative opportunity cost (½) is lower than Colombia (1). Likewise, Colombia has the comparative advantage in sugar, their opportunity cost (1) is lower than Japan's (2), and they will specialize in sugar.

	Wheat	Sugar
Japan	40	20
Colombia	20	20

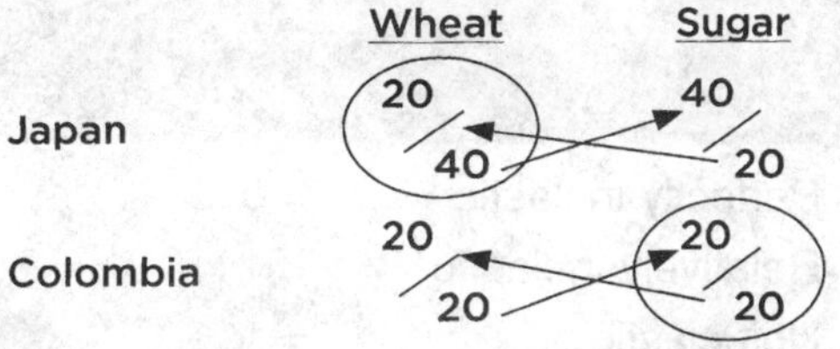

30. **(B)** (Chapter 11) This is the typical tendency for monopolistic competitors—price equals average total cost (not at minimum ATC), allowing firms normal profits (zero economic profits). At MC = MR, price is at OD and output is at OX.

31. **(E)** (Chapter 11) See the answer for 30 above for zero economic profits. The firm operates inefficiently since ATC is above minimum level, and P > MC.

32. **(C)** (Chapter 7) With economies of scale, as production increases there are savings in average costs of production. When output increases more than proportionately to increases in input, the firm is getting more output per added input or, in effect, there is a decrease in cost of production.

33. **(A)** (Chapter 7) In other words (in contrast to the other answers or choices), supply is able to adjust fully to changes in demand in the long run. In the short run, all inputs are not variable; some are fixed in quantity. In the short run, supply is unable to adjust fully to the changes in demand.

34. **(C)** (Chapter 5) Using the price elasticity of demand formula, 30/15 = an elasticity coefficient of 2, which makes demand relatively elastic.

$$\frac{\%\ \Delta\ \text{Quantity}}{\%\ \Delta\ \text{Price}}$$

Table 5.2

Elasticity Coefficient Value	
Type of Elasticity	**Elasticity Value**
Perfectly inelastic	= 0
Relatively inelastic	< 1
Unit elastic	= 1
Relatively elastic	> 1
Perfectly elastic	∞ (infinity)

35. (D) (Chapter 5) Only one copy available means the supply is fixed (vertical supply curve) and does not change with changes in price (perfectly inelastic).

36. (C) (Chapter 9) This is the only choice that is not a characteristic of perfectly competitive markets; instead, it is a characteristic of oligopolies or other forms of imperfect competition.

37. (C) (Chapter 7) The two types of costs, fixed and variable, are added together to get total cost. Variable costs can change in the short run, while fixed costs stay constant in the short run.

38. (E) (Chapter 11) A major characteristic of monopolistically competitive firms is that they produce where P = ATC, but not at minimum ATC, only when ATC is falling, which results in excess capacity. Also, there is strong competition, as firms can easily enter and exit.

39. (C) (Chapter 10) Consumer surplus is that excess of utility over price paid for goods or services. If you measure total utility as the area under the demand curve up to the amount of output consumed (AEKO), and if you subtract the cost (GOKE), you are left with the consumer surplus, triangle AGE. This is in reference to the graph for Questions 39–41.

40. (B) (Chapter 10) To find the deadweight loss, find the difference between the allocatively efficient output (quantity K, where P = MC) and the monopolist's profit-maximizing quantity (quantity J, where MR = MC). Between these two quantities, the area above marginal cost and below the demand curve is the deadweight loss; hence, the answer area BFE.

41. (A) (Chapter 10) The original surplus is AGE. If the monopolist's profit is HGFB and if the deadweight loss is BFE, then the reduced consumer surplus must be the remaining triangle, AHB.

42. (C) (Chapter 5) The after-tax price is $6, so the consumer surplus is the area under the demand curve, and above the price of $6, or area A. While consumers pay $6, the tax is $4 so the sellers only receive $2 after the tax. The producer surplus is the area above the supply curve, below the price received by sellers, area G.

43. (A) (Chapter 5) The tax incidence is the amount of the tax burden sellers and buyers pay. The tax burden for consumers is the difference between the before and after tax prices × quantity, or ($6 – $4) × q, and that is the area BC. For producers, it is the difference between the price received before and after the tax × quantity, or ($4 – $2) × q, and that is the area F.

44. (B) (Chapter 5) From where the supply curve + tax meets the demand curve, head to the axes to see the price ($6) and quantity (10) for buyers. From the after-tax equilibrium quantity of 10, go to the original supply curve before tax, and over to the price axis for the price received by sellers ($2). Or take the after-tax price minus the size of the tax to get the after-tax price received by sellers ($6 – $4 = $2).

45. **(A)** (Chapter 8) This is an essential concept to understand, diminishing marginal returns or productivity, the eventual decline in productivity as more and more of a variable input are added in short-run production.

46. **(D)** (Chapter 12) This is a very important concept, derived demand.

47. **(B)** (Chapter 4) If the increases in price of one good causes demand to go up for another product, then they are substitute goods, like coffee and tea. If a price increase of one good causes demand to go down for another product, then they are complementary goods, like hot dogs and hot dog buns.

48. **(E)** (Chapter 12) A monopsony, where one firm controls the market for labor, hires less labor at and at lower wages than would a competitive labor market. The quantity hired is where Marginal Factor Cost (MFC) = Marginal Revenue Product (MRP), but note the wage paid is at the supply curve at the quantity where MFC and MRP meet, not the wage where MFC = MRP. A competitive labor market would have a wage of $10 at Q_2.

49. **(A)** (Chapter 12) All firms will continue to hire up until the point where Marginal Revenue Product (MRP) = the Marginal Factor Cost (MFC). If the MRP > MFC, a firm will continue to hire until MRP = MFC.

50. **(C)** (Chapter 12) When a production possibilities curve has this shape, it is indicative of increasing opportunity costs. This means resources are not completely adaptable to other uses so as more of one product is produced, gradually more and more of the other product is sacrificed.

51. **(A)** (Chapter 7) When output is 0, total cost is $20, meaning that is a fixed cost. As output moves from 3 to 4, total cost moves from $50 to $80. The difference between these is the marginal cost, or $30. The average total cost is calculated by taking the total cost at an output of 4, $80, divided by 4, which is $20.

52. **(B)** (Chapter 11) A dominant strategy is a player's best choice regardless of the opponent's actions. Firm X's dominant strategy is to go high and earn $60 if Firm Y goes high and $50 if Y goes low. If X went low and Y goes high then Firm X would earn $50 as opposed to $60. If X went low and Y goes low, X would earn $15 as opposed to $40 if Y went high. Firm Y does not have dominant strategy as if X goes high, Y would be better off going high, but if X went low, Y would be better off going low.

53. **(D)** (Chapter 11) If the two firms collude, they would both price high, as this would give each the highest daily profit.

54. **(A)** (Chapter 7) Economic profit is different from accounting profit in that it considers both implicit and explicit costs. She has $20,000 in accounting profit, but she could have earned $30,000 as an artist and earned $2,000 in interest if she invested her restaurant money. So she could have earned a total of $32,000 as an artist compared to $20,000 as a restaurateur. So her economic loss is $12,000.

55. **(E)** (Chapter 10) For a nonprice-discriminating monopolist, marginal revenue is less than price. For a monopolist to increase sales, he must lower prices for all buyers. So when price falls for all buyers, marginal revenue falls at a greater rate than price. For any firm that has a downward sloping demand curve and charges all customers the same prices, marginal revenue will be less than price.

56. **(C)** (Chapter 4) The decreasing supply in the hot dog market will increase the price of hot dogs. As mustard and hot dogs are complementary goods, the increase in price of hot dogs will decrease the demand for mustard, shifting the mustard demand curve to the left. If the price of one good increasing causes demand to decrease for another good, they are complementary goods. If the price of one good increasing causes another good's demand to increase, they are substitute goods.

57. **(A)** (Chapter 13) The bigger the curve or "banana" shape of the Lorenz curve, the greater income inequality. This graph shows the degree of income inequality in a country. So line C displays greater income inequality, and line A shows perfect income equality.

58. **(C)** (Chapters 4, 5) If labor demand is relatively inelastic, firms will continue to hire workers despite wage increases. So as wages increase, firms with relatively inelastic labor demand curves will continue to hire more labor than if labor demand was more elastic, where labor demand would be more sensitive to wage increases.

59. **(B)** (Chapters 13) A regressive tax takes a greater percentage of total income from lower income groups. So even though this seems like a proportional tax, lower income groups may spend all of their income, whereas higher income groups are more likely to have saved some income. Lower income groups are thus likely to pay a greater percentage of their income on the food tax.

60. **(B)** (Chapter 6) The formula for utility maximization is $MU_x/P_x = MU_y/P_y$. When solving these problems, it is helpful to also make a chart of the MU/P for each good. Start by choosing and circling the goods that give the highest utility per dollar on your chart and continue until you run out of money. As you can see on the table below, the utility-maximizing combination of going to the movies and trampoline park 3 times each, given the $45 to spend, is correct.

Number of Times	Marginal Utility from Movies	Marginal Utility/Price, MU/P	Marginal Utility from Trampoline Park	Marginal Utility/Price, MU/P
1	30	(3)	15	(3)
2	20	(2)	10	(2)
3	10	(1)	5	(1)
4	5	.5	2	.40
5	0	0	1	.2

FREE-RESPONSE ANSWERS 开放式题目答案

Here are the correct answers for the Free-Response section. Please be advised that you can earn partial credit if at least some of your answer is correct. You can also receive points for labeling your graphs correctly, even if you make the wrong shift.

1.

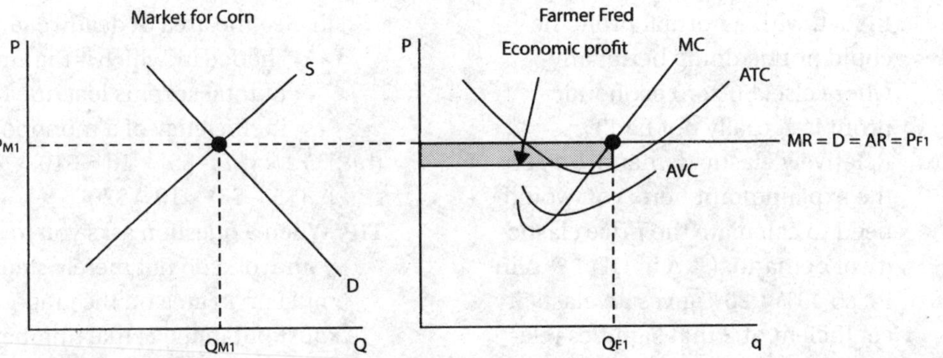

(a) Note that Farmer Fred is a price-taker and takes the price in the corn market. The profit-maximizing quantity is at MR = MC, from there head to the demand curve and quantity axis for P_{F1} and Q_{F1}. Note that a perfectly competitive firm has a perfectly elastic demand curve, labeled MRDARP (Marginal revenue, demand, average revenue, and price). P at the end is labeled P_{F1} giving the correct point for the correct label. For labeling profit, go to the profit-maximizing quantity, and start drawing the profit box between the demand curve and the ATC, and head over to the price axis to complete the profit rectangle.

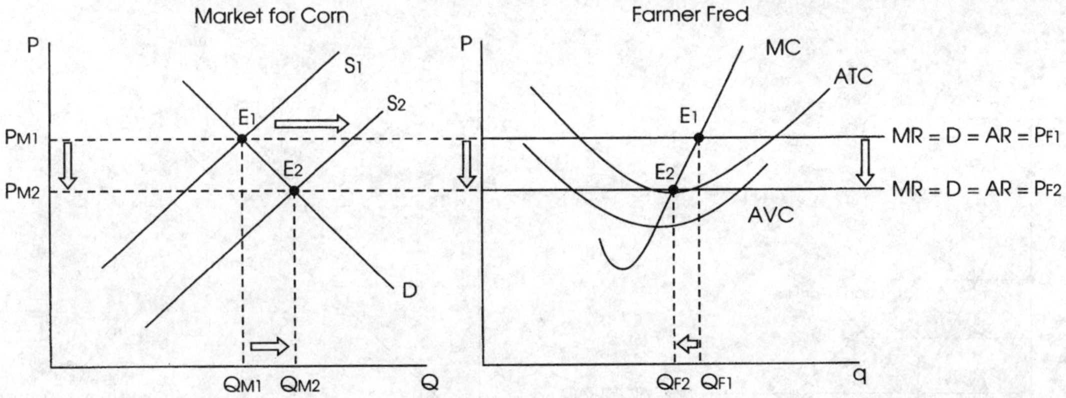

(b) Economic profits being made in a perfectly competitive market attract competition, as there is easy entry and exit for firms. The economic profit causes the supply curve in the market on the left to increase, causing the market price of corn to fall to P_{M2}. Farmer Fred has no control over the price at which he sells, so he "takes" that price, and his economic profit is gone. His price then falls to MR = D = AR = P_{F2}, and the quantity falls to Q_{F2} at his new equilibrium, E_2, at the minimum of the ATC.

(c) Fred is earning a normal profit because price = ATC. A normal profit = zero economic profit. (Remember the difference between accounting and economic profit? Zero economic profit does not mean there is no accounting profit. In fact, with a normal profit, he could not be doing better anywhere else. So zero economic profit is actually not bad!)

(d) Relatively elastic demand. To get the explain point here, you would need to calculate the price elasticity of demand. (% Δ in QD / % Δ in P), so 40% / 20% gives an elasticity coefficient of 2 that signifies relatively elastic demand. Here is the chart for elasticity coefficients that is important to know.

Elasticity Coefficient Values

Type of Elasticity	Elasticity Value
Relatively elastic	> 1
Perfectly elastic	∞ (infinity)
Relatively inelastic	< 1
Perfectly inelastic	= 0
Unit elastic	= 1

2.

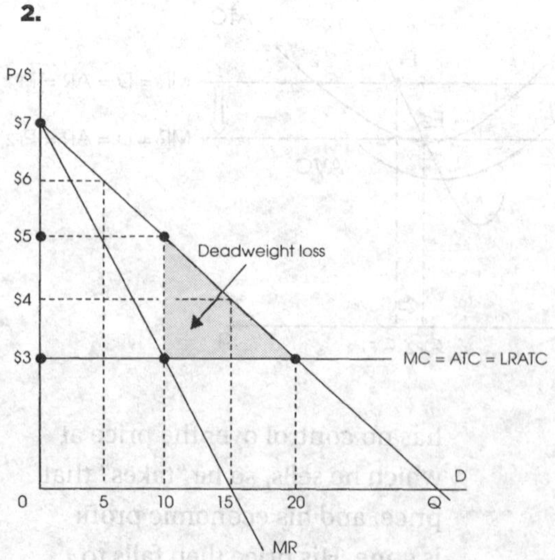

(a) i. The profit-maximizing quantity is 10. Find MR = MC and go down to the Q-axis to find the quantity, and for price, head to the demand curve from Q = 10 and over to the price axis to find the price of $5.

ii. 20 – 10 = 10. The allocatively efficient output is where P = MC, or the quantity 20. A monopoly does not produce at the allocatively efficient quantity.

iii. See the area of deadweight loss shaded in, which is the amount of total surplus lost due to the inefficiency of a monopoly.

(b) i. ½ × ($7 – $5) × 10 = $10

ii. ($5 – $3) × 10 = $20

TIP: When a question asks you to show your work, do not merely state a formula or an area on the graph. You must put in the actual numbers.

(c) 15. Producing beyond this range is when marginal revenue is negative and total revenue is decreasing, or the inelastic portion of the demand curve. Note on the graph that marginal revenue goes below the Q-axis here. A monopolist always produces in the elastic range of the demand curve. If a monopoly lowers the price of a product in the inelastic range, both total revenue and marginal revenue fall.

3.

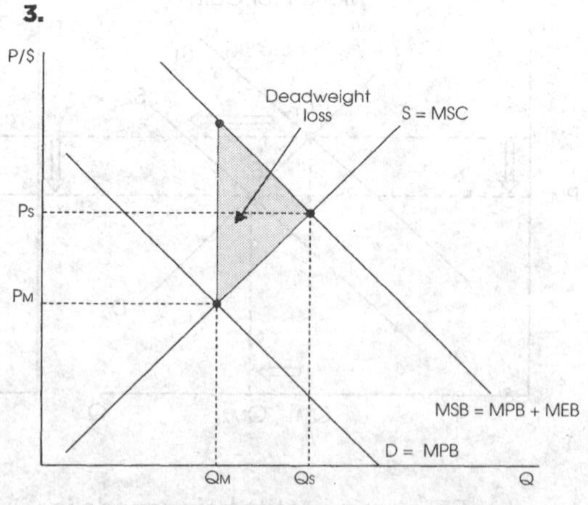

(a) i. The private market underproduces when a positive externality is present. The market quantity is Marginal Private Benefit (MPB) equals the Marginal Social Cost (MSC).

ii. The socially optimal output a good is where MSB = MSC.

(b) i. To correctly find the area of the deadweight loss, imagine it is an arrow pointing to the socially optimal quantity, originating from the side with two curves, with the length of the arrow tip the difference between Q_M and Q_S. It would be pointing the other way with a negative externality.

ii. The MSB is greater than the MPB at the market quantity. The difference between these two points is the Marginal External Benefit (MEB) that the market does not produce.

(c) An effective policy solution would be a per-unit subsidy equal to the Marginal External Benefit. A per-unit subsidy lowers the marginal cost of production by giving money to a firm for each additional unit produced. As a review, a lump-sum subsidy gives a fixed payment to a firm regardless of production quantity. A per-unit tax (for negative externalities) is more effective for solving externalities than a lump-sum subsidy or tax.

Macroeconomics

宏观经济学

As you work toward achieving that 5 on your AP Macroeconomics exam, here are five essentials that you **MUST** know above everything else:

Barron's Essential 5

巴朗总结的五个要点

1 **Understand the aggregate supply/aggregate demand model.** This concept is critical for doing well on the exam. It is likely to appear on a free-response question and will be used to answer multiple-choice questions.

- As with any diagram, be able to label all axes and curves.
- You should know what can shift the aggregate supply and aggregate demand curves.
- You should be able to use the model to conclude what will happen in the long run and in the short run when one or both of the curves shifts.

2 **Vocabulary is important.** Very few, if any, of the questions on the AP exam will ask you to define a specific term but you need to know the definition of technical ones.

- For instance, a multiple-choice question may ask about closing an inflationary gap. You will be at a total loss if the term "inflationary gap" is not in your vocabulary.
- Be sure you know the terms listed at the end of each chapter.

3 **Monetary and fiscal policy are critical concepts.** One of the most important things a student learns in introductory macroeconomics is that monetary and fiscal policy can be used to help fight unemployment and inflation.

- Be able to demonstrate how monetary and fiscal policy work on an aggregate supply/aggregate demand diagram.
- There are several reasons why monetary and fiscal policy may not work. You should be able to list and explain these reasons.
- Monetary and fiscal policy are not as effective in economies that rely heavily on international trade and have flexible exchange rates. You should be able to explain why.

4 **Diagrams are more important than formulas.** Important formulas are listed at the end of each chapter. However, calculators are not allowed on the exam, so complex calculations will not be required.

- Easy formulas such as Fisher's hypothesis or the formula for the unemployment rate are more likely to come into play on the exam.
- Specific diagrams, such as the supply and demand for loanable funds, are often required. Be sure to label all axes and curves. If you forget a label, use something general like "Q" for quantity or "D" for demand.

5 **Be definite in your conclusions to free-response questions.** Some questions are complex and have different conclusions in different circumstances. Nevertheless, be definite in your response.

- If you use the wrong approach on a free-response question but your conclusion is correct, you will still earn points. State your conclusion clearly.
- You can earn points on a free-response question just for having the appropriate graph correctly labeled. To obtain full credit, explain what is happening on the graph and reach the correct conclusion.

The National Economic Accounts 国民经济核算

14

- → GROSS DOMESTIC PRODUCT (GDP)
- → REAL GDP
- → THE UNDERGROUND ECONOMY
- → GROSS NATIONAL PRODUCT (GNP)
- → NATIONAL INCOME
- → PERSONAL INCOME

THE ACCOUNTS 核算

The National Economic Accounts (NEA) make up a comprehensive group of statistics that measure various aspects of the economy's performance. For instance, if everyone's income in the United States was summed together, how much would that be? The figure for personal income in 2013 was $14,134.7 billion. What were corporate profits in 2013? $2,102.1 billion. Personal income and corporate profits are two examples of the hundreds of statistics included in NEA.

NEA includes a variety of measures of income and production. The most recent updates on these figures are published by the Department of Commerce in a periodical titled the "Survey of Current Business." On the Internet, updates are available at *www.bea.gov*, the home page of the Bureau of Economic Analysis (BEA), an agency within the Department of Commerce.

GROSS DOMESTIC PRODUCT 国内生产总值

The premier statistic for measuring the overall performance of the economy is gross domestic product (GDP). GDP measures the dollar value of production within the nation's borders. Generally speaking, the more that is produced, the healthier the economy.

The BEA provides "flash" estimates of GDP for each quarter about 30 days after the quarter ends, but these rough estimates are subject to large revisions. The annual estimates of GDP are more reliable, but they, too, are subject to revision.

An amazing feature of these estimates is that they are available on such a timely basis. Consider all of the goods and services produced in the United States in a year, from toothpicks and cellular phones to haircuts and surgery. How does the BEA keep track of all this production? For 2013, GDP was estimated to be $16,799.7 billion.

How did the BEA arrive at this figure? A small army of statisticians and analysts keeps track of production and sales of a wide variety of goods and services. For instance, one person is responsible for Popsicle sticks, toothpicks, and tongue depressors. This person gets in touch with the major suppliers and retailers of these products. From this survey an estimate of the number of toothpicks sold is obtained. There is a difference between the number of toothpicks sold and the number produced, but this difference will be allowed for later. The survey of manufacturers and retailers also yields an average price of toothpicks. Then the number of toothpicks sold is multiplied by their price to get the dollar value of toothpick sales.

The dollar values of all other products sold are added to the figure for toothpicks to obtain an estimate of total sales of goods and services. The resulting figure is known as "final sales" and is part of NEA. But it is not GDP. GDP measures *production* not sales. There may be goods that are produced but not sold. They will show up in inventories at the manufacturers or at the retailers. Therefore, the change in business inventories is added to final sales to arrive at GDP.

Table 14.1 shows the calculation of GDP for a hypothetical economy that produces only two products—pizza and soda. In the year 2012, four pizzas are produced at an average retail price of \$10; 12 sodas are produced at a price of \$2. GDP is \$64. In the year 2013, pizza production is up to five pizzas and the price has increased to \$11. Soda production is up to 15 units, but the price has fallen to \$1. GDP is \$70.

Table 14.1

Calculating GDP

Year 2012		
Production	**Price**	**Value**
4 Pizzas	\$10	\$40
12 Sodas	\$2	\$24
		GDP = \$64
Year 2013		
Production	**Price**	**Value**
5 Pizzas	\$11	\$55
15 Sodas	\$1	\$15
		GDP = \$70

This is a general overview of how GDP is estimated. In practice, many more complications arise. Some of these complications will come to light as we examine the expenditure and the income approaches to calculating GDP.

THE EXPENDITURES APPROACH 支出算法

Consumption Expenditures 消费支出

If you look up the estimates of GDP online don't expect to see the dollar value of toothpicks sold or produced. That level of detail would require a publication much thicker than the

Oxford English Dictionary. Instead, the BEA lumps together all the goods and services sold to households and calls this consumption expenditures.

Government Expenditures 政府支出

However, state, local, and federal governments also make expenditures. The things that are produced and sold to governments are summed together and referred to as government expenditures. Some of the products that governments buy are unique to this category. For instance, fighter jets are sold to our federal government but not to individual households. On the other hand, our government purchases many of the same items bought by households, such as personal computers; but the value of personal computers purchased by the government will be different than that of households.

Investment Expenditures 投资支出

Expenditures by businesses on plant and equipment are called investment expenditures; thus, the term "investment" means something very different in its economic sense. It does not refer to households buying stocks or bonds. The complete definition of investment is business expenditures on plant and equipment plus residential construction plus the change in business inventories. The change in business inventories was mentioned in the previous section. It changes the figure for final sales into GDP. The BEA lumps the change in inventories in with business spending on plant and equipment and residential construction to get what it calls investment.

Exports and Imports 出口和进口

Many goods and services are produced here and sold abroad. These are called exports. Some of the expenditures made by households, government, and businesses will be on goods and services from abroad. These imports should not be included in our GDP since they represent production outside our nation's borders. That is why imports are subtracted from exports to get "net exports."

GDP represents production. Some of the goods and services produced go to households, some to government, some to businesses, and some are sold abroad. Imports are subtracted out because these products were not made domestically, yet they are counted in consumption expenditures by households, purchases by government, and investment by firms.

The expenditure approach to calculating GDP is often summarized with the formula:

$$GDP = C + I + G + X$$

where C is consumption expenditures by households
I is investment by firms
G is government purchases
X is net exports = exports − imports

The formula appears deceptively simple. Remember that to obtain the figure for C, consumption expenditures, quite a bit of effort is required. The average price and quantity sold of millions of products must be gathered. The same must be done for I, G, and X.

Table 14.2 shows the components of the expenditures approach to calculating GDP with their values for 2013. Notice that about 70 percent of all the goods and services produced go to households.

Table 14.2

The Expenditure Approach to GDP—2013

(Billion of Dollars)	
Consumption expenditures	11,501.5
Government expenditures	3,125.5
Investment	2,670.0
Net exports	−497.3
GDP	16,799.7

Source: U.S. Department of Commerce, Bureau of Economic Analysis

THE INCOME APPROACH 收入算法

The BEA takes the trouble to calculate GDP in a manner completely different from the expenditures approach outlined above. This second way of calculating GDP is known as the income approach. The income approach yields several statistics that are incorporated into NEA and provides a check on the expenditures approach.

Theoretically, both techniques for calculating GDP will result in exactly the same figure because when anything is produced, whether it is a stick of gum or a skyscraper, just enough income is generated in the production process to equal the value of what is produced.

Consider a toaster that retails for $15. Suppose it costs $10 to manufacture:

Labor	**$6**
Materials	**$3**
Overhead	**$1**

Since the toaster retails for $15, then $5 in profits were made when it was sold. So, if everyone who had anything to do with the manufacture of the toaster chipped in the income they made, it would equal $15 exactly. Workers made $6; raw material owners made $3; the utility company (overhead) made $1; and the owner of the toaster company made $5. Altogether, this comes to $15.

Notice that if the toaster sold for $15.01, then $5.01 in profits would have been earned and the principle would still hold true: whenever anything is produced, just enough is earned to buy it back. Therefore, an alternate way to measure GDP, which measures production, would be to add up all the income that was earned in the economy. That is the income approach to calculating GDP.

Table 14.3 outlines the income approach for calculating GDP. Wages and salaries are the predominant type of income. But there is also proprietors' income, rental income, and interest income. Corporate profits must also be included because this represents corporate income and corporations are owned by their shareholders. There are some adjustments that must be made once all the types of income are summed together. Specifically, indirect business taxes (such as business licenses) and depreciation must be added in.

Table 14.3

The Income Approach to GDP—2013

(Billion of Dollars)	
Compensation of employees	8,859.4
Proprietors' income	1,348.8
Rental income	590.6
Interest income	469.2
Corporate profits	2,102.1
Taxes on production and imports	1,088.0
Net business transfer payments	124.4
Government enterprise surplus	−40.1
Depreciation	+2,257.3
GDP	16,799.7

Source: U.S. Department of Commerce, Bureau of Economic Analysis

ADJUSTING FOR PRICE CHANGES 价格变动调整

GDP measures production, but one cannot conclude that more was produced simply because this year's GDP was greater than last because prices may have risen. The rise in prices could offset a decline in production volume, resulting in a higher figure for GDP. Clearly, if the prices of the goods and services produced changes, so will GDP, regardless of production.

There is, however, a simple way to correct for price changes: When calculating GDP for different years, use prices from just one of those years. This way the prices are constant from one year to the next and any change in GDP must be due to a change in production.

The BEA routinely makes this correction and the resulting figure is known as "real GDP," or "constant-dollar GDP." In order to make the distinction, regular GDP is sometimes referred to as "nominal" or "current-dollar GDP." The year from which prices are taken to calculate real GDP is called the base year. It does not matter which year is chosen as the base year. The important feature is that prices are held constant, so that any changes in real GDP are the result of changes in the amount of production.

TIP

Any economic statistic with the term "real" inserted in front of it means that statistic has been adjusted for inflation, i.e., real interest rate, real consumer spending.

Table 14.4 shows nominal and real GDP over the years. An astute reader could deduce that 2009 is the base year since real and nominal GDP are equivalent in that year. Once nominal and real GDP have been calculated, it is a simple matter to obtain a measure of price changes. But this statistic will be discussed in the next chapter when inflation and price indexes are taken up.

THE UNDERGROUND ECONOMY 地下经济

Each year there are trillions of dollars of goods and services that are produced and never counted in GDP. All of this production falls into what is called the underground economy. The first thing that comes to mind with regard to the underground economy is illegal items and activities, but illegal production and ill-gotten income are the smaller part of the underground economy.

Table 14.4

Nominal and Real GDP

	Nominal GDP (billions of $)	Real GDP (billions of chained 2009 $)
2003	11,512.2	13,270.0
2004	12,277.0	13,774.0
2005	13,095.4	14,235.6
2006	13,857.9	14,615.2
2007	14,480.3	14,876.8
2008	14,720.3	14,833.6
2009	14,417.9	14,417.9
2010	14,958.3	14,779.4
2011	15,533.8	15,052.4
2012	16,244.6	15,470.7
2013	16,799.7	15,761.3

Source: U.S. Department of Commerce, Bureau of Economic Analysis

Marry your auto mechanic, the saying goes, and you will lower GDP. This is true because when you took your car to the shop to be repaired, the BEA was able to estimate the transaction and include it in GDP under household consumption. Now that the mechanic is your spouse, the auto repairs are done out back under the shade tree. The BEA does not attempt to measure this sort of production.

Anything households do for themselves and that does not pass through a market goes unmeasured. This amounts to quite a bit of production. The backyard gardens, the lawn maintenance, the cleaning, the babysitting, etc. One estimate of underground household production puts it at 30 percent of official GDP.

Illegal gambling services, prostitution, and drugs are not counted in official GDP estimates. The housepainter who insists on being paid in cash to avoid taxes is part of the underground economy.

Adding together the legal and illegal sides of the underground economy, some analysts get a figure that is 150 percent of the official figure. That implies that production in the United States in 2013 was closer to $25,000.0 billion than the official figure of $16,799.7 billion.

OTHER THINGS NOT COUNTED IN GDP
GDP中未计算的其他项目

The underground economy is a subset of total production that is not counted in GDP but, technically speaking, should be. The illegal nature of the goods and services involved often prohibits estimation. However, there is a list of things that are not counted in GDP and rightly so.

1. For instance, it would be incorrect to count **secondhand sales** in GDP. When you sell your 1997 Ford truck, this does not represent production in the current year. The truck was counted in the GDP of 1997 and there is no reason to count it, or any portion of it, again simply because it is being resold.

2. **Transactions that are purely financial** are not, and should not be, counted in GDP. If you buy 100 shares of IBM stock, this does not directly represent any new production. Someone got your money and you got their shares of IBM. This swap does not affect GDP except for any brokerage services provided.
3. **Intermediate sales** are not included in GDP. These are sales to firms that will incorporate the item into their final product. An example will help here. When a corporation that makes Popsicles buys Popsicle sticks, this is an intermediate sale. When a person buys a Popsicle, he cannot avoid buying the stick as well. This latter transaction is counted in GDP and valued at the price of the Popsicle and the stick. So the stick would be counted twice if the purchase of sticks by the manufacturer was included in GDP and the final sale to the consumer was also counted.

   As another example of an intermediate transaction, the purchase of flour by a baker is not counted in GDP because the flour will get counted when the bread is purchased by a household. However, when a baker buys a delivery truck, this is not an intermediate transaction and the purchase gets counted in GDP under investment expenditures.

OTHER MEASURES IN THE NATIONAL ECONOMIC ACCOUNTS
国民经济核算中的其他计量

Table 14.5 highlights several other important measures in NEA aside from GDP. Again, GDP measures overall production, and therefore income as well, in the economy. Gross national product is similar to GDP except GNP includes production by American workers abroad and excludes production by foreign workers in America.

Table 14.5

GDP and Other Measures in NEA—2013

(Billions of Dollars)	
Gross Domestic Product (GDP)	16,799.7
Gross National Product (GNP)	17,057.5
National Income (NI)	14,542.4
Personal Income (PI)	14,134.7
Disposable Personal Income (DPI)	12,476.2

Source: U.S. Department of Commerce, Bureau of Economic Analysis

Another figure, national income (NI), measures the income earned by households and profits earned by firms after adjusting for depreciation and indirect business taxes. NI is often defined as the income earned by all the factors of production. The factors of production are land, labor, and capital.

NI represents the income earned by households and firms, but personal income (PI) represents the income received by households only.

Finally, disposable personal income (DPI) is the income of households after taxes have been paid. It is easily derived by subtracting personal taxes from PI. Disposable income represents the discretionary income of households. It can be spent or saved.

SUMMARY 小结

- NEA are a bank of internally consistent statistics that measure various aspects of the economy's performance. Basically, NEA measure production and income in their various forms. An implicit assumption behind the statistics is that more production and more income means a better economy.
- Some economists have questioned this assumption. Are we really better off when we produce more gadgets and gizmos, and pollute the environment in the process? Is it possible for more to be produced and more income to be earned while the quality of life deteriorates? Another criticism of NEA concerns leisure time. Don't rising production levels sometimes result in less leisure time? If so, this is not reflected in the statistics where the negative side effects of increased production levels are not taken into account.
- Despite these criticisms, NEA are the best measures available for gauging the economy's health. One final note: Other nations have similar statistics, but they may not be defined or collected in the same way. There are, however, some organizations that generate and publish international data that are comparable across countries. Putting the statistics on a per capita basis also facilitates international comparisons.

Table 14.6

GDP and GDP per Capita for Selected Countries, 2012

Country	GDP (billions of $)	GDP per Capita ($ per person)
Canada	1,779	51,206
China	8,227	6,091
Japan	5,961	46,731
Switzerland	631	78,928
United Kingdom	2,476	38,920
United States	16,245	51,749

Source: World Bank

TERMS 术语

Consumption Expenditures the dollar value of all the goods and services sold to households

Disposable Personal Income (DPI) the income of households after taxes have been paid

Government Expenditures the dollar value of goods and services sold to governments

Gross Domestic Product (GDP) dollar value of production within a nation's borders

Gross National Product (GNP) dollar value of production by a country's citizens

Intermediate Sales sales to firms that will incorporate the item into their final product

Investment Expenditures expenditures by businesses on plant and equipment plus residential construction and the change in business inventories

National Economic Accounts (NEA) a comprehensive group of statistics that measures various aspects of the economy's performance

National Income (NI) the income earned by households and profits earned by firms after subtracting depreciation and indirect business taxes

Net Exports exports minus imports

Personal Income (PI) income received by households

Real GDP GDP adjusted for price changes

Underground Economy all the illegal production of goods and services and legal production that does not pass through markets

FORMULAS 公式

GDP = C + I + G + X

$$\text{GDP per Capita} = \frac{\text{GDP}}{\text{Population}}$$

MULTIPLE-CHOICE REVIEW QUESTIONS 选择题

1. GDP is calculated for each ______ by ______.
   (A) quarter; The Bureau of Economic Analysis
   (B) week; The Bureau of Economic Analysis
   (C) month; The Bureau of Economic Analysis
   (D) month; The Bureau of Labor Statistics
   (E) quarter; The Bureau of Labor Statistics

2. "Flash" estimates of GDP
   (A) are subject to revision.
   (B) do not require revision.
   (C) are available after a thirty-day lag.
   (D) both (A) and (C)
   (E) both (B) and (C)

3. According to the way in which economists use the word, the bulk of "investment" is done by
   (A) households.
   (B) businesses.
   (C) government.
   (D) foreigners.
   (E) all of the above.

4. In the equation GDP = C + I + G + X, X stands for
   (A) exports.
   (B) expenditures.
   (C) exports minus imports.
   (D) imports minus exports.
   (E) export taxes.

5. GDP measures
   (A) production within a nation's borders.
   (B) production by a nation's citizens wherever they may be.
   (C) income earned by the factors of production plus depreciation and indirect business taxes.
   (D) (B) and (C)
   (E) (A) and (C)

6. Suppose a nation produces only two goods, pizza and soda. In 2015, 20 pizzas are sold at $4 each, and 10 sodas are sold at $2 each. If the price of pizza was $2 each and the price of soda was $1 each in 2014, the base year, then nominal 2015 GDP is
   (A) $100, real 2002 GDP is $50, and the GDP deflator is 50.
   (B) $50, real 2002 GDP is $100, and the GDP deflator is 200.
   (C) $50, real 2002 GDP is $100, and the GDP deflator is 2.
   (D) $40, real 2002 GDP is $100, and the GDP deflator is 50.
   (E) $100, real 2002 GDP is $50, and the GDP deflator is 200.

7. Imagine an economy that produces only two goods, cheese and crackers. Calculate GDP for this economy if cheese retails for $3 a pound and 10 pounds are produced while crackers sell for $2 a pound and 20 pounds are produced.
   (A) $35
   (B) $1,200
   (C) $70
   (D) $150
   (E) Not enough information is given to calculate GDP.

8. Assume Country Z only produces hot dogs and buns. Given the table below, what is the value of GDP in Country Z?

Production	*Price*
4 hot dogs	$1.00
4 buns	$0.50

   (A) $1.50
   (B) $12.00
   (C) $6.00
   (D) $8.00
   (E) $4.50

9. If XYZ Corporation buys an original Matisse painting to hang in its board room, then

(A) GDP decreases by the amount of the purchase because C decreases.
(B) GDP increases by the amount of the purchase because I increases.
(C) GDP is unaffected because it is a second hand sale.
(D) GDP decreases because I decreases.
(E) I increases, but C decreases.

10. The cabbages you grow in your summer garden are

(A) counted in GDP under C.
(B) counted in GDP under I.
(C) counted in GDP but not NDP.
(D) not counted in GDP.
(E) counted in final sales but not GDP.

11. If your grandparents have a new home built for their retirement, this would primarily affect

(A) consumption.
(B) government purchases.
(C) investment.
(D) exports.
(E) imports.

12. GDP measures

I. production
II. income earned during the production process
III. spending by consumers, businesses, governments, and foreigners

(A) Only I is correct.
(B) Only II is correct.
(C) Only III is correct.
(D) Only I and II are correct.
(E) I, II, and III are correct.

13. Real GDP

(A) is actual GDP as opposed to the estimate made by the BEA.
(B) is also called current-dollar GDP.
(C) is GDP adjusted for price changes.
(D) is not calculated for the United States.
(E) (B) and (C) are both correct.

14. Which of the following events has no effect on GDP?

(A) You buy a 1957 Chevy from a friend.
(B) The Department of Transportation repaves a road.
(C) Your friends make a music CD that doesn't sell any copies.
(D) A college buys computers.
(E) You buy a bottle of French wine.

15. Which of the following will have an effect on GDP?

(A) You lose $50 betting with a friend.
(B) You fix your brother's car without buying any new parts.
(C) Your father's firm makes computers and exports them to China.
(D) You buy 1,000 shares of stock in a corporation.
(E) Your wealthy uncle buys a painting by Picasso.

MULTIPLE-CHOICE REVIEW ANSWERS
选择题答案

1. (A)	**4.** (C)	**7.** (C)	**10.** (D)	**13.** (C)
2. (D)	**5.** (E)	**8.** (C)	**11.** (C)	**14.** (A)
3. (B)	**6.** (E)	**9.** (C)	**12.** (E)	**15.** (C)

FREE-RESPONSE REVIEW QUESTIONS 开放式题目

I. Explain the difference between nominal GDP, real GDP, and GDP per capita.

II. Suppose that production and prices rise from one year to the next, but population stays constant. Will each of the three statistics above rise, fall, or remain unchanged? Explain your reasoning.

III. In what type of situation is GDP per capita more appropriate than nominal or real GDP?

IV. Is GDP an under- or overestimate? Explain.

Free-Response Review Answers 开放式题目答案

I. Nominal GDP measures the production of goods and services within a nation's borders. Nominal GDP could increase because of an increase in output or an increase in the prices of the goods and services produced. Real GDP measures production, but adjusts for any price changes. Real GDP does not change if prices change because it values current output in terms of prices of the given base period. Only one thing can cause real GDP to change and that is a change in output. GDP per capita is production per person.

II. If production and prices rise while population stays constant, then all three statistics, GDP, real GDP, and GDP per capita will rise. GDP rises if production or prices rise. Real GDP rises if production rises. Per capita GDP rises if GDP rises and population does not.

III. GDP per capita is most appropriate for making international comparisons of GDP. The GDP of the United States is much greater than that of Switzerland, but production per person, and therefore living standards, are not all that different between the two nations.

IV. GDP is a vast underestimate of output because of all the production that is not counted. Items that do not go through standard markets are not counted. This includes illegal drugs and gambling, but also home car repair and household vegetable gardens. All of this uncounted production is known as the underground economy. Estimates are that the underground economy could be half the size of the official economy.

Inflation and Unemployment 通货膨胀与失业 15

→ CONSUMER PRICE INDEX (CPI)
→ GDP DEFLATOR
→ COSTS OF INFLATION
→ NOMINAL VS. REAL INTEREST RATE
→ TYPES OF UNEMPLOYMENT

THE TWIN EVILS 双重不幸

Both *inflation* and *unemployment* exert an enormous toll on the economy and, therefore, on our standard of living. The cost of unemployment is obvious: an important resource, labor, is being underutilized. This implies that we are not producing as much as if we were using our resources fully. In economic terms, we are producing inside the production possibilities frontier. Moreover, the households that are experiencing unemployment face real hardships.

The costs associated with inflation are less obvious. Many people understand that rising prices can hurt families on fixed incomes, but this is only a minor issue because most incomes keep pace with rising prices. When prices rise, someone benefits—the owners of the firms that produce the goods and services whose prices are rising. In general, rising prices imply rising incomes, so falling real incomes are not a major cost of inflation.

We will see that a more significant cost associated with inflation is the inefficiencies that ensue when people respond to rising prices. Again, we will be producing at a point inside the production possibilities frontier if we do not use our resources efficiently.

In addition, inflation arbitrarily takes purchasing power from some households and puts it in the hands of others. A massive redistribution of wealth is yet another cost of inflation.

The costs to society of rising prices are much more subtle than the blunt and obvious damages caused by unemployment. Nevertheless, it is unclear which economic evil is more pernicious. Only normative conclusions are possible on this question.

INFLATION 通货膨胀

How Inflation Is Measured 如何计算通货膨胀

Inflation is a sustained rise in most prices in the economy. The inflation rate is the rate at which prices are rising. It is much easier to define inflation than to measure it.

Each month the Bureau of Labor Statistics (BLS) checks prices on 90,000 items at more than 23,000 retail and service outlets. The BLS checks prices in urban, suburban, and rural areas. Because prices are liable to be different in different regions, the BLS must check prices on the same items in every part of the country.

The result of all this effort is the predominant measure of the cost of living in the United States—the consumer price index (CPI). The CPI measures the average change over time in the prices paid by urban consumers for a market basket of consumer goods and services. The BLS computes the CPI for each month.

Consider a simple example where the typical household in the economy consumes 5 packages of cheese and 8 boxes of crackers in a month. If the price of cheese rises to \$2.25 from \$2.00 and the price of crackers climbs to \$1.50 from \$1.25, then the CPI rises to 116.25 from 100. The calculations are shown in Table 15.1. The assumption is that period 1 is the base period, the period to which all other periods are compared.

Table 15.1

Calculating the Consumer Price Index

Peropd 1

Item	Price	Amount	Cost
Cheese	\$2.00	5	\$10.00
Crackers	\$1.25	8	\$10.00

Total cost = \$20.00

$$\text{CPI} = \frac{\text{Total Cost this Period}}{\text{Total Cost Base Period}} \times 100 = \frac{20.00}{20.00} \times 100 = 100$$

Peropd 2

Item	Price	Amount	Cost
Cheese	\$2.25	5	\$11.25
Crackers	\$1.50	8	\$12.00

Total cost = \$23.25

$$\text{CPI} = \frac{\text{Total Cost this Period}}{\text{Total Cost Base Period}} \times 100 = \frac{23.25}{20.00} \times 100 = 116.25$$

Peropd 3

Item	Price	Amount	Cost
Cheese	\$2.35	5	\$11.75
Crackers	\$1.60	8	\$12.80

Total cost = \$24.55

$$\text{CPI} = \frac{\text{Total Cost this Period}}{\text{Total Cost Base Period}} \times 100 = \frac{24.55}{20.00} \times 100 = 122.75$$

In period 3, the CPI rises to 122.75. To calculate the inflation rate between any two periods, take the percentage change in the CPI. For example, the inflation rate between periods 2 and 3 is:

$$\text{Inflation Rate} = (122.75 - 116.25)/116.25 = .0559 = 5.59\%$$

The inflation rate between periods 1 and 3 is:

$$\text{Inflation Rate} = (122.75 - 100.00)/100.00 = .2275 = 22.75\%$$

These calculations indicate that the cost of living for a typical family in this economy increased 5.59 percent between periods 1 and 2 and 22.75 percent between periods 1 and 3.

In the real world, many complications arise when calculating the CPI that are not apparent in this simple example. For instance, what should be done when the quality of a product changes? The price of automobiles has risen dramatically since the 1950s, but so has the quality of the product. A new car these days comes with seat belts and air bags—safety devices that were not available in earlier versions of the product. Quality improvements such as this account for some portion of the price increase. The CPI overstates the amount of inflation since it does not account for all quality improvements.

This is just one example of how the CPI can overstate cost of living increases. A 1996 study from a bipartisan commission concluded that the CPI overstates inflation by more than one percentage point a year. The discrepancy is important because most income maintenance programs, such as Social Security, adjust their benefit payments with the CPI.

The GDP Deflator GDP平减指数

Inflation can be measured with another statistic—the GDP deflator. In the previous chapter we discussed how GDP and real GDP are calculated. Both of these statistics can be used to obtain the GDP deflator through a simple formula:

$$\text{GDP Deflator} = (\text{GDP}/\text{Real GDP}) \times 100$$

In 2013 GDP was $16,799.7 billion, while real GDP equaled $15,761.3 billion. Therefore, the GDP deflator for 2013 was 106.6 (= (16,799.7/15,761.3) × 100). Table 15.2 shows GDP, real GDP, and the GDP deflator over the years.

To calculate the inflation rate between any two years simply take the percentage change in the GDP deflator. By what percent did prices rise from 2003 to 2013? 22.8 percent (= (106.6 – 86.8)/86.8)). In other words, there was 22.8 percent inflation between 2003 and 2013.

The GDP deflator, like the CPI, measures the level of prices in the economy. The inflation rates derived from the GDP deflator, however, do not match the inflation rates obtained from the CPI. Both inflation gauges suggest the same general pattern of inflation over the years.

The GDP deflator ignores import prices. If the price of imported beer increased, the CPI would rise in response, but not the GDP deflator. Still, for most years the CPI and the GDP deflator do not differ markedly.

Table 15.2

GDP, Real GDP, and the GDP Deflator

$$GDP\ Deflator = \frac{Nominal\ GDP}{Real\ GDP} \times 100$$

$$Real\ GDP = \frac{Nominal\ GDP}{GDP\ Deflator} \times 100$$

Year	Nominal GDP (billions of $)	Real GDP (billions of chained 2009 $)	GDP deflator
2003	11,512.2	13,270.0	86.8
2004	12,277.0	13,774.0	89.1
2005	13,095.4	14,235.6	92.0
2006	13,857.9	14,615.2	94.8
2007	14,480.3	14,876.8	97.3
2008	14,720.3	14,833.6	99.2
2009	14,417.9	14,417.9	100.0
2010	14,958.3	14,799.4	101.2
2011	15,533.8	15,052.4	103.2
2012	16,244.6	15,470.7	105.0
2013	16,799.7	15,761.3	106.6

Source: U.S. Department of Commerce, Bureau of Economic Analysis

TIP

Inflation can be measured with a variety of statistics. The most common measures of inflation are the percentage change in the consumer price index and the percentage change in the GDP deflator.

In some instances we may have data on the GDP deflator and GDP; then we can calculate real GDP with the following formula:

Real GDP = (GDP/GDP Deflator) × 100

In 2013 GDP was $16,799.7 billion and the GDP deflator equaled 106.6. Therefore, real GDP was $15,761.3 billion (= (16,799.7/106.6) × 100).

The Costs of Inflation 通货膨胀的成本

Many people think that the most damaging aspect of inflation is that it erodes purchasing power. It is true that any household whose income does not keep pace with inflation will be hurt. But for the vast majority of households, incomes keep pace with, if not exceed, price increases.

To understand why, consider the circular flow diagram presented earlier in the text (page 34). If the prices paid for goods and services produced by firms increases, firms take in more revenue. If this revenue is not passed back to households in the form of higher wages or rent, the firms make more profits. But someone owns the firms and the profits become their income. More specifically, the profits are returned to households in the form of dividends. So higher prices always translate into higher levels of income.

1. Inflation can be detrimental even if a household's income rises as fast as prices. This is because the value of savings accounts, trust funds, brokerage accounts, and other forms of financial wealth will be worth less than before the inflation. In other words, inflation erodes the purchasing power of savings. Savings play an important role in the economy. Households, businesses, and governments often need to borrow funds. Inflation discourages savings.
2. Another problem with inflation is the resources that are wasted dealing with higher prices. Firms have to print new brochures, restaurants need to produce new menus, and price lists in all the media will have to be revised. This takes time and effort. Resources that could have been used more productively are deployed to cope with rising prices. The misallocation of resources because of inflation is sometimes called "menu costs."
3. A final issue associated with inflation has to do with borrowing and lending in inflationary conditions. Lenders can be hurt by inflation because the dollars they loaned out are repaid at a later date with dollars that are not worth as much because of inflation. Imagine lending a friend $100 for a year at 10 percent interest. A year later the friend repays you $110. But suppose prices had risen 12 percent over the course of the loan. Your $110 could not even buy what your $100 could a year ago.

By the same token, borrowers could benefit from inflation because they get to repay their borrowings with inflated dollars. Why don't banks get hurt by inflation? Aren't they big lenders? They are, but they are also smart enough to add an inflation surcharge onto the interest rate that they charge. When a bank lends $100 dollars to your friend it might charge 22 percent—10 percent for his real return and 12 percent to cover the cost of inflation that he expects over the course of the loan.

The idea that some lenders would protect themselves from inflation by charging higher interest on loans was codified into a formula by Irving Fisher in the early 1900s; the formula is known as "Fisher's Hypothesis":

Nominal Interest Rate = Real Interest Rate + Expected Inflation

The nominal interest rate is the rate actually paid. The real interest rate is the actual return the lender receives net of inflation.

The end result is that lenders who do not anticipate inflation will be hurt, but the borrower would benefit in this case. The biggest lender in the economy is households if you consider putting money in a bank account a loan to the bank. Notice that the nominal interest rate paid by banks is not adjusted upward for expected inflation. Households are big lenders who do not anticipate inflation; therefore, they will be hurt by rising prices.

The federal government is the biggest borrower in the United States' economy. It stands to benefit from inflation because it can repay its borrowings with inflated dollars.

If you think about it, inflation works just like a tax, because households are major lenders and the government is a major borrower. It is as if Uncle Sam reaches into your wallet every night while you sleep and slips out just a little cash so that you don't even notice. The inflation tax is the result of the federal government benefiting from inflation while households are harmed. This redistribution of wealth from lenders to borrowers is yet another cost of inflation.

The costs of inflation are summarized in Table 15.3.

Table 15.3

The Costs of Inflation

- Financial wealth is eroded
- Savings are discouraged
- Menu costs—resources are misallocated with rising prices
- Inflation tax—wealth is redistributed from lenders to borrowers

UNEMPLOYMENT 失业

The costs associated with unemployment are obvious. Households will encounter hardships, maybe even hunger. Unemployment means that a resource, labor, is not being used to its fullest potential. We are producing inside the production possibilities frontier. We could be producing more and enjoying more goods and services.

Unemployment is a problem during recessions—periods when real GDP is declining. During a recession fewer goods and services are being produced. The amount of labor and other resources required for production is reduced and people find themselves out of work.

The unemployment rate is defined as the number of unemployed persons divided by the labor force. The labor force does not include retired persons, those too young to work, and anyone who has not been actively seeking employment. In order to be counted as unemployed you have to be out of work and looking for a job.

The Bureau of Labor Statistics (BLS) reports the unemployment statistics based on two broad surveys taken each month. One survey contacts employers and asks about employment levels at various business establishments, while the other survey interviews households.

Economists classify the unemployed into five general categories:

1. Those who are able to work, but not actively seeking employment because they are discouraged about their prospects for finding employment, are referred to as *discouraged workers* or the *hidden unemployed.* This situation is unfortunate because these people lack basic skills or suffer from other problems and have a difficult time finding work. Discouraged by their prospects, they no longer bother to pursue employment. These people do not show up in the unemployment statistics because they are not considered to be part of the labor force; thus the name "hidden" unemployment.
2. A form of unemployment that does show up in the official statistics is *structural unemployment.* The structurally unemployed are out of work because the economy is structured, or set up, to their disadvantage. For instance, there may be welders looking for work in Cleveland, but the welding jobs are in Dallas. Or welders may be out of work in Boston, but their are plenty of secretarial jobs open in that same area. Since it is often difficult for a person to relocate or retrain, structural unemployment is not easily remedied.
3. Some persons are able to find work for only a portion of the year due to the seasonal nature of their jobs. These individuals are considered to be *seasonally unemployed* as long as they actively look for work in the off-season. Farmers and construction workers may fall into this category.

4. As mentioned previously, unemployment rises during the contractionary phase of the business cycle. Individuals who lose their jobs during a recession and the corresponding slowdown in production are said to be *cyclically unemployed*. They are out of work specifically because of the business cycle. Hopefully, these people will be back to work when production picks up during the next expansion.
5. Finally, a number of persons are not working because they are in between jobs. Someone who is scheduled to begin a new job next month and does not presently hold a job is considered to be *frictionally unemployed*. It is unlikely that people will be able to switch jobs without some time off. Indeed, some people take advantage of this time to relax or move their households and get their affairs in order. Also, someone who quits one job to look for another is considered to be frictionally unemployed. Finally, new entrants into the labor market, such as graduates looking for work or a stay-at-home parent re-entering the work force, are considered frictionally unemployed.

TIP

People who are not actively looking for work are not in the labor force and therefore are not counted as unemployed.

In 2013 the labor force was estimated to be 155.3 million persons, while the unemployed numbered 11.4 million. This implies an unemployment rate of 7.4 percent (= 11.4/155.3). Some analysts contend that the unemployment picture is actually much worse than this figure indicates. For one, the 7.4 percent does not count hidden unemployment. Remember, those too discouraged to look for work are not counted as being unemployed or even in the labor force. They are simply not counted.

Another factor to consider is that persons who are working part time are counted as if they are fully employed, even if they would like to have a full-time job. Again, the reported statistic of 7.4 percent understates the unemployment problem.

A related point to keep in mind is that 7.4 percent is the average unemployment rate across the nation. There are sections of the country where the rate is much higher and sections where it is lower. Moreover, it is well known that the unemployment rate is worse for certain groups within the population, such as teenagers.

Many of the people counted as being unemployed are merely frictionally unemployed. In fact, it is estimated that of the 11.4 million persons unemployed in 2013, anywhere from 3 to 6 million are frictionally unemployed. Indeed, economists consider the economy to be at full employment when the unemployment rate reaches the 4 to 6 percent range since the frictionally unemployed account for about that much of the unemployment rate. If the unemployment rate were to fall further, inflation would most likely be a problem. The full employment rate of unemployment is sometimes called NAIRU for the nonaccelerating inflation rate of unemployment.

Despite the criticisms of the unemployment statistic, the fact remains that it is tabulated in the same manner each time, so that a drop in the rate means more people are working or the labor force has shrunk. The unemployment rate is a useful statistic, but care should be taken with its interpretation.

SUMMARY 小结

- Inflation and unemployment are serious economic problems. Inflation causes the misallocation of resources and an arbitrary redistribution of income. Inflation is typically a problem when the economy is overheated—growing faster than normal. But inflation can also occur during recessions. Later we shall see why.
- Unemployment occurs when the economy is operating below its potential. Our most important resource is labor, and unemployment exists when this resource is not being fully utilized. We could have produced more and enjoyed more goods and services if not for the unemployment.

- We have reviewed the major statistics that measure unemployment and inflation and found that they are not perfectly accurate. It is important to understand how the numbers are generated so that their potential deficiencies can be anticipated. For instance, if the price of imported oil is rising rapidly, it is critical to know that the GDP deflator will not reflect this increase. The GDP deflator does not include the prices of imported products. The CPI does.

The most important question concerning inflation and unemployment has been ignored in this chapter: What causes inflation and unemployment? A complete answer is provided in the chapters ahead.

TERMS 术语

Consumer Price Index (CPI) measure of the average change over time in the prices paid by urban consumers for a market basket of consumer goods and services

Cyclical Unemployment loss of jobs by individuals during a recession and the corresponding slowdown in production

Fisher's Hypothesis Nominal Interest Rate = Real Interest Rate + Expected Inflation

Frictional Unemployment state of being out of work because the person is in between jobs

GDP Deflator measure of the level of prices in the economy

Hidden Unemployment describing those who are able to work but who are not actively seeking employment because they are discouraged about their prospects for finding employment

Inflation a sustained rise in most prices in the economy

Menu Costs the misallocation of resources because of inflation

Nonaccelerating Inflation Rate of Unemployment (NAIRU) the full employment rate of unemployment; when employment falls below this rate, inflation accelerates

Seasonal Unemployment state of being out of work because of the time of year

Structural Unemployment state of being out of work because the economy is structured, or set up, to a person's disadvantage

Unemployment Rate the number of unemployed persons divided by the labor force

FORMULAS 公式

$$\text{CPI} = \frac{\text{Total Cost this Period}}{\text{Total Cost Base Period}} \times 100$$

$$\text{Inflation Rate} = \frac{\text{CPI (this period)} - \text{CPI (previous period)}}{\text{CPI (previous period)}} \times 100$$

GDP Deflator = (Nominal GDP/Real GDP) × 100

Real GDP = (Nominal GDP/GDP Deflator) × 100

Nominal Interest Rate = Real Interest Rate + Expected Inflation

Unemployment Rate = Number of Unemployed/Civilian Labor Force

MULTIPLE-CHOICE REVIEW QUESTIONS 选择题

1. The CPI is calculated for each ______ by ______

(A) week; The Bureau of Economic Analysis
(B) month; The Bureau of Economic Analysis
(C) month; The Bureau of Labor Statistics
(D) quarter; The Bureau of Economic Analysis
(E) quarter; The Bureau of Labor Statistics

2. If the CPI goes to 150 from 120, then prices have

(A) risen 20 percent.
(B) risen 25 percent.
(C) fallen 30 percent.
(D) risen 30 percent.
(E) risen 150 percent.

3. According to experts, the CPI

(A) overstates increases in the cost of living.
(B) understates increases in the cost of living.
(C) accurately estimates changes in the cost of living.
(D) could over- or underestimate changes depending on the season.
(E) should be abandoned in favor of the GDP Deflator.

4. When products improve in quality the CPI will

(A) automatically increase.
(B) automatically decrease.
(C) become negative.
(D) overestimate the inflation rate.
(E) underestimate the inflation rate.

5. The GDP Deflator

I. is used to calculate inflation rates.
II. is an alternative to the CPI.
III. is more accurate than the CPI.

(A) Only I is true.
(B) I and II are true.
(C) I and III are true.
(D) II and III are true.
(E) I, II, and III are true.

6. If nominal GDP equals $5,000 and real GDP equals $4,000, then the GDP Deflator equals

(A) 125
(B) 1.25
(C) 800
(D) .8
(E) 300

7. If nominal GDP equals $6,000 and the GDP deflator equals 200, then real GDP equals

(A) $30
(B) $3,000
(C) $12,000
(D) $1,200
(E) $1,200,000

8. Which of the following is NOT a major cost of inflation?

(A) Resources will be misallocated.
(B) Wealth will be redistributed.
(C) Savings will be discouraged.
(D) Real incomes will fall.
(E) Financial wealth will be eroded.

9. The term "menu costs" refers to

(A) less choices due to inflation.
(B) financial assets being worth less due to inflation.
(C) "à la carte" savings falling.
(D) food prices rising due to inflation.
(E) resource misallocation due to inflation.

10. Inflation

(A) encourages households to save more.
(B) does not affect savings in the economy.
(C) forces households to save more.
(D) forces households to save less.
(E) discourages savings.

11. Rising prices are a problem because

(A) money in household savings accounts can now buy fewer goods and services.
(B) household incomes generally do not rise with prices.
(C) the economy could run out of money.
(D) borrowers have to repay loans with more dollars.
(E) households are encouraged to save more.

12. Fisher's Hypothesis states that

(A) the real interest equals the nominal interest rate plus the inflation rate.
(B) the nominal interest rate equals the real interest rate minus the inflation rate.
(C) the nominal interest rate equals the unemployment rate plus the real interest rate.
(D) the nominal interest rate equals the unemployment rate minus the real interest rate.
(E) the nominal interest rate equals the real interest rate plus the inflation rate.

13. Sue loses her job at a shoe factory when the economy falls into a recession. Sue is

(A) frictionally unemployed.
(B) cyclically unemployed.
(C) seasonally unemployed.
(D) structurally unemployed.
(E) a discouraged worker.

14. There is a strong demand for welders in California but Bill, an unemployed welder, lives in New York. Bill is

(A) frictionally unemployed.
(B) cyclically unemployed.
(C) structurally unemployed.
(D) considered to be a hidden worker.
(E) not counted in the ranks of the unemployed.

15. It is unlikely that the unemployment rate will ever fall to zero because of

(A) frictional unemployment.
(B) cyclical unemployment.
(C) government policies.
(D) corporate policies.
(E) the aged and infirm in our population.

MULTIPLE-CHOICE REVIEW ANSWERS
选择题答案

1. (C) **4.** (D) **7.** (B) **10.** (E) **13.** (B)

2. (B) **5.** (B) **8.** (D) **11.** (A) **14.** (C)

3. (A) **6.** (A) **9.** (E) **12.** (E) **15.** (A)

FREE-RESPONSE REVIEW QUESTIONS 开放式题目

Inflation exerts significant costs on the economy. Specifically, explain how inflation

I. causes a misallocation of resources.

II. discourages savings.

III. redistributes wealth from lenders to borrowers.

Free-Response Review Answers 开放式题目答案

I. Inflation causes a misallocation of resources. Resources are spent dealing with rising prices and the repercussions of rising prices. Instead, these resources could have been spent producing more goods and services for the constituents of the economy to enjoy. For example, some firms will have to print new catalogs and revise their websites when the prices of their products change. This time and effort would not have been expended if prices had not risen. Some households will take the trouble to stock up on goods whose prices are expected to rise. The effort and storage costs are another misallocation of resources.

II. Inflation erodes the value of financial assets. Bank and brokerage accounts, trust funds, and other accounts cannot buy as many products when the prices of those products rise. Why save if inflation will simply eat away at the value of savings?

III. Inflation allows borrowers to repay their loans with dollars that are not worth as much as the ones they borrowed. Lenders, on the other hand, are being repaid with dollars that have lost some of their value. Shrewd lenders understand this and charge higher rates of interest to cover the inflation that may occur over the course of a loan. However, lenders who do not anticipate inflation will be hurt while those who borrow from them will benefit.

Aggregate Supply and Aggregate Demand
总供给和总需求

16

- → BUSINESS CYCLES
- → AGGREGATE SUPPLY
- → AGGREGATE DEMAND
- → EQUILIBRIUM

WHY THE ECONOMY MOVES IN CYCLES 为何经济周期性运行

1. The average growth rate of the United States economy, as measured by the percentage change in real GDP, is just over three percent per year for the postwar period, yet only in a very few instances has the economy grown at its average rate. It typically grows faster than average and then in some years real GDP falls or shows negative growth. We call these negative growth periods *recessions*.
2. All economies experience fluctuations in economic activity—contractions and expansions. The ups and downs in economic activity are recurrent but do not conform to a uniform schedule. The longest postwar recession in the United States lasted 18 months, the shortest just 6 months. The longest expansion was more than 10 years, while the shortest lasted only 12 months.
3. One business cycle is comprised of an expansion and a recession. The fact that business cycles do not conform to a time schedule and differ in other respects, such as their severity, makes them extremely difficult to predict. Economic forecasters get lower grades for accuracy than the weatherman.

Our task in this chapter, however, is not to predict when the next recession will occur, but to explain *why* the economy moves in cycles. We will build a replica, or model, of the economy and see if that model moves in fits and starts like the real economy. Our model should also display other well-known characteristics of capitalist economies. For instance, large increases in income tend to result in inflation. Does our model confirm this? Technological advances tend to increase output while putting downward pressure on prices. Does our model explain this? Inflation and unemployment tend to be inversely related—when one is up, the other is down—but not always. Does our model explain this tendency and is it flexible enough to allow for exceptions to the relationship?

The name of the model that addresses all of these questions is the *aggregate supply/aggregate demand (AS/AD) model*. The AS/AD model highlights the factors that determine output, income, employment, and prices in the economy. Before we begin to build the model, we must consider what Classical economic theory indicates are the important factors determining output, income, employment, and prices in the economy.

CLASSICAL ECONOMIC THEORY 经典经济学理论

Classical economic theory was the predominant paradigm in economic analysis from about 1800 until 1930. The basis of Classical thought is Say's Law—supply creates its own demand. As we pointed out earlier, whenever anything is produced, it generates an amount of income equal to its value. Say's Law indicates that it would be impossible to produce too much because of this fact. When something is produced (supplied), it generates enough income to purchase (demand) the item.

However, there is no rule that says the income generated in the production process must be used to purchase the item produced. Workers and managers may decide to save a portion of their earnings. Say had a response to this: The unpurchased items would collect in inventories. Swelling inventories would induce producers to lower prices, the items in inventory would now sell. In other words, even if wage earners do not use their incomes to purchase all that was produced, prices would adjust to ensure there was no excess production.

Therefore, demand for products was never a concern for Classical thinkers. There would always be enough demand. The most important factor determining output was supply. And the most important factors determining supply were the amount of resources in the economy and the state of technology. Classical analysis has a very simple response to the question, "What determines the amount of output in the economy?" Resources and technology.

Given this analysis it is easy to understand why Classical theory fell out of favor in 1930 during the Great Depression. Here, output in the economy had fallen sharply, yet there was no decrease in the amount of land, labor, and capital available. What's more, the productivity of those resources had not diminished either. That is to say, the state of technology was not deteriorating. The Classical economists could not explain why output fell so precipitously during the Great Depression.

KEYNESIAN THEORY 凯恩斯理论

In 1936 John Maynard Keynes (pronounced KANES), a British economist, published a book entitled *The General Theory of Employment, Interest, and Money*. The book pointed out flaws in Classical theory and went on to suggest another, more general, theory. Basically, Keynes suggested that the price adjustment the Classical economists relied upon to ensure that supply would always equal demand did not work under certain circumstances. Essentially, Keynes pointed out that Say's Law, the basis for Classical analysis, did not hold true in all cases.

Keynes' model of the way the economy works is handed down to us in the form of the AS/AD model. The model indicates that the Great Depression was caused by a lack of demand for goods and services. Based on this assessment of the situation, Keynes developed a brilliant remedy for the Great Depression. Unfortunately, the remedy Keynes suggested was considered too radical and the Great Depression lingered on until World War II when both Great Britain and the United States were forced to apply Keynes's remedy.

To truly appreciate Keynes's solution to the Great Depression (and to do well on the Advanced Placement exam) we have to build an AS/AD from scratch.

Aggregate Supply 总供给

Aggregate means "sum total"; aggregate supply is the supply of all goods and services by all suppliers in the economy. In other words, aggregate supply is the supply of everything by all producers.

We are specifically interested in how the supply of everything by all suppliers is affected by the level of prices in the economy. We already know from our look into the production possibilities frontier that output depends on the amount of resources available and the state of technology, not prices. So if we drew an aggregate supply curve in line with that reasoning, it would be perfectly vertical, indicating that the price level in the economy can be high or low, it doesn't matter, because output or supply is going to be the amount indicated by where the vertical aggregate supply curve touches the horizontal axis. In Figure 16.1 the horizontal axis is labeled *Real GDP*. In many textbooks it is labeled *Quantity of Output* since real GDP is a measure of the quantity of output.

TIP

Questions concerning the economy in the long run should be addressed using the vertical aggregate supply curve. For questions concerning the short run, use the upward sloping aggregate supply curve.

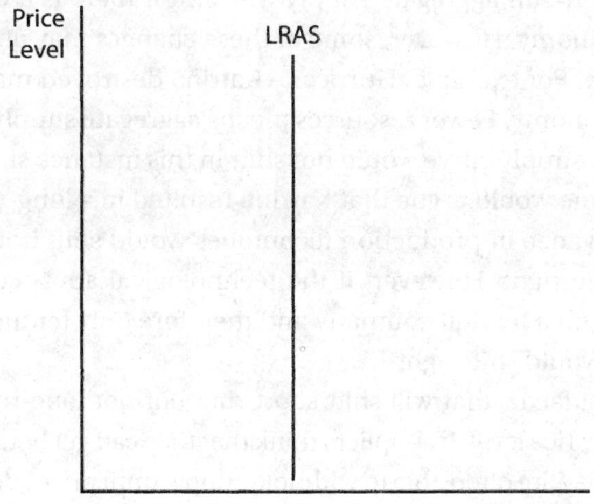

Fig. 16.1 A Long-Run Aggregate Supply Curve

The long-run aggregate supply curve touches the horizontal axis at the economy's potential GDP, Q_F. This is the amount that can be produced using the economy's resources fully and efficiently. It corresponds to an economy operating on its production possibilities frontier.

There may be situations, however, where the price level in the economy does indeed affect the amount supplied by all producers. For instance, in recessionary or depressionary conditions an increase in prices may result in an increase in supply. This is because it is easy to increase supply during a recession when there are plenty of unused resources. The increase in prices induces suppliers to provide more output. This idea is reflected in an aggregate supply curve that slopes upward from left to right.

If the aggregate supply curve is drawn as an upward sloping line, then it reflects the fact that supply can be increased or decreased in the short run in response to changes in the price level.

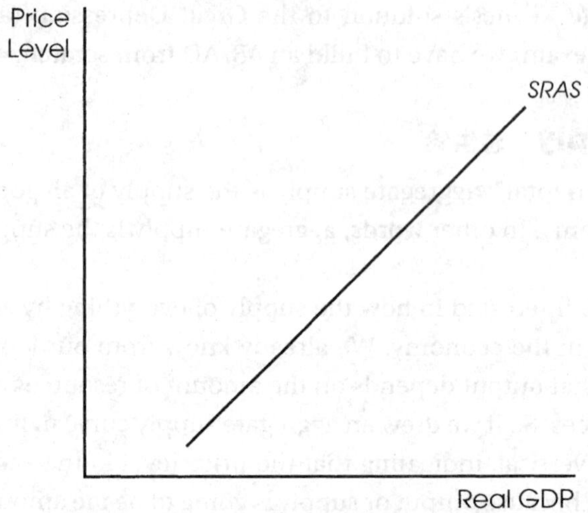

Fig. 16.2 A Short-Run Aggregate Supply Curve

Shifts in Aggregate Supply 总供给的变化

Both long-run and short-run aggregate supply will shift if there is a change in resources or productivity in the economy. However, some of these changes may affect only the short-run aggregate supply curve. For example, Hurricane Katrina destroyed many resources in a vast region of our macroeconomy. Fewer resources means aggregate supply shifted left. However, the long-run aggregate supply curve would not shift in this instance since the loss in resources was temporary. (Some would argue that Katrina resulted in a long-run loss of resources.)

A technological advance in production techniques would shift both short- and long-run aggregate supply to the right. However, if the technological advance was dependent on a licensing agreement with a foreign company and therefore only temporary, then only short-run aggregate supply would shift right.

There is one critical factor that will shift short run, but not long-run, aggregate supply: a change in the expected price level. If suppliers think that they can get better prices for their products in a month, then they are often able to withhold supply until prices do indeed rise. However, changing expectations about future price levels does not shift long-run aggregate supply.

FACTORS SHIFTING AGGREGATE SUPPLY

Changes in resource availability

- **Relaxing immigration laws to allow more labor into the country shifts aggregate supply right.**
- **Discovering new oil fields shifts aggregate supply right.**

Changes in productivity

- **New technologies that benefit producers shift aggregate supply right.**
- **Relaxing government regulations can increase productivity and shift aggregate supply right.**

Changes in the expected price level (shifts only short-run aggregate supply)

- **If suppliers expect prices to be lower in the future, they will supply more right now, shifting aggregate supply right.**

Aggregate Demand 总需求

The aggregate demand curve represents the total demand for goods and services in the economy by households, businesses, governments, and foreigners. In other words, aggregate demand is the demand for everything by everyone.

If the prices of goods and services rise, aggregate demand will fall, as shown in Figure 16.3.

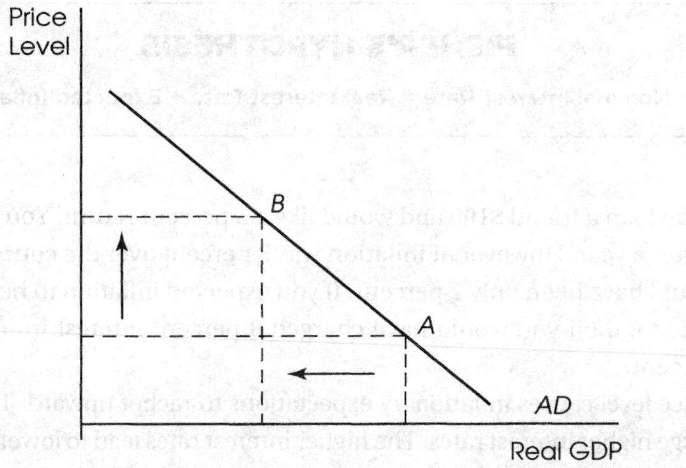

Fig. 16.3 An Increase in the Price Level Reduces Aggregate Demand

The question is why? Most people would say because high prices turn consumers off. But this answer is totally incorrect in this context. When the price level rises, incomes rise by the exact same proportion. Remember, whenever something is produced, it generates an equivalent amount of income. As prices rise in the economy, someone is benefiting. For example, the owners of businesses that manufacture the products that are rising in price are making more profits that eventually translate into more income for the owners. If incomes rise in proportion with prices, then why would aggregate demand fall?

There are three reasons why aggregate demand would fall when the price level rises: the wealth effect, the interest rate effect, and the foreign purchases effect. Each of these explanations takes into account that rising prices means rising incomes. They suggest aggregate demand would fall even though incomes are keeping pace with rising prices.

The aggregate demand curve slopes downward due to the

- **Wealth effect**
- **Interest rate effect**
- **Foreign purchases effect**

The Wealth Effect 财富效应

The wealth effect points to the fact that rising prices erode financial wealth. Suppose you had $200,000 saved up for your retirement. As the price level rises, that $200,000 can buy less and less. You may decide to begin saving at a greater rate. Therefore, as prices rise in the economy, the value of financial wealth declines and people respond to this by saving more and demanding fewer goods and services.

The Interest Rate Effect 利率效应

As the price level rises, so does the nominal interest rate. That is because lenders charge higher interest rates when they expect to be paid back with dollars that have lost some of their value due to inflation. Irving Fisher pointed this out long ago. The Fisher Hypothesis states that the nominal interest rate is equal to the real return lenders desire plus expected inflation.

> **FISHER'S HYPOTHESIS**
>
> **Nominal Interest Rate = Real Interest Rate + Expected Inflation**

Suppose you loan a friend $100 and would like a 5 percent return. You would ask for $105 to be repaid after a year. However, if inflation was 3 percent over the course of the loan, your real return would have been only 2 percent. If you expected inflation to be 3 percent over the course of the loan, then you would have charged 8 percent interest in order to have a real return of 5 percent.

A rising price level causes inflationary expectations to rachet upward. This, in turn, causes lenders to charge higher interest rates. The higher interest rates lead to lower aggregate demand because spenders often borrow the funds to make purchases. This is the interest rate effect.

> **THE INTEREST RATE EFFECT**
>
> **Price level ↑ → Interest rate ↑ → Interest-sensitive spending ↓ → Aggregate demand ↓**

The Foreign Purchases Effect 国外采购效应

If the price level in the United States rises, then its goods will be more expensive to foreigners. The nation will export less. Moreover, foreign goods will be more competitively priced, so U.S. imports will rise. Net exports will decline, the result being a direct decrease in aggregate demand.

> - **The wealth effect—if the price level rises, consumers feel less wealthy even if their income keeps pace with inflation because their financial assets are worth less. They therefore save more and spend less.**
> - **The interest rate effect—if the price level rises, so will the nominal interest rate. This reduces interest-sensitive spending.**
> - **The foreign purchases effect—if the U.S. price level rises, U.S. goods look more expensive to foreigners, and U.S. exports fall. Foreign goods are relatively less expensive, and U.S. imports rise. Thus, total demand for U.S. goods falls.**

It should be pointed out that all three effects work in reverse to ensure that a decrease in the price level causes an increase in aggregate demand.

Notice that a change in the price level will move the economy up or down the aggregate demand curve. We have not mentioned anything that will shift the aggregate demand curve. That is the subject of the next section.

Shifts in Aggregate Demand (AD) 总需求的变化

It is important to know what can shift the aggregate demand curve left and right. A change in the price level will cause the economy to move from one point to another along the same aggregate demand curve. It will not cause a shift.

Many things can shift aggregate demand. Remember, aggregate demand is demand from households, businesses, governments, and foreigners. An increase in consumer confidence can shift aggregate demand. An increase in income taxes causes consumers to spend less and shift aggregate demand left. If foreigners suddenly decided that they did not want American products, aggregate demand would decrease and therefore shift left. An increase in federal spending would shift aggregate demand to the right. If it was paid for with a tax increase, that would lessen the effect because taxes reduce spending.

Anything that affects total spending in the economy, except a change in the price level, will shift aggregate demand. The box below delineates some aggregate demand shifters.

FACTORS SHIFTING AGGREGATE DEMAND

Changes in consumer spending:

- A rise in consumer confidence would shift AD right.
- A tax hike would shift AD left.

Changes in investment spending:

- An increase in expected future sales would shift AD right.
- A rise in interest rates shifts AD left.

Changes in government spending:

- An increase in military spending shifts AD right.
- A decrease in spending on highway construction shifts AD left.

Changes in net exports:

- A decrease in the value of the dollar shifts AD right.
- The French begin to loathe American products, AD shifts left.

Anything that affects C or I or G or X (except the price level) shifts AD. Also, changes in the money supply shift AD. That's because an increase in the money supply would reduce interest rates and cause an increase in interest-sensitive spending.

Aggregate Supply and Aggregate Demand Together 合起来看总供给和总需求

The aggregate supply curves and the aggregate demand curve have the price level on the vertical axis and the quantity of output on the horizontal axis. We can, therefore, draw the curves on the same diagram.

You may recall that we discussed two different aggregate supply curves. Let's ignore the long-run aggregate supply curve for now and examine how the macroeconomy behaves in the short run.

The economy will have a tendency to operate at point E in Figure 16.4 with a quantity of output of Qe and price level of Pe. Say the price level was not Pe but P′. At P′ aggregate supply is greater than aggregate demand. This will cause inventories of products to bulge. Producers would respond by lowering prices.

A similar analysis suggests that if the price level was P″ aggregate demand would exceed aggregate supply. Inventories would fall. Producers would realize that they could raise their prices. In short, surpluses and shortages will drive the price level to Pe and the quantity of output Qe. Only then will there be no surplus or shortage of output.

The economy will produce Qe and experience price level Pe until something changes. Specifically, the equilibrium point will change when the aggregate supply curve or the aggregate demand curve shifts.

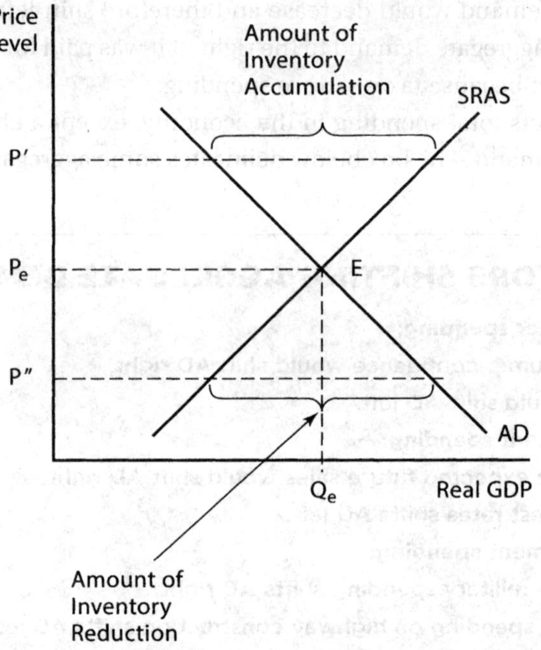

Fig. 16.4 Equilibrium of Aggregate Supply and Aggregate Demand

USING THE AS/AD MODEL 使用总供给/总需求模型

We are now in a position to put the AS/AD model through its paces. We can use the model to help us analyze what will happen under various conditions. For instance, suppose there is a technological advance that makes workers more productive. An example might be the development of the personal computer so that just about everyone can have one at his or her desk. In the 1970s computers were not developed to the point where one would fit on a desk and the cost of owning a personal computer was prohibitive. Now that productivity-enhancing computers are just about everywhere, how would this affect the economy?

Remember that a technological advance shifts the aggregate supply curve to the right. This is shown in Figure 16.5.

The original equilibrium is E_1. After the technological advance, the new equilibrium is E_2. Four specific conclusions can be made by comparing E_1 to E_2. First, prices are lower at E_2. Second, real GDP is higher. We are at Q_2 compared to Q_1. Because real GDP is higher we can draw two further conclusions: Unemployment will fall and income will rise.

Our AS/AD model tells us that we can expect lower prices, more output, less unemployment, and more income after a technological advance. Would a Classical economist respond differently? Let's redo the analysis using a long-run aggregate supply curve.

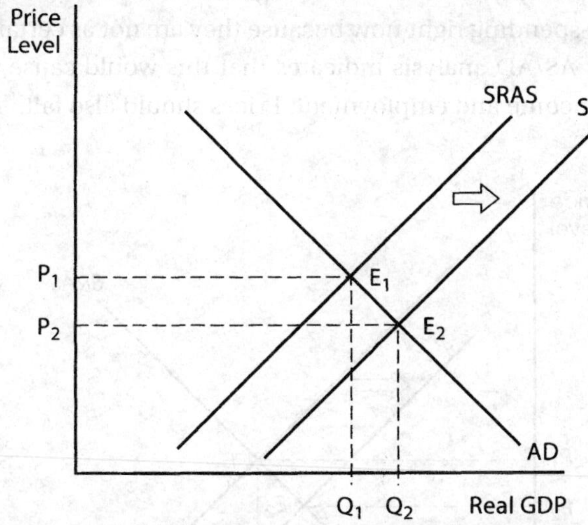

Fig. 16.5 The Effects of a Technological Advance

Figure 16.6 shows that an advance in technology would shift the long-run aggregate supply curve to the right. Comparing the original equilibrium, E_1, with the new equilibrium, E_2, gives the same results as when the aggregate supply curve was upward sloping: Prices are lower at E_2 and real GDP is higher. Higher output means unemployment will be lower and income will be higher. The results are the same using either aggregate supply curve.

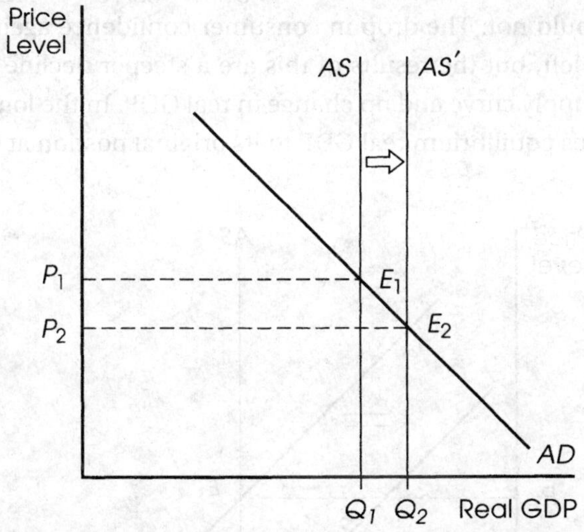

Fig. 16.6 The Effects of a Technological Advance with a Long-Run Aggregate Supply Curve

Let's try another example where the results will differ depending on what type of aggregate supply curve is used. This time let's consider the effects of a drop in consumer confidence on the economy. When consumers feel less confident about their future job prospects and income levels, they are not willing to spend as much of their current incomes. This causes the aggregate demand curve to shift to the left.

Comparing the initial equilibrium, E_1, with new equilibrium, E_2, in Figure 16.7 indicates that prices and real GDP will fall because of the decline in consumer confidence. Once real GDP falls we can conclude that unemployment will rise and income will fall. It seems that we have a self-fulfilling prophesy here. Consumers begin to think that the economic future will be bleak; so they reduce spending right now because they are not as certain of their job prospects in the future. Our AS/AD analysis indicates that this would cause a recession, where output falls along with income and employment. Prices should also fall.

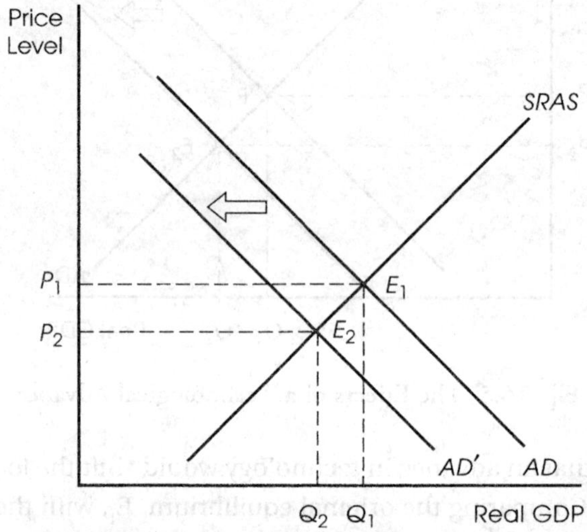

Fig. 16.7 The Effects of a Drop in Consumer Confidence

Would the same results hold if we used a long-run aggregate supply curve? Figure 16.8 indicates that they would not. The drop in consumer confidence again shifts the aggregate demand curve to the left, but the results of this are a steeper decline in prices than with a short-run aggregate supply curve and no change in real GDP. In the long run, prices fall even farther, and this pushes equilibrium real GDP to its original postion at Q_1.

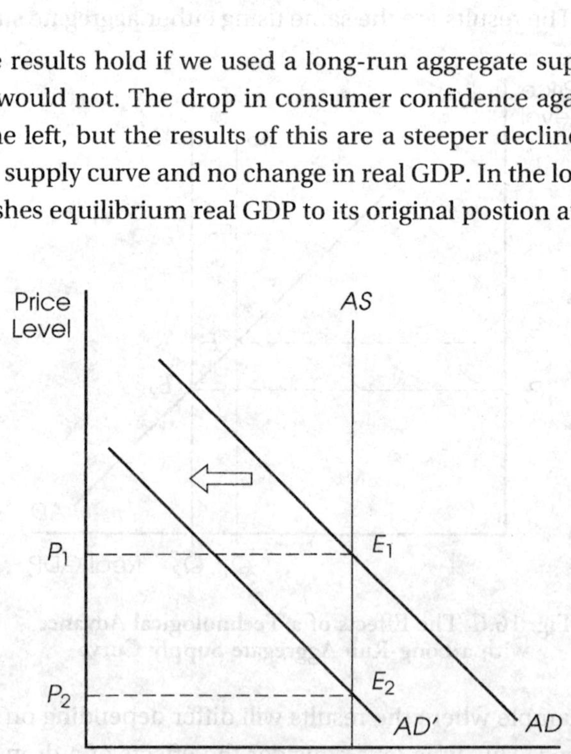

Fig. 16.8 The Effects of a Drop in Consumer Confidence with a Long-Run Aggregate Supply Curve

According to long-run analysis, when aggregate demand falls, prices fall, and this drop in prices should help maintain spending levels. Therefore, real GDP does not fall with the decline in aggregate demand.

The Short Run vs. the Long Run 长期和短期

We can consider the short- and long-run effects of any change in the economy with our aggregate supply and aggregate demand model. Figure 16.9 shows the effects of a tax cut on an economy that is already operating at its potential.

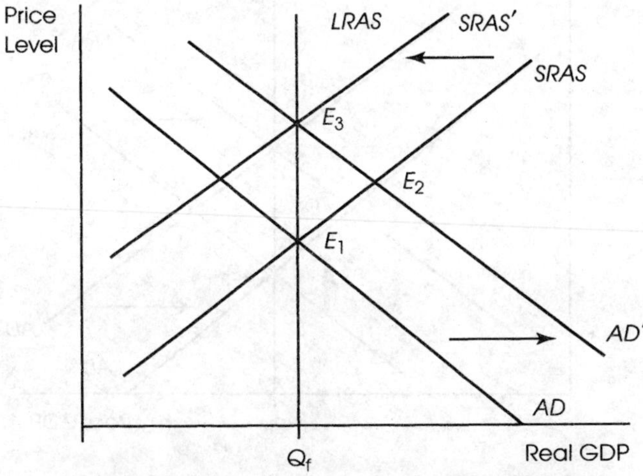

Fig. 16.9 The Effects of a Tax Cut on an Economy Operating at Potential GDP

Begin at E_1, where all three curves cross. This economy is operating at its potential because output is at Q_p, which represents potential GDP. The tax cut shifts the AD curve to the right, and the economy is now operating at E_2. This is the short-run effect of the tax cut. Output is up, which means that income and employment have increased as well. The price level is higher at E_2 than at E_1 as well.

Since E_2 is to the right of potential GDP, we know this economy is operating above potential. Resources are strained, and the price level is up. This leads to the expectation that prices will be higher in the future. If suppliers expect higher prices for their products in the future, many of them can reduce the supply right now. This shifts the AS curve to the left, and the economy winds up at E_3.

In the short run the tax cut stimulated the economy to produce beyond its potential. In the long run the economy was back at its potential. The price level is higher in the long run, but wages and incomes will be proportionally higher as well. The tax cut had no effect on living standards in the long run. This makes sense. Living standards in the long run depend on resources and technology, not tax cuts.

Let's use our model to understand the Great Depression. It is well known that the Great Depression was caused by a severe drop in aggregate demand. Several causes for the decline in aggregate demand have been highlighted by economic historians. First, the financial panic caused a 33 percent decline in the money supply. That would shift aggregate demand left. The stock market crash caused businesses and households to cut spending. Some say new tariffs on international trade added to the reduction in aggregate demand.

Figure 16.10 shows the short- and long-run effects of a reduction in aggregate demand. In the short run the economy moves to E_2. Production, income, and employment are down. The price level has fallen as well. The Great Depression evinced all these effects. In the long run, the expectation is that a depression will lead to a further drop in prices. This is because resources are idle and there is plenty of labor to be employed at low nominal wages. When suppliers expect prices to be lower in the future, they attempt to supply more right now. This causes the aggregate supply curve to shift right. The economy ends up at E_3, producing at its potential.

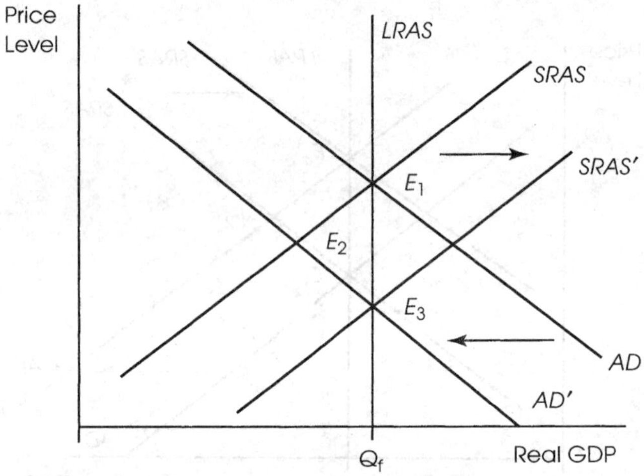

Fig. 16.10 The Effects of a Reduction in Aggregate Demand

There was just one problem with this analysis during the 1930s. Ten years went by, and the economy *still had* not returned to potential. Prices were *falling*, but some *said they had* not fallen enough. Government policies were put in place to prevent prices from falling because the lower prices were driving businesses into bankruptcy.

Keynesian economists like to point out that sticky prices do not allow the economy to return to its long-run potential as our analysis suggests. These economists say the government should take action during recessions because the long run may never come. Exactly what the government can do to move the economy toward its potential is the subject of the next two chapters.

SUMMARY 小结

At this point some readers may be thinking, which analysis is correct, long run or short run? It turns out that the two analyses can be reconciled. We will do so in the coming chapters.

- The AS/AD model is a very powerful tool for thinking about how an economy will respond to given events, such as a technological advance or a dip in consumer confidence. If you are interested in the long-run effects, then it is best to use a vertical aggregate supply curve. Use a short-run aggregate supply curve in the opposite circumstances.
- The question we asked at the beginning of this chapter got lost in all the details: What causes business cycles? The AS/AD model suggests that shifts in the aggregate supply and demand cause fluctuations in economic activity. We listed the factors that could shift these curves. The resulting changes in equilibrium output and prices are the business cycles that we observe in the real world.

Finally, keep in mind that the AP exam in Macroeconomics emphasizes the material in this chapter. It will pay for you to become familiar with the graphs and understand what can cause the curves in each graph to shift. You may think about repeating the chapter if you do not do well on the sample multiple-choice and free-response questions.

TERMS 术语

Aggregate Demand the demand for all goods and services by all households, businesses, governments, and foreigners

Aggregate Supply the supply of all goods and services by all producers in the economy

Business Cycle a wave of economic activity comprised of an expansion and a recession

Classical Economic Theory the predominant paradigm in economic analysis from about 1800 until 1930, based on Say's Law

Equilibrium Price Level the price level that equates aggregate supply and aggregate demand, the average level of prices in the economy

Equilibrium Quantity the amount of output that results in no shortage or surplus, the amount of goods and service bought and sold in the economy

Expansion a sustained improvement in economic activity

Potential GDP the amount that can be produced when all of the economy's resources are used fully and efficiently

Recession a sustained decline in economic activity

Say's Law theory that supply creates its own demand

MULTIPLE-CHOICE REVIEW QUESTIONS 选择题

1. Business cycles
   - (A) occur infrequently in capitalist economies.
   - (B) refer to reusing resources in production.
   - (C) are predictable ups and downs in economic activity.
   - (D) are each comprised of a recession and an expansion.
   - (E) are the same as depressions.

2. Recessions
   - (A) are a thing of the past.
   - (B) are very severe depressions.
   - (C) are marked by a sustained decline in output.
   - (D) occur at regular intervals.
   - (E) are typically accompanied by falling unemployment.

3. Say's Law
   - (A) is the basis of Keynesian economic analysis.
   - (B) is the basis of Classical economic analysis.
   - (C) states that demand creates its own supply.
   - (D) indicates that prices will be stable in capitalist economies.
   - (E) was verified by the Great Depression.

4. Keynes
   - (A) advanced Classical economic theory by making several refinements.
   - (B) showed how Say's Law operated in capitalist economies.
   - (C) was a great American economist.
   - (D) explained the cause of and cure for the Great Depression.
   - (E) advanced Classical economic theory by building on Say's Law.

5. Which of the following would NOT shift the aggregate supply curve?
   - (A) An increase in the price level.
   - (B) A decrease in the amount of resources in the economy.
   - (C) An increase in the amount of resources in the economy.
   - (D) An improvement in technology.
   - (E) A decrease in productivity.

6. Which of the following would shift the aggregate demand curve to the left?
   - (A) An increase in consumer confidence.
   - (B) Business firms reduce spending on plant and equipment.
   - (C) Foreigners develop a preference for our products.
   - (D) Government increases its level of spending.
   - (E) An increase in the money supply.

7. Which of the following would NOT shift the aggregate demand curve?
   - (A) A change in consumer confidence.
   - (B) A change in technology.
   - (C) A change in the money supply.
   - (D) A change in spending by state governments.
   - (E) A change in foreign tastes for our products.

8. What will happen to the equilibrium price level and the equilibrium quantity of output if the aggregate demand curve shifts to the right? Assume an upward-sloping aggregate supply curve.
   - (A) The equilibrium price level increases while the equilibrium quantity of output decreases.
   - (B) The equilibrium price level decreases while the equilibrium quantity of output increases.
   - (C) The equilibrium price level and quantity of output increase.

(D) The equilibrium price level and quantity of output decrease.
(E) The equilibrium price level increases while the equilibrium quantity of output remains unchanged.

9. What will happen to the equilibrium price level and the equilibrium quantity of output if consumer confidence increases? Assume an upward-sloping aggregate supply curve.

(A) The equilibrium price level increases while the equilibrium quantity of output decreases.
(B) The equilibrium price level decreases while the equilibrium quantity of output increases.
(C) The equilibrium price level and quantity of output increase.
(D) The equilibrium price level and quantity of output decrease.
(E) The equilibrium price level increases while the equilibrium quantity of output remains unchanged.

10. What will happen to the equilibrium price level and the equilibrium quantity of output if the aggregate demand curve shifts to the right? Assume a long-run aggregate supply curve.

(A) The equilibrium price level increases while the equilibrium quantity of output decreases.
(B) The equilibrium price level decreases while the equilibrium quantity of output increases.
(C) The equilibrium price level and quantity of output increase.
(D) The equilibrium price level remains unchanged while the equilibrium quantity of output increases.
(E) The equilibrium price level increases while the equilibrium quantity of output remains unchanged.

11. What will happen to the equilibrium price level and the equilibrium quantity of output if the aggregate supply curve shifts to the left? Assume an upward-sloping aggregate supply curve.

(A) The equilibrium price level increases while the equilibrium quantity of output decreases.
(B) The equilibrium price level decreases while the equilibrium quantity of output increases.
(C) The equilibrium price level and quantity of output increase.
(D) The equilibrium price level and quantity of output decrease.
(E) The equilibrium price level increases while the equilibrium quantity of output remains unchanged.

12. What will happen to the equilibrium price level and the equilibrium quantity of output if a major earthquake destroys much of the plant and equipment on the West Coast? Assume an upward-sloping aggregate supply curve.

(A) The equilibrium price level increases while the equilibrium quantity of output decreases.
(B) The equilibrium price level decreases while the equilibrium quantity of output increases.
(C) The equilibrium price level and quantity of output increase.
(D) The equilibrium price level and quantity of output decrease.
(E) The equilibrium price level increases while the equilibrium quantity of output remains unchanged.

13. What will happen to the equilibrium price level and the equilibrium quantity of output if the aggregate supply curve shifts to the left? Assume a long-run aggregate supply curve.

(A) The equilibrium price level increases while the equilibrium quantity of output decreases.

(B) The equilibrium price level decreases while the equilibrium quantity of output increases.
(C) The equilibrium price level and quantity of output increase.
(D) The equilibrium price level remains unchanged while the equilibrium quantity of output increases.
(E) The equilibrium price level increases while the equilibrium quantity of output remains unchanged.

14. An increase in the price level
(A) shifts aggregate demand left.
(B) increases real financial wealth and therefore decreases consumer demand.
(C) reduces real financial wealth and therefore increases consumer demand.
(D) increases real financial wealth and therefore increases consumer demand.
(E) reduces real financial wealth and therefore decreases consumer demand.

15. According to the interest rate effect, aggregate demand slopes downward because lower prices
(A) reduce interest rates and therefore decrease the quantity demanded in aggregate.
(B) increase interest rates and therefore decrease the quantity demanded in aggregate.
(C) reduce interest rates and therefore increase the quantity demanded in aggregate.
(D) increase interest rates and therefore increase the quantity demanded in aggregate.
(E) None of the above are correct.

MULTIPLE-CHOICE REVIEW ANSWERS
选择题答案

1. (D) **4.** (D) **7.** (B) **10.** (E) **13.** (A)

2. (C) **5.** (A) **8.** (C) **11.** (A) **14.** (E)

3. (B) **6.** (B) **9.** (C) **12.** (A) **15.** (C)

FREE-RESPONSE REVIEW QUESTIONS 开放式题目

I. Draw an aggregate supply/aggregate demand diagram. Label the axes of your diagram. Make the aggregate supply curve upward sloping. Show which curve shifts when foreigners suddenly develop a distaste for our products. What will happen to equilibrium output and the equilibrium price level in the short run?

II. Would you expect the same thing to happen to equilibrium output and the equilibrium price level in the long run? Redraw the aggregate supply/aggregate demand diagram using a long-run aggregate supply curve. Now what happens when foreigners develop a distaste for our products?

III. Explain why the long-run aggregate supply curve is drawn as a vertical line and the short-run aggregate supply curve is drawn upward sloping. Explain why the long-run effects of a change in foreign tastes are different from the short-run effects.

Free-Response Review Answers 开放式题目答案

I. AS/AD Model when foreigners develop a distaste for our products

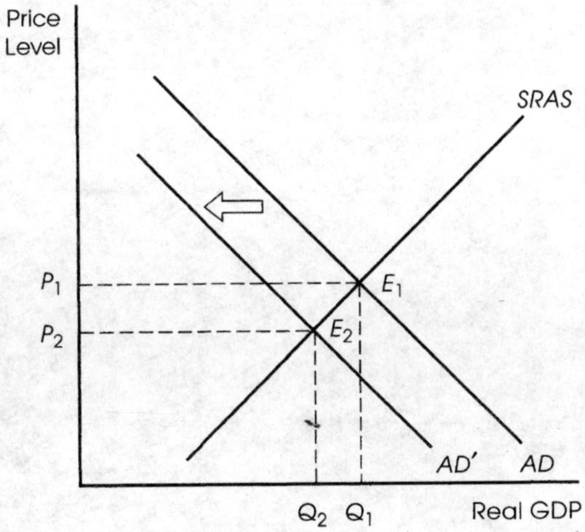

When foreigners develop a distaste for our products the aggregate demand curve shifts to the left. This causes the equilibrium price level and the equilibrium quantity of output to fall.

II. AS/AD Model when foreigners develop a distaste for our products (with long-run aggregate supply curve)

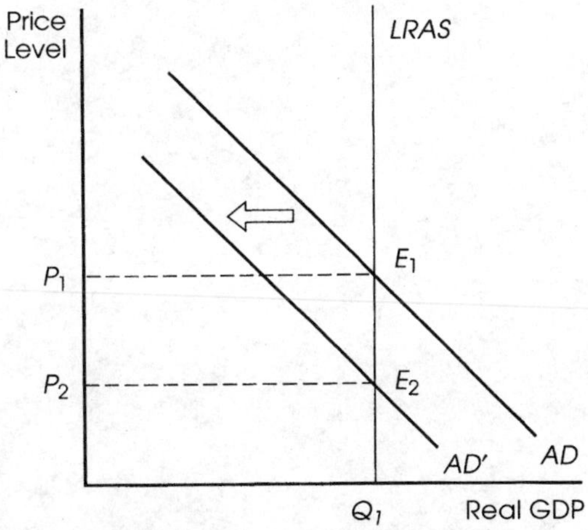

The long-run, or Classical, economic analysis indicates that the equilibrium price level will fall when foreigners develop a distaste for our products, but the equilibrium quantity of output will remain unchanged.

III. The long-run aggregate supply curve is drawn as a vertical line because aggregate supply is not affected by the price level in the long run. Only the amount of resources and the state of technology affect aggregate supply in the long run. In the short run, however, an increase in the price level induces suppliers in the economy to bring more product to market. Therefore, when foreigners develop a distaste for our products, prices fall and this reduces the amount of product that suppliers are willing to bring to market. But in the long run, the change in foreign tastes has not affected the amount of resources we have or our state of technology, so the quantity of output remains unchanged.

Fiscal Policy 财政政策

17

- → RECESSIONARY GAP
- → CROWDING OUT
- → LOANABLE FUNDS MARKET
- → INFLATIONARY GAP
- → PHILLIPS CURVE
- → STAGFLATION
- → RATIONAL EXPECTATIONS
- → AUTOMATIC STABILIZERS
- → MARGINAL PROPENSITY TO CONSUME
- → MULTIPLIER FOR FISCAL POLICY

KEYNES'S REMEDY FOR THE GREAT DEPRESSION 凯恩斯对大萧条的药方

Imagine an economy that is suffering from low levels of output and income. Unemployment is high and prices are falling. The AS/AD model (see Chapter 16) tells us that this is exactly what would occur in an economy where the aggregate demand curve has shifted to the left. Keynes concluded that the Great Depression was caused by a deficiency of spending, or aggregate demand, in our terms. His remedy was to get a boost in spending. But how? Consumers were tapped out and barely had enough to put food on the table. The unemployment rate was 25 percent in the United States. Why should businesses spend more on plant and equipment? Many of them were on the verge of bankruptcy. Maybe foreigners could be called upon to spend more? No, our major trading partners were experiencing depressions of their own.

Keynes recommended that the federal government boost its level of spending. That would shift the aggregate demand curve to the right where it belonged. The only catch was that the government couldn't tax more to pay for the increased spending. Increasing taxes would only shift the aggregate demand curve back to the left; the government would have to spend money it didn't have. It would have to run a deficit and borrow the money to increase spending. This was unheard of at the time. Prudent governments did not spend more than they took in by way of tax revenues.

In fact, during the Great Depression tax collections were down because so many businesses were not making any profits to tax and so many households were making no income to tax. There was talk of raising the tax rate. Our aggregate supply and demand model tells us that this is exactly the wrong thing to do—increasing taxes would only shift the aggregate demand curve further to the left.

No government was willing to try Keynes's radical new idea to remedy the Great Depression and the economic bad times persisted. It wasn't until the early 1940s that World War II forced many governments to spend more money than they had and borrow to make up the difference. That was how the Great Depression was finally put behind us.

TIP

To do well on the AP Macroeconomics exam you will have to understand how government spending and tax collections affect the economy.

Today, governments have gotten over their qualms about deficit spending. Governments have been known to deficit spend even when there was no recession. Keynes would be appalled. During expansions governments should spend less than they take in through taxes. Run a surplus. These surpluses could be used to pay off the borrowings from the deficits.

FISCAL POLICY 财政政策

Fiscal policy is changes in government spending and taxes to fight recessions or inflations. To remedy recessions the government should increase its level of spending and/or reduce taxes. In other words, the government should run a deficit.

The aggregate supply/aggregate demand (AS/AD) model can be used to show how deficit spending would work to cure a recession. Consider Figure 17.1, which shows an economy experiencing a recession. The aggregate demand curve and the short run aggregate supply curve cross to the left of the long run aggregate supply curve. Remember that the long run aggregate supply curve is vertical at the quantity of output the economy could produce if it used its resources fully and efficiently. Since the short run equilibrium is to the left of the vertical long run aggregate supply curve, the economy must not be using its resources fully and/or efficiently.

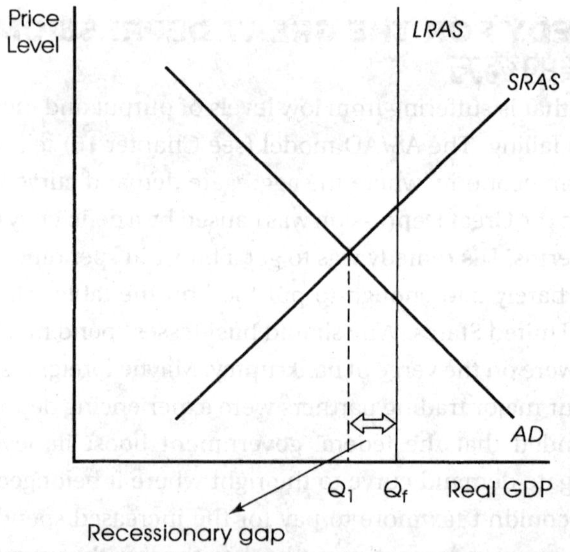

Fig. 17.1 A Recessionary Gap

The horizontal distance between the quantity of output the economy is producing, Q_1, and its potential, Q_f, is called the recessionary gap. The economy depicted in Figure 17.1 is experiencing a recession. Output is below potential and if output is low, so is income. And unemployment must be a problem if production is low. These are recessionary conditions.

Fiscal policy could be used to close the recessionary gap. An increase in government spending would shift the aggregate demand curve to the right. So would a decrease in taxes. Either of these policies would mean deficit spending on the part of the government. But when the aggregate demand curve shifts to the right, the recession is over. This is shown in Figure 17.2.

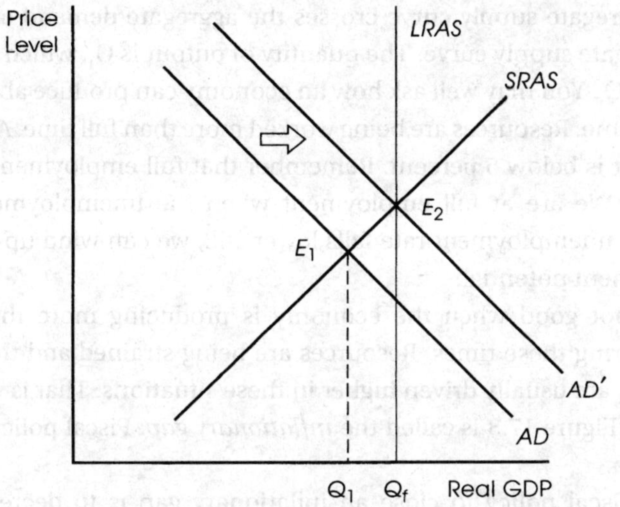

Fig. 17.2 Fiscal Policy to Close a Recessionary Gap

After the aggregate demand curve shifts to the right, the new equilibrium occurs where all three curves cross. The new quantity of output is Q_f (f for full employment) and the recession is ended. Unfortunately, the price level is higher at the new equilibrium. This means the economy experienced some inflation as a result of the fiscal policy that cured the recession. Hopefully, the costs of this inflation were worth the benefits of ending the recession.

An economy can experience the opposite sort of trouble from a recessionary gap. An inflationary gap occurs when an economy is producing above its potential. Figure 17.3 illustrates this situation.

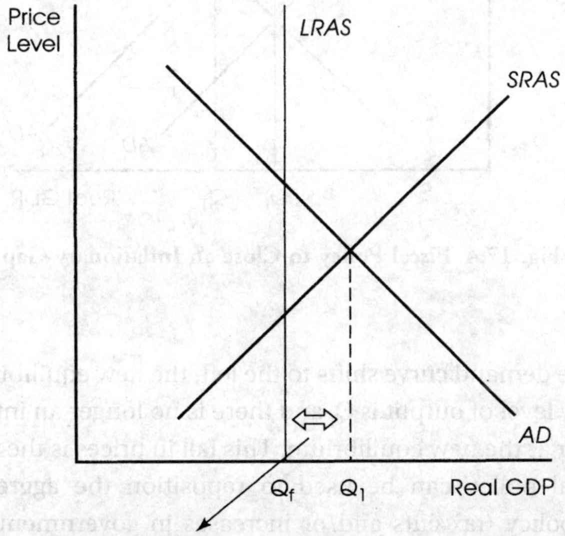

Fig. 17.3 An Inflationary Gap

The short-run aggregate supply curve crosses the aggregate demand curve to the right of the long-run aggregate supply curve. The quantity of output is Q_1, which is more than the economy's potential, Q_f. You may well ask how an economy can produce above its potential. One response is overtime. Resources are being worked more than full time. Another response is that unemployment is below 5 percent. Remember that full employment does not mean zero unemployment. We are at full employment when the unemployment rate reaches 5 percent or so. If the unemployment rate falls lower still, we can wind up producing more than our full employment potential.

The situation is not good when the economy is producing more than its potential. Inflation is typical during these times. Resources are being strained and the economy may be overheating. Prices are usually driven higher in these situations. That is why the distance between Q_f and Q_2 in Figure 17.3 is called the *inflationary gap*. Fiscal policy can be applied to resolve the problem.

The appropriate fiscal policy to close an inflationary gap is to decrease government spending and/or increase taxes. These policies would result in a surplus where government tax collections exceed government spending. This would slow the economy by curtailing the amount of spending that occurs. The aggregate demand curve shifts to the left when the government decreases its level of spending or raises taxes. This is shown in Figure 17.4.

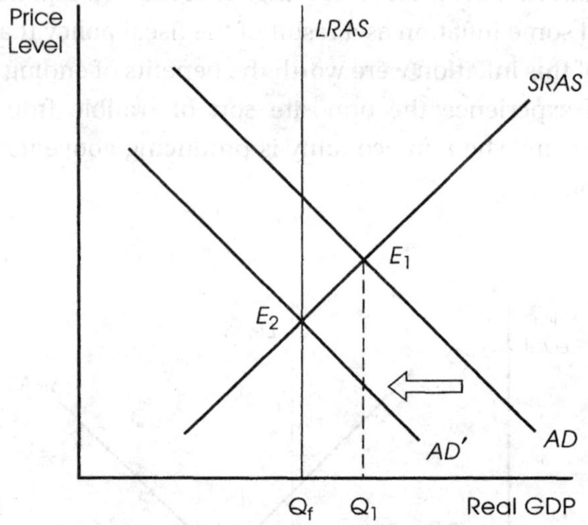

Fig. 17.4 Fiscal Policy to Close an Inflationary Gap

TIP

No matter what kind of trouble the economy finds itself in, recession or inflation, fiscal policy is a potential remedy.

After the aggregate demand curve shifts to the left, the new equilibrium is where all three curves cross. The new level of output is Q_f and there is no longer an inflationary gap; in fact, the price level is lower at the new equilibrium. This fall in prices is the inflation being cured.

To sum up, fiscal policy can be used to reposition the aggregate demand curve. Expansionary fiscal policy (tax cuts and/or increases in government spending) shifts the aggregate demand curve to the right. Contractionary fiscal policy shifts aggregate demand to the left.

MULTIPLIERS FOR FISCAL POLICY 财政政策的乘数

Imagine an economy in the midst of a recession. The appropriate fiscal policy is to increase government spending or reduce taxes. Either of these changes in the government's budget will have a magnified effect on the overall economy. This is because an increase in government spending will engender further spending.

The marginal propensity to consume (MPC) is how much is spent out of an extra dollar of income. Young people are well known to have an MPC =1. Give them an extra dollar, and it is spent. But middle-aged people thinking about their retirement or their children's education may save 15 cents out of any extra dollars they may earn, giving them an MPC = .85.

Suppose the MPC = .8 and government spending increases by $20 billion. If the government spends the $20 billion on new roads, then the company and crews that build these roads earn $20 billion in income. They will spend $16 billion of that since the MPC = .8. That $16 billion will become an increase in income for the people and businesses that sold products and services to the road builders. And the story goes on and on because the .8 of the $16 billion will be spent in the next round.

TIP

Be careful not to say that an increase in government spending increases the money supply. It does not. An increase in government spending increases aggregate demand which, in turn, increases real GDP, income, and prices in the short run. But the money supply is unchanged.

Round	Spending	MPC = 0.8
1	$20 billion	
2	$16 billion	
3	$12.8 billion	
4	$10.24 billion	
Total	$100 billion	

We know that the total increase in spending after all the ensuing rounds amounts to $100 billion. This figure was obtained from the formula:

Change in Real GDP = Initial Change in Spending × Multiplier

$100 billion = $20 billion × 5.0

The marginal propensity to save (MPS) is simply 1 – MPC. If the MPC is .85, then the MPS = .15. That is, given an extra dollar of income, 15 cents will be saved.

The multiplier is equal to 1/(1 – MPC) = 5.0 (= 1/(1 – .8) = 1/.2). This means any change in government spending will be magnified 5 times.

However, real GDP will not rise by $100 billion if the government lowers taxes by $20 billion. This is because when consumers get their tax breaks totaling $20 billion they will initially increase spending by $16 billion, assuming once again that the MPC equals 0.8. Households save $4 billion of the tax cut.

Change in Real GDP = Initial Change in Spending × Multiplier

$80 billion = $16 billion × 5.0

In this case, real GDP increases by $80 billion.

The fact that a $20 billion dollar change in government spending has a slightly more powerful impact on real GDP than a $20 billion change in taxes has an interesting implication. What would happen if the government were to increase spending by $20 billion while simultaneously *increasing* taxes by $20 billion? The increase in government spending of $20 billion would cause a $100 billion increase in real GDP, while the $20 billion increase in taxes would reduce real GDP by $80 billion. The net effect is a $20 billion increase in real GDP.

If the government has a balanced budget so that spending equals tax revenues, it can maintain the balanced budget and still stimulate real GDP. This is because if spending and tax revenues were both raised by some amount, say $20 billion, then real GDP would increase by $20 billion.

Table 17.1

Frequently Used Multipliers

MPC	Multiplier
.5	2
.75	4
.8	5
.9	10

Balanced-Budget Move 平衡预算变动

Whenever the government changes spending and taxes so that the effects on the budget are neutral, this is known as a "balanced-budget" move. So an increase in government spending of $5 million and an increase in taxes of $5 million is a balanced-budget move. Similarly, a decrease in government spending of $4 billion and a decrease in taxes of $4 billion is a balanced-budget move.

In each of these cases, the change in government spending has a stronger impact than the change in taxes. Real GDP will be affected by the amount of the spending and tax change. For instance, when government increases spending by $5 million and taxes by the same amount, real GDP will increase by $5 million.

If government decreases spending by $4 billion and lowers taxes by the same amount, real GDP will decrease by $4 billion. You can arrive at this conclusion the long way: calculate the impact of the government spending change and the impact of the tax change. Then figure the net effect. Or you can take the shortcut: the balanced-budget multiplier is equal to 1. This means an increase in government spending of x dollars that is matched by an increase in tax revenues of x dollars results in an increase in real GDP of x dollars. Based on the same reasoning, a decrease in government spending of x dollars that is matched by a decrease in tax revenues of x dollars results in a decrease in real GDP of x dollars.

The Phillips Tradeoff 菲利普斯曲线

Fiscal policy, however, has its drawbacks. We have already seen that a fiscal policy designed to remedy a recession will result in inflation. Similarly, a fiscal policy designed to combat inflation will result in declines in output and possibly a recession. It seems that fiscal policy cannot remedy both unemployment and inflation at the same time.

The idea that inflation and unemployment move in opposite directions was first noticed by a British economist, A. W. Phillips. Looking back over 100 years of British economic history he discovered that when inflation was high, unemployment was low. When inflation was low, unemployment tended to be high. The inverse relationship between inflation and unemployment became known as the Phillips tradeoff.

Phillips graphed the relationship between inflation and unemployment. The results were similar to Figure 17.5. A high inflation rate, such as point A, is associated with a low unemployment rate. A low inflation rate, such as point B, is associated with a high unemployment rate.

Phillips published his findings in 1958, and his relationship has been looked for in many economies over various time periods. For instance, it is well known that unemployment and inflation behaved according to this relationship in the United States in the 1960s, but the 1970s defied the Phillips tradeoff—both inflation and unemployment were high in the mid-1970s.

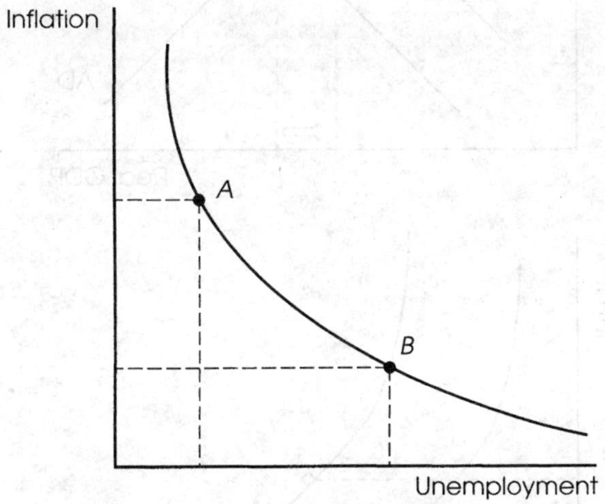

Fig. 17.5 The Phillips Curve

Economists are now able to explain why the Phillips relationship holds in some periods and not in others. Notice that when the aggregate demand curve shifts to the left, it results in the price level falling (lower inflation) and the quantity of output falling (higher unemployment). When the aggregate demand shifts to the right, just the opposite occurs—inflation rises and unemployment falls. All of this is in line with what Phillips discovered. This indicates that the aggregate demand curve must have been shifting about in the United States in the 1960s, while the aggregate supply curve remained stable.

Now consider what happens when the aggregate supply shifts left. Figure 17.6 depicts this event for the short run. The initial equilibrium is E1. Then the aggregate supply curve shifts left and the new equilibrium is E2. Prices are higher at E2 (inflation is up) and output is lower (unemployment is up). This goes against the Phillips relationship. Indeed, it is the worst of all situations, with both inflation and unemployment rising. Economists call this *stagflation*.

If the aggregate demand curve shifts right, then the economy will slide up the Phillips curve from a point such as B in Figure 17.5 toward point A. However, if the aggregate supply curve shifts left, as in Figure 17.6, then the whole Phillips curve shifts right. The rightward shift of the Phillips curve reflects the fact that the economy has to suffer higher levels of inflation and unemployment.

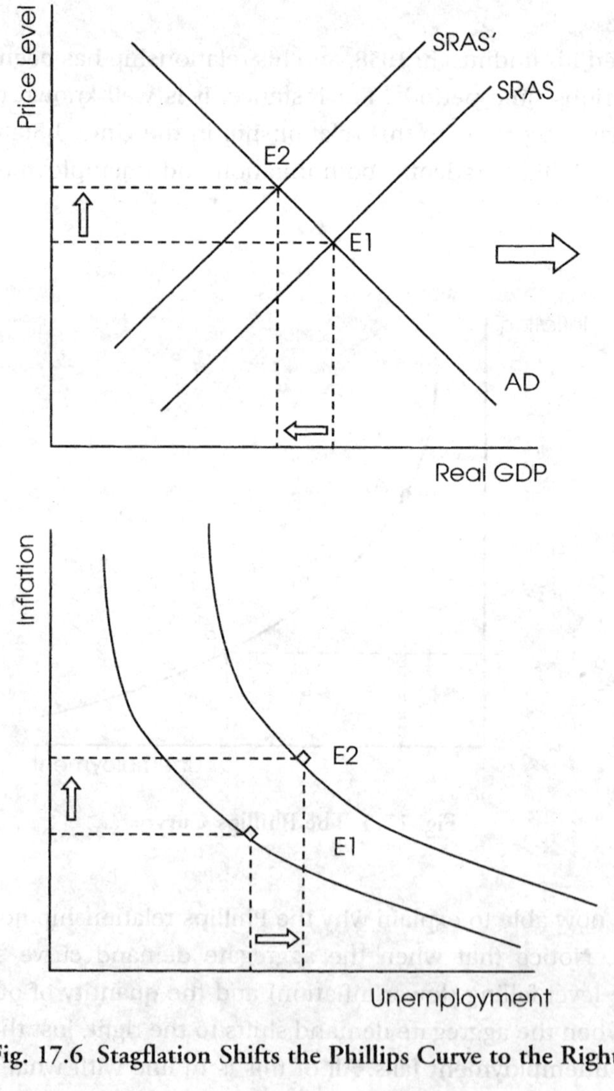

Fig. 17.6 Stagflation Shifts the Phillips Curve to the Right

The Phillips curve portrays the tradeoff between inflation and unemployment in the short run. In the long run, it is doubtful that such a relationship exists. Consider an increase in aggregate demand with a long-run aggregate supply curve:

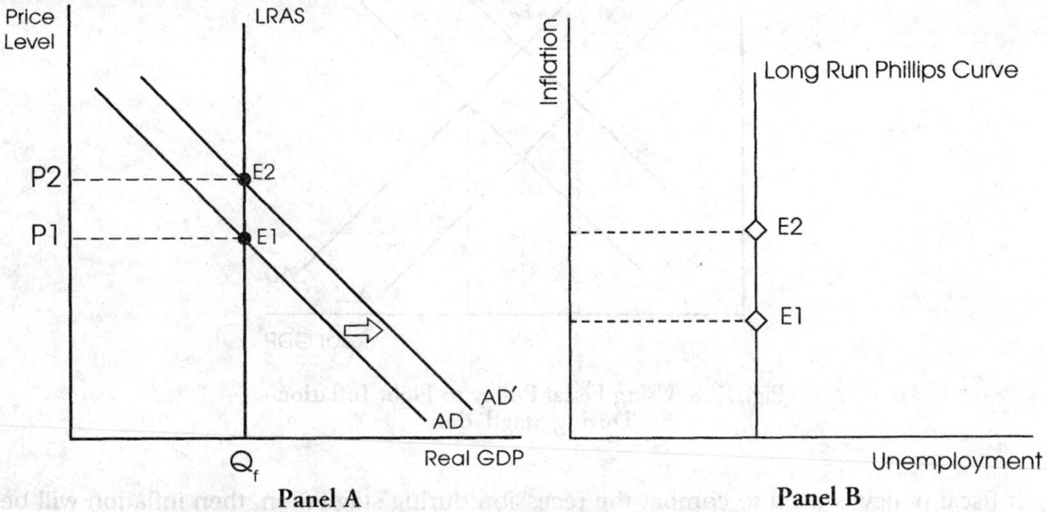

Fig. 17.7 The Phillips Curve Is Vertical in the Long Run since Changes in Aggregate Demand Affect Only Prices

The result is an increase in the price level from P1 to P2, but output does not change from Q_f. Therefore, unemployment will not change. We have an increase in the price level but no change in unemployment. In other words, the Phillips relationship is a vertical line in the long run.

> **POINTS TO REMEMBER**
>
> **If the aggregate demand curve shifts right, the economy slides up the Phillips curve.**
> **If the aggregate demand curve shifts left, the economy slides down the Phillips curve.**
> **If the short-run aggregate supply curve shifts left, the Phillips curve shifts right. If the short-run aggregate supply curve shifts right, the Phillips curve shifts left.**

Stagflation 滞涨

Stagflation occurs whenever the aggregate supply curve shifts to the left. Since both inflation and unemployment are rising, this defies the Phillips relationship, which concludes that unemployment and inflation move in opposite directions.

Stagflation occurred in the 1970s in the United States when the supply of a very important resource, oil, was curtailed by the formation of an oil cartel. Notice that stagflation poses a special problem for fiscal policy. If both inflation and unemployment are high, should fiscal policy be used to fight the high unemployment or the high inflation? It cannot remedy both at the same time.

Figure 17.8 shows what would happen if fiscal policy were used to fight inflation during stagflation. The initial equilibrium is E1. Then the aggregate supply curve shifts to the left because resources are not as available. This results in stagflation and takes us to E2. Then the government runs a surplus by raising taxes and/or lowering spending. This shifts the aggregate demand curve to the left and we end up at E3. The price level is brought back down to its original level, but the quantity of output has fallen to new lows. The inflation has been cured but the recession has been made worse.

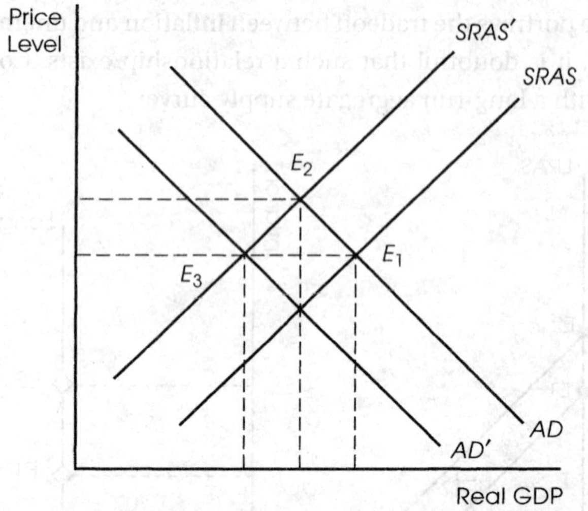

Fig. 17.8 Using Fiscal Policy to Fight Inflation During Stagflation

If fiscal policy is used to combat the recession during stagflation, then inflation will be taken to even higher levels. This is a major drawback of fiscal policy. It cannot cope with stagflation because it can remedy only one problem at the expense of another.

The true solution to stagflation is to get the aggregate supply curve to shift back to the right. This can be accomplished by making resources more available or a technological advance. There are no standard government policies that can accomplish this quickly and effectively. *Supply-side economics* is an attempt to shift the aggregate supply curve to the right to cure stagflation. Supply-side economists recommend special tax policies and less government regulation to accomplish the task. So far, however, these policies have not been fully tested.

In any event, the Phillips relationship poses a problem for advocates of fiscal policy. The relationship indicates that fiscal policy can remedy only one of the two economic evils at a time. When both inflation and unemployment rear their heads simultaneously, fiscal policy is not appropriate.

Crowding Out 挤出效应

Crowding out can render fiscal policy ineffective. Crowding out is the increase in interest rates and subsequent decline in spending that occurs when the government borrows money to finance a deficit.

To see how crowding out works, imagine an economy mired in a recessionary gap. Suppose the government implements the appropriate fiscal policy and runs a deficit. This means the government will need to borrow money. However, we have been ignoring the fact that if the government borrows a large portion of the funds available for lending, then interest rates would rise.

TIP

Recent AP exams have tested students' understanding of crowding out by asking questions concerning the market for loanable funds.

To understand this consider what would happen if you walked into a bank for a car loan just after the government had borrowed a good portion of the bank's loanable funds. They could give you the car loan, but probably at a higher rate of interest than before.

Now, you may decide that the monthly payments on the car and loan would be too high. You do not buy the car and hundreds of people make decisions similar to yours. The demand for cars drops and autoworkers are laid off.

Crowding out can be shown in a diagram of the market for loanable funds such as Figure 17.9, panel A. The supply of loanable funds is upward sloping to reflect the idea that more people, banks, and institutions are willing to loan funds when interest rates are higher.

The demand for funds is downward sloping to indicate that more loans are desired when the real interest rate is lower.

Do not confuse the supply and demand for loanable funds with the supply and demand for money. The supply of money is vertical because the Federal Reserve controls it. The supply of loanable funds is upward sloping because loans can come from many sources. Households are the biggest lenders in the economy if you consider depositing money in a bank a loan to the bank. Foreign central banks have become a welcome source of loanable funds in the U.S. economy.

One of the largest demanders of loanable funds in the U.S. is the federal government. When the federal government deficit-spends in order to stimulate the economy, the demand for loanable funds shifts right in Figure 17.9, panel A. This results in a higher equilibrium real interest rate. The higher interest rate discourages borrowing and spending, especially for investment. The decrease in investment spending by businesses can offset the government's expansionary fiscal policy.

Diagrammatically, crowding out is reflected in an aggregate demand curve that shifts back to the left after a fiscal policy has just shifted it to the right. This is shown in Figure 17.9, Panel B. Originally the economy is in a recession at E_1. An expansionary fiscal policy is used to shift the aggregate demand curve to the right. The new equilibrium is E_2 and the recessionary gap is closed. However, interest rates rise because of the government borrowing associated with the fiscal policy. This is shown in the loanable funds market in Panel A. The higher rates of interest induce consumers and businesses to borrow and spend less than before. This drop in consumer and business spending shifts the aggregate demand curve back to its original position and the economy ends up back at E_1 and in recession.

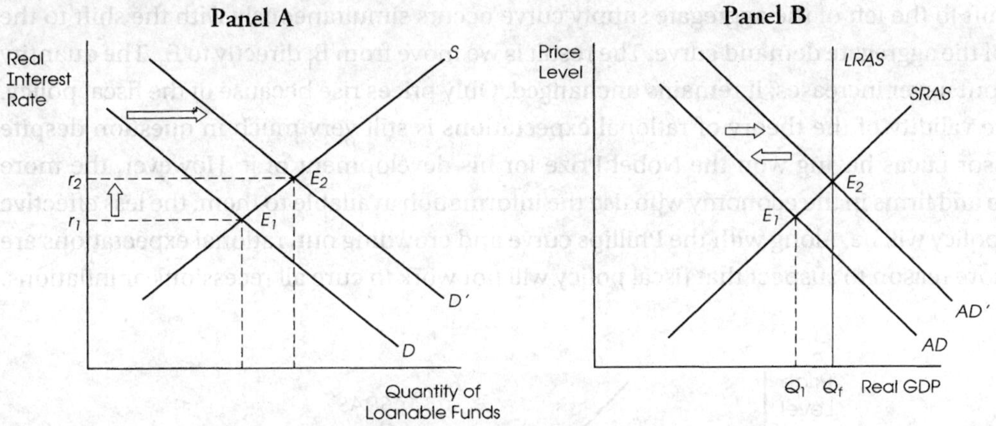

Fig. 17.9 Crowding Out

This is how crowding out can nullify the beneficial effects of fiscal policy. Crowding out is not always an issue. Sometimes there are plenty of loanable funds available and the government can borrow and deficit spend without an adverse effect on fiscal policy. Other times, the government borrowing raises interest rates, which chokes off consumer and business spending. The declines in consumer and business spending offset the increase in government spending and fiscal policy is ineffective.

Rational Expectations 理性预期

In 1995 Robert Lucas of the University of Chicago won the Nobel Prize in economics "for having developed and applied the hypothesis of rational expectations, and thereby having transformed macroeconomic analysis and deepened our understanding of economic policy."

This hypothesis is based on the idea that households and businesses will use all the information available to them when making economic decisions. This seems like a logical and harmless assumption, but carried to its logical conclusion, rational expectations implies that fiscal policy will be ineffective at changing the quantity of output.

Suppose the government tries to stimulate the economy through expansionary fiscal policy. The government deficit-spends. People understand that such a policy results in higher prices. Even if they don't have the economic education to make this conclusion, others will, and they will read about it in the press: prices are expected to rise with expansionary fiscal policy. When households and firms expect prices to be higher in the future, they supply less labor and products right now. Why supply labor and products now when you can supply them next month at a higher price?

This reduction in supply nullifies the expansionary effect of the fiscal policy. Only prices rise because of the deficit spending by the government. The situation is illustrated in Figure 17.10.

Initially the economy is in equilibrium at E_1. The government then deficit spends in order to increase the quantity of output. This shifts the aggregate demand curve to the right. Normally we would end up at E_2 and that would be the end of the story. However, under rational expectations we never get to E_2 because households and firms realize that the expansionary fiscal policy will result in higher prices. They are simply using the information in any economics text to reach this conclusion. Rational expectations are that people will use all the information available when making economic decisions.

Expecting higher prices for their labor and products, people and firms reduce their supply of labor and products right now. This causes the aggregate supply curve to shift to the left. The shift to the left of the aggregate supply curve occurs simultaneously with the shift to the right of the aggregate demand curve. The result is we move from E_1 directly to E_3. The quantity of output never increases; it remains unchanged. Only prices rise because of the fiscal policy.

The validity of the theory of rational expectations is still very much in question despite Professor Lucas having won the Nobel Prize for his development of it. However, the more people and firms in the economy who use the information available to them, the less effective fiscal policy will be. Along with the Phillips curve and crowding out, rational expectations are one more reason to suspect that fiscal policy will not work to cure all recessions or inflations.

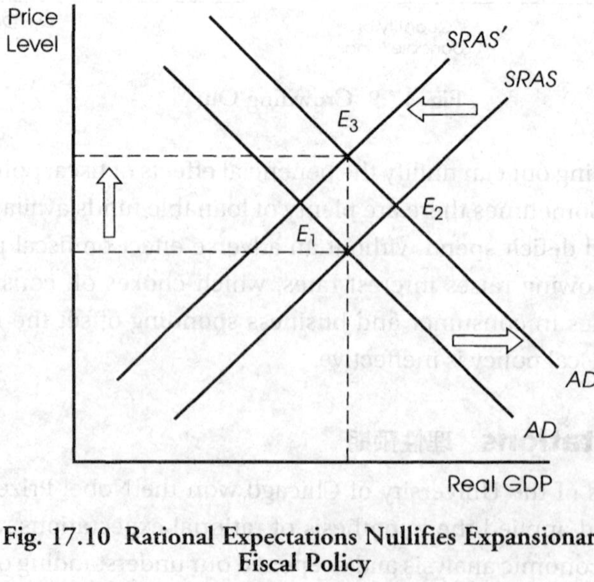

Fig. 17.10 Rational Expectations Nullifies Expansionary Fiscal Policy

Automatic Stabilizers 自动稳定器

Automatic, or built-in, stabilizers are government policies already in place that promote deficit spending during recessions and surplus budgets during expansions. These policies prevent recessions from becoming depressions. They also help keep inflations from turning into hyperinflations.

Income taxes and antipoverty programs such as Temporary Aid to Needy Families (TANF) are examples of automatic stabilizers. Consider how income taxes are affected as the economy falls into a recession. More and more people become unemployed or make less income as the recession progresses. But when a household makes less income, it owes less in taxes. In other words, government tax revenues will automatically fall during a recession and this is exactly the type of fiscal policy called for to fight a recession.

Automatic stabilizers cannot prevent a recession because the drop in income is necessary for them to begin working. However, built-in stabilizers can prevent a recession from becoming a depression.

Let's consider how a program like TANF would work as an automatic stabilizer. Again, imagine an economy slipping into a recession. More and more households will qualify for TANF funds. Government spending on antipoverty programs automatically increases during a recession and a boost in government spending is just the sort of fiscal policy that is required to fight a recession.

Also notice that income taxes and TANF would work to prevent an expansion from becoming too exuberant. As the expansion continues, inflationary pressures build as households make more and more income. But more income means higher tax payments for households. Higher taxes are the appropriate fiscal policy to fight inflation. Also, fewer households will qualify for TANF funds as the economy expands. This means government spending on this program will be falling. Cuts in government spending are the appropriate fiscal policy to fight inflation.

Automatic stabilizers work to prevent business cycles from becoming too extreme in either direction. Many economists credit automatic stabilizers, not fiscal policy, for the decreased amplitude of business cycles since World War II.

SUMMARY 小结

- Fiscal policy is just one of several options policymakers can use to address economic concerns such as unemployment or inflation. The appropriate fiscal policy to combat unemployment and recessions is to have the government run a deficit by spending more and/or lower tax collections. To fight inflation, the government should run a surplus by cutting government spending and raising tax rates. These policies shift the aggregate demand curve to a more suitable position.
- Students may wonder why we have recessions and inflations if fiscal policy can be used against them. The answer is that fiscal policy has drawbacks and is not completely effective. One drawback of fiscal policy is that the same policies that fight recessions promote inflation. And if the economy is suffering from stagflation, recession, and inflation simultaneously, fiscal policy can address only one of these problems while making the other worse.
- Crowding out and rational expectations can make fiscal policy completely or partially ineffective. Crowding out refers to the rise in borrowing costs to firms and households after the government borrows to deficit spend. Higher borrowing costs can result in lower spending by households and firms that would offset the expansionary

fiscal policy. Rational expectations assumes that people and firms will know that an expansionary fiscal policy will result in higher prices. Because prices are expected to be higher in the future, people work less and firms supply less right now. They would prefer to work and supply more later when wages and prices are higher. The reduction in supply offsets the expansionary fiscal policy.

- Yet another problem with fiscal policy is the fact that Congress and the President have to first realize the economy is in trouble, then design a fiscal policy to combat the recessionary or inflationary gap. All of this takes time. Fortunately, there are laws and programs already on the books that will work to fight recessions or inflations. These laws and programs are called automatic stabilizers. Tax laws and antipoverty programs are examples of built-in stabilizers. Automatic stabilizers cannot prevent recessions or inflations, but they can prevent recessions from becoming depressions and inflations from becoming hyperinflations.

TERMS 术语

Automatic Stabilizers government policies already in place that promote deficit spending during recessions and surplus budgets during expansions

Crowding Out the increase in interest rates and subsequent decline in spending that occurs when the government borrows money to finance a deficit

Deficit situation that exists when government spending exceeds tax revenues

Fiscal Policy changes in government spending and taxes to fight recessions or inflations

Inflationary Gap what occurs when the equilibrium quantity of output is above potential output

Marginal Propensity to Consume (MPC) the amount of an extra dollar of income that is spent

Multiplier the degree of magnification that an initial change in spending will have on the economy

Phillips Tradeoff the inverse relationship between inflation and unemployment

Rational Expectations the idea that households and businesses will use all the information available to them when making economic decisions

Recessionary Gap what occurs when the equilibrium quantity of output is below potential output

Stagflation term used to describe the situation when the economy experiences inflation and a recession simultaneously

Surplus spending by the government that is less than tax revenues

FORMULAS 公式

$$\text{Marginal Propensity to Consume} = \frac{\text{Change in Spending}}{\text{Change in Income}}$$

Multiplier = 1/(1 – MPC)

Total Change in Income = Initial Change in Spending × Multiplier

MULTIPLE-CHOICE REVIEW QUESTIONS 选择题

1. Fiscal policy refers to
   (A) increases in taxes to fight recessions.
   (B) decreases in taxes to fight inflations.
   (C) changes in government spending and taxes to fight recessions or inflations.
   (D) federal deficits.
   (E) federal surpluses.

2. A federal deficit occurs when
   (A) exports exceed imports.
   (B) imports exceed exports.
   (C) federal tax collections exceed spending.
   (D) federal spending exceeds federal tax revenues.
   (E) the federal government spends less than last year.

3. The appropriate fiscal policy to remedy a recession
   (A) calls for the federal government to run a deficit.
   (B) calls for the federal government to run a surplus.
   (C) is increased taxes and government spending.
   (D) is decreased government spending and taxes.
   (E) is increased taxes and reduced government spending.

4. The appropriate fiscal policy to remedy inflation calls for
   (A) the federal government to run a deficit.
   (B) the federal government to run a surplus.
   (C) increased taxes and government spending.
   (D) decreased government spending and taxes.
   (E) decreased taxes and increased government spending.

5. To close a recessionary gap with fiscal policy
   (A) the aggregate demand curve should be shifted to the right.
   (B) the aggregate demand curve should be shifted to the left.
   (C) the aggregate supply curve should be shifted to the right.
   (D) the aggregate supply curve should be shifted to the left.
   (E) prices should be raised.

6. To close an inflationary gap with fiscal policy
   (A) the aggregate demand curve should be shifted to the right.
   (B) the aggregate demand curve should be shifted to the left.
   (C) the aggregate supply curve should be shifted to the right.
   (D) the aggregate supply curve should be shifted to the left.
   (E) prices should be lowered.

7. One drawback of using fiscal policy to close a recessionary gap is that

(A) unemployment will rise.
(B) taxes will have to be raised.
(C) the equilibrium price level will rise.
(D) government spending on important programs will have to be cut.
(E) equilibrium output will fall.

8. Use the following three responses to answer the question: Fiscal policy is not always effective because of

I. crowding out.
II. rational expectations.
III. the balanced budget amendment.

(A) I only
(B) II only
(C) II and III
(D) I and II
(E) I, II, and III

9. Stagflation occurs when

(A) inflation falls and unemployment rises.
(B) inflation rises and unemployment falls.
(C) inflation and unemployment both rise.
(D) Inflation and output both rise.
(E) Inflation and output both fall.

10. Study the diagram below.

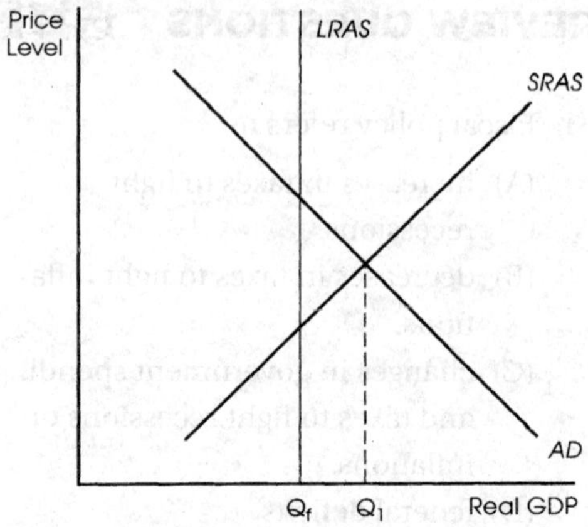

(A) It is incorrect since Q_f can never be to the left of Q_1.
(B) It is incorrect because AD should slope upward and AS should slope down.
(C) It portrays a recessionary gap.
(D) It portrays an inflationary gap.
(E) It portrays Phillips curves.

11. Crowding out

(A) is one reason fiscal policy is so effective.
(B) occurs when interest rates fall due to government borrowing.
(C) occurs when consumers and firms spend less offsetting expansionary fiscal policy.
(D) causes the aggregate demand curve to shift to the right.
(E) occurs when rising interest rates cause cuts in government spending.

12. The theory of rational expectations
   (A) assumes that consumers and businesses anticipate rising prices when the government pursues an expansionary fiscal policy.
   (B) implies that fiscal policy will be effective even during stagflation.
   (C) supports the notion of a Phillips tradeoff.
   (D) assumes that consumers and businesses do not use all the information available to them.
   (E) was developed by Keynes as a remedy for the Great Depression.

13. Study the diagram below.

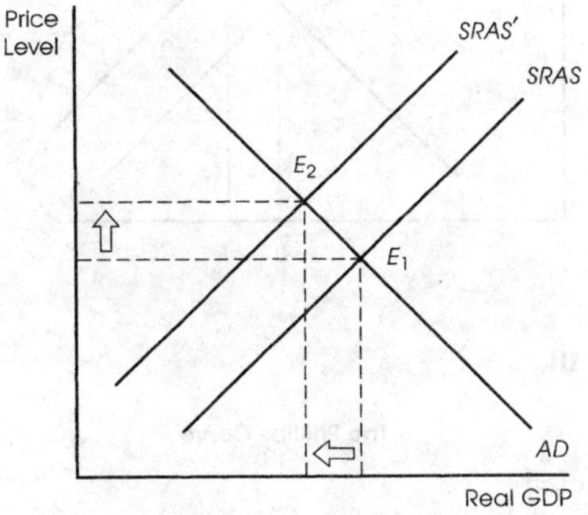

   (A) It shows how fiscal policy can work to cure inflation.
   (B) It shows how fiscal policy can work to close a recessionary gap.
   (C) It portrays the Phillips tradeoff.
   (D) It is incorrect because AD should slope upward and AS should slope down.
   (E) It portrays stagflation.

14. Automatic, or built-in, stabilizers
   (A) prevent inflation.
   (B) prevent recessions from occurring.
   (C) prevent inflation and recessions from occurring.
   (D) are government policies already in place that promote deficit spending during expansions and surplus budgets during recessions.
   (E) are government policies already in place that promote deficit spending during recessions and surplus budgets during expansions.

15. The Phillips curve
   (A) shows how government spending and tax collections are related.
   (B) is upward sloping from left to right.
   (C) indicates that inflation will be high when unemployment is low.
   (D) shows how the equilibrium price level is related to fiscal policy.
   (E) shows how output and prices are related.

MULTIPLE-CHOICE REVIEW ANSWERS
选择题答案

1. (C)	**4.** (B)	**7.** (C)	**10.** (D)	**13.** (E)
2. (D)	**5.** (A)	**8.** (D)	**11.** (C)	**14.** (E)
3. (A)	**6.** (B)	**9.** (C)	**12.** (A)	**15.** (C)

FREE-RESPONSE REVIEW QUESTIONS 开放式题目

I. Draw a diagram that portrays a recessionary gap. Be sure to label the axes of your diagram and the aggregate demand curve, the upward sloping aggregate supply curve, and the long run aggregate supply curve.

II. Describe the fiscal policy that would be appropriate to close the recessionary gap. On the diagram show how the fiscal policy works to close the recessionary gap.

III. Draw a Phillips curve. Be sure to label the axes of your diagram. An economy that is in recession would have a low inflation rate but a high unemployment rate. Mark such a point on your Phillips curve and label it "R." Suppose a fiscal policy is implemented and this policy closes the recessionary gap. Mark and label another point on the Phillips curve to demarcate the new inflation/unemployment combination and label it "AFP" for "after the fiscal policy." Explain how you concluded where AFP would be.

Free-Response Review Answers 开放式题目答案

I.

A Recessionary Gap

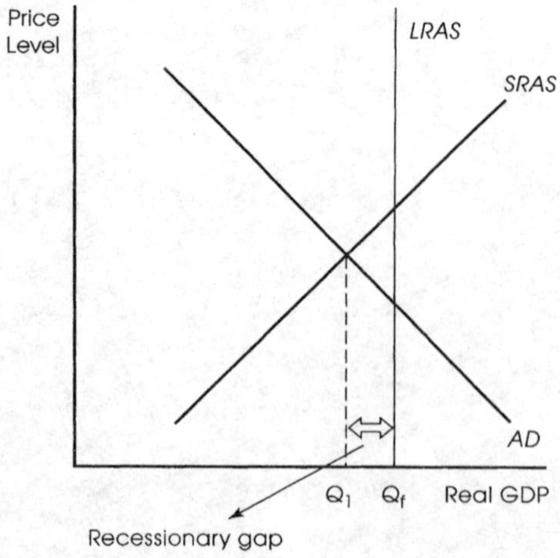

II. The appropriate fiscal policy to close a recessionary gap is for the federal government to run a deficit. This can be accomplished by the federal government increasing spending or by reducing taxes or both. Any of these policies will serve to increase aggregate demand. This is shown on the AS/AD model by a shift to the right of the aggregate demand curve.

Fiscal Policy to Close a Recessionary Gap

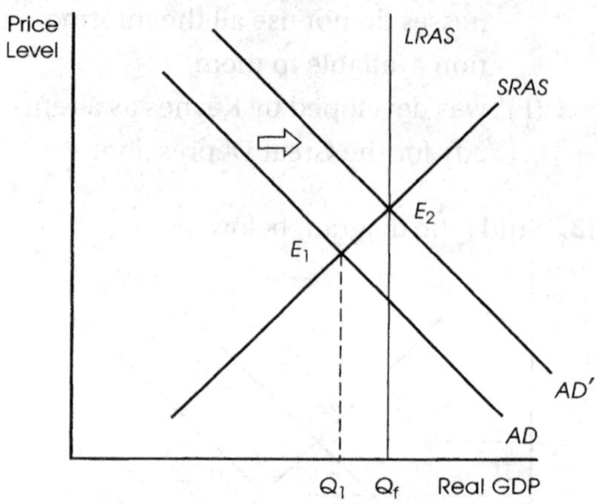

III.

The Phillips Curve

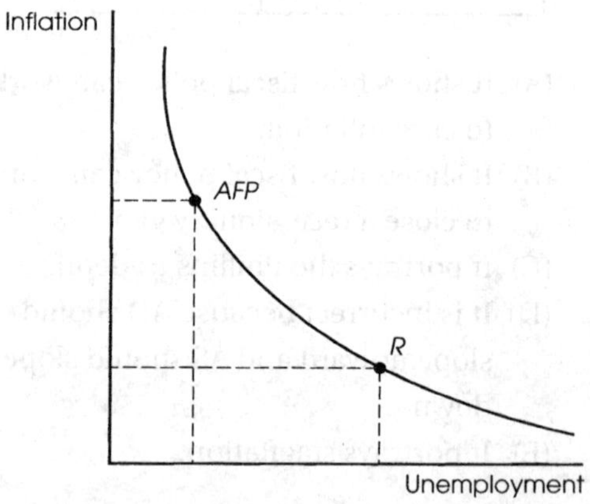

Beginning at point R, an expansionary fiscal policy would lower the unemployment rate but raise prices. After the fiscal policy the economy would have lower unemployment but higher inflation. This is the case at point AFP. Thus, an expansionary fiscal policy serves to slide the economy up the Phillips curve.

Money and Banking 货币与银行业

18

- → M1
- → M2
- → FIAT MONEY
- → FUNCTIONS OF MONEY
- → T-ACCOUNTS
- → FRACTIONAL RESERVE BANKING
- → MONEY MULTIPLIER
- → POLICY TOOLS OF THE FEDERAL RESERVE

THE SUPPLY OF MONEY 货币供给

It is best to avoid the word "money" when talking about fiscal policy. It is incorrect to say that an increase in government spending increases the amount of money in the economy and, therefore, aggregate demand. Replace the word "money" with "income" in the previous sentence and it becomes accurate.

The money supply in the United States is controlled by the Federal Reserve. When the government deficit-spends, this does not change the money supply. The money in circulation may be used more intensely, but the number of dollars does not change with fiscal policy.

Money is anything that society generally accepts in payment for a good or service. This is a very broad definition and allows for many things to be counted as money. There have been societies that accepted beads and clamshells in exchange for goods and services.

Experts in the field of money and banking disagree on what should be included in the money supply because they disagree on what our society generally accepts in exchange for goods and services. Certainly, currency—coins and paper money—is the most widely accepted form of money in our society. And checks written on bank deposits are accepted almost as readily as currency. Bankers refer to checking accounts, and accounts that function like checking accounts, as *transaction accounts*. In the opinion of many experts, currency, transaction accounts, and travelers' checks are the only items generally accepted in payment in the United States. This definition of money is referred to as M1 and totaled $2.55 trillion in 2013.

Credit Cards 信用卡

Credit cards are perhaps more widely accepted than checks, but credit cards are not part of the money supply—they are merely a convenient way of taking out a loan from a bank. When you pay for something with your credit card, the bank that sponsors your credit card is actually paying the merchant for the item purchased. The bank records this transaction like a loan on its books. Then the bank hounds you for repayment of the loan and interest is charged if you do not pay the entire amount in a short period of time. Credit cards are one way banks use their depositors' money to make loans. Since we count the amount of money deposited into checking accounts as part of M1, it would be redundant to count credit cards also.

TIP

Most people think of money as currency, but transaction accounts (checking accounts) are 50 percent of M1 and savings accounts are the biggest part of M2.

Savings Accounts and CDs 存款账户与信用卡

Many experts think that more than just the three items included in M1 should be counted in the money supply. For instance, money in savings accounts might be part of the money supply. True, hardly any merchants will accept your passbook savings account and deduct from it when you make a purchase, but it is very easy to withdraw money from your savings account and make the purchase. Similarly, certificates of deposit are easily cashed (although there are stiff penalties for early withdrawal on these accounts), although no merchant will accept one for payment.

The issue here is liquidity—the ability to turn an asset into cash rapidly and without loss. Savings accounts and certificates of deposit are not generally accepted to pay for things, but they are very liquid and should, therefore, be counted as money. The definition of money known as M2 includes everything in M1 plus money deposited in savings accounts, certificates of deposit, and retail money funds.

M1 and M2 are the most common definitions of money. However, there are several alternative definitions such as "M3" and "MZM." These alternative definitions of money include items that are less liquid such as eurodollars.

Table 18.1

The Money Supply in the United States, 2013 (Billions of Dollars)

M1		M2	
Currency	1,127.5	M1	2,547.3
Transaction accounts	1,416.1	Savings accounts	6,914.1
Travelers' checks	3.7	Certificates of deposit	583.8
Total	2,547.3	Retail money funds	645.9
		Total	10,691.1

Source: Federal Reserve Bank of the United States

FIAT MONEY 法定货币

There is a lot of gold in Fort Knox and a smaller stash in the vault of the Federal Reserve Bank of New York, but none of this gold is used to back the money supply. The United States, and most nations of the world, use *fiat money*. This means that the coins and paper money have nothing standing behind them except the fact that they are *legal tender*.

Legal tender means that the coin or paper money must be accepted in exchange for goods or services by the decree of the government. Still, Confederate currency was legal tender during the Civil War and even die-hard Southerners wouldn't accept it. That is because far too much of it was supplied by the Confederate authorities. This reveals the key to understanding how fiat currency works—its supply must be kept relatively limited.

From 1873 until 1933 the United States was on some form of the gold standard. The money supply was backed by gold or a combination of gold and silver. The primary advantage of the gold standard is that the supply of money must be kept limited since the supply of gold is limited. However, this system can be too confining when an increase in the supply of money is warranted and there is not an increase in the amount of gold held by the government.

A fiat monetary system is more flexible in that the gold holdings of the government need not increase in order to expand the nation's supply of money. By the same token, nations that do not keep the supply of their fiat currency limited will see it diminish in value, sometimes to the point of becoming worthless.

What Is Money Good For? 货币商品是干什么用的?

Most people think that money is good for only one thing—spending. True, textbooks refer to money as a "medium of exchange." Money is a much more efficient way to exchange goods and services than barter. Barter requires a double coincidence of wants; you have to find someone who has what you want and wants what you have in exchange. Money obviates the need for this and allows us to spend our time more productively.

However, people use money in another way all the time: to make comparisons. Which corporation is bigger, Procter and Gamble or Pfizer? The assets of Pfizer are worth about $190 billion, while the assets of Procter and Gamble are worth $220 billion; Pfizer is smaller than Procter and Gamble by this measure. Notice that dollars figures were used to make this comparison. This is using money as a unit of account. Consider another example. Suppose you win a drawing and you can have the grand prize, a Ford Mustang, or $10,000. Most people would take the car based on the comparison that a new Ford Mustang is worth well over $10,000. Again, money is being used to compare things.

Finally, money also serves as a store of value. You can work hard for 40 years and stuff 20 percent of each paycheck under your mattress. After you retire you can live like a king. This is using money to store the value of your hard labor during your working years. Of course, money is a poor store of value during inflationary times. The $600,000 under the mattress can buy less and less as prices rise. On the other hand, money is an excellent store of value during deflations. The $600,000 can buy more and more goods and services as prices fall.

Table 18.2

The Functions of Money

- Medium of exchange—money is used to buy goods and services
- Unit of Account—money is used to measure and compare
- Store of value—money is used to accumulate wealth

THE FEDERAL RESERVE SYSTEM 联邦储蓄系统

To understand how the money supply can be changed, it is necessary to understand the Federal Reserve System, or Fed, for short. The Fed is the central bank of the United States. This means that it controls the money supply and supervises all the depository institutions within the country. All of the banks, savings and loans, credit unions, and mutual savings banks report to the Fed each week. The Fed can audit any of these institutions at any time and would have to approve any mergers and acquisitions.

The Fed operates as the bank of banks. If you need a loan, you might go to a bank. If a bank needs a loan, it may borrow from the Fed. If you feel uncomfortable carrying around a lot of cash, you might deposit some of that cash in your account at a bank. If a bank feels uncomfortable having a lot of cash in its vault, it may deposit some of that vault cash in its account at the Fed.

FACTS ABOUT THE FED

1. There are 12 branches of the Fed located in major cities throughout the nation. This makes it convenient for banks and other depository institutions to do their banking.
2. The main headquarters of the Fed is in Washington, D.C.
3. The President of the United States appoints the seven members of the Board of Governors of the Federal Reserve System.
4. The President also appoints one of the members to be the chairman of the Board of Governors and another member to be the vice chairman.
5. All the members of the Board of Governors serve 14-year terms.
6. The Board of Governors makes the important decisions concerning the money supply. Should M1 and M2 be increased? Decreased? Held steady?

The Fed is a quasi-governmental institution. The people working at the Fed are paid by the federal government, but the Fed is not part of the executive, legislative, or judicial branches of government. The Board of Governors makes decisions concerning the money supply in complete autonomy. The Fed is not responsible to the President or Congress, although it regularly reports to both on its operations and intentions for the money supply.

Fractional Reserve Banking 部分准备金银行制

Banks and other depository institutions keep only a fraction of the money deposited with them on hand. Most of any given deposit is used to make loans or other investments. Nevertheless, banks have plenty of cash on hand to meet their withdrawal needs. A bank manager's worst nightmare is to run short of cash.

The Fed's regulation D requires all depository institutions to keep 10 percent of the funds deposited in transactions accounts as reserves. Transaction accounts are checking accounts and other accounts that function as checking accounts, such as NOW accounts and share draft accounts. Reserves must be held against transaction deposits only. Savings accounts and certificates of deposit have no reserve requirement. Banks can hold their required reserves in their vault or in their account at the Fed. By the way, currency held in a bank's vault is not counted as part of the money supply.

Many people think that the Fed requires banks to keep aside 10 percent of the money deposited in transaction accounts to insure that there will be cash on hand to meet withdrawal needs. This is not true. As stated, bankers will make sure to have enough money on hand to meet withdrawal needs without any requirements from the Fed. Reserve requirements, as we shall see below, help the Fed control the money supply.

T-accounts 丁字形账户

In order to understand fractional reserve banking, it can be instructive to look at the balance sheet, or T-account, of a hypothetical commercial bank. Recent exams in AP Macroeconomics have featured multiple-choice and free-response questions that require knowledge of T-accounts.

T-accounts are an accounting tool that may be used for recording transactions. On the left side of a T-account, we record transactions involving the bank's assets. Changes in the bank's liabilities are recorded on the right-hand side of the ledger. Consider the balance sheet of Bank A when a customer deposits $100 into a checking account:

Commercial Bank A

Assets	Liabilities
+$100 currency	+$100 demand deposits

The bank has $100 more currency in its vault. That is an asset. But the bank also has a new liability: $100 in a customer's checking account that it must be prepared to reimburse at any moment. Notice that this transaction, by itself, has no effect on the money supply. The currency inside a bank's vault is not part of M1 or M2, but demand deposits are included in both. The customer's deposit lowers currency holdings of the public by $100. However, checking accounts are increased by $100.

As you know, $10 of this deposit are required reserves and the remaining $90 are excess reserves. The transaction above could just as well be recorded as:

Commercial Bank A

Assets	Liabilities
+$10 required reserves	+$100 demand deposits
+$90 excess reserves	

Now consider what happens when the bank makes a loan with its excess reserves.

Commercial Bank A

Assets	Liabilities
+$10 required reserves	+$100 demand deposits
+$90 excess reserves	
–$90 excess reserves	
+$90 loan	

TIP

A balance sheet must always stay balanced. If an amount is deducted from one side, then an equal amount must be added to the same side, or deducted from the other side.

The bank no longer has $90 in excess reserves, but it has another asset –$90 in loans that hopefully will be repaid some day in the future with interest.

Assume the loan was used to buy flowers and at the end of the day the florist deposits the $90 in his checking account at Bank B.

Commercial Bank B

Assets	Liabilities
+$9 required reserves	+$90 demand deposits
+$81 excess reserves	

The bank holds 10 percent of the deposit aside as required reserves. The remaining $81 is excess reserves. However, it is critical to notice that this deposit increased the money supply, be it M1 or M2, by $90. How so? Demand deposits are part of the money supply, and they went up by $90. Did the currency holdings of the public decrease by $90? Did demand deposits at any other bank fall because of this transaction? No. When a bank makes a loan it creates money because it leads to increases in transaction accounts while no transaction account, or currency holdings of the public, are affected by the loan.

A similar scenario occurs if Bank A uses its $90 in excess reserves to buy an investment rather than make a loan. Suppose Bank A buys a collectible doll as a financial investment. Whoever sold Bank A the doll deposits the $90 in their bank, say Bank B:

Commercial Bank A		Commercial Bank B	
Assets	**Liabilities**	**Assets**	**Liabilities**
–$90 excess reserves		+$9 required reserves	+$90 demand deposits
+$90 collectible doll		+$81 excess reserves	

Bank B shows an increase in demand deposits of $90, which are part of M1 or M2, and no bank has lost demand deposits because of the transaction. The point of this analysis is to show that banks create money when they make loans or buy financial investments.

The process works in reverse as well. Banks destroy money when loans are repaid or they sell financial investments. To show money destruction, let's say Bank A sells its collectible doll some years later for $90. (Alas, the doll did not provide any financial reward.) The doll's new owner pays with a check from Bank B:

Commercial Bank A		Commercial Bank B	
Assets	**Liabilities**	**Assets**	**Liabilities**
–$90 collectible doll		–$9 required reserves	–$90 demand deposits
+$90 excess reserves		–$81 excess reserves	

Demand deposits in the banking system decrease by $90 without a compensating increase, thus decreasing M1 or M2. You may be thinking that the money supply is uncontrolled since it depends on banks' preferences for making loans or buying financial investments. But that is incorrect. Under normal circumstances, banks can be counted on to use just about all their excess reserves for loans or investments because that is how profits are maximized. In the next section, we shall see that the Fed controls the money supply by controlling the amount of reserves banks have for loans and investments.

The Money Expansion Process 货币扩张过程

Imagine that a counterfeiter prints up $1,000 in phony bills and spends the fake money at a jewelry store. At the end of the day the jeweler deposits the counterfeit money into his bank. The bank, not detecting the phony bills, credits the jeweler's transaction account by $1,000. The bank must hold $100 of the $1,000 aside as required reserves. The remaining $900 can be used as the bank sees fit. Typically, excess reserves such as these $900 are used to make loans or buy investments since that is how the bank makes profits.

Now suppose the bank loans the $900 to someone applying for a home improvement loan. The $900 ends up being spent on paint. The owner of the paint store deposits the $900 into a transaction account. Notice that this deposit is boosting transaction accounts by $900 and transaction accounts are part of the money supply as measured by M1 or M2. In other words, the money supply is increased when banks make loans with their excess reserves.

And this is not the end of the story. The bank that received the $900 deposit from the paint store must hold 10 percent of the deposit, or $90, as required reserves. The rest of the deposit is excess reserves and the bank can use these in any way they wish. Suppose the bank buys some real estate as an investment with the $810 in excess reserves. Whoever sold the real estate to the bank now has a check for $810. If this check is deposited into a transaction account, the money supply will be going up again, this time $810.

Again, this is not the end of the story. The bank that receives the deposit of $810 will hold 10 percent, or $81, aside as required reserves. The remaining $729 is excess reserves that the bank may use to make a loan or buy an investment.

When all is said and done, the original $1,000 in counterfeit money will have led to a $10,000 increase in the money supply. This is because of the money expansion process where banks create transaction account money by using their reserves to make loans or buy investments. Table 18.3 outlines the money expansion process for this example.

Remember that money deposited into transaction accounts is part of the money supply. When counterfeiters deposit $1,000 into their transaction account, the money supply ends up increasing by $10,000. This is because of all the subsidiary deposits that occur because of the original $1,000 deposit. The column labeled "deposits into transaction accounts" sums to $10,000.

Two formulas help us determine how much the money supply will increase because of a deposit from outside the system. The first formula is for the money multiplier:

Money Multiplier = 1 / reserve requirement

In our case the reserve requirement is 10 percent:

Money Multiplier = 1 / .10 = 10

Table 18.3

The Money Expansion Process

	Deposits into transaction accounts	Required reserves	Excess reserves
Bank 1 (Counterfeiter's bank)	$1,000	$100	$900 (used to make a loan)
Bank 2 (Paint store's bank)	900	90	810 (used to buy real estate)
Bank 3 (Real estate seller's bank)	810	81	729
Bank 4	729	72.90	656.10
.	.	.	.
.	.	.	.
.	.	.	.
	$10,000		

This tells us that any deposit from outside the banking system, such as counterfeit money, will change the money supply by 10 times the amount of the deposit.

The second formula gives the change in the money supply because of the initial change in bank reserves:

Change in the Money Supply = Money Multiplier × Change in Bank Reserves

In our example the money multiplier is 10 and the initial change in bank reserves is the $1,000 in counterfeit money:

Change in the Money Supply = 10 × $1,000 = $10,000

If the reserve requirement was five percent and the counterfeiters deposited $4,000 in fake money, the change in the money supply would be:

Money Multiplier = 1 / .05 = 20

Change in the Money Supply = 20 × $4,000 = $80,000

Policy Tools of the Federal Reserve 联储政策工具

The previous examples illustrate why counterfeiting is considered to be such a serious crime. A small amount of counterfeit money can lead to a significant change in the money supply because of the monetary expansion process, but the examples also indicate how the Fed could change the money supply.

The Fed could print money and deposit it into a bank and the monetary expansion process would take over. The money supply would increase by a multiple of the Fed's deposit. And what's more, the initial deposit isn't counterfeit.

As it turns out, there are several ways the Fed could change the reserves of the banking system and, therefore, the money supply. These methods are the policy tools of the Fed.

1. The Fed could *raise or lower the reserve requirements* for depository institutions. If the reserve requirement was lowered, banks would have more excess reserves and could make more loans and investments. This would increase the money supply. To decrease the money supply the Fed would raise reserve requirements.

2. Another policy tool involves the *discount rate*. The discount rate is the rate of interest the Fed charges when it makes loans to depository institutions. Remember that if you want a loan you might go to a bank, whereas a bank that needs a loan may go to the Fed. The Fed charges banks a rather low rate of interest on the loans it makes, thus the name discount rate.

   If the Fed lowers the discount rate, more banks are encouraged to borrow. These borrowings by banks from the Fed increase bank reserves. The money supply will increase by a multiple of the borrowings from the Fed.

   As an illustration, suppose the Fed lowers the discount rate by half of a percentage point. Say that the lower discount rate encourages banks to borrow $12 million more than usual from the Fed. Assuming a 10 percent reserve requirement, the money supply would then increase by $120 million:

   Money Multiplier = 1 / Reserve Requirement

   Money Multiplier = 1 / .10 = 10

   Change in the Money Supply = Money Multiplier × Change in Bank Reserves

   Change in the Money Supply = 10 × $12 million = $120 million

If the Fed wanted to decrease the money supply, then the discount rate should be raised. Raising the discount rate discourages banks from borrowing from the Fed, and banks, therefore, have less reserves. A decrease in reserves translates into a multiple decrease in the money supply.

During the recent financial crisis the Fed made loans to non-depository institutions. For the first time, so-called term auction facilities allowed the Fed to make loans to troubled financial institutions.

3. The third policy tool available to the Fed to initiate changes in the money supply is *open market operations*. Open market operations is when the Fed buys and sells government securities in the secondary market. Government securities are IOUs that the government issues when it borrows money. They sometimes go by the names Treasury bills, bonds, or notes. The federal government of the United States has borrowed trillions of dollars from individuals and corporations, both foreign and domestic.

The Fed expanded its open-market operations as it dealt with the financial crisis of 2008–2009 and set precedent by buying assets other than government securities from a variety of entities holding those assets. For instance, the Fed bought mortgage-backed securities from Fannie Mae, Freddie Mac, and the Federal Home Loan Bank.

Secondary Market 次级市场

When the government borrows money it issues a government security to the lender that states the amount of the loan, the rate of interest, and the length of the loan. However, the lender need not hold the government securities until it matures. At any time the lender may sell the government security to another investor. This is done in the *secondary market.*

Lenders wishing to sell government securities that have a relatively high rate of interest attached to them will experience a profit in the secondary market, while those with relatively low rates will experience a loss. But the Fed does not buy and sell government securities in the secondary market with an eye toward making financial gains. The Fed participates in the secondary market for government securities in order to change the money supply.

Imagine what happens when the Fed buys government securities in the secondary market. The Fed pays for the securities with a check that the seller deposits in a bank account. This deposit is an increase in bank reserves from outside the system. The money supply will increase by a multiple of this increase in bank reserves.

To take a specific example, if the reserve requirement is 10 percent and the Fed wants to increase the money supply by \$50 million, then the Fed would buy \$5 million worth of government securities in the secondary market.

$$\text{Money Multiplier} = 1 \;/\; \text{Reserve Requirement}$$

$$\text{Money Multiplier} = 1 \;/\; .10 = 10$$

$$\text{Change in the Money Supply} = \text{Money Multiplier} \times \text{Change in Bank Reserves}$$

$$\text{Change in the Money Supply} = 10 \times \$5 \text{ million} = \$50 \text{ million}$$

If the Fed wanted to decrease the money supply, it would sell government securities in the secondary market. Persons or corporations that buy the securities will pay with a check. The Fed cashes the check to draw the reserves out of the banking system and does not deposit proceeds of the sale back into the banking system. In this way bank reserves are depleted. The money supply falls by a multiple of the decline in bank reserves.

Specifically, if the Fed sells \$6 million worth of government securities in the secondary market, and the reserve requirement is five percent, then the money supply will fall by \$120 million.

$$\text{Money Multiplier} = 1 / \text{Reserve Requirement}$$

$$\text{Money Multiplier} = 1 / .05 = 20$$

$$\text{Change in the Money Supply} = \text{Money Multiplier} \times \text{Change in Bank Reserves}$$

$$\text{Change in the Money Supply} = 20 \times -\$6 \text{ million} = -\$120 \text{ million}$$

Table 18.4 summarizes the policy tools of the Fed.

Table 18.4

Policy Tools of the Federal Reserve

Tool	Description	To Increase Money Supply	To Decrease Money Supply
Change reserve requirements	Change the percentage of each deposit that banks must hold aside	Lower the reserve requirement	Raise the reserve requirement
Change the discount rate	Change the rate of interest the Fed charges on bank borrowings	Lower the discount rate	Raise the discount rate
Open market operations	Buy or sell government securities in the secondary market	Buy government securities	Sell government securities

SUMMARY 小结

- Money is anything generally accepted to pay for goods and services. Certainly, currency, transaction accounts, and travelers' checks are generally accepted. This definition of money is known as M1. Many experts think that other highly liquid assets should be considered money. These include savings accounts, certificates of deposit, and other liquid assets. Adding these three items to M1 gives M2, another prevalent definition of money.
- The money supply in the United States, like most nations, is not backed by gold or silver or any precious commodity. Fiat money is money because the government says it is money. Experience has shown that it is extremely important to keep the supply of a fiat money relatively limited if it is to function correctly.
- Money is good for spending (a medium of exchange), comparing things (a unit of account), and as an investment vehicle (a store of value). The United States is on a fractional reserve system where depository institutions keep only a fraction of each deposit on hand. Most of the money deposited in a bank is used to make loans and buy investments.

- The Federal Reserve is the central bank of the United States and controls the money supply. It does this mostly with open market operations, but can also alter the discount rate or change reserve requirements. Any of these three techniques changes the reserves of the banking system. The money supply changes by a multiple of the change in bank reserves.

TERMS 术语

Certificate of Deposit debt instrument that is similar to a savings account except the interest rate is slightly greater and the deposit cannot be drawn on without penalty

Currency coins and paper money

Discount Rate the rate of interest the Fed charges when it makes loans to depository institutions

Excess Reserves the amount of any deposit that does not have to be held aside and may be used to make loans and buy investments

Federal Reserve the central bank of the United States

Fiat Money money that is not backed by any precious commodity

Government Securities IOUs that the government issues when it borrows money

Liquidity the ability to turn an asset into cash rapidly and without loss

M1 currency, transaction accounts, and travelers' checks

M2 M1 plus savings accounts, certificates of deposit, and other liquid assets

Money anything that society generally accepts in payment for a good or service

Money Multiplier = 1 / reserve requirement, the multiple by which the money supply will change because of a change in bank reserves

Open Market Operations activities in which the Fed buys and sells government securities in the secondary market

Required Reserves the amount of any deposit that must be held aside and not used to make loans or buy investments

Reserve Requirement the percentage of any deposit that must be held aside and not used to make loans or buy investments

Savings Account an account at a depository institution that earns interest while the funds are readily available but cannot be withdrawn with checks

Secondary Market place where government securities that have already been issued may be bought or sold

Transaction Account a checking account at a bank or a similar account at some other depository institution

FORMULAS 公式

Money Multiplier = 1 / reserve requirement

Change in the Money Supply = Money Multiplier × Change in Bank Reserves

MULTIPLE-CHOICE REVIEW QUESTIONS 选择题

1. Which of the following is not included in M1?

(A) Coins.
(B) Paper money.
(C) Travelers' checks.
(D) Credit cards.
(E) Transaction accounts.

2. Which of the following is not included in M2?

(A) Currency.
(B) Travelers' checks.
(C) Certificates of deposit.
(D) Savings accounts.
(E) Credit cards.

3. Which of the following statements is true?

(A) Some of the things included in M2 are not as liquid as the things in M1.
(B) M2 is smaller than M1.
(C) M1 is backed by gold and M2 is backed by silver.
(D) The biggest component of M1 is currency.
(E) The biggest component of M2 is currency.

4. Fiat money

(A) is not backed by any precious commodity.
(B) can be exchanged for gold.
(C) is backed by gold, but cannot be exchanged for it.
(D) is not legal tender.
(E) can be backed by gold or silver.

5. The Federal Reserve is

(A) part of the legislative branch of government.
(B) the monetary authority for banks, but not other depository institutions.
(C) part of the judicial branch of government.
(D) in control of the money supply.
(E) in control of government spending.

6. Required reserves

(A) can be used by banks to make loans or buy investments.
(B) can be held in a bank's vault or its account at the Fed.
(C) must be kept in a bank's vault.
(D) must be used to make loans.
(E) ensure that banks will have enough cash on hand to meet their withdrawals.

7. The secondary market for government securities is

(A) where used items are traded.
(B) located in smaller cities.
(C) where the government borrows money.
(D) where government securities that have already been issued may be bought or sold.
(E) where government securities are issued.

8. If the reserve requirement is 2 percent, then the money multiplier is

(A) 5
(B) 5 percent
(C) 50
(D) 50 percent
(E) one half

9. If the Fed buys bonds in the secondary market

(A) the money supply will increase.
(B) the money supply will decrease.
(C) the money supply will not be affected.
(D) the discount rate would be affected.
(E) reserve requirements would have to be increased in tandem.

10. Which of the following would lead to an expansion of the money supply?

(A) The Fed raises the discount rate.
(B) The Fed buys government securities in the secondary market.
(C) The Federal government deficit-spends.
(D) The Fed raises reserve requirements.
(E) Taxes are reduced.

11. Assume the reserve requirement is 10 percent. If the Fed sells \$29 million worth of government securities in an open market operation, then the money supply can

(A) increase by \$2.9 million.
(B) decrease by \$2.9 million.
(C) increase by \$290 million.
(D) decrease by \$290 million.
(E) increase by \$26.1 million.

12. Assume the reserve requirement is 5 percent. If the Fed buys \$4 million worth of government securities in an open market operation, then the money supply can

(A) increase by \$1.25 million.
(B) decrease by \$1.25 million.
(C) increase by \$20 million.
(D) decrease by \$20 million.
(E) increase by \$80 million.

13. When the Fed lowers the discount rate its intention is to

(A) give depository institutions a break on their borrowings.
(B) signal participants in financial markets that a recession is coming.
(C) signal participants in financial markets that an inflationary period is coming.
(D) lower prices in the economy.
(E) encourage borrowing by depository institutions so that the money supply may expand.

14. Lowering reserve requirements would

(A) force banks to hold more reserves and make more loans.
(B) allow banks to make more loans and buy more investments thus decreasing the money supply.
(C) allow banks to make more loans and buy more investments thus increasing the money supply.
(D) allow banks more freedom to merge and acquire other businesses.
(E) force banks to sell investments so that fewer funds are held in reserve.

15. The Fed's Board of Governors has ______ members, each serving ______ -year terms.

(A) 14, 7
(B) 7, 14
(C) 8, 8
(D) 50, 2
(E) 8, 10

MULTIPLE-CHOICE REVIEW ANSWERS
选择题答案

1. (D)	**4.** (A)	**7.** (D)	**10.** (B)	**13.** (E)
2. (E)	**5.** (D)	**8.** (C)	**11.** (D)	**14.** (C)
3. (A)	**6.** (B)	**9.** (A)	**12.** (E)	**15.** (B)

FREE-RESPONSE REVIEW QUESTIONS 开放式题目

I. Assume the reserve requirement is 10 percent. If the Fed buys $10,000 worth of government securities in the secondary market, will the money supply expand or shrink? By exactly how much after all is said and done?

II. Explain why the money supply changes when the Fed buys $10,000 worth of government securities in the secondary market. Why is the change in the money supply not $10,000?

III. Suppose that depository institutions did not use all of their excess reserves to make loans and buy investments. For example, if the reserve requirement was 10 percent, depository institutions would hold 20 percent of their deposits idle. How would this affect your answer to I. above?

Free-Response Review Answers 开放式题目答案

I. If the Fed buys $10,000 worth of government securities in the secondary market, the money supply expands. When the Fed pays for the securities the sellers will deposit their checks into the banking system. The reserves of the banking system will increase by $10,000. The money supply will increase by ten times that amount, or $100,000 because the money multiplier is 10 in this case. (Money multiplier = 1 / .10 = 10.)

II. The money supply increases because when the Fed buys securities in the secondary market, this increases the reserves of banks where the checks are deposited. The reserves of these banks go up by $10,000. Now these banks are holding more reserves than they are required to by the Fed's reserve requirements. The banks make loans and buy investments with these excess reserves and this serves to increase transaction accounts. Transaction accounts are part of the money supply.

III. If banks do not use all of their excess reserves to make loans and buy investments, then money expansion process is not as effective. When a bank makes a loan, this money ends up as a deposit elsewhere, usually at another bank. If banks prefer to hold extra reserves, then the loans will not be as large and the increase in the money supply because of the $10,000 increase in reserves also will not be as large. If banks have a 10 percent reserve requirement and hold 10 percent more in extra reserves, this means that the money multiplier is 5 (= 1 / .2) and the money supply will expand to only $50,000, not $100,000.

Monetary Policy 货币政策 19

→ EQUATION OF EXCHANGE
→ QUANTITY THEORY OF MONEY
→ MONETARISTS VS. KEYNESIANS
→ FEDERAL FUNDS RATE

DEFINITION 定义

Test your economic intuition by answering this question: If the economy is mired in a recession, should the money supply be increased or decreased? The correct answer is *increased*. Congratulate yourself for having good economic intuition if you answered correctly.

Here is a much more difficult, and less intuitive question: Why does an increase in the money supply stimulate a sluggish economy? After a moment of thought, most people respond that an increase in the money supply would motivate spending. Not bad. But if households and corporations wanted to spend more, why don't they simply use the existing money supply more intensely? They could spend more without increasing the money supply if each dollar was turned over more often. If households and corporations don't want to increase spending, would an increase in the money supply force them to spend more?

You will be able to answer the more difficult questions posed above shortly. First, let's define monetary policy—changes in the money supply to fight recessions or inflations. The Board of Governors of the Fed designs and executes monetary policy in the United States. Suppose the Board of Governors decides to increase the money supply. In Chapter 18 we saw that this could be accomplished with a decrease in reserve requirements, a decrease in the discount rate, or an open market purchase of government securities.

The Federal Open Market Committee (FOMC) helps the Board of Governors decide which tool to use. If the open market purchases are selected, then the FOMC plots out exactly how many government securities will be purchased at what time. The FOMC is comprised of twelve members. All seven of the members of the Board of Governors sit on the FOMC, as well as five of the presidents of the twelve Fed regional banks.

CHANGES IN THE MONEY SUPPLY 货币供给的变动

Classical View 经典观点

Classical economic analysis concludes that changes in the money supply have no effect on the equilibrium quantity of output; only prices and wages are affected. According to Classical theory, an increase in the money supply would increase aggregate demand, but the increase in aggregate demand would result in higher prices.

Workers would immediately realize that their wages could not buy as many goods and services at the higher prices and they would demand wage increases. When the dust settled, if the money supply was raised 10 percent, prices and wages would rise 10 percent and nothing else would be changed.

If the economy was in a recession and the unemployment rate was high, an increase in the money supply would not help. After the money supply was increased, prices and wages would be higher, but the unemployment rate would be unchanged.

The Classical view on how an increase in the money supply affects the economy is reflected in the aggregate supply/aggregate demand (AS/AD) model in Figure 19.1. The increase in the money supply shifts the aggregate demand curve to the right. But suppliers respond to this increase in the demand for their products by raising prices from P_1 to P_2, but not output. Remember, the Classical aggregate supply curve is vertical. So the increase in aggregate demand has no effect on the quantity of output. Since output is unaffected, so is unemployment.

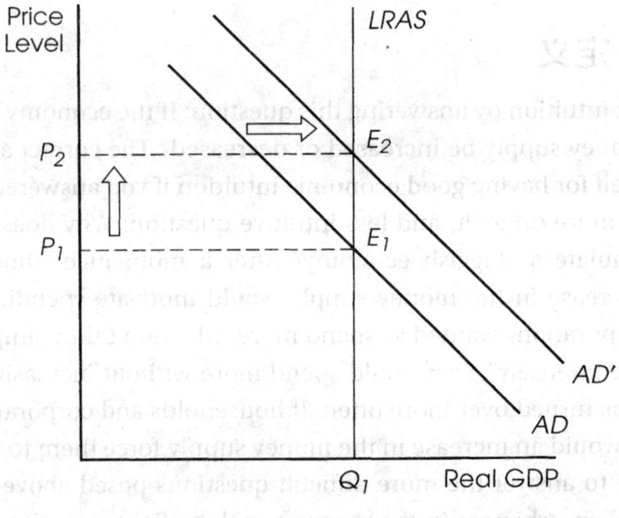

Fig. 19.1 An Increase in the Money Supply: Classical View

The Classical economists based their conclusions about how money affects the economy on the equation of exchange:

$$M \times V = P \times Q$$

Where M is the money supply
V is the velocity of money
P is the price level and
Q is the quantity of output or real GDP.

The money supply can be defined as M_1 or M_2. The velocity of money is the number of times the typical dollar of M_1 or M_2 is used to make purchases during a year. The price level is the average price of a good or service in the economy, the same as the vertical axis in the AS/AD model. The quantity of output can be measured with real GDP and is the same as the horizontal axis in the AS/AD model.

The equation of exchange is a *tautology*, meaning it is true by definition. No economist, Classical or not, disputes the fact that $M \times V = P \times Q$. But the Classical economists take this a step further and assume that V and Q are constant. If this is true, then the arithmetic of the situation tells us that if M increases 10 percent, P must also increase 10 percent.

The Classical economists referred to this result as *monetary neutrality* or the *Quantity Theory of Money*. A change in the money supply would result in a proportional change in prices. The quantity of output, real GDP, the rate of unemployment, and other real variables are unaffected. This analysis is in line with the Classical notion that the only things that can affect the quantity of output are resource availability and technology.

Monetarist View 货币主义观点

It is easy to shoot down the Classical theory of monetary neutrality. The theory is based on the assumption that V and Q are constant. In the United States, the velocity of M1 was 3.6 in 1960 and 6.8 in 2013. Clearly, V is not constant. Similarly, Q, or real GDP, has increased 410 percent in the same time span. With a nonconstant V and Q, we can no longer conclude that a change in the money supply causes a proportional change in prices.

The Monetarist view on how a change in the money supply affects the economy is more realistic. The Monetarist view starts with the assumption that V and Q are stable, but not constant, in the short run. Now if the money supply is increased 10 percent, it is by no means definite that P will increase by 10 percent. Monetarists claim that both P and Q will increase and not necessarily by 10 percent.

According to the Monetarist view, a change in the money supply affects the economy in many ways. For one, interest rates will be affected and this will affect spending levels and, therefore, aggregate demand. For another, more money directly translates into more spending as households and firms try to spend and invest the increment in the money supply. And there are other channels through which a change in the money supply will affect the economy. They are "too numerous to enumerate," according to Milton Friedman, a Nobel Prize-winning economist who is often called the father of monetarism.

TIP

The Fed can affect interest rates in the economy by raising or lowering the money supply. Raising the money supply lowers interest rates.

On the AS/AD model, an increase in the money supply results in an increase in aggregate demand. This translates into an increase in the price level and the quantity of output. We get a different result than the Classical analysis because the aggregate supply curve is drawn upward sloping from left to right instead of vertical.

The Monetarist view on how a change in the money supply affects the economy, like the Classical view, is based on the equation of exchange. However, the Monetarist view is not as rigid. The Classical view maintains that V and Q are constant, so that an increase in M will have a proportional effect on P. Q is not affected. The Monetarist view is that V and Q are stable in the short run, but not constant. This means that both P and Q will be affected when M is increased. Indeed, the Monetarists assert that most of the fluctuations in Q over the years are the result of the Fed changing M.

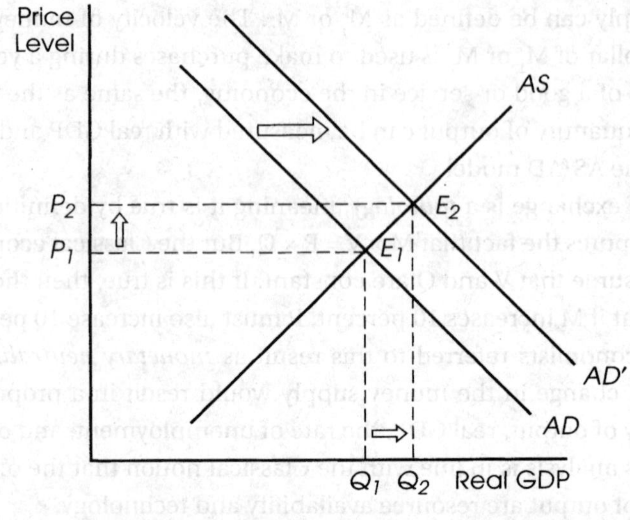

Fig. 19.2 An Increase in the Money Supply: Monetarist View

The Monetarists are highly critical of the Fed. If changes in output are caused primarily by changes in the money supply, then all the Fed need do is allow the money supply to increase at a reasonable constant rate, say three percent a year. When the Fed undertakes monetary policies that reverse the direction of money growth, this results in the recessions and inflations we observe in the economy.

Keynesian View 凯恩斯观点

A third perspective on how a change in the money supply affects the economy is that of the Keynesians. This view, like the monetarist view, is concerned with short run effects and uses an upward sloping aggregate supply curve. The difference is that the Keynesians believe that a change in the money supply affects the economy through one channel, not many—and that channel is the interest rate.

An increase in the money supply would lower interest rates, since more money is available to be borrowed. Lower interest rates encourage households and firms to take out loans in order to increase spending and investment in plant and equipment. This means more aggregate demand.

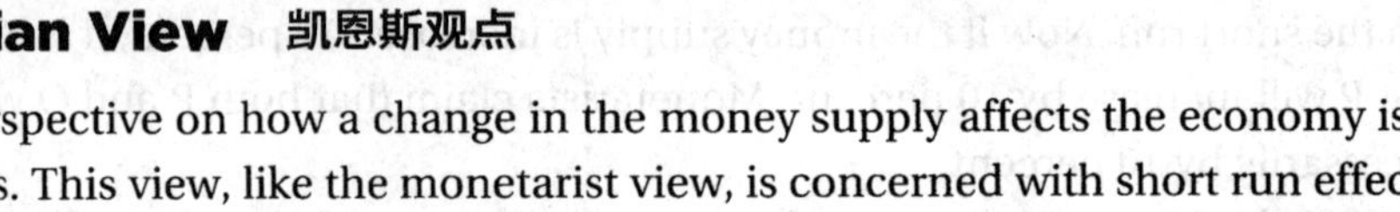

Fig. 19.3 How an Increase in the Money Supply Affects the Economy: Keynesian View

However, Keynesians argue that the increase in aggregate demand will be small. The increase in the money supply will only lower interest rates a bit according to Keynesian analysis. To see this consider Figure 19.4, which shows the supply and demand for money.

The supply of money is vertical because it is not related to the nominal rate of interest. The Federal Reserve determines the money supply. The demand for money is downward

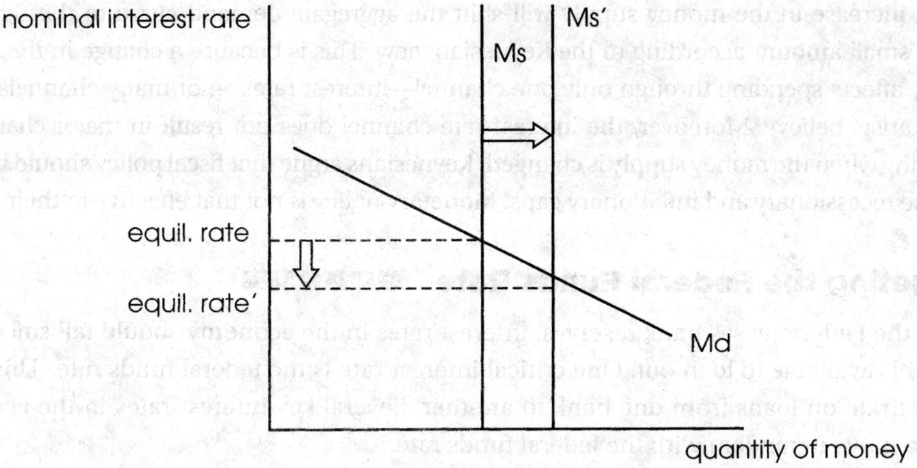

Fig. 19.4 An Increase in the Money Supply Lowers the Interest Rate

sloping to reflect the fact that it is negatively related to interest rates. When interest rates rise, households and firms decrease their money holdings. They would rather put their money where it can earn the higher rates of interest, usually in bonds.

The demand for money is also affected by prices and income. If either of these increase, the demand for money will shift to the right. If prices increase, then households and firms will need more money to pay for the things they buy. If income increases, then households will want to buy more things and this means larger money holdings in their wallets or in their checking accounts.

Keynesians believe that the money demand curve is rather flat. That way, if the money supply is increased as in Figure 19.4, then interest rates do not fall very much. Moreover, Keynesians claim that even if the interest rate did fall appreciably, borrowing and spending would not increase all that much.

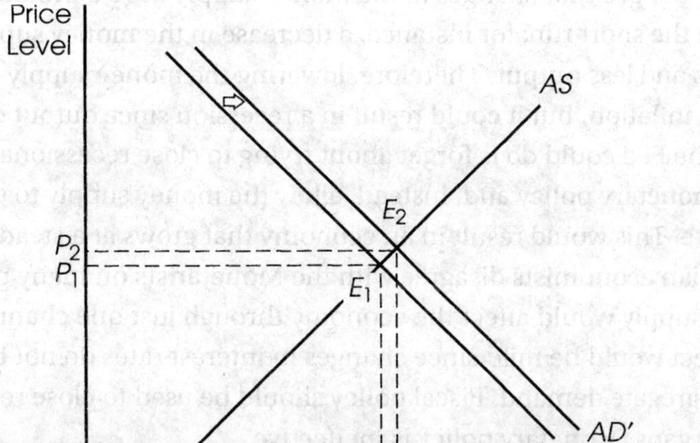

Fig. 19.5 An Increase in the Money Supply: Keynesian View

An increase in the money supply will shift the aggregate demand curve to the right, but only a small amount according to the Keynesian view. This is because a change in the money supply affects spending through only one channel—interest rates—not many channels as the Monetarists believe. Moreover, the interest rate channel does not result in major changes in spending when the money supply is changed. Keynesians argue that fiscal policy should be used to close recessionary and inflationary gaps. Monetary policy is not that effective in their eyes.

Targeting the Federal Funds Rate 联邦基金利率

When the Fed increases bank reserves, interest rates in the economy should fall since more money is available to loan out. One critical interest rate is the federal funds rate. This is the interest rate on loans from one bank to another. Several key interest rates in the economy tend to move in tandem with the federal funds rate.

The current practice of the Fed is to raise or lower bank reserves in order to peg the federal funds rate at some desired level. The Fed targets the federal funds rate in order to know if more or less money is required in the economy.

For example, if the federal funds rate began to rise, it would indicate that loanable funds are becoming more scarce. If the Fed wants to head off a recession, it would add reserves to the banking system, perhaps through open-market operations, in order to keep the federal funds rate from rising.

SUMMARY 小结

- The term "demand management policy" refers to both monetary and fiscal policy because, like fiscal policy, monetary policy shifts the aggregate demand curve. If the government decides to increase total spending in the economy, shifting the aggregate demand curve to the right, this could be accomplished by increasing the money supply, or increasing government spending, or reducing taxes.
- Most economists believe that a change in the money supply will affect both prices and output in the short run. Classical economic theory tells us that in the long run a change in the money supply will only affect prices. Only resources and technology can affect output in the long run, a change in the money supply cannot.
- Monetarists believe that changes in the money supply have a profound effect on the economy in the short run; for instance, a decrease in the money supply would result in lower prices and less output. Therefore, lowering the money supply would be a good way to fight inflation, but it could result in a recession since output decreases. The best thing the Fed could do is forget about trying to close recessionary and inflationary gaps with monetary policy and, instead, allow the money supply to grow at a steady, constant rate. This would result in an economy that grows at a steady, constant rate.
- The Keynesian economists disagree with the Monetarists on many points. A change in the money supply would affect the economy through just one channel, interest rates. And the effect would be mild since changes in interest rates do not have a profound effect on aggregate demand. Fiscal policy should be used to close recessionary and inflationary gaps. Monetary policy is ineffective.
- The Fed targets the federal funds rate. That is to say, the Fed increases or decreases bank reserves in order to put the interbank loan rate at the desired level. For instance, increasing bank reserves lowers the federal funds rate. This should stimulate borrowing and spending.

At the outset of this chapter we asked if households and corporations don't want to increase spending, would an increase in the money supply force them to spend more? Hopefully at this point you can see that the answer is Yes, although "induce" may be a better word than "force." Monetarists think that a significant amount of spending would be induced by an increase in the money supply. Keynesians disagree.

Table 19.1

Perspectives on the Money Supply

	Classical	Monetarist	Keynesian
A change in the money supply affects	the price level	the price level and output	the price level and output
through	many variables	many variables	the interest rate
The effect is	strong but limited to prices and wages	strong	weak
V and Q are	constant	stable	variable

TERMS 术语

Board of Governors executive board of the FED that makes major monetary policy decisions

Demand Management Policy monetary and fiscal policy

Equation of Exchange $M \times V = P \times Q$; the money supply times its velocity equals the price level times output

Federal Funds Rate the interest rate charged when a bank makes a loan to another bank.

Federal Open Market Committee (FOMC) a committee within the Fed that designs and executes the particulars of monetary policy

Monetarist one who believes that changes in the money supply have a profound effect on the economy

Monetary Neutrality (Quantity Theory of Money) policy in which a change in the money supply would result in a proportional change in prices while real variables, such as the unemployment rate, would be unaffected

Monetary Policy changes in the money supply to fight recessions or inflations

Money Demand the amount that households and firms want to hold in currency and deposits

Velocity of Money describing the number of times the typical dollar of M_1 or M_2 is used to make purchases during a year

FORMULAS 公式

Equation of Exchange: $M \times V = P \times Q$

MULTIPLE-CHOICE REVIEW QUESTIONS 选择题

1. The Federal Open Market Committee
- (A) advises the President of the United States.
- (B) is part of the Federal Reserve System.
- (C) has seven members.
- (D) promotes free trade.
- (E) is part of the legislative branch of government.

2. According to Classical economic theory, a decrease in the money supply would
- (A) raise the price level and output in the economy.
- (B) lower the price level and output in the economy.
- (C) raise the price level in the economy.
- (D) lower the price level in the economy.
- (E) raise the price level and lower output in the economy.

3. According to monetarist analysis, a decrease in the money supply would
- (A) raise the price level and output in the economy.
- (B) lower the price level and output in the economy.
- (C) raise the price level in the economy.
- (D) lower the price level in the economy.
- (E) raise the price level and lower output in the economy.

4. According to Keynesian analysis, a decrease in the money supply would
- (A) raise the price level and output in the economy.
- (B) lower the price level and output in the economy.
- (C) raise the price level in the economy.
- (D) lower the price level in the economy.
- (E) raise the price level and lower output in the economy.

5. In the equation of exchange
- (A) M stands for the money supply and Q stands for quality.
- (B) V stands for the velocity of GDP and Q stands for quality.
- (C) P stands for the price level and Q stands for quarter.
- (D) P stands for the price level and V stands for the velocity of money.
- (E) P stands for population and V stands for the velocity of money.

6. The velocity of money
- (A) cannot be calculated for an actual economy.
- (B) is how fast money can be transferred.
- (C) is required to calculate the money multiplier.
- (D) is the number of times a typical dollar changes hands.
- (E) is the number of times a typical dollar is used to make a purchase in a year.

7. In the equation of exchange, if V and Q are constant, then

(A) changes in the price level must be proportional to changes in the money supply.
(B) changes in the money supply have no effect on the price level.
(C) changes in the price level cause changes in the money supply.
(D) the equation is invalid.
(E) the money supply must be zero.

8. In the United States over the years, V and Q

(A) have not changed significantly.
(B) are perfectly constant.
(C) have decreased significantly.
(D) have increased significantly.
(E) changed once since World War II.

9. According to Monetarist theory, when the money supply is changed, the economy is affected

(A) only because a change in the money supply affects interest rates.
(B) unpredictably.
(C) because interest rates change and so do many other factors that affect spending.
(D) because many factors that affect spending change, but not interest rates.
(E) but only insignificantly.

10. According to Keynesian theory, a decrease in the money supply would

(A) lower interest rates, which would encourage borrowing and, therefore, increase spending.
(B) raise interest rates, which would discourage borrowing and, therefore, increase spending.
(C) raise interest rates, which would discourage borrowing and, therefore, reduce spending.
(D) lower interest rates, which would discourage borrowing and, therefore, reduce spending.
(E) raise interest rates, which would encourage borrowing and, therefore, reduce spending.

11. Which of the following could cause the aggregate demand curve to shift to the left?

(A) An increase in the money supply.
(B) Contractionary demand management policies.
(C) Expansionary demand management policies.
(D) An increase in government spending.
(E) There is more than one correct answer here.

12. According to Monetarist theory,

(A) the Fed should actively conduct monetary policy.
(B) changes in the money supply do not have significant effects.
(C) fiscal policy is the preferred way of shifting the aggregate demand curve.
(D) the Fed should allow the money supply to grow at a constant rate.
(E) the Fed should randomly change the money supply.

13. According to Keynesian theory,

(A) the Fed should not conduct monetary policy.
(B) changes in the money supply have significant effects.
(C) fiscal policy is the preferred way of shifting the aggregate demand curve.
(D) the Fed should allow the money supply to grow at a constant rate.
(E) the Fed should randomly change the money supply.

14. In order to conduct expansionary monetary policy, the Fed could use open market operations to

(A) buy Treasury bonds in order to raise the federal funds rate.
(B) buy Treasury bonds in order to lower the federal funds rate.
(C) sell Treasury bonds in order to raise the federal funds rate.
(D) sell Treasury bonds in order to lower the federal funds rate.
(E) buy Treasury bonds in order to lower the discount rate.

15. Monetarists believe that V and Q are

(A) constant.
(B) stable.
(C) variable.
(D) not critical for understanding how money affects the economy.
(E) unstable.

MULTIPLE-CHOICE REVIEW ANSWERS
选择题答案

1. (B)	**4.** (B)	**7.** (A)	**10.** (C)	**13.** (C)
2. (D)	**5.** (D)	**8.** (D)	**11.** (B)	**14.** (B)
3. (B)	**6.** (E)	**9.** (C)	**12.** (D)	**15.** (B)

FREE-RESPONSE REVIEW QUESTIONS 开放式题目

I. Suppose the money supply is increased. What would happen to the equilibrium price level, the equilibrium quantity of output, and the unemployment rate according to

A. Classical economic theory?

B. Monetarist theory?

C. Keynesian theory?

II. Explain why the three schools of economic thought in Part I. reach different or similar conclusions concerning how an increase in the money supply will affect the economy.

Free-Response Review Answers 开放式题目答案

I. If the money supply were increased then

A. according to Classical economic theory the equilibrium price level would increase and the equilibrium quantity of output would remain unchanged. Since the quantity of output is unchanged, the unemployment rate is unchanged.

B. according to Monetarist theory the equilibrium price level would increase and the equilibrium quantity of output would increase as well. Since the quantity of output increased, the unemployment rate would fall.

C. according to Keynesian theory the equilibrium price level would increase slightly and the equilibrium quantity of output would increase slightly as well. Since the quantity of output increased slightly, the unemployment rate would decrease slightly.

II. All three schools of thought agree that an increase in the money supply will raise the equilibrium price level. However, the Keynesians believe that the price level will only rise slightly. This is because they believe that an increase in the money supply will stimulate only a small amount of extra spending. Another way of saying this is that the Keynesians feel that an increase in the money supply will shift the aggregate demand curve to the right, but only by a small amount.

Similarly, the Keynesians feel that the equilibrium level of output will increase only slightly because total spending is not that sensitive to changes in the money supply. Therefore, unemployment falls modestly. The Monetarists, on the other hand, believe that an increase in the money supply has a significant impact on the economy. The equilibrium quantity of output rises substantially because spending is boosted by the increase in the money supply. Therefore, unemployment falls significantly.

Only the Classical thinkers believe that the equilibrium level of output and the unemployment rate will be completely unaffected by the increase in the money supply. This is because of the Classical emphasis on the long run effects of any change in the economy. The amount of output that an economy can generate depends on the amount of resources available and the state of technology. An increase in the money supply affects neither of these and so the Classical conclusion is that output is not affected by an increase in the supply of money. It only serves to raise prices.

Economic Growth 经济增长 20

→ PRODUCTIVITY
→ HUMAN CAPITAL
→ POTENTIAL GDP

LIVING STANDARDS 生活水准

In 1948 real GDP per capita (in 2009 dollars) in the United States was $13,758. By 2013 it had risen to $49,804. These figures indicate that the standard of living almost quadrupled in those 65 years. Real GDP per capita represents how much was produced, per person in the nation. When more goods and services are produced, this implies more material wealth. This is the essence of economic growth—increments in material wealth. The percentage change in real GDP, or real GDP per capita, is the customary measure of economic growth.

Of course, not all growth is good. Some bemoan the congestion, pollution, and loss of simplicity that sometimes accompany economic growth. Nevertheless, generally speaking, more output per person implies higher living standards. Life is more harsh in Tanzania, where GDP per capita is less than $1,000, than in Australia where GDP per capita is over $20,000.

In the United States since World War II, real GDP typically grows about three percent a year. Real GDP per capita has an average growth rate of just under two percent for the same period. This means that American citizens enjoy a standard of life that improves just under two percent a year.

Even small differences in the rate of growth can add up over the years. Imagine two economies, both with a real GDP per capita of $30,000. If real GDP per capita grows by one percent a year in the first economy and two percent a year in the second, then in 25 years the first economy will have a real GDP per capita of $38,500, while in the second it will rise to $49,200.

This brings us to the "rule of 70." It will take 10 years for GDP, or any variable, to double if it grows by seven percent a year. More generally, a variable will double in 70/x years, where x is the annual growth rate of the variable. So if the standard of living grows at five percent a year, we can expect the standard of living to double in 14 (= $^{70}/_{5}$) years.

It is well known that the fruits of economic growth are not shared equally among the population in America. Since income is unequally distributed, so is the economic bounty.

In fact, America has one of the more skewed distributions of income in the industrialized world. Roughly half of all the income goes to 20 percent of the families. The poorest 20 percent of the population earns only five percent of all the income. Growth theorists argue about what can be done about disparities in living standards within a nation. Some see the disparity as a natural consequence of growth, while others insist that economic growth need not result in economic inequality.

DETERMINANTS OF ECONOMIC GROWTH 经济增长的决定因素

The production possibilities frontier can be used to summarize the factors that cause an economy to grow. Our previous analysis indicated that two factors could cause the production possibilities frontier to shift outward: (1) an increase in the amount of resources, and, (2) a technological advance that increases productivity. When the production possibilities frontier shifts outward, it implies that the economy's potential for production has increased. Potential GDP is the amount that can be produced using resources fully and efficiently.

Figure 20.1 illustrates how an increase in a particular resource, labor, would affect the production possibilities frontier. If the economy was producing at point A before the increase in the amount of labor in the economy, it could now produce at a point such as B, where more guns and butter are consumed.

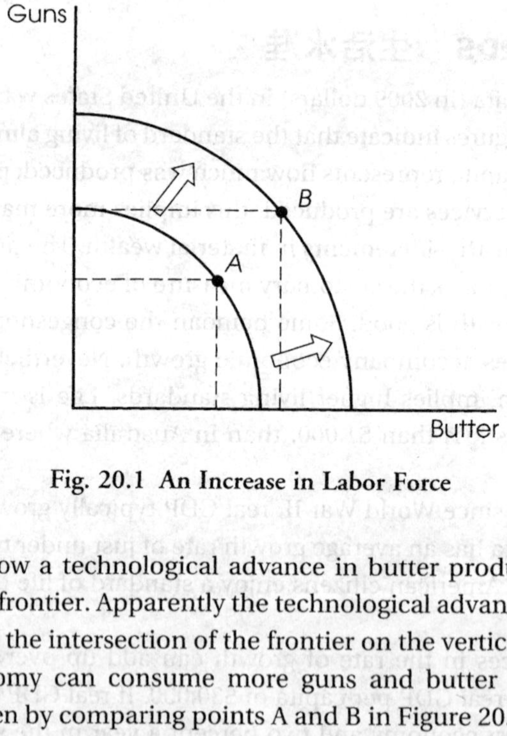

Fig. 20.1 An Increase in Labor Force

Figure 20.2 shows how a technological advance in butter production would affect the production possibilities frontier. Apparently the technological advance has no application in gun production because the intersection of the frontier on the vertical axis has not changed. Nevertheless, the economy can consume more guns and butter after the technological advance. This can be seen by comparing points A and B in Figure 20.2.

The aggregate demand/aggregate supply (AS/AD) model can also illustrate economic growth. If the long run aggregate supply curve is used, then shifts in aggregate demand have no effect on the equilibrium quantity of output. Only a shift to the right of the long run aggregate supply curve can increase equilibrium output. This is shown in Figure 20.3.

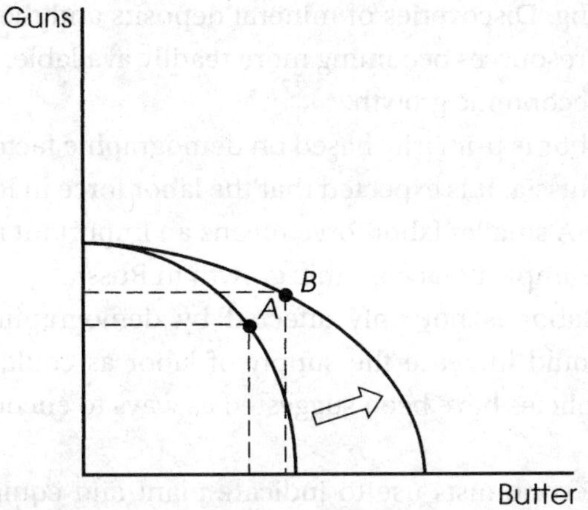

Fig. 20.2 A Technological Advance in Butter Production

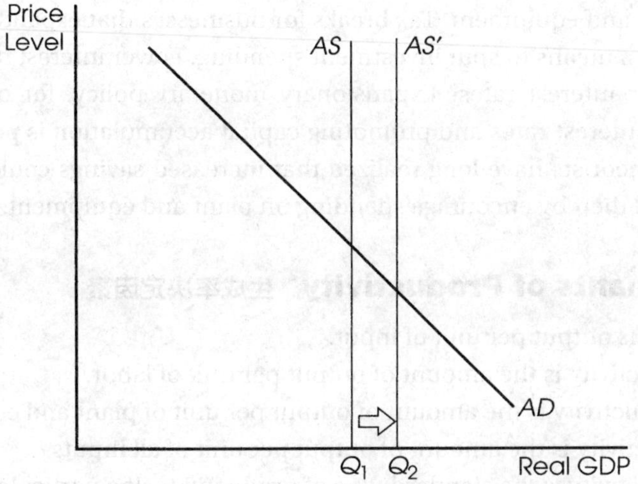

Fig. 20.3 An Increase in Long-Run Aggregate Supply

The only question that remains is, what can cause the long-run aggregate supply curve to shift to the right? Readers with good retention will remember that there are two factors that could cause the long-run aggregate supply curve to shift to the right: (1) an increase in the amount of resources, and (2) a technological advance that increases productivity. These are the same two factors that can cause the production possibilities frontier to shift outward.

Our investigation of the production possibilities frontier and the AS/AD model indicates that there are two general factors affecting economic growth: (1) resource availability, and (2) the productivity of those resources. To dig deeper, we now ask what can affect resource availability and productivity.

TIP

Economic growth can be portrayed with an outward shift of the production possibilities frontier or a rightward shift in the long-run aggregate supply curve.

The Determinants of Resource Availability 可用资源的决定因素

Recall that resources are classified into three categories—land, labor, and capital. One way to promote economic growth is to promote the availability of each of these classes of resources. For instance, you might think that the amount of natural resources, what economists call land, is strictly limited, but that is not true. New deposits of oil, natural gas, and minerals are continually being discovered. Also, advances in agriculture and irrigation can make more land available for farming. Discoveries of mineral deposits and the creation of arable fields are examples of natural resources becoming more readily available. This results in more production and, therefore, economic growth.

The availability of labor is primarily based on demographic factors. These demographics are a major concern in Russia. It is expected that the labor force in Russia will shrink due to a decline in the birth rate. A smaller labor force means an important resource is less available. This will have a negative impact on economic growth in Russia.

But the supply of labor is not only affected by demographic factors. Government-subsidized child care could increase the supply of labor as could education and training programs. Both these policies have been suggested as ways to encourage the supply of labor and economic growth.

TIP

Many theories of economic growth focus on the idea that savings can be used to increase the amount of capital in the economy.

Capital is the term economists use to indicate plant and equipment. An expansion of the amount of plant and equipment in the economy would shift the production possibilities frontier outward or the long run aggregate supply curve to the right. In either case, the result is economic growth. Economists have advocated a variety of policies that would promote spending on plant and equipment. Tax breaks for businesses that expand their capital stock have been tried as a means to spur investment spending. Lower interest rates may also help. What would lower interest rates? Expansionary monetary policy, for one thing. Another idea for lowering interest rates and promoting capital accumulation is policies to stimulate savings. Growth theorists have long realized that increased savings could lower borrowing costs for firms and thereby encourage spending on plant and equipment.

The Determinants of Productivity 生成率决定因素

- Productivity is output per unit of input.
- Labor productivity is the amount of output per unit of labor.
- Capital productivity is the amount of output per unit of plant and equipment.
- Total productivity is the amount of output per unit of all inputs.
- Labor productivity is the standard type of productivity. If a particular sort of productivity is not mentioned, it is safe to assume the discussion is about labor productivity.

Table 20.1 highlights the fact that labor productivity is important for economic growth. From 1948 until 1973 the United States enjoyed robust growth in labor productivity and living standards, as measured by real GDP per capita, increased accordingly. From 1973 until 1999, the growth rate of labor productivity has slowed and so has economic growth.

Table 20.1

Labor Productivity and the Standard of Living in the United States

Period	Average Growth Rate of Labor Productivity (%)	Average Growth Rate of Real GDP Per Capita (%)
1948–1973	2.9	2.1
1973–1999	1.6	1.4

Source: U.S. Bureau of Labor Statistics; Bureau of Economic Analysis; U.S. Bureau of the Census

What determines the productivity of labor? One of the most important factors is the amount of capital relative to the amount of labor. An increase in the amount of plant and equipment per worker will increase labor productivity.

Also, technology can affect the productivity of labor. The innovations that brought a personal computer to almost every office worker's desk undoubtedly raised productivity.

Another factor affecting productivity is the skill level of work force. Education and training can raise labor productivity. Economists call attempts to improve the quality of the labor force investments in "human capital." Human capital is the skill and knowledge embodied in the labor force. A labor force with high levels of human capital is more productive.

TIP

When the word *growth* appears in a question, you should think about the long run and the factors that affect economic long-run growth—resources and technology.

SUMMARY 小结

- Economic growth is defined as the growth of output usually as measured by real GDP or real GDP per capita. In the United States, real GDP per capita has grown about two percent a year since World War II. However, the fruits of economic growth are not shared equally by all Americans. The top 20 percent of families garner 50 percent of all the income earned.
- Economic growth is the result of increased resource availability or increased productivity. Long run output can increase only if more resources are on hand or those resources are more productive; however, there are a variety of factors that can impact resource availability and productivity. Table 20.2 delineates these factors.
- Finally, economists recognize that economic growth has its price. Economic growth can degrade the environment, cause congestion, and lead to more hectic lifestyles. Still, most people would prefer to live where real GDP per capita is high than where it is low.

Table 20.2

Determinants of Economic Growth
Increased Resource Availability
■ Discovery of new natural resources
■ Growth of the labor force
■ Growth of the capital stock
Increased Productivity
■ More capital per unit of labor
■ Technological progress
■ Better educated and trained work force

TERMS 术语

Capital plant and equipment

Capital Productivity the amount of output per unit of plant and equipment

Economic Growth growth of output usually measured by the percentage change in real GDP or real GDP per capita

Human Capital the skill and knowledge embodied in the labor force

Labor Productivity the amount of output per unit of labor

Potential GDP the amount that can be produced using resources fully and efficiently

Productivity output per unit of input

Total Productivity the amount of output per unit of all inputs

FORMULAS 公式

Rule of 70 Years it takes a variable to double = 70/the annual growth rate of the variable

MULTIPLE-CHOICE REVIEW QUESTIONS 选择题

1. Economic growth is
   (A) measured by the number of businesses in the economy.
   (B) shared equally among the population.
   (C) critical in determining the standard of living in a nation.
   (D) measured by the amount of government spending.
   (E) measured by the unemployment rate.

2. The standard of living is measured by
   (A) GDP.
   (B) GDP per capita.
   (C) Real GDP per capita.
   (D) Actual GDP per capita.
   (E) the unemployment rate.

3. Which of the following will result in economic growth?
   (A) A decrease in the unemployment rate.
   (B) An increase in the unemployment rate.
   (C) An increase in the size of the labor force.
   (D) A decrease in the population.
   (E) A change in political leadership.

4. Which of the following will promote economic growth?
   (A) Government regulation.
   (B) A new production technique that lowers costs.
   (C) Increased taxes.
   (D) More strict pollution standards for corporations.
   (E) Reduced taxes.

5. Which of the following will promote economic growth?
   (A) An increase in the amount of capital.
   (B) Lower wages.
   (C) Price controls that keep prices low.
   (D) Increased government spending.
   (E) A decrease in the money supply.

6. If real GDP per capita was $10,000 in 1990 and $15,000 in 2000, then the amount of economic growth is
   (A) 0.5 percent.
   (B) 5.0 percent.
   (C) 50 percent.
   (D) 3.3 percent.
   (E) More information is required to determine the amount of economic growth.

7. If real GDP per capita was $20,000 in 1980 and $21,000 in 1990, then we conclude that the standard of living has increased
   (A) 0.5 percent.
   (B) 5.0 percent.
   (C) 50 percent.
   (D) 3.3 percent.
   (E) More information is required to determine the amount of economic growth.

8. The standard of living will increase if
   (A) everyone takes more leisure time.
   (B) the population grows.
   (C) GDP increases.
   (D) real GDP increases.
   (E) real GDP increases at a greater rate than the population.

9. Output in country A is 1,200 units and its population is 100 persons. Output in country B is 2,400 units and its population is 400 persons.

(A) Country A has a higher standard of living than country B.
(B) Country A has a lower standard of living than country B.
(C) Country A and B have identical living standards.
(D) Country A is less productive than country B.
(E) More information is needed to determine which country has the higher standard of living.

10. Output in country X is 30,000 units and there are 3,000 persons working, while country Z has an output of 40,000 units and 8,000 workers.

(A) The productivity of labor in country Z is 33 percent higher than in country X.
(B) The productivity of labor in country Z is 25 percent higher than in country X.
(C) The productivity of labor in country X is 33 percent higher than in country Z.
(D) The productivity of labor in country X is 25 percent higher than in country Z.
(E) The productivity of labor in country X is twice as much as country Z.

11. The government can promote economic growth by

(A) setting a minimum wage.
(B) regulating industry.
(C) taxing firms that waste resources.
(D) job training programs.
(E) restricting imports.

12. Private industry can promote economic growth by

(A) implementing innovative production techniques.
(B) offering products at artificially low prices.
(C) giving a significant amount of profits to charity.
(D) hiring workers who are not really needed.
(E) adhering to environmental standards.

13. The size of the labor force in Japan is expected to shrink as a large segment of its population retires. This will

(A) affect labor productivity more than economic growth.
(B) affect economic growth more than labor productivity.
(C) not have a major effect on economic growth or labor productivity.
(D) affect labor productivity and economic growth equally.
(E) shift Japan's aggregate supply curve to the right.

14. If the standard of living increases, we can conclude that

(A) output must have increased.
(B) population must have increased.
(C) output and population must have increased.
(D) population must have decreased.
(E) output must have increased proportionally more than population.

15. If real GDP per capita grows at a rate of 10 percent a year, then we can expect the standard of living to double in

(A) 10 years.
(B) 9 years.
(C) 8 years.
(D) 7 years.
(E) 5 years.

MULTIPLE-CHOICE REVIEW ANSWERS
选择题答案

1. (C)	**4.** (B)	**7.** (B)	**10.** (E)	**13.** (B)
2. (C)	**5.** (A)	**8.** (E)	**11.** (D)	**14.** (E)
3. (C)	**6.** (C)	**9.** (A)	**12.** (A)	**15.** (D)

FREE-RESPONSE REVIEW QUESTIONS 开放式题目

I. Use the production possibilities frontier to illustrate the effects of a very successful government policy to train the labor force so that workers became more productive. Be sure to label the axes of your diagram.

II.

A. Use the AS/AD model to show the effects of a decrease in the availability of timber due to a depletion of the supply of trees. Be sure to use a long run aggregate supply curve and label the axes of your diagram.

B. Now suppose the government reduced taxes while the supply of timber was depleted. What effect would this have?

Free-Response Review Answers 开放式题目答案

I. The effects of a more productive labor force due to training.

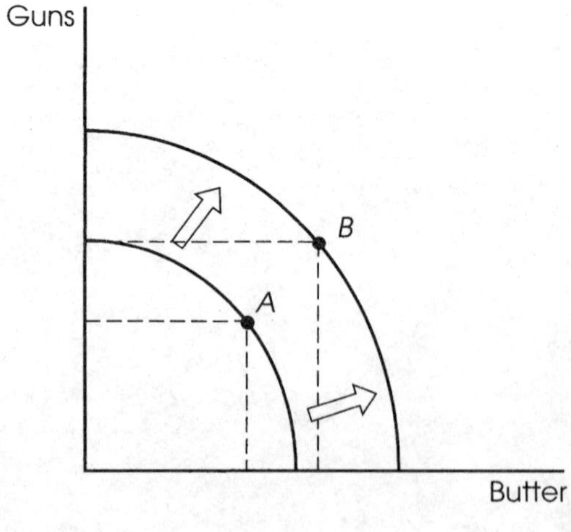

II. A. A decrease in the supply of timber shifts the aggregate supply curve to the left. This will raise the equilibrium price level and lower the equilibrium quantity of output.

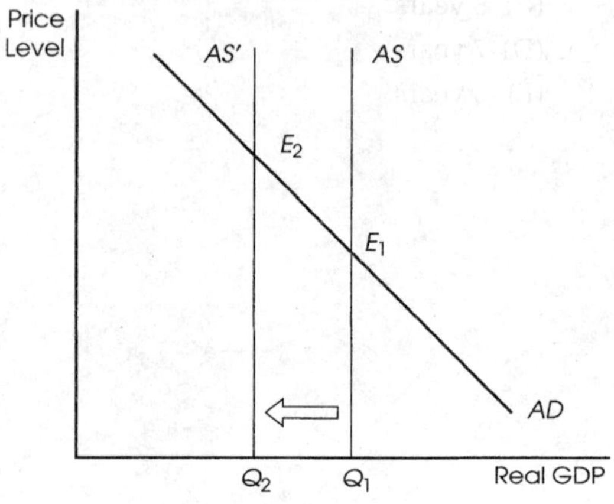

B. If the government reduced taxes while the supply of timber was depleted, this would shift the aggregate demand curve to the right. The equilibrium quantity of output would still fall to Q2, but the equilibrium price level would be higher than if the government did not reduce taxes.

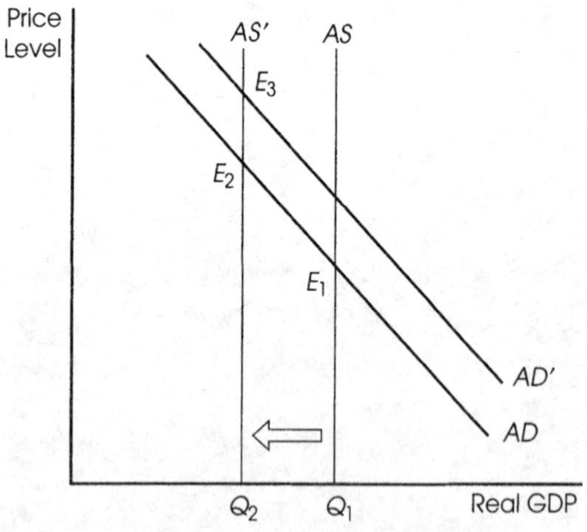

International Trade and Exchange 国际贸易和外汇

21

→ TARIFFS AND QUOTAS
→ BALANCE OF PAYMENTS
→ GOLD STANDARD
→ EXCHANGE RATES
→ MONETARY AND FISCAL POLICY IN AN OPEN ECONOMY

THE BALANCE OF TRADE 贸易平衡

In 2013 the United States was the world's second largest exporting nation, shipping $2.3 trillion worth of goods and services abroad. However, in that same year, the United States imported $2.8 trillion worth of goods and services. The fact that our imports exceeded our exports by almost $500 billion is troubling to some people. Don't foreigners want our products? We buy their products, but they don't buy as many of ours. Won't this have adverse economic effects? Will we owe foreign nations money? Doesn't this cost American jobs?

A nation's balance of trade is equal to its exports minus its imports. Earlier we called this figure net exports. For the United States in 2013, the balance of trade was negative $500 billion (= $2.3 trillion – $2.8 trillion). When the balance of trade is negative, it can be referred to as a *trade deficit*. The last time America had a trade surplus was 1975. Are these chronic trade deficits a problem, and what, if anything, can be done about them?

Trade deficits can indeed be symptomatic of underlying economic problems. For instance, if a nation's exports are of inferior quality or cost too much relative to the competition, then it may experience a trade deficit. Or a country might rely heavily on imports just to meet its subsistence needs while it has nothing to export. This dire situation would result in a trade deficit as well. Finally, a nation's currency may be overpriced for one reason or another. This would make it expensive for foreigners to buy their products. A trade deficit could be the result.

But there is a more likely explanation for the chronic trade deficits in the United States: We have higher incomes than our trading partners. We are doing so well that we can afford the best of everything no matter where in the world it might be produced. This makes America's imports swell. Unfortunately, many other countries are not doing as well. They cannot afford to buy our exports and our trade balance suffers. If this idea about the origin of our trade deficits is correct, then we should see smaller deficits, or even surpluses, when our economy is experiencing a recession. During the 1991–92 recession the trade deficit shrank to $30 billion. The last trade surplus in the United States was in 1975 on the tail end of a severe 16-month recession.

TRADE RESTRICTIONS 贸易限制

Arguments for Trade Restrictions 贸易限制的理由

Even if our trade deficits spring from the high standard of living we enjoy, they may still be problematic. When we buy foreign textiles, that means there is less demand for domestic textile workers. Imported textiles could mean unemployment for domestic textile workers.

Barriers to free trade across nations have been erected for a variety of reasons. One argument is to protect jobs from foreign competition. However, there is a steep price to pay for this protection. Everyone who buys textiles will be paying more for them because competition was thwarted. We know from our earlier analysis of comparative advantage that free trade enables the countries involved to consume more than under restricted trade.

Other reasons for trade restrictions include the infant industry argument, the diversity argument, and dumping. Infant industries are those that are just getting started. At this point they are in no condition to compete with foreign industries that have all the advantages of being well established. The argument is that these infant industries will be able to compete after they have developed. At that point, the trade restrictions could be dropped.

Another reason to protect an industry from foreign competition is for the sake of diversity. A nation should not rely too heavily on others. What if a war broke out? Do you think our enemies would continue to export to us? We need to encourage some industries despite their inefficiencies because diversity is healthy. Trade barriers can promote diversity.

Dumping is a technical term in international trade. It describes a situation where foreign producers are selling a product in the domestic market for less than it cost to produce it. The foreign firms would like to establish a foothold in our markets, so they are willing to absorb the loss. Domestic producers argue that prices will soon rise once the foreign firms have put them out of business. Trade barriers can be used to prevent dumping.

Table 21.1 lists major arguments for trade restrictions. Most economists think that the benefits of free trade outweigh any of these reasons for restricting the flow of goods and services between nations.

Table 21.1

Arguments for Trade Restrictions
■ Promote domestic employment ■ Infant industry argument ■ Diversity of production ■ Prevent dumping

Instituting Trade Restrictions 设立贸易限制

There are a variety of ways to discourage or prevent imports from coming into a country. Quotas, tariffs, and licensing requirements are the most common.

1. **AN IMPORT QUOTA IS A LIMIT ON THE AMOUNT OF A PRODUCT THAT CAN BE IMPORTED.** When the import quota is set at zero, domestic producers are completely protected from foreign competition. Figure 21.1 shows the effects of an import quota on the domestic market for rice.

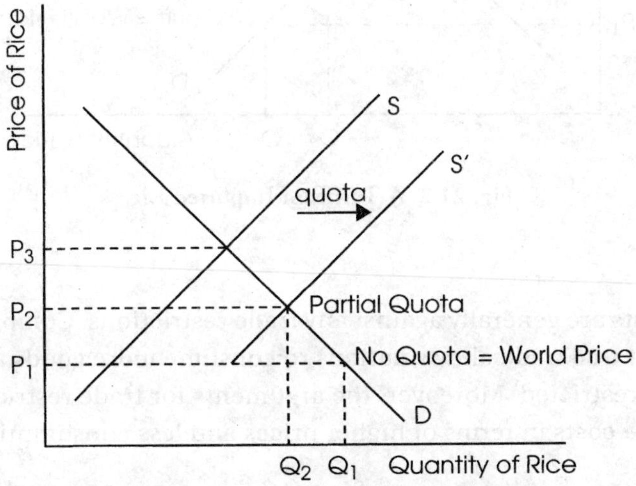

Fig. 21.1 A Quota on Rice Imports

If free trade is allowed, then the price of rice will be P_1, the world price. If no trade in rice is allowed, then the price will be P_3, the domestic price in the absence of trade. If a quota allows in some rice, then the supply of rice curve will shift to the right by that amount. As shown, compared to free trade, the quota raises the domestic price of rice and less rice is consumed. In addition, it can be shown that consumer surplus is reduced by the quota as is total surplus.

2. **AN IMPORT TARIFF IS A TAX ON THE SPECIFIED IMPORTED PRODUCT.** The tariff serves to raise the price of the imported product in the eyes of domestic consumers. This gives the edge to domestic producers. Figure 21.2 shows the effects of an import tariff.

   The price of rice would be P_1 except that the tariff raises it to P_2. The higher price causes a decrease in the quantity of rice demanded and the amount actually bought and sold is now lower (Q_2). The tariff, like the quota, raises the domestic price of rice and lowers the amount bought and sold. These higher prices and reduced amounts of consumption are the costs of trade restrictions.

3. **CLEVER ADMINISTRATORS CAN STIFLE TRADE IN MANY WAYS ASIDE FROM QUOTAS AND TARIFFS.** Arcane rules and regulations are often developed with no other purpose in mind than to discourage competition. Governments may require businesspersons to obtain a license granting them the right to import a specific product. The government need only limit the number of licenses it grants and the amount to be imported by each license holder in order to restrict trade. The effects of licensing agreements and rules and regulations that stifle trade are shown in exactly the same manner as the import quota diagram in Figure 21.1.

TIP

Trade restrictions are bad for consumers because they raise prices and limit choices.

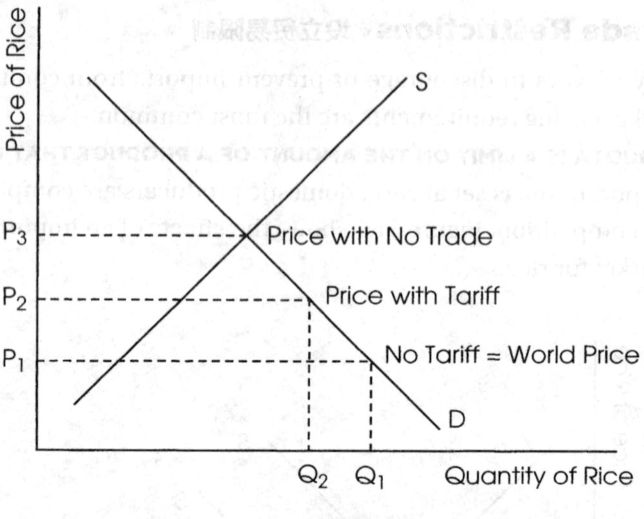

Fig. 21.2 A Tariff on Imported Rice

Economists are generally against any trade restrictions. Comparative advantage suggests that free trade allows nations to consume more goods and services than if trade was restricted. Moreover, the arguments for trade restrictions are dubious while the costs in terms of higher prices and less consumption are more definite.

Table 21.2

Trade Restrictions
■ Quotas ■ Tariffs ■ Licensing requirements

THE BALANCE OF PAYMENTS 收支平衡

The balance of payments is composed of the current account, the financial account, and the capital account. The current account is primarily net exports with some additional items. The financial account measures investment dollars flowing into the United States minus investments by U.S. entities abroad. For 2013 the financial account balance is positive, meaning more investment dollars flowed into the United States than flowed out in foreign-asset investments. The capital account is mainly debt forgiveness. Table 21.3 delineates the balance of payments for the United States in 2013.

Table 21.3

The Balance of Payments for the United States in 2013 (Billions of $)

Current Account Balance		–379.3
Balance of trade	–478.9	
Net investment income	228.8	
Net transfers	–133.2	
Financial Account Balance		351.3
Foreign purchases of U.S. assets		
Minus U.S. purchases of foreign assets	353.1	
Net financial derivatives	–1.8	
Capital Account Balance		0.4
Net Errors and Omissions		27.6
		0

Source: **Bureau of Economic Analysis**

The current account, the financial account, and the capital account should sum to zero. This is an accounting necessity. When the current account is negative, as it was in 2013, this means that we have been spending more abroad than foreigners have been spending here, whether it is on goods and services, or investment payments or gifts and aid. This excess spending abroad puts dollars in foreign hands.

The financial account accounts for those dollars that were put in foreign hands. The financial account for 2013 indicates that most of the dollars that wound up in foreign hands were used to buy assets in the United States. Had foreigners not wanted to use their dollars to buy investments in the United States, they could have just held on to them. Even so, that is an investment—an investment in U.S. currency.

The financial account plus the capital account must be positive by the same magnitude that the current account is negative. This is because all the dollars that wind up overseas must be accounted for. Measuring all these dollar flows is fraught with error. In 2013 these errors and omissions amounted to a significant sum: $27.6 billion.

EXCHANGE RATES 汇率

The exchange rate is the value of one country's currency in terms of another's. Exchange rates are determined, as we shall see, by supply and demand. Table 21.4 shows selected exchange rates.

Let us consider the exchange rate between the U.S. dollar and the Indian rupee. One dollar was worth about 60 rupees in June 2014. This implies that one rupee is worth about 1⁄60 of a dollar, or less than 2 cents. Why isn't the rupee worth more or less? Because the supply and demand for rupees intersected at less than 2 cents per rupee. This is illustrated in Figure 21.3.

Table 21.4

Selected Exchange Rates on June 5, 2014

One U.S. dollar equals:	
1.08	Australian dollar
0.60	British pound
1.09	Canadian dollars
5.48	Danish kroner
0.73	Euro
59.27	Indian rupees
102.51	Japanese yen
12.92	Mexican pesos
10.70	South African rand

Source: Federal Reserve Bank of New York

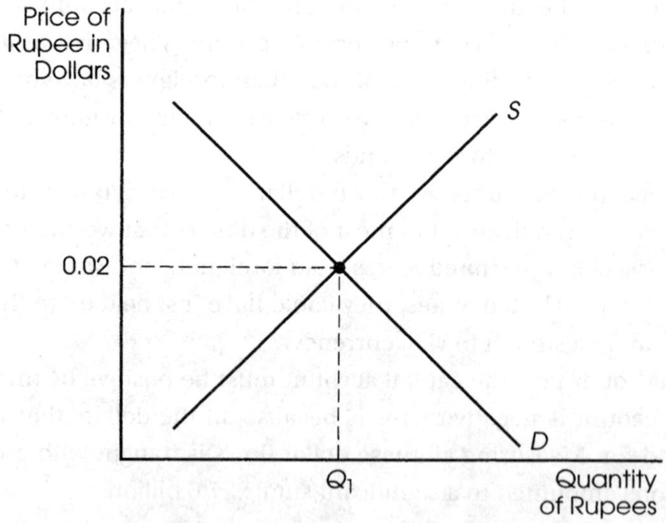

Fig. 21.3 The Supply and Demand for Rupees

The demand for rupees in the international market is downward sloping, which implies that the quantity of rupees demanded will be greater when the dollar price is lower. This makes sense: More people and firms would want to acquire rupees if they could get a lot of them for each dollar. The supply curve for rupees is upward sloping, which implies that the quantity of rupees supplied will be greater when the dollar price is higher. Again, this makes sense: More people would be willing to part with their rupees if they could get more cents for each one.

Changing Rates 变动率

The exchange rate between the rupee and the dollar is changing constantly because the supply and the demand for rupees in terms of dollars are shifting constantly. If Americans began to appreciate Indian products more, then the demand for rupees would increase. That's because importers of Indian products would have to place bigger orders and pay for those orders in rupees.

When the demand for rupees increases, the demand curve for rupees shifts to the right as shown in Figure 21.4. The result is a rise in the dollar value of the rupee and an increase in the amount of rupees exchanged.

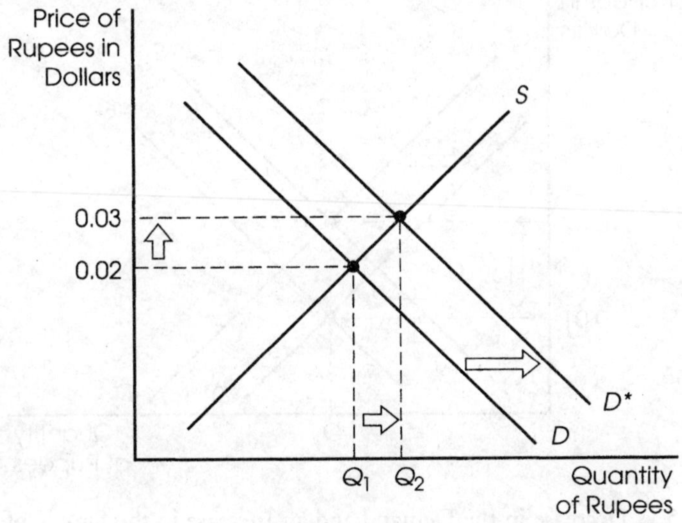

Fig. 21.4 An Increase in the Demand for Rupees

When the value of the rupee increases against the dollar as in Figure 21.4, this is known as an "appreciation" of the rupee. Or looked at from the other side, the dollar has "depreciated" vis-à-vis the rupee. Previously, a rupee cost 2 cents. Now a rupee costs 3 cents.

Interest Rates 利率

Changing tastes are just one of several factors that influence exchange rates between countries. Interest rates are another. If interest rates in India rise relative to interest rates in America, then it will be more rewarding to lend money in India. However, an American wanting to lend money in India must first turn her dollars into rupees. This increases the demand for rupees. The result will be the same as in Figure 21.4 where the demand for rupees shifts to the right. The rupee will appreciate and more rupees will be exchanged for dollars.

There is an additional curve shift that will occur with a change in interest rates. The supply of rupees will decrease as fewer Indian investors will want to place their funds overseas. The domestic return has become more attractive. If the supply curve is shifted to the left as well in Figure 21.4, it will serve to appreciate the rupee further.

Political Stability 政治稳定

Political stability can also affect exchange rates. If the Indian government finds itself in turmoil with its credibility for maintaining peace and justice in question, fewer foreigners will want to invest in India. The demand for rupees would fall even if interest rates were relatively higher in India. This would shift the demand for rupees to the left. Moreover, Indian citizens will want to store more of their wealth abroad. Who knows what might happen to bank accounts and financial assets in a country where the government is losing control? When Indian citizens want to place some of their wealth in America, they typically start by trading their rupees for dollars. This is reflected in a shift to the right in the supply of rupees.

So political instability in India would decrease the demand for rupees and increase the supply. This is shown in Figure 21.5. The result is a significant depreciation of the rupee.

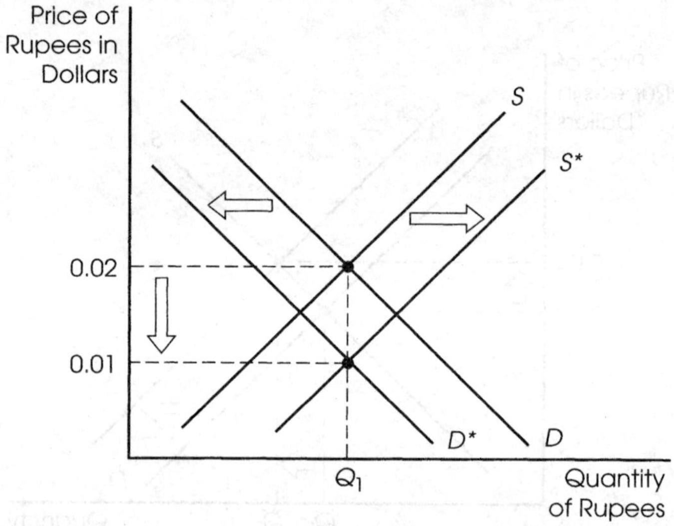

Fig. 21.5 A Decrease in the Demand and an Increase in the Supply of Rupees

Relative Levels of Income 收入相对水平

The relative levels of income in India and America will influence the exchange rate between dollars and rupees. If America is better off than India in terms of income, Americans will be able to afford more of the finer things India has to offer. And India will not be able to enjoy America's exports to the same extent because of her relatively lower standard of living. So if the standard of living in America advanced while India slipped into a recession, the situation would be just the opposite of that portrayed in Figure 21.5—the demand for rupees would increase because Americans could afford Indian exports. The supply of rupees would fall, not increase, since Indians would not be demanding as many American exports as before the recession.

Relative Prices 相对价格

Relative prices in India and America can also impact exchange rates. If prices rise in India while they hold steady in America, the value of the rupee will depreciate. This is because some Americans will balk at purchasing Indian products because of the higher prices, thus reducing the demand for rupees. And Indian citizens will buy more American products since the prices of these items have held steady. This will increase the supply of rupees. The situation is just as depicted in Figure 21.5.

Astute readers may take the analysis a step further. Once the value of the rupee depreciates, the higher-priced Indian products will appear cheaper to Americans and the lower-priced American products will appear more expensive to Indians. This is because the currencies must be exchanged to obtain each other's products. If you reasoned this way, congratulate yourself—you have outlined the theory of purchasing power parity. This theory states that the same product, say, a pencil, will cost the same if it is bought domestically or imported because exchange rates change to erase any price differential that may exist. It's an interesting theory, but the real world abounds with counterexamples.

Speculation 投机

Speculators have an important impact on exchange rates. Individuals and institutions buy and sell currencies with an eye toward making a profit. As with all financial transactions, these speculators want to "buy low and sell high." If it is expected that the rupee will depreciate in the near future, speculators will try to sell their rupees now before the price falls. In Figure 21.6, this would increase the supply of rupees, shifting the supply curve to the right. Notice that the result is a depreciation of the rupee from 2 cents to 1 cent. Speculation often results in self-fulfilling prophecies.

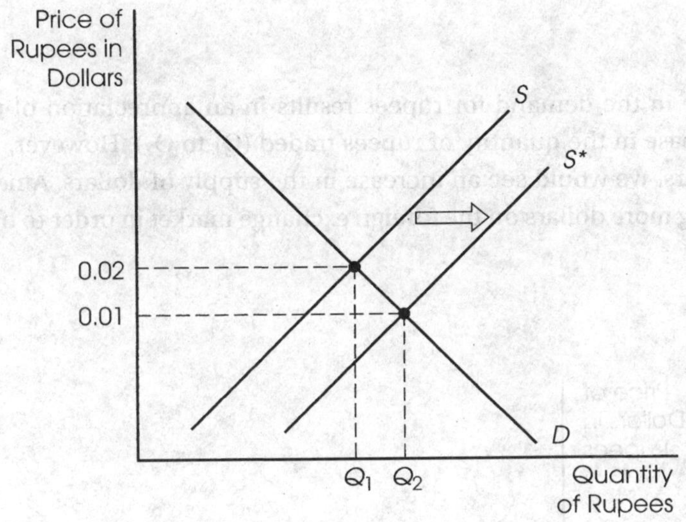

Fig. 21.6 An Increase in the Supply of Rupees

Side-by-Side Foreign Exchange Graphs 并列式外汇图表

At least two currencies will be affected by a change in any of the factors affecting foreign exchange rates: the currency under consideration and that of its trading partner or partners. In order to illustrate these effects, side-by-side exchange rate graphs may be used.

Consider a case where Americans suddenly develop a passion for India's exports. If we look at the market for rupees, we will see an increase in demand for rupees. American importers will be required to obtain rupees in order to obtain the goods Americans desire from India.

The increase in the supply of dollars results in a depreciation of the dollar (D_1 to D_2) and an increase in the quantity of dollars traded (Q_1 to Q_2). Thus, we may conclude that when Americans increase their preference for Indians goods, the rupee will appreciate while the dollar depreciates. Figures 21.7 and 21.8 are often placed side-by-side to illustrate these simultaneous effects on the two currencies.

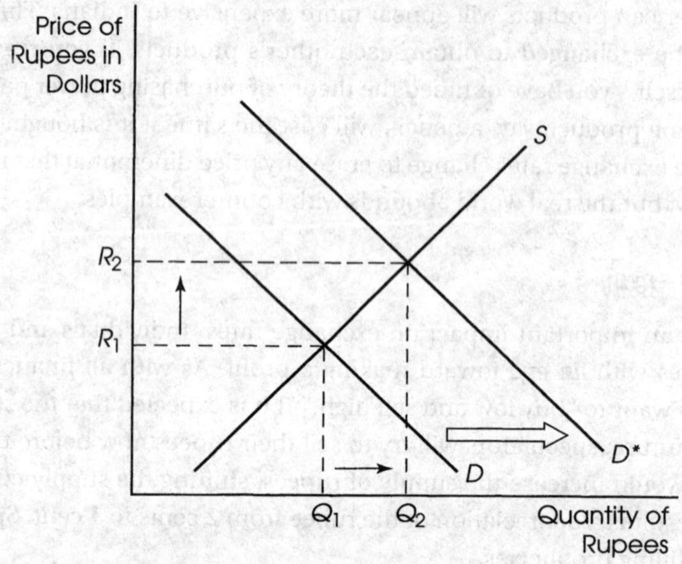

Fig. 21.7 Market for Rupees: An Increase in the Demand for Rupees

The increase in the demand for rupees results in an appreciation of the rupee (R_1 to R_2) and an increase in the quantity of rupees traded (Q_1 to Q_2). However, if we look at the market for dollars, we would see an increase in the supply of dollars. American importers will be supplying more dollars on the foreign exchange market in order to obtain the rupees they want.

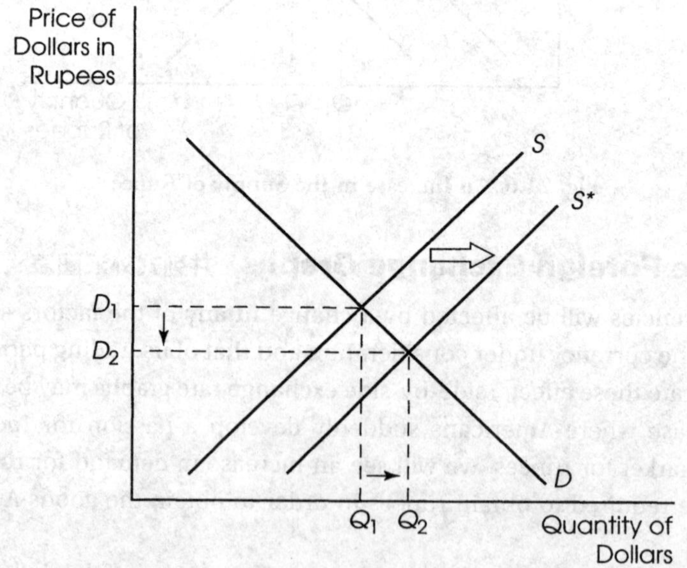

Fig. 21.8 Market for Dollars: An Increase in the Supply of Dollars

Table 21.5

Determinants of Exchange Rates

- Demand for a nation's exports (tastes)
- Relative interest rates
- Political stability
- Relative level of income
- Relative prices (theory of purchasing power parity)
- Speculation

Exchange Rate Regimes 汇率制

Before the Great Depression, most of the large economies of the world were on a gold standard. Essentially, the gold standard kept exchange rates between countries fixed. Since the dollar was worth a certain amount of gold and the franc was worth a given amount of gold, the value of the dollar versus the franc would be established. If the value of the franc appreciated vis-à-vis the dollar, people could use their dollars to buy gold and then use that gold to buy francs, and then use those francs to buy more dollars than they started with.

Arbitrage of this sort kept exchange rates between nations fixed, but the gold standard was not without flaws. If tastes changed and Americans clamored for French products, the exchange rate did not rise to choke off some of this foreign demand. In such a situation the United States would develop a balance of payments deficit as French citizens and institutions piled up dollar holdings. Many historians and economists point to balance of payment crises caused by the gold standard as one of the central causes of the Great Depression.

Modern international exchange is no longer based on gold. The Bretton Woods regime replaced the fixed exchange rate system based on gold in 1944. In the Bretton Woods system the dollar was as good as gold. Countries pegged the value of their currencies to the dollar, and the United States stood ready to trade any dollar holdings of foreign governments to gold at $35 an ounce. This system broke down in 1971 when the United States, running chronic trade deficits, could no longer support the $35 an ounce price of gold.

Managed Float 管理浮动汇率

The current system for determining international exchange rates is referred to as a *managed float*. Supply and demand determine exchange rates between currencies as outlined above. But if exchange rates change in a manner deemed to be detrimental, nations will intervene. Intervention involves coordinated buying and selling of currencies in order to adjust their equilibrium values determined by supply and demand.

For example, because the United States runs chronic trade deficits there is an abundant supply of dollars in international markets. This tends to depress the value of the dollar. A depreciated dollar would lower America's demand for foreign products. This would help with our chronic trade deficits, but it would hurt the countries that export to us. If governments decide to support the dollar, they would intervene by buying dollars. This results in the dollar appreciating in value.

A managed float allows supply and demand to determine exchange rates within a range of values. Once exchange rates exceed that range, governments use their currency holdings to intervene.

MONETARY AND FISCAL POLICY IN AN OPEN ECONOMY
开放经济下的货币政策和财政政策

Monetary and fiscal policy can be used to fight inflation or recession. However, our previous discussion of these policies ignored their effects on the exchange rate and the balance of trade. The impacts of monetary and fiscal policy in the context of an open economy are more complicated.

TIP

Monetary and fiscal policies are less effective when exchange rates are perfectly flexible.

An expansionary monetary policy still stimulates the economy in the short run by increasing the quantity of output and putting upward pressure on prices. This will worsen the balance of trade since the increase in output means an increase in income. Rising incomes tend to drive imports, worsening the balance of trade. And rising prices tend to discourage exports, again, worsening the balance of trade.

Policymakers need to keep in mind the effects of monetary policy on imports and exports. In a closed economy, an increase in the money supply stimulates output and income in the short run. In an open economy these effects will be dampened because imports will rise. That is to say, some of the stimulatory effect will be spent overseas, and exports will fall because of the inflation resulting from the increase in the money supply.

The effects of an expansionary fiscal policy are tempered in the same way in the context of an open economy. An increase in government spending and a reduction in taxes will increase output and income in the short run, while putting upward pressure on prices. Higher levels of income tend to raise imports while higher prices tend to discourage exports. This worsens the balance of trade and implies that the effects of the fiscal policy will not be as pronounced.

Also notice that monetary and fiscal polices will affect exchange rates because these policies alter incomes and prices. Remember that exchange rates are impacted by the relative level of income and the relative level of prices in a nation.

SUMMARY 小结

- The United States has been importing more than it has been exporting since the mid-1970s. However, our trade deficits are more a symptom of how well off we are relative to our trading partners than a cause for alarm. Most economists agree that trade restrictions, such as import tariffs, quotas, and licensing agreements, are harmful. Free trade, where countries specialize according to the law of comparative advantage, benefits consumers in the countries involved.
- Nevertheless, most nations restrict trade in one way or another. The arguments for trade restrictions vary from promoting employment to preventing dumping. Infant industries and the benefits of a diverse manufacturing base are two more reasons put forward to justify trade restrictions. However valid the reason, economic analysis shows that the cost of restricting trade is higher prices to the consumer.
- A nation's balance of payments accounts for the funds that flow into and out of the country. If there is a deficit in the current account, there must be a corresponding surplus in the financial and capital accounts.
- The exchange rate is the price of one nation's currency in terms of another. In today's world, exchange rates are determined by the supply and demand for a nation's currency—up to a point. Occasionally, nations will intervene in the market by supplying more or less of a particular currency or demanding more or less. Nations use their official reserves during these interventions in order to prop up or devalue a given currency. In other words, countries can adjust the position of the supply and demand curves for a currency, but only if they have the cooperation of the major trading

nations. Without cooperation no single nation has enough reserves to make much of an adjustment to the supply or demand curves of most currencies. This international monetary system, where supply and demand determine exchange rates with the occasional intervention by a consortium of trading partners, is known as a managed float.

- Exchange rates, therefore, are free to float about where supply and demand might take them—just so long as they don't go too far and trigger an intervention. Anything that can affect the supply or the demand for a nation's currency will affect its exchange rate. The demand for a nation's exports affects the demand for its currency, as do relative interest rates. Relative prices and income also affect exchange rates. And speculation can play a role. If market participants expect a particular currency to appreciate in the near future, they will try to buy as much as they can now. As we have seen, this increases the demand for the currency, which, in turn, causes it to appreciate, the fulfillment of a self-fulfilling prophecy.
- Exchange rates are affected when a country pursues monetary and fiscal policy because, in the short run, these policies affect income and prices. Moreover, the balance of trade will be affected by monetary and fiscal policy because imports and exports are impacted by changes in income and prices as well. The short run effects of monetary and fiscal policy are not as pronounced in an open economy.

TERMS 术语

Appreciation the increase of the value of a currency in terms of another currency

Balance of Payments an accounting of the funds that flow into and out of a country comprised of the capital account and the current account

Balance of Trade a nation's exports minus its imports

Capital Account a portion of the balance of payments comprised of foreign purchases of U.S. assets minus U.S. purchases of foreign assets, plus the change in official reserves

Closed Economy a hypothetical economy with no foreign trade

Current Account a portion of the balance of payments comprised of the trade balance, net investment income, and net transfers

Depreciation the decrease of the value of a currency in terms of another currency

Dumping the practice of foreign producers selling a product in the domestic market for less than it cost to produce it

Exchange Rate the value of one country's currency in terms of another's

Gold Standard a unit of currency that is equivalent to a stated amount of gold

Import Quota a limit on the amount of a product that can be imported

Import Tariff a tax on a specified imported product

Infant Industries those industries that are just getting started, perhaps requiring trade restrictions

Intervention situation in which a nation or group of nations use their official reserves to supply or demand a currency in order to alter the exchange rate

Managed Float an exchange rate regime where supply and demand determine exchange rates with occasional intervention when warranted

Net Investment Income amount U.S. citizens earned as interest and dividends from abroad minus how much was paid to foreigners in interest and dividends

Net Transfers money our government and citizens send as gifts or aid to foreigners minus how much foreigners send to us in gifts and aid

Official Reserves government's holdings of foreign currencies

Open Economy an economy with foreign trade

Trade Deficit excess of a nation's imports over its exports

Trade Surplus excess of a nation's exports over its imports

FORMULAS 公式

Balance of Payments = Current Account + Capital Account + Financial Account

MULTIPLE-CHOICE REVIEW QUESTIONS 选择题

1. When a country has a balance of trade deficit

(A) it must make up the difference by shipping gold to its creditors.
(B) its exports exceed its imports.
(C) its currency will appreciate.
(D) corrective actions must be taken.
(E) its imports exceed its exports.

2. A balance of trade surplus can be the result of

(A) a loose monetary policy.
(B) foreigners having no taste for this country's products.
(C) an appreciation of the country's currency.
(D) low levels of income relative to other nations.
(E) high domestic prices.

3. One strategy a corporation may use to gain market share in a foreign market is

(A) raising the price of its product.
(B) convincing its government to put an import tariff on the product.
(C) convincing its government to place a quota on the product.
(D) cornering.
(E) dumping.

4. Tariffs and quotas on imports

(A) result in higher domestic prices.
(B) promote trade between nations.
(C) do not necessarily affect domestic prices.
(D) affect domestic prices: the former raises them while the latter lowers them.
(E) are ways to fight inflation.

5. Tariffs and quotas on imports

(A) result in lower domestic prices.
(B) sometimes raise and sometimes lower the amount of the product sold domestically.
(C) lower the amount of the product sold domestically.
(D) raise the amount of the product sold domestically.
(E) do not affect domestic prices or quantities.

6. Which of the following is NOT an argument for restricting trade?

(A) to protect infant industry
(B) to promote employment
(C) to fight inflation
(D) to promote a diversity of industries
(E) to prevent dumping

7. If the value of the U.S. dollar depreciates, *ceteris paribus*, then U.S.

(A) imports will rise.
(B) unemployment will rise.
(C) net exports will fall.
(D) exports will rise.
(E) net exports will be unaffected.

8. If a country has a negative value on its current account, then it must

(A) pay that amount to its trading partners.
(B) have a positive value of equal magnitude on its capital plus financial account.
(C) depreciate its currency.
(D) appreciate its currency.
(E) send gold abroad.

9. With a managed float

(A) countries occasionally intervene in foreign exchange markets.
(B) countries never have to intervene in foreign exchange markets.
(C) countries must constantly intervene to maintain the value of their currencies.
(D) exchange rates are fixed.
(E) each currency is worth a stated amount of gold.

10. Expansionary fiscal policy

(A) increases unemployment in an open economy.
(B) lowers the nominal interest rate, which results in currency appreciation.
(C) is less effective in an open economy with floating exchange rates.
(D) will not affect the nominal interest rate.
(E) lowers the nominal interest rate, which results in currency depreciation.

11. In the balance of payments, the trade balance

(A) is ignored.
(B) appears in the capital account.
(C) appears in the current account
(D) is included in the official reserves.
(E) is counted as part of "net transfers."

12. If interest rates rise in the United States relative to other nations, then

(A) the value of the dollar will tend to appreciate.
(B) the value of the dollar will tend to depreciate.
(C) exchange rates will be affected but not the value of the dollar.
(D) the exchange rate will not be affected.
(E) the balance of trade will tend toward a surplus.

13. If prices rise in the United States relative to other countries, then

(A) the value of the dollar will tend to appreciate.
(B) the value of the dollar will tend to depreciate.
(C) exchange rates will be affected but not the value of the dollar.
(D) the exchange rate will not be affected.
(E) the balance of trade will tend toward a surplus.

14. If the demand for dollars rises while the supply of dollars falls, then the

(A) dollar will appreciate.
(B) dollar will depreciate.
(C) exchange rates will be affected but not the value of the dollar.
(D) exchange rate will not be affected.
(E) balance of trade will tend toward a surplus.

15. If the demand for our exports rises while our tastes for foreign goods falls off, then

(A) the value of the dollar will tend to appreciate.
(B) the value of the dollar will tend to depreciate.
(C) exchange rates will be affected but not the value of the dollar.
(D) the exchange rate will not be affected.
(E) the balance of trade will tend toward a surplus.

MULTIPLE-CHOICE REVIEW ANSWERS
选择题答案

1. (E)	**4.** (A)	**7.** (D)	**10.** (C)	**13.** (B)
2. (D)	**5.** (C)	**8.** (B)	**11.** (C)	**14.** (A)
3. (E)	**6.** (C)	**9.** (A)	**12.** (A)	**15.** (A)

FREE-RESPONSE REVIEW QUESTIONS 开放式题目

I. Suppose two counties, Alpha and Beta, trade freely and allow investments to flow across their borders as well. Draw two graphs, one of the supply and demand for Alpha's currency and one of the supply and demand for Beta's currency. Be sure to label the axes of your graphs. Show how the value of each currency will be affected if the interest rate on investments in Alpha rises while the return on investments in Beta remains unchanged.

II. Given your response above, how will the imports and exports of each country be affected?

Free-Response Review Answers 开放式题目答案

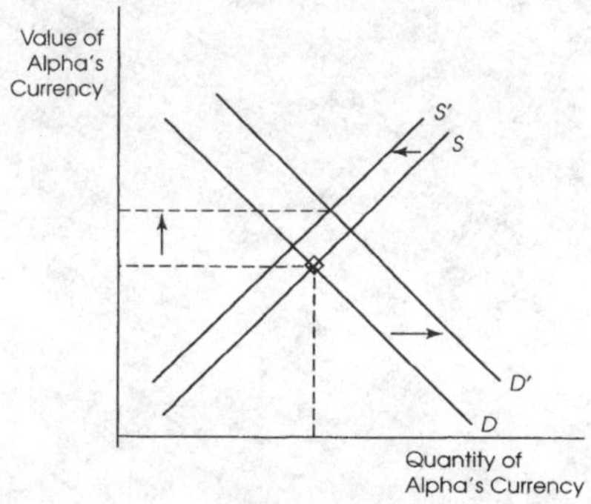

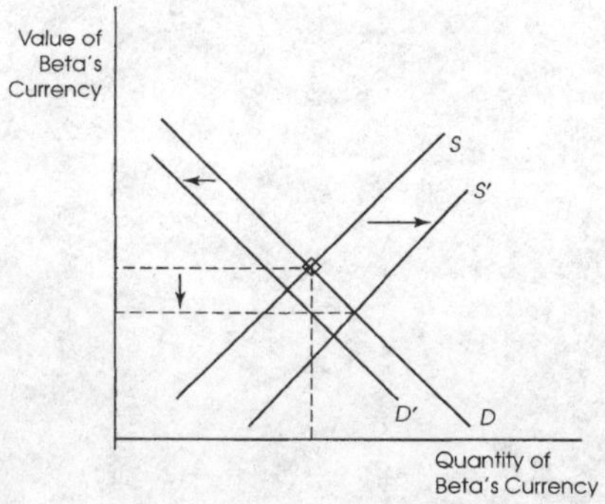

I. With higher returns in Alpha, the demand for Alpha's currency will rise. Foreigners will want to invest in Alpha and need its currency to do so. It also is possible that the supply of Alpha's currency will decline as more domestic investments are undertaken. These two shifts are shown in Figure 21.7. Alpha's currency will appreciate in value.

With higher returns in Alpha, the supply of Beta's currency will rise. It also is possible that the demand for Beta's currency will decline as more of Alpha's investors undertake domestic investments. These two shifts are shown in Figure 21.8. Beta's currency will depreciate in value.

II. Since Alpha's currency is appreciating, Alpha's exports will fall and its imports will rise. Alpha's net exports will fall. Since Beta's currency is depreciating, Beta's exports will rise and its imports will fall. Beta's net exports will rise.

These changes make sense. Alpha's current account is declining, but its financial account is rising. Beta's current account is improving, but its mirror image, the financial account, is worsening.

Model AP Exam in Macroeconomics

AP宏观经济学考试样题

答题纸 ANSWER SHEET
宏观经济学 Macroeconomics
MULTIPLE-CHOICE QUESTIONS 选择题

1. Ⓐ Ⓑ Ⓒ Ⓓ Ⓔ	21. Ⓐ Ⓑ Ⓒ Ⓓ Ⓔ	41. Ⓐ Ⓑ Ⓒ Ⓓ Ⓔ
2. Ⓐ Ⓑ Ⓒ Ⓓ Ⓔ	22. Ⓐ Ⓑ Ⓒ Ⓓ Ⓔ	42. Ⓐ Ⓑ Ⓒ Ⓓ Ⓔ
3. Ⓐ Ⓑ Ⓒ Ⓓ Ⓔ	23. Ⓐ Ⓑ Ⓒ Ⓓ Ⓔ	43. Ⓐ Ⓑ Ⓒ Ⓓ Ⓔ
4. Ⓐ Ⓑ Ⓒ Ⓓ Ⓔ	24. Ⓐ Ⓑ Ⓒ Ⓓ Ⓔ	44. Ⓐ Ⓑ Ⓒ Ⓓ Ⓔ
5. Ⓐ Ⓑ Ⓒ Ⓓ Ⓔ	25. Ⓐ Ⓑ Ⓒ Ⓓ Ⓔ	45. Ⓐ Ⓑ Ⓒ Ⓓ Ⓔ
6. Ⓐ Ⓑ Ⓒ Ⓓ Ⓔ	26. Ⓐ Ⓑ Ⓒ Ⓓ Ⓔ	46. Ⓐ Ⓑ Ⓒ Ⓓ Ⓔ
7. Ⓐ Ⓑ Ⓒ Ⓓ Ⓔ	27. Ⓐ Ⓑ Ⓒ Ⓓ Ⓔ	47. Ⓐ Ⓑ Ⓒ Ⓓ Ⓔ
8. Ⓐ Ⓑ Ⓒ Ⓓ Ⓔ	28. Ⓐ Ⓑ Ⓒ Ⓓ Ⓔ	48. Ⓐ Ⓑ Ⓒ Ⓓ Ⓔ
9. Ⓐ Ⓑ Ⓒ Ⓓ Ⓔ	29. Ⓐ Ⓑ Ⓒ Ⓓ Ⓔ	49. Ⓐ Ⓑ Ⓒ Ⓓ Ⓔ
10. Ⓐ Ⓑ Ⓒ Ⓓ Ⓔ	30. Ⓐ Ⓑ Ⓒ Ⓓ Ⓔ	50. Ⓐ Ⓑ Ⓒ Ⓓ Ⓔ
11. Ⓐ Ⓑ Ⓒ Ⓓ Ⓔ	31. Ⓐ Ⓑ Ⓒ Ⓓ Ⓔ	51. Ⓐ Ⓑ Ⓒ Ⓓ Ⓔ
12. Ⓐ Ⓑ Ⓒ Ⓓ Ⓔ	32. Ⓐ Ⓑ Ⓒ Ⓓ Ⓔ	52. Ⓐ Ⓑ Ⓒ Ⓓ Ⓔ
13. Ⓐ Ⓑ Ⓒ Ⓓ Ⓔ	33. Ⓐ Ⓑ Ⓒ Ⓓ Ⓔ	53. Ⓐ Ⓑ Ⓒ Ⓓ Ⓔ
14. Ⓐ Ⓑ Ⓒ Ⓓ Ⓔ	34. Ⓐ Ⓑ Ⓒ Ⓓ Ⓔ	54. Ⓐ Ⓑ Ⓒ Ⓓ Ⓔ
15. Ⓐ Ⓑ Ⓒ Ⓓ Ⓔ	35. Ⓐ Ⓑ Ⓒ Ⓓ Ⓔ	55. Ⓐ Ⓑ Ⓒ Ⓓ Ⓔ
16. Ⓐ Ⓑ Ⓒ Ⓓ Ⓔ	36. Ⓐ Ⓑ Ⓒ Ⓓ Ⓔ	56. Ⓐ Ⓑ Ⓒ Ⓓ Ⓔ
17. Ⓐ Ⓑ Ⓒ Ⓓ Ⓔ	37. Ⓐ Ⓑ Ⓒ Ⓓ Ⓔ	57. Ⓐ Ⓑ Ⓒ Ⓓ Ⓔ
18. Ⓐ Ⓑ Ⓒ Ⓓ Ⓔ	38. Ⓐ Ⓑ Ⓒ Ⓓ Ⓔ	58. Ⓐ Ⓑ Ⓒ Ⓓ Ⓔ
19. Ⓐ Ⓑ Ⓒ Ⓓ Ⓔ	39. Ⓐ Ⓑ Ⓒ Ⓓ Ⓔ	59. Ⓐ Ⓑ Ⓒ Ⓓ Ⓔ
20. Ⓐ Ⓑ Ⓒ Ⓓ Ⓔ	40. Ⓐ Ⓑ Ⓒ Ⓓ Ⓔ	60. Ⓐ Ⓑ Ⓒ Ⓓ Ⓔ

Model AP Exam in Macroeconomics
AP宏观经济学考试样题

Two hours are allotted for this exam: 1 hour and 10 minutes for Section I, which consists of multiple-choice questions; and 50 minutes for Section II, which consists of three mandatory essay questions.

SECTION I—MULTIPLE-CHOICE QUESTIONS
第一部分——选择题

Time—1 hour and 10 minutes
Number of Questions—60
Percent of Total Grade—66⅔

Directions 说明

Each of the questions or incomplete statements beginning on page 322 is followed by five suggested answers or completions. Select the one that is best in each case and then fill in the corresponding oval on the answer sheet.

1. In the long run an increase in the money supply results in

(A) a proportional increase in the quantity of output.
(B) stagflation.
(C) an increase in the real rate of interest.
(D) an economic expansion.
(E) a proportional increase in the price level.

2. You buy 100 shares in XYZ Corporation on the Internet and your broker charges you $29.95.

(A) This will increase the investment component of GDP and therefore overall GDP.
(B) This has no effect on GDP.
(C) This will increase GDP by $29.95.
(D) This will increase GDP by the cost of the shares minus $29.95.
(E) This will increase GDP by the cost of the shares plus $29.95.

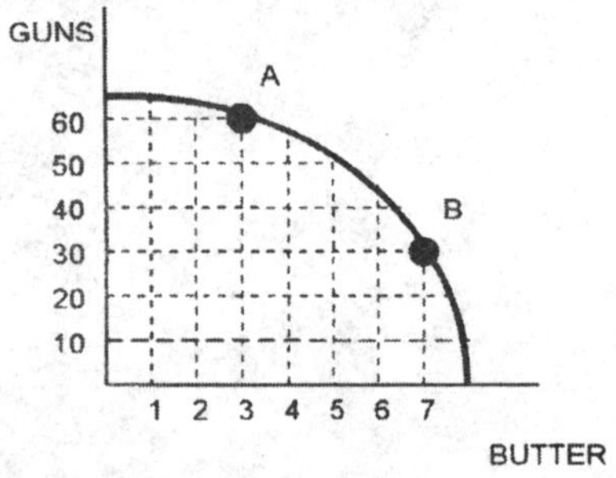

3. Given the graph above, the opportunity cost of four additional units of butter as the economy moves from A to B is

(A) seven units of butter.
(B) 30 units of guns.
(C) 60 units of guns.
(D) unobtainable.
(E) indeterminant.

4. In the short run, contractionary monetary policy causes aggregate demand to ______, output to ______, and the price level to ______.

	Aggregate Demand	Output	Price Level
(A)	Increase	Increase	Increase
(B)	Increase	Increase	Decrease
(C)	Decrease	Decrease	Increase
(D)	Decrease	Decrease	Decrease
(E)	Decrease	Increase	Increase

5. Assume the reserve requirement is five percent. If the Fed sells $10 million worth of government securities in an open market operation, then the money supply can potentially

(A) increase by $200 million.
(B) decrease by $200 million.
(C) increase by $50 million.
(D) decrease by $50 million.
(E) increase by $150 million.

6. Given the table below, which statement is true?

Labor hours needed to produce a unit of:

Country	Wine	Cheese
France	40	80
Belgium	15	60

(A) France has the absolute advantage in both products.
(B) France should specialize in and export wine while Belgium should specialize in and export cheese.
(C) France has the comparative advantage in cheese.
(D) France has the absolute advantage in cheese.
(E) Belgium has the comparative advantage in both products.

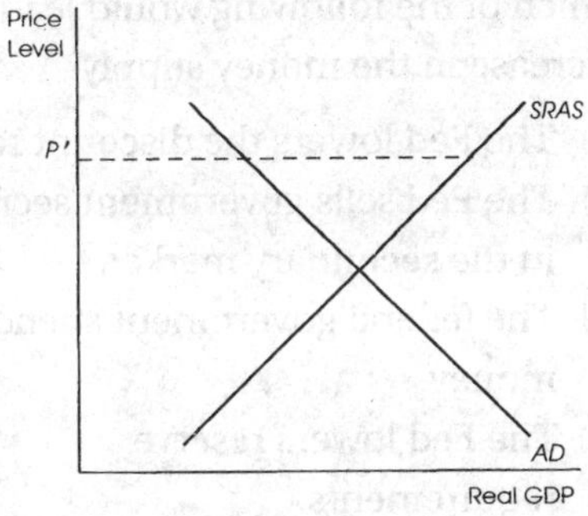

7. At P′ in the diagram above,

(A) inventories will be unintentionally drawn down, and the price level will fall.
(B) inventories will be unintentionally increased, and the price level will fall.
(C) inventories will be unintentionally drawn down, and the price level will rise.
(D) inventories will be unintentionally increased, and the price level will rise.
(E) inventories will be unintentionally drawn down, but prices will not be affected.

8. Suppose taxes are cut in an economy that is in equilibrium at full employment. In the long run the tax cut will

(A) raise real output and raise the price level.
(B) lower real output and raise the price level.
(C) raise real output and lower the price level.
(D) lower real output and lower the price level.
(E) raise the price level.

9. As a result of automatic stabilizers, during economic expansions government expenditures

(A) and taxes fall.
(B) and taxes rise.
(C) rise and taxes fall.
(D) fall and taxes rise.
(E) remain stable.

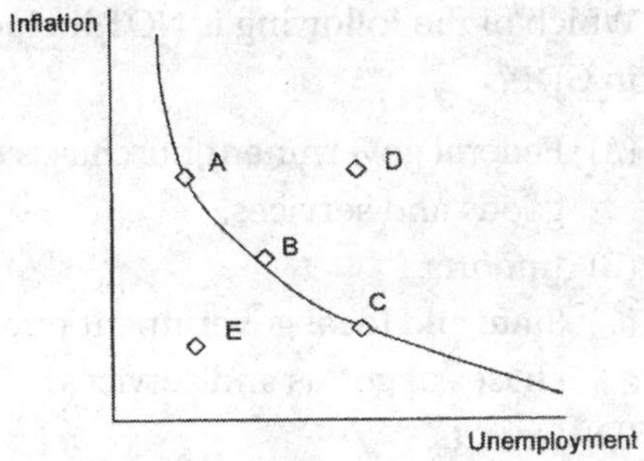

10. Consider the diagram above. In the short run, stagflation will move the economy from point B to

(A) point A.
(B) point A and then back to point B.
(C) point C.
(D) point D.
(E) point E.

11. Which of the following shifts the production possibilities frontier outward?

(A) A decrease in the price level.
(B) An increase in labor productivity.
(C) An increase in the money supply.
(D) A decrease in the unemployment rate.
(E) An increase in the minimum wage.

12. In the circular-flow diagram households send ________ to firms in return for ________.

(A) resources; spending
(B) spending; resources
(C) resources; wages and profits
(D) goods and services; wages
(E) goods and services; spending

13. An Italian company opens a shoe factory in the U.S. The production from this shoe company is included in

(A) the Italian GDP.
(B) the U.S. GDP.
(C) both the Italian and U.S. GDP.
(D) both the Italian and U.S. GDP split 50/50.
(E) neither the Italian nor U.S. GDP.

14. Which of the following is NOT included in GDP?

(A) Federal government purchases of goods and services.
(B) Imports.
(C) State and local government purchases of goods and services.
(D) Exports.
(E) The change in business inventories.

15. An increase in the price level reduces total spending in the economy because

I. consumers' incomes cannot go as far now that prices have risen.
II. foreigners buy less.
III. higher prices result in higher interest rates, which lower spending.

(A) Only I is correct.
(B) I and II are correct.
(C) I and III are correct.
(D) II and III are correct.
(E) I, II, and III are correct.

16. Suppose real GDP increases. We can conclude without a doubt that

(A) prices are higher.
(B) employment is higher.
(C) production is higher.
(D) prices and output are greater.
(E) unemployment is lower.

17. The appropriate fiscal policy to remedy a recession is to

(A) increase government spending and taxes.
(B) reduce government spending and taxes.
(C) increase government spending and reduce taxes.
(D) decrease government spending and increase taxes.
(E) increase the money supply.

18. Which of the following would lead to a decrease in the money supply?

(A) The Fed lowers the discount rate.
(B) The Fed sells government securities in the secondary market.
(C) The federal government spends less money.
(D) The Fed lowers reserve requirements.
(E) Taxes are reduced.

19. If interest rates rise relatively more in country A than in country B, then the value of country A's currency will

(A) appreciate.
(B) depreciate.
(C) remain unchanged.
(D) change indeterminately.
(E) depreciate by the difference in interest rates.

20. If the marginal propensity to consume equals .75 and government spending increases by $100 million, then overall real GDP can be expected to

(A) decrease by $133.33 million.
(B) increase by $133.33 million.
(C) decrease by $400 million.
(D) increase by $400 million.
(E) increase by $75 million.

21. Inflation

(A) hurts creditors who do not anticipate it.
(B) hurts creditors who anticipate it.
(C) hurts debtors.
(D) benefits debtors.
(E) both A and D are correct.

22. Which of the following persons is considered to be unemployed?

I. Mary, who has quit her job to look for another.
II. John, who fulfilled his dream by retiring from work at age 45.
III. Diane, who works part-time but would like to work full-time.

(A) I only
(B) II only
(C) III only
(D) I and III
(E) II and III

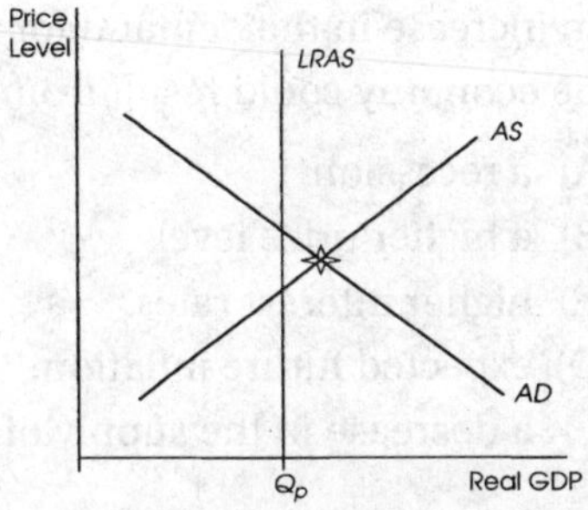

23. The economy depicted in the figure above is experiencing ________. In the absence of monetary or fiscal policy, the economy will eventually move to a point where the price level is ________.

(A) a recession; higher
(B) a recession; lower
(C) extremely high production; higher
(D) extremely high production; lower
(E) extremely high production; unchanged

24. The population of country X is exactly the same as country Y, but country X produces twice as much output as country Y. We can conclude that

(A) the people of country X are smarter than the people of country Y.
(B) the people of country X enjoy a standard of living twice as much as country Y.
(C) the people of country Y enjoy a standard of living twice as much as country X.
(D) the people of country Y work twice as hard as the people of country X.
(E) country X is bigger than country Y.

25. If the government of country Z increases spending by $12 million dollars and raises tax collections by the same amount, then what will be the overall impact of these moves on real GDP in country Z?

(A) Real GDP will increase by $6 million.
(B) Real GDP will decrease by $6 million.
(C) Real GDP will remain unchanged.
(D) Real GDP will increase by $12 million.
(E) Real GDP will decrease by $12 million.

26. Suppose you observe an economy where prices are falling and real GDP is rising. This may have been caused by

(A) stagflation.
(B) an advance in technology.
(C) an increase in government spending.
(D) a decrease in government spending.
(E) a decrease in the money supply.

27. Which of the following would reduce economic growth?

(A) A decline in investment.
(B) An increase in immigration from abroad.
(C) A technological advance.
(D) An increase in the labor force.
(E) An increase in the savings rate.

28. Currency held by the public

(A) is not part of the money supply, but currency held by banks is.
(B) is part of M1 but not M2.
(C) is part of the money supply, but currency held by banks is not.
(D) and by banks is part of the money supply.
(E) or banks is not part of the money supply since it is not included in M1.

29. The equation of exchange demonstrates the neutrality of money only if the

(A) velocity of money supply and the quantity of output are constant.
(B) money supply and its velocity are equal.
(C) velocity of money supply equals the speed of transactions.
(D) money supply and its velocity are inversely related.
(E) money supply and the exchange rate are inversely related.

30. Economy X is an open economy with flexible exchange rates. Economy Y is closed. *Ceteris paribus* expansionary monetary policy is

(A) more effective in X because the policy will increase net exports.
(B) more effective in X because the policy will decrease net exports.
(C) equally effective in X and Y.
(D) less effective in X because the policy will increase net exports.
(E) less effective in X because the policy will decrease net exports.

31. An increase in the price of forklifts imported into the United States from Belgium will

(A) increase the consumer price index and the GDP deflator.
(B) increase the consumer price index but not the GDP deflator.
(C) increase the GDP deflator but not the consumer price index.
(D) increase the GDP deflator and the producer price index.
(E) have no effect on the consumer price index or the GDP deflator.

32. An increase in the demand for money in the economy could result from

(A) a recession.
(B) a higher price level.
(C) higher interest rates.
(D) expected future inflation.
(E) a decrease in the supply of money.

33. The international value of the dollar will appreciate if

(A) American income falls relative to the rest of the world.
(B) American interest rates fall relative to interest rates in other countries.
(C) American prices rise.
(D) foreigners boycott American products.
(E) speculators expect the value of the dollar to depreciate.

34. The potential amount of money created after the Fed increases bank reserves will be diminished if

(A) the public prefers to hold less cash.
(B) the velocity of money falls.
(C) depository institutions decide to hold more excess reserves.
(D) the marginal propensity to consume falls.
(E) the international value of the dollar falls.

35. An increase in the federal deficit may affect the demand for loan funds and therefore the real interest rate and investment spending. Which of the following gives the correct direction of these effects?

	Demand for loanable funds	Real interest rate	Investment spending
(A)	Increase	Increase	Increase
(B)	Decrease	Decrease	Decrease
(C)	Decrease	Decrease	Increase
(D)	Increase	Increase	Decrease
(E)	Increase	Decrease	Increase

36. If the inflation rate is expected to increase in the immediate future, then

(A) consumers will begin saving more now.
(B) the velocity of money will fall.
(C) this will put upward pressure on the nominal interest rate.
(D) this will put downward pressure on the real interest rate.
(E) the international value of the dollar will rise.

37. If the economy is in disequilibrium where the price level is such that the aggregate quantity of products demanded exceeds the aggregate quantity of products supplied, then

(A) prices will be driven upward to restore equilibrium.
(B) supply will increase.
(C) demand will decrease.
(D) supply will decrease.
(E) a recession is inevitable.

38. If 200 computers with a retail value of $100,000 are domestically produced in 2005, but not sold until 2006, then GDP in 2005 is

(A) $100,000 higher because of the computers.
(B) 200 higher because of the computers.
(C) unaffected until 2006 when the computers are sold and the figure for GDP in 2005 is revised.
(D) higher by the wholesale value of the computers.
(E) unaffected and the computers are counted in GDP for 2006.

39. Appropriate fiscal and monetary polices during the contractionary phase of the business cycle include

(A) budget surpluses and higher discount rates.
(B) tax reductions and open market purchases.
(C) budget surpluses and lower discount rates.
(D) increases in government spending and higher discount rates.
(E) decreases in government spending and lower discount rates.

40. A change in government spending will have a greater short run impact on real output when

(A) the marginal propensity to consume is lower.
(B) the velocity of money is lower.
(C) the velocity of money is higher.
(D) the marginal propensity to consume is larger.
(E) interest rates rise.

41. Suppose a country produces only two goods, pizza and soda. Given the information in the table below, nominal GDP, real GDP, and the GDP deflator in 2005 are (assume 2004 is the base year):

Year	Pizza Production	Soda Production	Price of a Pizza	Price of a Soda
2004	8	20	$10	$1
2005	10	30	$17	$3

	Nominal GDP	Real GDP	GDP deflator
(A)	800	400	200
(B)	130	260	50
(C)	260	130	200
(D)	260	196	133
(E)	800	400	400

42. If the economy experienced a decrease in real GDP and price level, this could best be explained by

(A) a decline in labor productivity.
(B) a technological advance.
(C) a decline in investment.
(D) an uptick in net exports.
(E) a reduction in interest rates.

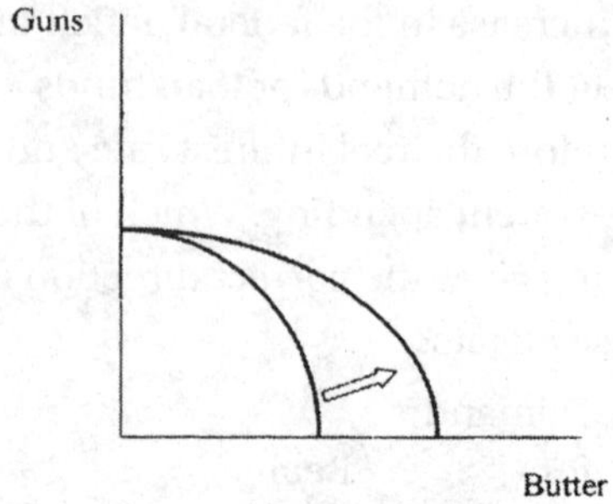

43. The shift depicted in the diagram above could have been caused by

(A) better production methods in the gun industry.
(B) an increase in the number of cows in the economy.
(C) an increase in the number of workers in the economy.
(D) a technological setback in the gun industry.
(E) a reduction in farmland available due to pollution.

44. Suppose the real interest rate in a country rises. What can be expected to happen to the demand for this nation's currency and, therefore, the value of its currency and net exports?

	Demand for currency	Value of currency	Net exports
(A)	Decrease	Appreciate	Decrease
(B)	Decrease	Depreciate	Decrease
(C)	Decrease	Depreciate	Increase
(D)	Increase	Appreciate	Increase
(E)	Increase	Appreciate	Decrease

45. According to Keynesian analysis, the Great Depression was caused by

(A) a lack of spending.
(B) a sharp rise in the marginal propensity to consume.
(C) too much investment.
(D) too much foreign influence on the economy.
(E) a sharp decline in labor productivity.

46. An economy in a recession can return to full employment in the long run through

(A) falling wages and prices.
(B) rising wages and prices.
(C) expansionary monetary policy.
(D) increased government spending.
(E) decreased government spending.

47. If the cost of the basket of goods and services the Bureau of Labor Statistics uses to calculate the consumer price index rises from $200 in the base period to $400 in the current period, then the consumer price index

(A) equals 0.5 in the current period.
(B) has risen 5 percent from the base to the current period.
(C) equals 50 in the current period.
(D) equals 200 in the current period.
(E) has risen 200 percent.

48. Contractionary monetary policy implies which of the following about the discount rate, the nominal interest rate, and aggregate demand?

	Discount rate	Nominal interest rate	Aggregate demand
(A)	Decrease	Increase	Decrease
(B)	Increase	Increase	Decrease
(C)	Decrease	Decrease	Decrease
(D)	Increase	Increase	Increase
(E)	Increase	Decrease	Decrease

49. A decline in the demand for money could be the result of

(A) higher prices.
(B) more money placed in checking accounts.
(C) higher returns on bonds.
(D) fewer credit cards.
(E) open market purchases by the Fed.

50. An important assumption underlying monetarism is that

(A) the marginal propensity to consume is constant.
(B) the money supply is continuous.
(C) the exchange rate is fixed.
(D) the velocity of money is stable.
(E) the exchange rate is flexible.

51. Which of the following policies is most likely to bring about economic growth in the long run?

(A) Imposing tariffs to protect domestic industries from foreign competition.
(B) Placing taxes on savings.
(C) Increasing government spending.
(D) Increasing the money supply.
(E) Promoting improvements in the education of the population.

52. An increase in the price level and a decrease in real GDP in the short run could be the result of

(A) a prolonged period of very bad weather.
(B) a decrease in the money supply.
(C) a decrease in consumer confidence.
(D) an increase in consumer confidence.
(E) an increase in the money supply.

53. In 2010, the United States had a trade deficit of $600 billion; therefore,

(A) net exports were positive.
(B) Americans consumed more than they produced.
(C) America's government spent more than it took in.
(D) $600 billion worth of capital flowed out of America.
(E) the government had to make payments to foreign countries of $600 billion.

54. GDP measures a country's level of

I. production.
II. stability.
III. income.

(A) I only.
(B) II only.
(C) III only.
(D) I and II.
(E) I and III.

55. Which of the following lists contains only Fed actions that will increase the money supply?

(A) Raise reserve requirements; lower the discount rate; sell bonds.
(B) Raise reserve requirements; lower the discount rate; buy bonds.
(C) Raise reserve requirements; raise the discount rate; sell bonds.
(D) Lower reserve requirements; lower the discount rate; sell bonds.
(E) Lower reserve requirements; lower the discount rate; buy bonds.

56. Which of the following lists contains only policies that will close an inflationary gap?

(A) Increase the money supply; run a federal budget deficit.
(B) Decrease the money supply; run a federal budget deficit.
(C) Decrease the money supply; increase taxes; reduce government spending.
(D) Increase the money supply; increase taxes; reduce government spending.
(E) Decrease the money supply; decrease taxes; reduce government spending.

57. Suppose the exchange rates are 0.5 British Pound per dollar; 10 Mexican Pesos per dollar; and 100 Chinese Yuan per dollar. Further suppose that a Big Mac costs 3 dollars in America; 2 pounds in England; 50 pesos in Mexico; and 200 yuan in China. In which country is a Big Mac most expensive?

(A) America.
(B) England.
(C) Mexico.
(D) China.
(E) England and China are equally most expensive.

58. Potential GDP will fall, *ceteris paribus*, if

(A) the unemployment rate rises.
(B) the retirement age is lowered.
(C) tariffs protecting domestic jobs are eliminated.
(D) more immigration is allowed.
(E) the minimum wage is raised.

59. Suppose that an expansionary fiscal policy leads to a large increase in real output and a small increase in the price level. From this it can be inferred that

(A) inflation had already impacted the economy before the fiscal stimulus.
(B) the economy initially had some unemployed resources.
(C) aggregate supply decreased.
(D) aggregate demand is steeply sloped.
(E) aggregate supply is steeply sloped.

60. Imagine someone who is not looking for work because he is embarrassed in the interview process when his inability to read is revealed. However, this person would take just about any job that was offered. According to the Bureau of Labor Statistics this person is

(A) in the labor force and unemployed.
(B) in the labor force and employed.
(C) not in the labor force.
(D) not in the labor force, but counted as unemployed.
(E) not in the labor force, but counted as employed.

SECTION II—FREE-RESPONSE QUESTIONS
第二部分——开放式题目

Planning Time—10 minutes
Writing Time—50 minutes
Percent of Total Grade—33⅓

DIRECTIONS 说明

You have 50 minutes to answer all three of the following questions. It is suggested that you spend approximately half your time on the first question and divide the remaining time equally between the next two questions. In answering the questions, you should emphasize the line of reasoning that generated your results; it is not enough to list the results of your analysis. Include correctly labeled diagrams, if useful or required, in explaining your answers. A correctly labeled diagram must have all axes and curves clearly labeled and must show directional changes.

Students should consider doing a "sketch" (main points, quick graph, etc.) of the answer before actually answering the free-response questions. When you use graphs on the free-response questions, label the axes and make direct references to any symbols, e.g., MR, P, output, on the graphs when you respond to questions.

NOTE

Recent Advanced Placement exams require *three* questions. Some of the questions may be based on material covered in the common chapters, such as production possibilities frontier or curve when applied to international trade. For these questions, please refer to those chapters.

1. Country X is a closed economy experiencing a falling price level and a low level of real GDP.

(a) Draw a correctly labeled graph of aggregate demand and aggregate supply that depicts the recession in Country X.

(b) Assume income taxes are reduced in Country X.

(i) Explain how a cut in income taxes would affect the equilibrium price level and equilibrium real GDP in Country X.

(ii) Show the effects of the tax cut on your graph from part (a). Be clear about which curve(s) is/are shifting which way.

(c) Draw a correctly labeled graph of money supply and money demand showing the equilibrium nominal interest rate.

(i) Explain how the changes in the equilibrium price level and equilibrium real GDP from part (b) above will affect the equilibrium nominal interest rate.

(ii) Show the effects of the changes in the equilibrium price level and equilibrium real GDP on your graph of money supply and money demand.

(iii) Explain how the change in the equilibrium nominal interest rate will impact the macroeconomy.

2. Suppose that interest rates in the United States fall relative to the rest of the world. Explain how this will affect

(a) the value of the dollar.

(b) net exports.

(c) Now suppose the monetary authorities in the United States did not want the value of the dollar to change as you explained in part (a) above. Explain how the value of the dollar could be held stable in this situation.

3. Describe how an open market purchase of $7 million by the Federal Reserve Bank will affect the money supply.

(a) Assuming a required reserve ratio of five percent, what is the maximum amount by which the money supply can change due to the open market operation?

(b) How will your answer to (a) above change if banks decide to hold reserves over and above the required amount?

(c) Suppose a large corporation makes the open market purchase of $7 million. Explain how the money supply will be affected in this case.

答案 ANSWER KEY
宏观经济学 Macroeconomics
MULTIPLE-CHOICE QUESTIONS 选择题

1. E	**16.** C	**31.** E	**46.** A
2. C	**17.** C	**32.** B	**47.** D
3. B	**18.** B	**33.** A	**48.** B
4. D	**19.** A	**34.** C	**49.** C
5. B	**20.** D	**35.** D	**50.** D
6. C	**21.** E	**36.** C	**51.** E
7. B	**22.** A	**37.** A	**52.** A
8. E	**23.** C	**38.** A	**53.** B
9. D	**24.** B	**39.** B	**54.** E
10. D	**25.** D	**40.** D	**55.** E
11. B	**26.** B	**41.** C	**56.** C
12. C	**27.** A	**42.** C	**57.** C
13. B	**28.** C	**43.** B	**58.** B
14. B	**29.** A	**44.** E	**59.** B
15. D	**30.** E	**45.** A	**60.** C

ANSWERS EXPLAINED
答案解析

MACROECONOMICS
宏观经济学

Multiple-choice questions 选择题

1. **(E)** (Chapter 19) The Classical notion of monetary neutrality is based on the idea that the money supply and the price level are proportionally related.
2. **(C)** (Chapter 14) Financial transactions are not counted in GDP, but brokerage services are counted.
3. **(B)** (Chapter 2) At point A the economy is producing 60 guns and 3 units of butter. At Point B production is 30 guns and 7 units of butter. The 4 additional units of butter come at a cost of 30 guns.
4. **(D)** (Chapter 19) Contractionary monetary policy is a decrease in the money supply. This shifts aggregate demand to the left. A leftward shift in aggregate demand results in a higher level of output and a higher price level. This is seen in the aggregate demand–aggregate supply model:

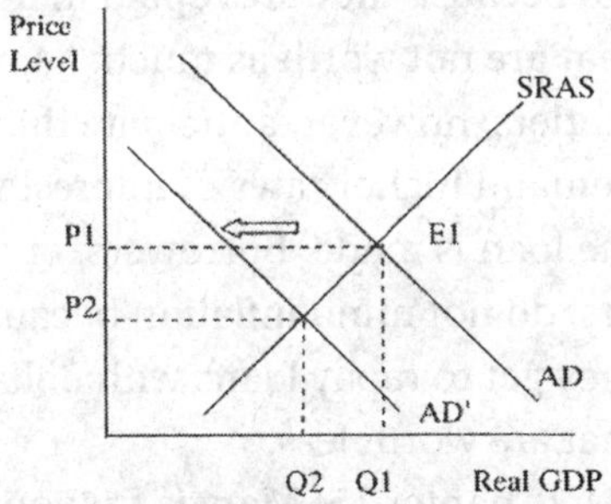

5. **(B)** (Chapter 18) If the reserve requirement is 5 percent, then the money multiplier is 20 (= 1/.05). Bank reserves fall by $10 million because of the open market operation. The money supply falls by $200 million (= $10 million × 20).
6. **(C)** (Chapter 2) Since Belgium can produce both wine and cheese with fewer labor hours than France, Belgium has the absolute advantage in both products. The opportunity cost of cheese in Belgium is 60/15 = 4 wine; the opportunity cost of cheese in France is 80/40 = 2 wine. France has the lower opportunity cost of producing cheese and therefore the comparative advantage in cheese production.
7. **(B)** (Chapter 16) Since AS > AD at P′, inventories will unintentionally increase. In order to lower excess inventories, firms will be forced to lower prices, and the price level falls.
8. **(E)** (Chapter 16) The trick to answering this question correctly is to use a vertical aggregate supply curve. You know to do so because the question asks about the long run. The tax cut shifts AD right to AD′. This results in a higher price level (P_2), but the same level of output (Q_1).

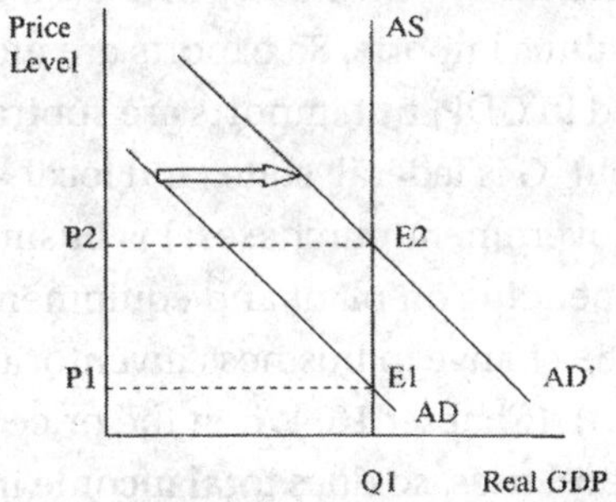

9. **(D)** (Chapter 17) During an economic expansion output, income, and employment increase. This results in fewer households qualifying for income maintenance programs such as food stamps and housing subsidies. Government expenditures fall, but tax collections rise because more income means more tax revenue for the government.

MODEL MICROECONOMICS EXAM

10. **(D)** (Chapter 17) Stagflation is inflation and recession (unemployment) at the same time. The only point shown with higher inflation and unemployment than B is point D. Indeed, stagflation causes the Phillips curve to shift right through a point such as D.
11. **(B)** (Chapter 2) Only changes in technology/productivity or changes in resource availability can shift the production possibilities frontier. Many students choose D here, but notice that a decrease in unemployment will move the economy onto the frontier from a point inside the frontier.
12. **(C)** (Chapter 2) Households own the resources (land, labor, capital) in the economy. They sell them to firms in exchange for wages and profits.
13. **(B)** (Chapter 14) It does not matter where the company has its headquarters. GDP counts production within a nation's borders.
14. **(B)** (Chapter 14) Consider the equation GDP = C + I + G + X. X is exports minus imports. So exports are included in GDP, but imports are subtracted out. G is federal, state, and local government purchases; I is business spending on plant and equipment plus the change in business inventories.
15. **(D)** (Chapter 16) When the price level rises, so does total income in the economy. Therefore I is not correct. However, foreign incomes do not rise, so foreigners buy less of our products. II is correct. III is a statement of Fisher's Hypothesis and is also correct.
16. **(C)** (Chapter 14) When real GDP rises it can only be due to more production. Price changes do not affect real GDP. Employment (and therefore unemployment) may or may not change with changes in real GDP.
17. **(C)** (Chapter 17) Increasing government spending and reducing taxes stimulate aggregate demand and fight recessions. Increasing the money supply does this as well, but that is monetary policy.
18. **(B)** (Chapter 18) When the Fed sells securities in the secondary market they get paid with checks drawn on bank accounts. Bank reserves fall and the money supply falls by a multiple of the decline in bank reserves.
19. **(A)** (Chapter 21) When interest rates rise in country A, people from country B will want to buy bonds there. People from country B will need to obtain the currency of country A in order to do this. The demand for country A's currency rises. This causes it to appreciate.
20. **(D)** (Chapter 16) If the marginal propensity to consume is .75, then the multiplier is 4 (= 1/(1 – .75)). The increase in government spending gets multiplied by 4 to determine the overall increase in spending and therefore real GDP. 4 × \$100 million = \$400 million.
21. **(E)** (Chapter 15) Inflation hurts lenders because they are repaid in dollars that are not worth as much. Some lenders, however, anticipate this and demand higher rates of interest when the loan is made. Borrowers, or debtors, do not mind inflation because they get to repay loans with dollars that are worth less.
22. **(A)** (Chapter 15) Mary is frictionally unemployed. Retired persons presumably are not looking for work, so they are not part of the labor force. People who work part-time are counted as employed even if they would like to work full-time.

23. **(C)** (Chapter 16) The economy is experiencing an extremely high production level since it is in short-run equilibrium to the right of potential, or long-run, real GDP. In the absence of government policies to correct the situation, the AS curve will shift to the left. Prices are expected to be higher in the future, and so aggregate supply decreases right now. The aggregate supply curve shifts left until a new equilibrium is reached at potential, or long-run, aggregate supply.

24. **(B)** (Chapter 20) The standard of living depends on real GDP per capita. Country X has twice the output per person as country Y.

25. **(D)** (Chapter 17) This is a balanced-budget move—government spending is increasing and tax collections are increasing by the same amount. It is not necessary to know the MPC. In this situation the net impact on real GDP is a change equivalent to the change in government spending.

26. **(B)** (Chapter 16) A technological advance shifts the aggregate supply curve to the right.

27. **(A)** (Chapter 20) Less investment implies less plant and equipment in the future. That reduces economic growth, whereas choices B through E all enhance growth.

28. **(C)** (Chapter 18) Currency in the vaults of depository institutions is not counted as part of the money supply. However, if you withdraw $100 from your checking account, M1 is unaffected. When the money comes out of the bank's vault and goes into your pocket, that in itself raises the money supply by $100—but your checking account went down by $100 because of the withdrawal. It's a wash.

29. **(A)** (Chapter 18) The velocity of money supply and the quantity of output must be constant in the equation of exchange or else, by algebra, a change in the money supply will not have a proportional effect on output in the equation of exchange.

30. **(E)** (Chapter 21) The more open an economy, the less effective monetary policy will be. Consider an increase in the money supply. This will raise real GDP and prices in the short run. However, if the economy is open, then the increase in real GDP will boost incomes and therefore importation (which reduces real GDP somewhat), and the increase in prices will reduce exports (which also reduces real GDP somewhat).

31. **(E)** (Chapter 14) The consumer price index will not be affected by the increase in the price of the forklifts because forklifts are an industrial product, not a consumer product. The GDP deflator is not affected because import prices are ignored by the deflator.

32. **(B)** (Chapter 19) When prices rise people and firms want more money in their wallets and checking accounts in order to conduct their transactions.

33. **(A)** (Chapter 21) If income in America falls relative to the rest of the world, then Americans' demand for imports will decrease. Therefore, the supply of dollars will decrease relative to the demand for dollars. In turn, the value of the dollar increases.

34. **(C)** (Chapter 18) If the Fed increases bank reserves, but banks decide to simply hold onto the new reserves, then the money expansion process will be curtailed. The process depends on banks using their new reserves to make loans out or buy investments.

35. (D) (Chapter 17) The government must borrow to finance the federal deficit and this raises the demand for loanable funds. The result will be an increase in the real interest rate and decrease in investment spending. This chain of events is known as crowding out.

36. (C) (Chapter 15) Fisher's Hypothesis states that the nominal interest rate equals the real interest rate plus expected inflation.

37. (A) (Chapter 16) If the price level in the economy is below the equilibrium price level, then the quantity of products demanded will exceed the quantity supplied. There will be a shortage, and shortages drive prices up.

38. (A) (Chapter 14) Products get counted in GDP in the period they are produced. If they produced but not sold, then they are in inventory. The change in inventories is part of GDP. Inventory changes are included in investment.

39. (B) (Chapter 19) Reducing taxes is a stimulatory fiscal policy, and open market purchases are expansionary monetary policy.

40. (D) (Chapter 17) The multiplier is 1/(1 – MPC). Therefore, the higher the MPC, the higher the multiplier. With a higher multiplier, changes in government spending will have more impact on real GDP.

41. (C) (Chapters 14 and 15)

Calculating GDP for 2005

Production	Price	Value
10 Pizzas	$17	$170
30 Sodas	$3	$90
		GDP = $260

Calculating real GDP for 2005

Production	Price	Value
10 Pizzas	$10	$100
30 Sodas	$1	$30
		Real GDP = $130

Calculating the GDP deflator for 2005

$260/130 \times 100 = 200$

42. (C) (Chapter 16) Aggregate demand must decrease for real GDP and the price level to fall. A decline in investment causes aggregate demand to decrease.

43. (B) (Chapter 20) Shifts such as these are the result of a technological advance or increase in resources that benefit only one of the two industries. If the economy produced only guns, then an increase in the number of cows would not help increase production.

44. (E) (Chapter 21) Higher real interest rates attract foreign investors. These investors demand the nation's currency, which in turn appreciates its value. This makes domestic products more expensive to foreigners and foreign products less expensive to domestic citizens. Thus, net exports decrease.

45. (A) (Chapter 17) Real output declined and the price level fell during the Great Depression. This can only be the result of aggregate demand shifting left—a lack of demand or spending.

46. **(A)** (Chapter 16) In Classical theory, a recession causes wages and prices to fall. The falling prices stimulate demand for products, while the falling wages stimulate demand for labor. This pickup in demand ends the recession and brings about full employment.

47. **(D)** (Chapter 15)

$$CPI = \frac{\text{Total Cost This Period}}{\text{Total Cost Base Period}} \times 100 = \frac{400}{200} \times 100 = 200$$

48. **(B)** (Chapter 19) Contractionary monetary policy means lowering the money supply. The Fed would increase the discount rate, which results in a higher nominal interest rate. Higher interest rates discourage spending, which decreases aggregate demand.

49. **(C)** (Chapter 19) When the return on bonds and other assets rises, people and firms want to hold less money in their wallets and checking accounts and, instead, put the money into these assets with high returns.

50. **(D)** (Chapter 19) Monetarists feel that changes in the money supply have a profound impact on nominal GDP. According to the equation of exchange, this would not be true if the velocity of money fluctuated in the opposite direction of the change in the money supply.

51. **(E)** (Chapter 20) Economic growth is stimulated by investment in resources. Education enhances one of the most important resources in the economy—labor.

52. **(A)** (Chapter 16) Only a decrease in short run aggregate demand could cause an increase in the price level and a decrease in real GDP. It sounds odd, but a prolonged period of bad weather (droughts, monsoons, etc.) destroys resources such as farmland and other plant and equipment. Aggregate supply shifts left when fewer resources are available.

53. **(B)** (Chapter 21) A trade deficit means a country's imports exceed its exports. In this case a country is consuming more than it is producing.

54. **(E)** (Chapter 14) The income and expenditure approaches to calculating GDP highlight the fact that GDP measures not only production, but income as well.

55. **(E)** (Chapter 19) The three primary tools at the Fed's disposal for increasing the money supply are lowering reserve requirements, lowering the discount rate, and buying bonds on the open market.

56. **(C)** (Chapters 17 and 19) Aggregate demand needs to be decreased to close an inflationary gap. This can be accomplished with contractionary monetary policy (decreasing the money supply) or contractionary fiscal policy (increasing taxes or reducing government spending).

57. **(C)** (Chapter 21) One way to solve this problem is to put all the different prices in dollar terms:

Country	$ Price of a Big Mac
America	$3
England	2 pounds ÷ 0.5 = $4
Mexico	50 pesos ÷ 10 = $5
China	200 yuan ÷ 100 = $2

The Mexican Big Mac costs 50 pesos, which translates into $5. This is the most expensive Big Mac.

58. **(B)** (Chapter 21) Potential GDP is how much could be produced using all resources fully and efficiently. In order for potential GDP to fall, resources must become less available or inefficiencies must be introduced into the production process. Lowering the retirement age means less labor is available.

59. **(B)** (Chapter 17) Expansionary fiscal policy increases aggregate demand. Increases in aggregate demand raise prices and output. However, if there is a lot of unemployment and capacity to begin with, then the increase in aggregate demand can easily be met by increasing output.

60. **(C)** (Chapter 15) People like this are neither employed nor unemployed according to the Bureau of Labor Statistics because they are not counted as part of the labor force. To be in the labor force, one must be actively seeking employment or employed.

Free-Response Answers
开放式题目答案

1. **(a)**

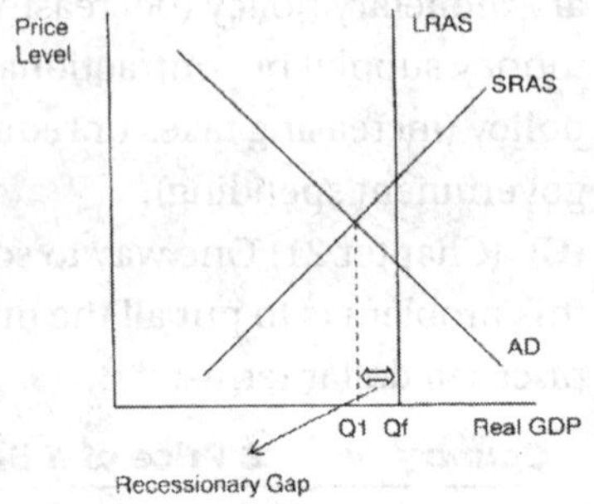

(b) (i) An income tax cut leaves households with more disposable income, which results in an increase in spending. Aggregate demand would increase. This would cause the equilibrium price level and the equilibrium level of real GDP to increase.

(ii) Aggregate demand would shift to the right:

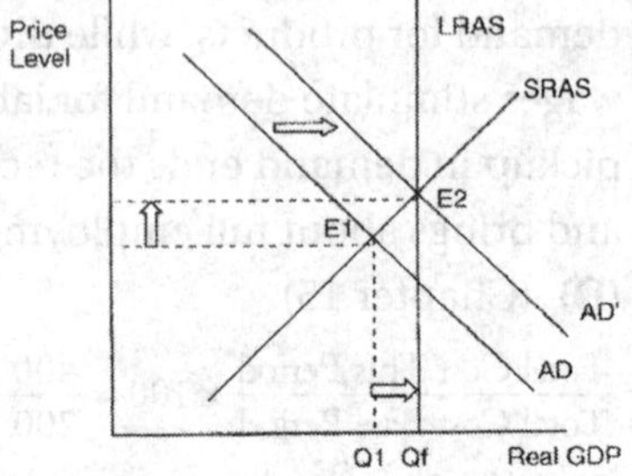

The equilibrium point moves from E_1 to E_2 with the income tax cut. The graph shows that this implies a higher equilibrium price level and a higher level of real GDP.

(c)

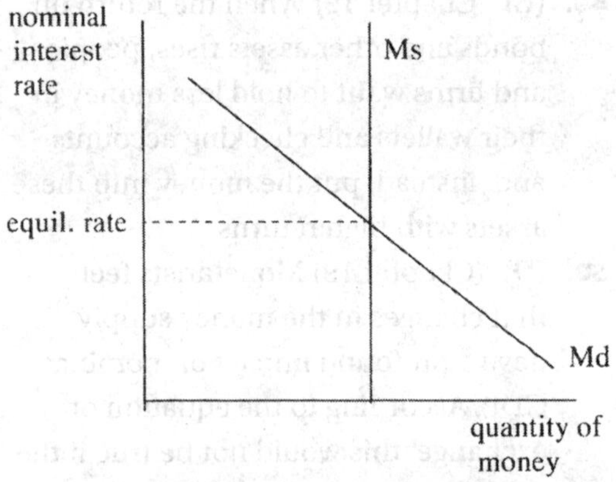

(i) The increase in the equilibrium price level serves to increase the demand for money, as does the increase in the level of real GDP. The increased demand for money, in turn, raises the nominal rate of interest.

(ii)

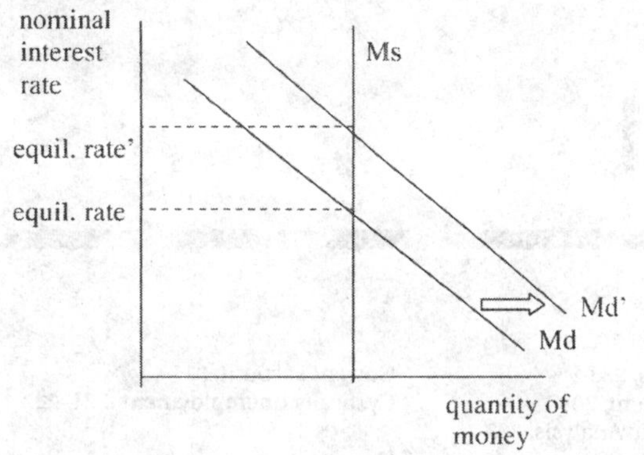

The increase in the demand for money serves to raise the equilibrium nominal interest rate.

(iii) The increased nominal rate of interest will impact the economy in a variety of ways: (1) Higher interest rates will encourage saving and reduce consumption; (2) investment will fall; and (3) higher interest rates will increase the value of the dollar and thereby lower net exports. All in all, higher interest rates tend to reduce aggregate demand and thus reduce the impact of the initial tax cut. The tendency of interest rates to rise with expansionary fiscal policy and consequently reduce the fiscal thrust is called "crowding out."

2. **(a)** The value of the dollar will decrease because the drop in interest rates will mean that fewer foreigners will want to invest in the United States. This, in turn, implies that the demand for the dollar will fall. A decline in demand for the dollar results in a depreciation.

(b) Net exports will rise because the value of the dollar has depreciated. A fall in the value of the dollar will raise U.S. exports (our goods are less expensive to foreigners) and lower U.S. imports (foreign goods are more expensive to Americans after the depreciation of the dollar).

(c) The Federal Reserve, in conjunction with the Department of the Treasury, could prevent the depreciation of the dollar outlined above. Basically, the Federal Reserve would use its foreign currency reserves to buy U.S. dollars on the international market. This increase in the demand for dollars would offset decline in demand due to lower interest rates.

3. An open market purchase of $7 million by the Federal Reserve Bank will serve to increase the money supply by more than $7 million. The purchase itself puts $7 million in new reserves into the banking system. Banks then make loans or buy investments with these additional reserves. The loans and investments generate new deposits, which are additions to the money supply.

(a) When the reserve ratio is 5 percent, the money multiplier is 20 (= 1/.05). This implies that any change in bank reserves could possibly be magnified 20 times. Therefore, the open market purchase of $7 million could lead to a $140 million (= $7 million × 20) increase in M1.

(b) The $140 million figure is based on the assumption that banks use their additional reserves as much as possible to make loans or buy investments. If banks hold reserves over and above the requirements, then the money expansion process will be diminished. The money supply will expand by less than $140 million if banks hold reserves above the required amount.

(c) The money supply is unaffected in this case. The corporation's bank account declines by $7 million while the seller's account rises by the same amount. No new reserves are added to the system, so the money supply does not change.

Index 索引